WHITE ROBES
SILVER SCREENS

WHITE ROBES
SILVER SCREENS

MOVIES AND THE
MAKING OF THE
KU KLUX KLAN

TOM RICE

INDIANA UNIVERSITY PRESS
Bloomington & Indianapolis

This book is a publication of

INDIANA UNIVERSITY PRESS
Office of Scholarly Publishing
Herman B Wells Library 350
1320 East 10th Street
Bloomington, Indiana 47405 USA

iupress.indiana.edu

The paper used in this publication
meets the minimum requirements of
the American National Standard for
Information Sciences – Permanence of
Paper for Printed Library Materials,
ANSI Z39.48–1992.

Manufactured in the
United States of America

Library of Congress
Cataloging-in-Publication Data

Rice, Tom.
    White robes, silver screens :
movies and the making of the
Ku Klux Klan / Tom Rice.
    pages cm
    Includes bibliographical
references and index.
    ISBN 978-0-253-01843-4 (pbk. : alk.
paper) – ISBN 978-0-253-01836-6 (cloth
: alk. paper) – ISBN 978-0-253-01848-9
(ebook) 1. Ku Klux Klan (1915-) –
In motion pictures. 2. Ku Klux Klan
(1915–) – History. 3. Motion picture
industry – Political aspects – United
States – History – 20th century.
4. Motion pictures in propaganda –
United States – History – 20th century.
5. Birth of a nation (Motion picture) –
Influence. I. Title.
    PN1995.9.K75R53 2015
    791.43'655 – dc23

                              2015017063

1 2 3 4 5   20 19 18 17 16 15

Contents

Acknowledgments

I AM WELL AWARE THAT MOST PEOPLE WHO READ ACKNOWL-
edgments do so in the hope of finding their own names. I must therefore
begin with an apology to those missing from these pages. What follows
is certainly not an exhaustive list of those deserving thanks, and I am
extremely grateful to everyone who has offered me support, suggestions,
and distractions during the writing of this book.

The project began many years ago while I was studying at the University of Southampton, and would not have progressed beyond an initial
idea without the inspiring teaching of Mike Hammond and John Old-
field. Since then I have been extremely fortunate to work more closely
with Lee Grieveson, who has had an enormous influence on my work.
Over the last decade, Lee has been a constant source of support, reading every page, challenging every idea, and answering every question.
Occasionally he has done so without complaint. Writing any book – and
perhaps more so one that takes as its subject the Ku Klux Klan – can be
a lonely experience, but Lee has provided sage advice and friendship
throughout, for which I am enormously grateful.

The manuscript has benefitted from the many other readers who
have offered suggestions, in particular Mike Allen, Melvyn Stokes, and
Brian Jacobson. I am especially grateful to Greg Waller, who read two
versions of the manuscript and whose constructive feedback greatly
shaped the final work. I was very fortunate to conduct my doctoral
study at King's College London and University College London, and
I have completed this work in the company of supportive and generous
colleagues at the University of St. Andrews. It seems churlish not to

thank them all, but for more direct assistance, I am grateful to Robert Burgoyne, Dina Iordanova, Katherine Hawley, Leshu Torchin, David Martin-Jones, Mike Arrowsmith, Karen Drysdale, Bregt Lameris, and especially Josh Yumibe. Among the many others who have provided valuable information or material along the way are Jason Lantzer, Kevin Brownlow, and Thomas R. Pegram.

There are inevitable challenges in researching American history while based in the UK, and I am particularly indebted to the many archivists who have given so much of their time and expertise in responding to my many requests. Of the institutions that I visited, I would like to thank archivists and librarians at the University of North Carolina; the New York Public Library; the Billy Rose Theatre Collection; the Library of Congress; the Indiana State Library; the Indiana Historical Society; Ohio State University; the Ohio Historical Society; the British Library; and the British Film Institute. Many others have responded to my requests from the UK, and I am extremely pleased to acknowledge and thank, in no particular order, Boise State University (ID) (Alan Virta); the New Haven Public Library (CT) (Allison Botelho); the Hamilton East Public Library (IN) (Nancy Massey); the New Jersey State Library (Robert Heym); the New Jersey Historical Society; the Historical Society of Delaware; the Monmouth County Historical Association (NJ); the Margaret Herrick Library at the Academy of Motion Picture Arts and Sciences (Barbara Hall); the Shreve Memorial Library (LA); Kent State University (OH); the Oklahoma Historical Society; the Tulsa Historical Society and Museum (OK) (Ian Swart); the George Eastman House (Nancy Kauffman); the Warner Bros. Archives of the University of Southern California (Jennifer Prindeville); the Charlie Chaplin Archive, Cineteca di Bologna (Cecilia Cenciarelli); the Georgia State University Library (Sarah King Steiner); and the American Legion Library (Joseph J. Hovish). I have also benefitted from the emergence of online archival resources over the past decade, and would like to acknowledge, in particular, the Media History Digital Library and Newspaper Archive.

I would also like to thank everyone at Indiana University Press for their expertise and direction in developing the manuscript and bringing it to print. I am especially grateful to Raina Polivka, Jenna Whittaker, David Miller, and Eric Schramm, and to Kay Banning for her work on the index. I have also been very fortunate to receive financial support throughout my research, in particular from the Arts and Humanities Research Council. This work would not have been possible without their assistance.

Finally, I would like to thank my friends and family for providing distractions, support, and perspective, and for sitting next to me even when I insisted on reading Klan histories on public transport. I owe an enormous debt to my parents, to my brother and sister, and to Richard and Mary Bipps. I would also like to thank Caryl and John and my two inspirational grandmothers.

Above all, this book is for Suzie, Lottie, and Ernest.

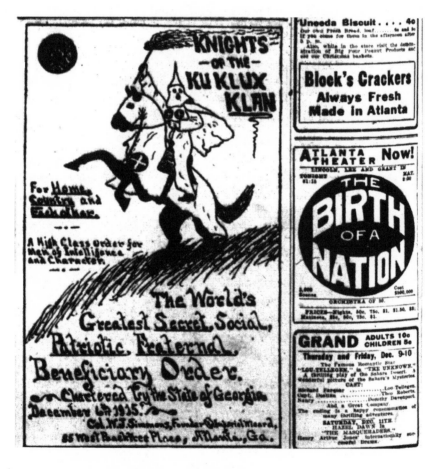

o.1. Advertisement for Knights of the Ku Klux Klan and *The Birth of a Nation, Atlanta Journal,* 9 December 1915.

Preface

ON MONDAY, 6 DECEMBER 1915, THE NIGHT OF THE ATLANTA premiere of *The Birth of a Nation,* the recently formed Ku Klux Klan, "mounted and on foot, paraded down Peachtree Street and fired rifle salutes in front of the theatre." Ten months earlier, at the film's national premiere at Clune's auditorium in Los Angeles, actors in full Ku Klux Klan regalia had sat on horseback outside the theater, re-creating the on-screen image. Much had changed between these two dates, however. In Los Angeles, which was fast becoming the center for film production, theatrical "Klansmen" were there to provide publicity for the film. In Atlanta, a city increasingly riven by Jim Crow segregation and by national reports of mob violence, active Klansmen now used the film to introduce and publicize a new group that was emerging at the exact moment of the film's local release.[1]

A few days after the Atlanta premiere, an advertisement appeared in both the *Atlanta Constitution* and *Atlanta Journal* for "The World's Greatest Secret Social Patriotic Fraternal Beneficiary Order." The advertisement, hand-drawn by William Simmons, the founder and self-appointed Imperial Wizard of the Knights of the Ku Klux Klan, showed a Klansman riding a horse while carrying a flaming cross. It unabashedly imitated the image initially used to promote D. W. Griffith's film, an association made all the more apparent in the *Atlanta Journal,* where Simmons's advertisement appeared next to a small poster for *The Birth of a Nation* (fig. 0.1).[2]

The events surrounding the Atlanta premiere a century ago represent, for many, the extent of the Klan's relationship with cinema. The initial release of *The Birth of a Nation* has variously been presented as a formative moment in the history of the modern Klan and of the modern film industry, yet it is a moment at which the histories of these two emerging phenomena are invariably said to have diverged. This book argues instead that these initial events presage a longer, more complex history of interwar America, as the Klan tried to use film in a variety of ways to establish itself as one of the most influential and recognizable groups of the twentieth century. In the process, the book examines how a conservative social and political force, and pressure groups more broadly, began to grapple with media to visualize and make material their particular agendas.

The appearances of the Klan around the Atlanta premiere reveal a group that, from its reemergence in the winter of 1915, was (re)using and contemporizing film as a way to publicize and define itself within the local community. The methods deployed – performing at the site of exhibition and reworking promotional devices used for the film – served to transfer the historical activities on-screen out onto the streets. Indeed, while Simmons's so-called "modern" Klan was largely distinct from the long-deceased original model, founded fifty years earlier in the aftermath of the Civil War, it managed, through its exploitation of *The Birth of a Nation,* to manufacture a historical lineage from the short-lived, romanticized Reconstruction group.[3]

Beyond this, the Klan's appearance and advertisements show a modern group specifically exploiting and commercializing the visual iconography of Griffith's film. Much of the modern Klan's imagery – such as the fiery cross and insignia – was derived directly from Griffith's film and, more specifically, from Thomas Dixon's novel and play on which *The Birth of a Nation* was based. As such, the Klan mobilized an image (the Klan costume) that was now manufactured for, and advertised through, film. Of particular interest for the present book, the advertisements and accompanying publicity highlight the modern Klan's use of media, from its point of reemergence, engaging with and appropriating film through the printed press.

If we move forward eight years to January 1924 and examine another Klan advertisement, we see developments in the ways the group imag-

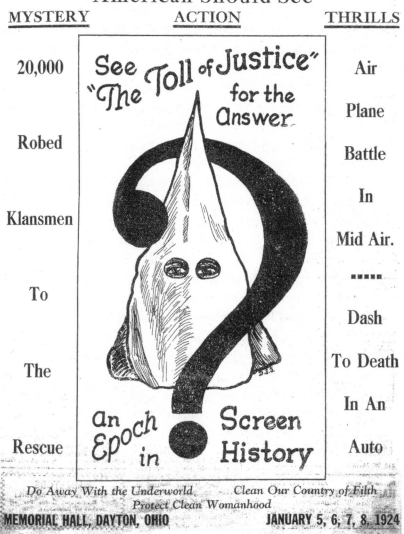

0.2. Advertisement for *The Toll of Justice* in a Klan newspaper, *Kluxer,* 5 January 1924, 29.

ined and used cinema. *Kluxer,* a modern Klan newspaper, ran a full-page advertisement for *The Toll of Justice* (1923), a film produced in Ohio by Klan interests and featuring genuine Klansmen (see fig 0.2). The Klan now had an elaborate media network, with *Kluxer* just one of many newspapers that connected local and national Klan interests during the 1920s. As part of this network, the Klan was also producing and exhibiting its own films. Furthermore, the Klan's success and popularity had moved well beyond Atlanta, with the Klan exercising particular influence in the Midwest, specifically in Ohio and Indiana.

If the activities in Atlanta in 1915 evidence a new group attempting to appropriate and monetize a cinematic image, the poster for *The Toll of Justice* hints at the implications of such moves. In this instance, the advertisement foregrounds a picture of the Klan hood, which was by now the financial cornerstone of the Klan's commercial operations, with each new recruit paying $6.50 for their Klan regalia. The image itself had come to signify mystery and excitement, as the question mark in the advertisement suggests, with the Klan's own media attempting both to exploit this popular curiosity and to take control of the image, to extricate it from the intimations of racial violence and corruption that antagonistic factions of the media propagated. Through film, the Klan now promised to unmask the Klansmen by presenting its own "authentic," inside view of Klan activities.

The poster may then be understood as part of an ideological battle, not only over the image, identity, and function of the Klan, but more broadly over its place within American society. A promotional tool not only for the film, the movie poster also functioned as an advertisement for the Klan, serving to recruit likeminded individuals. More specifically, in emphasizing three instructions – "Do away with the Underworld," "Clean Our Country of Filth," and "Protect Clean Womanhood" – which served as directives from the Klan, the poster sought to publicize the Klan's idealized vision of modern America.

There are two further points to note here. First, a close examination of Klan newspapers, films, and promotional materials challenges popular perceptions of the group, many of which were established from *The Birth of a Nation.* For example, the Klan's dealings with film – whether protesting or producing – reveal a group far more concerned with Jewish and Catholic influences on American society than with African Americans. This marks a significant shift from the earlier Klan of the Reconstruction era memorialized by Dixon and Griffith; that group operated within a fresh social context. These shifts have been blurred by more recent film and media representations, which have often presented a monolithic Klan over almost 150 years of history and, within this, at least three distinct movements: the Reconstruction Klan, the interwar "modern Klan" that is the subject of this study, and the Klan of the civil rights movement. Examining the Klan's relationship to film after 1915 and its formative media operations helps to explain both these distinct historical movements and the dominant contemporary representations of the group.

Second, the Klan imagined film, and the discourses around it, as a means of shaping public behavior, of defining and creating Klansmen and, by extension, American citizens. In so doing, the Klan joined American identity to its own, promoting "The Picture that every red-blooded American should see." The tagline serves a further function by 1924, with the group looking to differentiate its film from the supposedly "foreign" industry pictures, such as Charlie Chaplin's *The Pilgrim* (1923), against which it was widely criticizing and protesting. The Klan was, by now, a prominent social reform group, protesting against film as one emblematic instance of the modernity it sought to counter. This modernity was defined, through its protests of film, in religious terms as the product of a Jewish-controlled industry. In response, the Klan now made films to visualize an alternative conception of American identity.

The posters reveal a myriad of imagined uses for cinema – to recruit, define, and inculcate citizens – and present film outside of traditional exhibition contexts, with the Klan now finding various sites in which to make cinema useful for its purposes. Before the Saturday night performance of *The Toll of Justice*, advertised in *Kluxer*, a thousand Klansmen marched to the town hall where the film was showing. Led by a Klan band, they delivered a magnified version of the modest spectacle offered at the Atlanta premiere eight years earlier.[4] Significantly, the march was not outside a designated theater or cinema, but to Memorial Hall. Typical of the non-theatrical venues utilized by the Klan, *The Toll of Justice* would play at schools, churches, and city halls, reaching out and defining the Klan as an educative, religious, and legitimate part of the local community.

If this example highlights the need to look beyond 1915, it also highlights a need to revisit that year. The *Kluxer* advertisement and resulting parade demonstrates the continuing influence of Griffith's film on the Klan – it emphasizes the scale of the production and refers to an "epoch in screen history," a phrase widely used for *Birth* – while other advertisements directly compared the *The Toll of Justice* to *Birth*. The *Birth of a Nation* has been widely acknowledged as a formative work in the development of both Classical Hollywood and a vertically integrated film industry, its economic success having consolidated ongoing formal and industrial shifts, expediting, for example, a move from Nickelodeons to middle-class "movie palaces." Yet what is less well known is the film's crucial position in a concurrent history of sponsored screenings within rural communities. From its initial appearance in Atlanta, *The Birth of a Nation* – and film more generally – became useful for social and political organizations like the Klan, which looked to exploit the mass media to define, promote, and position themselves within the American mainstream.

In this way, *Birth* becomes part of a far bigger question that filmmakers, exhibitors, audiences, moral crusaders, and the state are all attempting to answer at this moment: What is the role of cinema? Twenty years after the first public projection of moving images, these groups were still configuring the function and *place* of cinema within society. Two examples from 1915 reveal the parameters of this debate. First, in February, the Supreme Court passed its first verdict on the film industry, determining that the exhibition of moving pictures was "business pure and simple" and should not be viewed as "part of the press of the country, or as organs of public opinion."[5] A month later, D. W. Griffith gave an interview in the *New York Times,* in which he provocatively envisaged a time "in less than ten years" when public school children would be taught history by moving pictures and when public libraries would contain "long rows of boxes in a scientifically prepared room" at which you would "actually see what happened."[6] This parallel cinema – instructional, educational, non-theatrical – would grow up alongside the more famous and entrenched studio-based form that Griffith had helped establish.

In many respects this book is a response to the Supreme Court's verdict. In short, a close examination of the Klan's engagement with cinema – as producer, exhibitor, social pressure group, or on-screen subject – provides one answer to these questions on cinema's function. Such an answer, in illustrating how the Klan imagined and used film as part of the media, challenges both the Supreme Court's ruling and dominant histories of silent cinema that focus on entertainment and Hollywood. This is not to say that the Klan does not operate within these areas, as the book frequently reveals, but certainly a study of the Klan illustrates the overlooked ways in which a myriad of social and political groups began to use cinema to further their own agendas.

In examining the role of film in both contributing to and revealing Klan histories, it is essential to look beyond 1915 and beyond the initial exhibition of *Birth*. While its release directly coincided with the formation of a modern Klan, this newly formed group would remain a marginal presence, predominantly confined to parts of Georgia until 1920. There were a couple of important changes at that point, which facilitated the group's extensive expansion across the country, namely, shifts both in the political landscape of America and in the Klan's own organization. The "Red Scare" of 1919, fueled by a media panic that followed a series of worker strikes, reached its apex with raids and deportations on supposedly foreign socialist sympathizers. Within this context, Americanization campaigns spread, supported by government, industry, and educational centers, and, of most interest here, "patriotic" fraternal groups like the Klan. As Lee Grieveson has demonstrated, film would now play a prominent role in "shap[ing] the allegiance of the population."[7] Significantly, the concurrent reorganization of the Klan was instigated by two publicity managers, who established a "propagation department" and immediately looked to engage fully with cinema. While reactionary in its politics, the Klan would now embrace the modern mass media, establishing local and national newspapers, controlling radio stations, publishing houses, and, of particular relevance here, film exhibition.

By the time of the advertisement in *Kluxer*, the Klan was approaching its peak and exercising a considerable influence in many aspects of social and political life. The Johnson-Reed Immigration Act of May 1924, which restricted immigration into the United States, may be indicative of the institutionalization of Klan values, but there are also plenty of local examples that highlight the Klan's legitimacy within local communities. Newspapers reported Klansmen making donations at church services, attending school bake sales in full regalia, and establishing baseball leagues. The group would by now claim almost five million members from all walks of life and, as such, is best understood not as an anomaly of the period or social pariah, but rather as one of a number of prominent conservative groups that helped to shape and define American society and, in its virulent criticisms of Hollywood, American culture.

What follows covers the period of the modern Klan's existence, from its rebirth in 1915 to its eventual disbandment in 1944. The book adds to our understanding of the Klan's history and the often-neglected aspects of interwar American cinema. In particular, it contributes to an emerging body of work on non-theatrical uses of cinema and on the ways in which conservative groups have used and shaped media agendas.[8]

In revisiting *The Birth of a Nation,* the first chapter examines the role of the film in the rebirth of the Klan, but equally the role of the Klan in the rebirth of the film during the 1920s. Such a formation highlights the fragile, unstable dynamics at play between the Klan and cinema. By charting the group's early development, the opening chapter confronts a series of questions. Why 1915? Why Atlanta? What role did *The Birth of a Nation* play in this rebirth and, in particular, what role did film play after 1920, when the Klan embraced modern publicity and spread across the nation? In answering these questions, I chart a history that begins with the stage presentation of Dixon's play *The Clansman* in 1905, revisits Atlanta in 1915, takes in the Klan's extensive exploitation of William Fox's *The Face at Your Window* in 1921, and concludes with Griffith's 1924 production of a new historical epic, *America.*

Having considered how the Klan exploited and appropriated film, chapter 2 explores the relationship between the Klan and the film industry on a discursive level, through a close examination of Klan newspapers. From the Klan's protests against actress Pola Negri, Paramount, and Chaplin's *The Pilgrim* to its literal presence within Hollywood, the chapter highlights the Klan's role as a social reformer and as a significant conservative pressure group, directing and renegotiating the widespread calls for industrial reform. As calls for censorship escalated, and as manufactured scandals engulfed Hollywood, the Klan used its criticisms of film and Hollywood to position itself as a legitimate social force, protecting Protestant values against the perceived threats of a social modernity, exemplified by Jewish and Catholic interests. In this way, the battle fought between traditional conservative American Protestant interests – of which the Klan was now front row center (or, perhaps, front row right) – and an industry presented as modern, decadent, and foreign is a microcosm of a national struggle that raged over postwar American national identity.

The Klan's own forays into film production and exhibition, discussed briefly here through the advertisement of *The Toll of Justice,* are the focus of chapter 3. The chapter introduces the Klan as film producer and exhibitor and, in exploring its non-theatrical uses of film, positions the Klan in relation to respected religious and patriotic groups such as The American Legion; it also positions its films alongside stage shows, initiations, and "Klantauquas" as part of the Klan's broader entertainment and pedagogical programs.[9] How did the Klan articulate its values and policies through its cinema, and what do the Klan's experiences in producing and exhibiting film reveal more broadly about the development – and indeed challenges and limitations – of independent and non-theatrical forms of cinema in the United States?

The first three chapters focus predominantly on the Klan's activities, its active engagement with film as "textual poacher," reformer, censor, and independent producer and exhibitor. What, then, did the mainstream industry do in response, and what are the repercussions of these exchanges for the Klan, the American film industry, and more broadly for American society? These questions form the backdrop to chapter 4, which looks more closely at the industry's responses to the Klan. It examines industrial representations of the group – from Mary Pickford's appearance as a night rider in *Heart o' the Hills* (1919) to Humphrey Bogart's starring role in *Black Legion* (1937) – exploring and explaining how producers and exhibitors represented and exploited the Klan, in various guises, on mainstream screens. The chapter examines less celebrated industrial output, from westerns and children's cartoons to comedy shorts and, later, exploitation films. In covering the full period of the modern Klan's activity, from 1915 to 1944, the chapter also considers the decline of the Klan, played out on and through film. The Klan's increasing marginalization, both from society and from film discourse, can be understood through its failed film endeavors – for example, many of its leaders who were involved in a succession of well-publicized scandals at the time were directly involved in Klan cinema – and, in particular, by examining the industry's changing representation of the Klan on-screen during the 1930s.

Taken together, the chapters in this book provide a multi-faceted story of interwar America, one that exposes the fierce debates around Americanism, race, religion, and citizenship that defined this era. Cinema, in all its forms, shaped and articulated these debates and in turn was fashioned within this context.

WHITE ROBES
SILVER SCREENS

ONE

Re-*Birth*

THE BIRTH OF A NATION AND THE GROWTH OF THE KLAN

The Ku Klux Klan has become a serious menace to American Institutions. A careful investigation has revealed that the ease with which Klan solicitors are able to sell memberships is directly attributable to the romantic color cast about the Klan name by your motion picture The Birth of a Nation. Whatever we may think of the Klan of 1865, we must agree that the Klan of 1923 is far from romantic or heroic. We feel that it is your duty to use your tremendous power to undo the damage unwittingly done [to] the country when your [film The] Birth of a Nation was shown and we call upon you to cooperate with all good American citizens to stamp out this growing evil. May we have an expression of your personal opinion of the Klan and such assurance as you feel necessary that you will take steps to tear away the mantle of heroism in which you once dressed the nightriders [?]

Telegram written by W. N. Kramer, publisher of *The Spotlight*, to David W. Griffith, 10 January 1923

On 10 January 1923, W. N. Kramer, the publisher of *Spotlight,* an anti-Klan newspaper in Minneapolis, wrote these words to D. W. Griffith, challenging him to respond to his earlier work and to "paint the Ku Klux Klan in its true light."[1] Kramer argued that Griffith's representation of an idealized historical Klan in *The Birth of a Nation* was now helping Kleagles (Klan "solicitors") to sell memberships for a new incarnation of the Ku Klux Klan, which had formed in Atlanta in 1915 and had now spread throughout the country. While *Spotlight,* like most historians subsequently, referred to the film's initial release, Griffith's film had, by 1923, become a prominent and prototypical component of the modern Klan's publicity. The group utilized *The Birth of a Nation* throughout the decade, whether arranging its own screenings, making very public appearances at cinemas showing the film, or using the discussions surrounding the film to define and promote itself within American society. The Klan would closely reference and rework particular images from the film, and when it began producing, distributing, and exhibiting its own pictures in the 1920s, *Birth* would become a touchstone for this "Klan cinema."

The Klan's engagement with *Birth* was intended in part to connect the modern incarnation to the long-disbanded historical group represented on-screen. It partly achieved this by "dressing" the modern group in the theatrical robes of Dixon and Griffith's historical fantasy. Indeed, the costume adopted by Griffith on-screen would serve as an emblematic connection to, and advertisement for, a new modern group. In this instance, *Spotlight* rather generously exonerated Griffith of responsibility for the film's afterlife – the telegram refers to "damage unwittingly done" – but it still acknowledged a film completely transformed by the modern Klan and, what's more, now outlined the filmmaker's "duty" to reassert his authorial control and, in Klan parlance, to unmask the modern night riders.

At the same moment in January 1923, Thomas Dixon, the author of *The Clansman,* the novel and play on which *The Birth of a Nation* was based, spoke in New York at the invitation of the American Unity League, a largely Catholic group devoted to the eradication of the re-emergent Klan. Dixon used the speech to offer his "outspoken contempt" for the modern group. "The Klan assault upon the foreigner is," he stated, "the acme of stupidity and inhumanity. We are all foreigners except the few Indians we haven't killed."[2] Dixon was also seeking financing at this time for a film based on his 1907 novel *The Traitor,* which he claimed in the stock promotional circular would "strike a deadly blow" to the organization. In direct response to this "anti-Klan film," a Klan group planned a picture of its own, *Armageddon.* Their preferred director for the project was D. W. Griffith.[3]

By 1923 both sides of the Klan divide were seeking out, using, and critiquing Griffith and Dixon. Their work was discussed in relation to the modern Knights of the Ku Klux Klan, although, perhaps unsurprisingly, both rejected any direct responsibility for their perceived progeny. "It may be flattering," Griffith wrote shortly afterward, "to find out that the present Klan has copied the picture so closely, but it is not a welcome thought to me, that I have been in any way responsible for the spread of this order." When Dixon learned in 1922 that a local branch of the Klan in Baltimore had taken his name ("Thomas Dixon Klan Number One"), he stated that he knew nothing about this and "am opposed to it root and branch." The *Baltimore Afro-American* newspaper, commenting on Dixon's response, described this as "another example of a Southern Aristocrat denying his own child."[4]

This notion that *The Birth of a Nation* had spawned a new national, socially active Klan was, by 1923, widely and uncritically endorsed. *Spotlight* stated categorically that "Birth of Nation [had] established [the modern] Klan in [the] U.S.," and argued that this "single motion picture is practically the only agent" in its growth. When the National Association for the Advancement of Colored People (NAACP) telegraphed Kansas governor Jonathan M. Davis in the same year, urging him to prevent the film from being exhibited in his state, it justified its protests by similarly arguing that the film "is largely responsible for [the] present day revival of the Klan."[5]

These traditional causative arguments, which suggest that a single film engineered one of the most prominent social and political organizations in American history, oversimplify what is a far more complex, stuttering, and far-reaching history. By 1923, *Birth* had become a central component of and generative text for a modern Klan, with the Klan looking to use the film, in varied ways, not simply at its formation in 1915, but as the group developed and grew in the 1920s. While there is an enormous amount of literature on *Birth* and its initial spectacular theatrical success, what remains less well known is the film's afterlife during the 1920s in smaller theaters – some owned by the Klan – and other kinds of spaces. As the Klan reappropriated the film – becoming something of a "textual poacher," to borrow Henry Jenkins's phrase – it pulled, stretched, and deepened the divides occasioned by the film's initial release.[6] This text, made malleable by promotional devices fashioned by Dixon when the original play first toured in 1905 and by Griffith upon the film's release a decade later, was now reworked and maneuvered as it became politically useful to this conservative group. As such, this chapter not only examines the role of the film in the rebirth of the Klan but, moreover, of the Klan in the rebirth of the film during the 1920s.

The *Spotlight* telegram also showcases the media's role in the fiercely contested growth of the Klan, published as it was in one of the emerging anti-Klan newspapers, a response, in turn, to the rapid growth of the Klan press. This chapter traces the proliferation of Klan media across the nation, from Atlanta in 1905 to Ohio two decades later. In examining the shared contexts in which the film and the modern Klan emerged in Atlanta, I consider how both Dixon's play and the subsequent film responded to, negotiated, and engendered social, political, and racial tensions within the city. After considering how these traveling national productions contributed to a new, local Klan in Atlanta, I then examine how Klan leaders, Kleagles (recruiters), and local groups used *Birth* as a promotional and recruiting vehicle as the order enjoyed a rapid and spectacular spread across the nation during the first half of the 1920s. The story begins, however, in Atlanta in 1905.

ATLANTA 1905: BEGINNINGS

On Monday, 30 October 1905, Thomas Dixon walked onto the stage at the Grand Opera House during the Atlanta premiere of his new play, *The Clansman*. Before the final act – entitled "The Ku Klux Klan" – Dixon offered a defense of his work, providing his own historical take on the Reconstruction Klan of the 1860s by recalling his father's time as a member of the organization. The *Atlanta Constitution* reported that Dixon was "cheered for several minutes by the audience and he was several times interrupted by applause."[7]

These audience reactions attest to Dixon's showmanship and also, more strikingly, to the mounting racial tensions that his work both responded and contributed to. The cries of "lynch him," emanating from white members of the audience during the staged trial of the African American named Gus, were reportedly met by hisses and taunts from the balcony where the segregated African Americans watched. The *Atlanta Independent*, an African American weekly, claimed that the situation had become so tense that the management kept the house lights on throughout the performance and stopped the sale of soda bottles for fear that they would be hurled around the theater. Further reports explained that "every suggestion of equality is met with howls of approval from the third gallery and storms of hisses from every other section of the house."[8]

The theater was presented within the press as a site of racial confrontation, a site through which contemporary racial fears were channeled and as a microcosm of society at large. *The Clansman* opened with an election in which inebriated African Americans discuss exactly how they intend to engage in voter fraud. The issue of racial equality and, more specifically, black enfranchisement would become the defining issue of the 1906 Democratic primary in Atlanta, foregrounded and championed by the former populist Tom Watson and the victorious candidate Hoke Smith. Dixon described his play not as a "reminiscence" but as a "prophecy," and was quick to use his own personality both to generate publicity and to engineer a connection between his historical work and the contemporary situation.[9] In January 1906 he sent an open letter to African American leader Booker T. Washington, who was about to go onstage at a fundraising event for the Tuskegee Institute in New York's Carnegie Hall. "In response to your appeal for funds," Dixon wrote, "I hereby offer to contribute $10,000 from the profits of 'The Clansman' to Tuskegee Institute, provided you give complete and satisfactory proof that you do not desire social equality for the Negro, and that your school is opposed to the amalgamation of the races."[10]

Washington did not respond to Dixon, but this was largely immaterial for Dixon. We see here Dixon's confrontational and divisive racial politics used as part of the play's promotional strategies, strategies that would be reapplied a decade later when *The Clansman* was adapted for the screen. When Dixon was challenged on the historical veracity of his play, he proposed submitting his work to a "jury of the American Historical Society" and offered a thousand dollars if the verdict went against him. In a rhetoric later famously used by Griffith, Dixon claimed that he had "sworn documentary evidence" for every incident referenced and had "mastered the contents" of more than 4,000 books.[11] However, it was not simply the view of history offered by Dixon that was problematic, but the ways in which this history was represented through the live performance.

The Clansman brought the spectacle of a just and heroic Klan into the theater, offering two distinct modes of Klan representation, which would prefigure, and be reimagined in, the Klan's later on-screen appearances.[12] *The Clansman's* final act opens with the shrouded figures dashing across the stage on horseback. Advertisements highlighted the excitement generated by the Klan's ride to the rescue, promoting a "thrilling story of the Ku Klux Klan" and a "stupendous dramatic spectacle." As with *The Birth of a Nation,* which would advertise the 18,000 people and 3,000 horses involved in the production, the scale of this display was prioritized often at the expense of the narrative. Posters for *The Clansman* noted the "Forty Principals. Two carloads of scenery. Army of supernumeraries and horses" on the stage.[13] Despite the play's title, which suggests an individual Klan protagonist, the play's denouement encouraged audiences to position themselves alongside a collective mass of largely anonymous robed figures.

Aside from the concluding sequence of the Klan in action, "mounted, masked and costumed" and riding in vengeance, *The Clansman* also displayed the more private rituals of the group. A scene inside the "cave of the invisible kingdom," where Klansmen gathered around a fiery cross for the "trial" of Gus, offered theater viewers access to the "unseen" nighttime ceremonial activities of the group and foreshadows later screen appearances of the Klan that would promise to show the inner workings of the secret organization.[14] Even the *New York Dramatic Mirror,* in its critical bashing of this "peculiarly obnoxious melodrama," acknowledged that "one must admit that the night meeting of the Klan was an impressive stage episode." "It is no wonder," the review concluded, "that nervous women have been hysterical at that point of the performance."[15]

The reactions to the Klan sequences, not just from "nervous women," hint at the ways in which the staging invited audiences to respond collectively and viscerally to the group activities of the Klan. A review of a performance in South Carolina saw "the spirit of the mob" within the audience, while Dixon would use similar language when dismissing the critical and institutional opposition to his play, describing the audience as the "supreme court of public opinion."[16] There are clear parallels with the reception of the film a decade later, as the play invited debates on the social impact of stage entertainment at a moment when, with the proliferation of Nickelodeons, these discussions were extended to moving pictures. While initially the discussions speculated on the ways in which the play might incite racial violence, by the play's second season in the latter half of 1906, a more prescriptive approach was adopted and the play was banned or withdrawn in a number of areas, chief among them Atlanta. A closer look at the aborted staging of the play in Atlanta in 1906 reveals an early recognition of and concern for the social impact that Dixon's work (and his methods of exploitation) could exercise within a racially divisive local community. Furthermore, it positions *The Clansman* within a sequence of events, culminating in the riots and the intensification of Jim Crow segregation, that would reconstitute and mold the increasingly volatile, racially divided city in which the modern Klan would ride a decade later.

The *Atlanta Georgian,* a newspaper that was supportive both of Dixon's play and politics, published an editorial on 26 September 1906 entitled "Let us Postpone Clansman." The paper positively avoided condemning the play, "which has some great points," but warned against the planned return at the Grand Opera House in October.

> If the upper gallery should be filled with blacks, as it was when The Clansman was here before, and the lower house with white people, and if the whites, applauding wildly every allusion to white supremacy and eternal superiority, as they did before, should be answered by the blacks as they were before, breaking into eager yells at the strong statement of racial equality and intermarriage, this particular act might be concluded with a tragedy akin to one in Booth's theater in the April of 1865.
>
> If Gus, the negro villain of the play, should be seen by the second gallery skulking in the shadow of that tender little girl with rape in his head and his eyes, the chances are not small that Gus (who is a fine fellow in his own character [and a white actor in blackface]) might go home with a bullet to his body today as a reminder of the second gallery's excited prejudices.[17]

The *Atlanta Constitution* contributed its own editorial the following day, in which it "unqualifiedly condemns the production of this dangerous theatrical performance in Atlanta," describing it as a "highly inflammatory, if not incendiary, melodrama." The *Atlanta Journal,* which had serialized the novel a year earlier, surmised that the play's appearance "could result in no good and would possibly be the cause of additional disasters." On the same day, Henry DeGive, the manager of the Grand Opera House, contacted the touring company and agreed that the play would not return at present.[18]

DeGive's decision came at the end of a week in which Atlanta had faced the deadliest race riots in its history. Those reading the *Atlanta Constitution* on 23 September would awake to this headline: "Atlanta is swept by raging mob due to assaults on white women; 16 Negroes reported to be dead." A city previously considered racially progressive and a model for the New South was now beset by mob violence. This mob violence was responding primarily, as the headline suggested, to a fear surrounding the sexual threat of African Americans on white womanhood. These fears were exacerbated throughout the acrimonious gubernatorial election campaign, which was finally resolved in Hoke Smith's favor in August. The campaigners served up a tirade of racist rhetoric, as Smith encouraged voters to use any means "to remove the present danger of Negro domination." The printed press – with which both Smith and his opponent Clark Howell had very close connections – exploited this racial discourse in a "scramble for circulation," publishing lurid accounts of sexual assaults and warning of a "negro crime wave."[19] A decade later, Dixon would fan these fears as he presented the NAACP's objections to *The Birth of a Nation* as evidence of a contemporary African American threat, informing white audiences that the NAACP encouraged members "to fight the whites and to make mongrel marriages."[20]

These tales of imperiled white women, littered across the city's front pages in the summer of 1906, evoked the climax of Dixon's play. The *Atlanta Georgian*, in its warning against the reengagement of *The Clansman*, had suggested that it was the staged rape of the "tender little girl" that might elicit a violent response from the audience.[21] Significantly, Dixon altered the conclusion of his novel when he brought it to the stage in 1905. Where previously the Klan had ridden to save Phil Stoneman from execution, onstage it also now rode to save his sister Elsie from the advances of Silas Lynch. The Klan now responded to the imperiled white woman, imagining a role that resonated with contemporary popular fears.

In depicting a manufactured racial problem, *The Clansman* was part of a social and political assault on the African American, which precipitated the riots of September 1906. The *Atlanta Constitution* suggested that some of the present race troubles in the city could "date their psychological incentive" to the play's initial appearance, reevaluating the play's initial reception in the context of recent events. The paper opposed the play's reengagement by arguing that it was "designed to inflame the most elemental passions of race against race" and served as a "passionate incentive to riot and murder." *The Clansman* had already been banned in a number of states and had been described elsewhere as a "riot breeder" and as "about as elevating as a lynching." It did, however, remain enormously popular. During its second year, touring from September 1906 to April 1907, *The Clansman* played in 250 prominent towns in the South, traveling 32,000 miles in the process. The racial discourses surrounding the play traveled with the company, attaching to local incidents as they journeyed. The decision to postpone the staging of *The Clansman* in Atlanta was fueled by these traveling discourses and controversies, but it also highlighted a specific local response to the disintegration of race relations there since the play's previous appearance.[22]

In transposing a historical tale of South Carolina to local, contemporary situations, Dixon's play was credited with visualizing, exploiting, and inciting racial tensions. The play imagined not only a problem but also a possible solution in the white robes of the Ku Klux Klan. Dixon's Klan provided what was seen as a thrilling, just, and necessary white response to the threat of the African American rapist and, as the reports of sexual assaults escalated during the summer of 1906, the local papers now speculated on the resurrection of the group as part of this white response.[23]

The *Atlanta Evening News* ran a front-page headline in August 1906 stating that "Ku Klux Klans will doubtless be organised in the suburbs of Atlanta for the purpose of punishing the negroes who assault white women." Alongside the headline was a list of six women "assaulted" in Fulton County and the "punishments" meted out ("identified; legally executed," "Assailant still at large," or "identified and lynched"). The paper was manufacturing both demand and response, with an accompanying editorial, written by Charles Daniel, presenting a "call for 1,000 Good and True men," who would "at any and all costs . . . wreak swift and terrible punishment upon the guilty." A few days later, the *Atlanta Journal* reported that petitions were being circulated for the formation of the "famous midnight band of Reconstruction time" and that "recent outrages" were the cause of this movement.[24]

While Daniel's new Klan – a so-called "News Protective League" – was not realized, reports suggested that vigilante groups had emerged elsewhere in the South and, on occasion, the formation of these groups was directly aligned to the staging of *The Clansman*. When the play reached Mississippi in October 1906, newspapers described a "nightmare scenario" in which the play was "so stirring in race prejudice" that "lawless bands of both races" had formed. After claims that a new Ku Klux Klan was organized in the area, African Americans were reported to have formed a band of "White Caps."[25]

In the same month, "a mob of several thousand negroes" attacked the Walnut Street Theatre in Philadelphia, where *The Clansman* was showing. After meeting with prominent African Americans, the mayor banned further productions of the play, explaining that he was convinced that the tendency of the play was to "produce" and "intensify racial hatred." Significantly, Mayor John Weaver blamed the producers and promoters of the play for encouraging this agitation "for the purpose of advertising the production." In a typically feisty response, Dixon argued that the closure of the theater by a "Negro mob" marked the "most infamous outrage in the history of America." Dixon used the closure to fuel the rhetoric of his play (as he would do again in 1915), speaking of a political submission to the "Negro criminal." While the African American response to the play was not fully organized (the NAACP formed in 1909), its staging provided a public arena through which contemporary racial tensions could be played out. On this occasion, Dixon enlisted lawyers to argue his case before Pennsylvania judge Mayer Salzberger, who ruled in his favor. Buoyed by the victory and the publicity generated, Dixon brought the play back to the Walnut Street Theatre in April 1907 for what he now described as an "indefinite period."[26]

In drawing parallels, both on and off the stage, between the progressive politics of the Reconstruction era and the modern-day rise of an urban African American class, Dixon ensured that his play would continue to resonate with audiences as it traveled. Despite the withdrawal of *The Clansman* in 1906, his work would return to Atlanta throughout the next decade. *The Traitor*, the final part of his trilogy, a "wonderful story of the decline and fall of the Ku Klux Klan," played at the Grand Opera House in November 1908 before *The Clansman* successfully returned to the same venue in February 1909 and again in October 1911.[27] When *The Clansman* returned in 1909, the *Atlanta Georgian* reported that Civil War veterans were in attendance. This followed the play's recent run in Tennessee, the birthplace of the original Klan, at which surviving founders and leaders of the group had assembled. Newspapers listed the prominent former Klansmen present, including a congressman, a governor, and a secretary of state, with the appearance of the veterans helping to validate both the play's representation of history and the supposedly secret past of these men. The synthesis between staged fiction and history, between performers and spectators, blurred traditional boundaries of theatrical performance. Reports explained that the interest of the audience was divided between the actors onstage and the "grand old 'vets'" in the boxes. The crowd responded to and cheered not only the performers but also the historical figures that this fiction was mythologizing. The event illustrates the integration and agency of Klan figures within the theatrical space, aligning themselves with the staged activities. Intriguingly, the veterans also offered to extend this appearance outside the theater, to provide a "real" Ku Klux Klan parade to mark *The Clansman's* run.[28]

The veterans' offer may be understood as a reenactment, but it also shows, on a modest scale, *The Clansman* as an event regenerating particular aspects of the Reconstruction Klan, namely the display and public performance of the group. *The Clansman* provided a means of taking this historical Klan back off the stage and out onto the streets. On this occasion the offer was "respectfully declined," but when *The Clansman* returned to Atlanta in December 1915 through the medium of film, a new, recently formed group of Klansmen would mark its premiere by parading outside the theater.[29]

ATLANTA 1915: THE BIRTH OF A NEW KLAN

The poster for *The Birth of a Nation's* much-heralded appearance in Atlanta in December 1915, which was featured alongside Simmons's hand-drawn advertisement for his new group, depicted the film's title within a circle or globe. While Simmons had taken inspiration from – or rather directly imitated – the familiar image of the rearing horseman used in Dixon's books and in earlier publicity for *Birth*, by the time Griffith's film reached Atlanta a "global" poster was also offered. The poster, which often included the tagline "The eighth wonder of the world" alongside the new moniker that had replaced "The Clansman" shortly after its New

York premiere in February 1915, was emblematic of the film's national and global ambitions. While the stage show of *The Clansman* had been advertised as "a play every Southerner should see," by the time *The Birth of a Nation* began its Southern tour, the film's assimilation narrative had enjoyed unprecedented success in the North and would help open up international markets, such as South America. By reinserting and fore-grounding a new local Klan at the film's premiere, Simmons sought to localize and contemporize this national history, just as Dixon had done previously with his play, now offering an outlet and solution for the local racial tensions exacerbated during the film's run.[30]

Simmons's advertisement was noted in the African American weekly *The New York Age*, which in a prophetic editorial warned of its potential impact: "Here we have 'The Birth of a Nation' not merely set forth in a moving picture show, BUT PERPETUATED in an active organization; an organization which will grow and spread, and whose virulent power compared with that of 'The Birth of a Nation' will be a cancer compared to a cat boil."[31] The editorial reserved particular criticism for the state of Georgia. On the day of the film's premiere in Atlanta, Simmons had been granted a charter for his new Klan from Secretary of State Phil Cook. "Here we have the State itself authorizing and sanctioning a rever-sion to a whole epoch of blackness," the editorial wrote, notably using language adopted within the film's publicity campaigns. Griffith and his partners, the Aitken brothers (Harry and Roy), had set up the Epoch Producing Company to distribute the film in the United States. Dixon's novel had been described as "an epoch-making book," while the play was advertised with a quote from an early review in the *Norfolk Register* as an "epoch-making play." For the *New York Age*, this epoch was defined not by form but ideology, signaling a return to a dark era in American and African American history.[32]

The editorial presented the Klan as institutionalized, an accepted facet of the state. *The Birth of a Nation* contributes to this process, pri-marily by referencing President Woodrow Wilson both within the film and within the film's promotional discourses (the famous and oft-quoted claim that Wilson described the film as "like history written with light-ning"). Wilson had been a classmate of Dixon at Johns Hopkins Univer-sity, a point that Dixon never tired of mentioning, and it is Wilson whose words first introduce the Klan in the film. Fully half an hour before the Klan appears on-screen, a title provides a quotation from Wilson's *A History of the American People*. "The white men were roused by a mere instinct of self-preservation . . . ," it states, "until at last there had sprung into existence a great Ku Klux Klan, a veritable empire of the South, to protect the Southern country." Using the current president to introduce the Klan not only legitimized its historical portrayals, but also served to institutionalize its represented values and actions within a modern context. Despite the language often adopted by the Klan – as a victimized minority – Griffith's film and the modern Klan arrived into a pervasive culture of fear and racial intolerance, evident on a national level but magnified within the city of Atlanta.

As in 1906, contemporary accounts suggested that racial tensions ripened Atlanta for a new Klan. Most famously, Tom Watson, who had fueled racial animosity during the gubernatorial campaign of 1906, suggested in September 1915 that "another Ku Klux Klan may be organized to restore home rule." Watson was responding here to the recent lynching of Leo Frank, a Jewish factory manager from the North, who was dragged from Milledgeville State Prison to the woods outside Marietta, Georgia (twenty miles from Atlanta), in the early hours of 17 August by the night-riding "Knights of Mary Phagan." The official Georgia state historian noted the similarities between the lynching of Frank and the work of the original Klan when he claimed that "no finer piece of Ku-Kluxing was ever known in Georgia."[33] Frank's coroner, John Booth, was a former Klansman who similarly noted this link, while some press reports imagined these contemporary events through Dixon's historical, fictional framework. "If Dixon were to rewrite his story [*The Clansman*], following the lynching of Leo Frank," wrote the *Fort-Wayne Sentinel*, "he would have to make only small changes in detail."[34]

In this hugely publicized case, Frank was tried and convicted of the murder of thirteen-year-old Mary Phagan, who was found beaten and strangled in the basement of the National Pencil Company factory, part-owned and supervised by Frank, in April 1913. The prosecutor, Hugh Dorsey, who had enjoyed dinner with Dixon after the initial Atlanta performance of *The Clansman* in 1905, presented Frank as a Jewish metropolitan capitalist, coming down from the North and preying on young rural, Southern girls. Frank's case might appear at first to reveal a shift in racial ideology. After all, Frank was convicted despite a convincing level of evidence pointing toward the African American factory janitor, Jim Conley. Yet Frank represents the modern embodiment of the historical enemy presented in *Birth*. Cartoons and newspaper reports depicted Frank, in the words of one detective on the case, as a "racial descendant of the carpetbaggers," suggesting that his lynching offered a "vicarious atonement for the rule of the carpetbagger in the South during the Reconstruction period." While in *Birth*, the target of the lynch mob is an African American, he is described as a "product" of the carpetbaggers. The ultimate targets at the film's conclusion are the Northerner, Stoneman, and the mulatto, Lynch. As a white Jewish Northerner, Frank represented the amalgamation of these two enemies. His Jewish identity, concealed by his white skin, was indicative of a blurring of racial boundaries, brought about by increased European immigration, which was now seen to challenge both Southern and national identity.[35]

Similarly, Mary Phagan came to represent both a historical and contemporary victim. On the one hand, Mary Phagan was increasingly portrayed, and manufactured, as the incarnate of Flora from *Birth*. Just as Flora had jumped to her death in *Birth* to preserve her honor, white Southerners retained a "staunch insistence that Phagan died to preserve her chastity."[36] Yet on the other hand, Phagan contemporized and localized the fictional character of Flora for audiences in Atlanta. Her death foregrounded fears about changing gender roles, and the impact of industrialization and urbanization on Southern society. Simmons's displays and advertisements are thus part of a process that renegotiates the historical activities of the Klan on-screen, transposing new enemies, victims, and solutions to a local populace.[37]

While audiences may have transposed Mary Phagan into *Birth* through the character of Flora, her backstory as a young rural girl drawn to the city for work also anticipated the popular and controversial white slave pictures, such as *Traffic in Souls*, released shortly after her death (the film reached Atlanta in January 1914). The comparison, noted by Matthew Bernstein, is significant in understanding both a popular reaction against Frank and the antecedents of a modern antisemitic Klan. The white slave traders were widely presented as European immigrant Jews, and while their victims were also often European immigrants, racial discourse clearly distinguished between the "foreign" slave dealer and the "white" victim. Richard Maltby suggests that the terms of the debates allowed feminists and male reformers "to see themselves as rescuers of slaves," and this imagery also offered an important precursor both to *Birth* and to the establishment of a modern Klan. The white slave discourses presented European Jews as a threat within American society. Immigration, America's imperialist ambitions, and now the impending European conflict all brought America into closer contact with these foreign groups and, as we shall see with the Red Scare of 1919, this threat extended beyond a literal, physical danger to a more abstract threat on American national identity. It was this abstract threat that would prove so lucrative for the modern Klan.[38]

The example of Leo Frank attests to a popular fascination with, and fetishizing of, the lynched body shortly before the premiere of *Birth* in Atlanta. When Leo Frank was hanged in August 1915, an estimated 15,000 went to see his body. Postcards with photographs of the lynching were sold in local shops, and immediately exhibitors sought to bring these images to their theaters. Kevin Brownlow writes that one of the theater managers in Atlanta advertised a Pathe newsreel a week after Frank's death by driving a truck around town with a sign promising "actual scenes of the lynching at The Georgian today."[39] A number of Klan historians have noted a more literal link between the Frank lynching and the reemergent Klan, claiming that a group of thirty-six men who met to reform the Klan largely comprised men involved in Frank's murder. Nancy MacLean believes that the "truth" of the link lies less in personnel than in a common vigilante spirit.[40] Either way, *The Birth of a Nation* spoke to a populace for whom questions and images of race and vigilante justice transcended the screen.

In writing about the reception of *The Birth of a Nation* in Lexington, Kentucky, Gregory Waller argues that, while exhibitors there adopted generic promotional and advertising tactics used throughout the nation, the ways in which the film was exhibited and possibly received was a "reflection of quite specific local conditions, particularly of racial relations in Lexington."[41] This paradigm is especially apparent in Atlanta, where the existing national advertising campaign (the posters of a Klansman on horseback, the parade of actors outside the theater) was adapted for local conditions (the advertisement for a local Klan, the parade of local Klansmen). Indeed, as the picture traveled across the country, it resonated with local discourses and generated local responses. In 1905, Thomas Dixon had looked to adapt his play to local contexts in order to increase box office receipts. For William Simmons, a decade later, localizing this film now served to boost his nascent fraternal group commercially. In an interview with *Collier's* in 1928, Simmons acknowledged the important role Griffith's film played in the launch of his group, saying that "The Birth of a Nation helped the Klan enormously."[42] Simmons had not actually seen the film before its arrival in Atlanta, suggesting that for this serial fraternalist it was the event, and the publicity generated by it, that initially appealed to him more than the specific ideology or racial politics contained within the film. Simmons identified the arrival of *Birth* as the ideal moment to launch his latest group using *Birth* in very specific, local ways that years later would shape and influence the national organization. In particular, Simmons manufactured and fostered the visual Klan image and adopted prototypical promotional strategies that entwined the Klan and visual media.

Simmons explained that he had conceived of the modern Klan while recuperating for three months after a motor accident. "I drew many figures of Klansmen on horseback and on foot," he explained. "I planned the robes and the pointed helmet and the mask. I worked out all the emblems and all the ritual." His account illustrates an almost child-like emphasis on image, display, and ritual. Many of these images and rituals were inspired not by historical accounts of the original Klan, but rather by the work of Thomas Dixon. For example, when asked where he got the idea of the fiery cross, emblematic of the modern Klan but not a feature of the original group, Simmons responded, "Oh, you keep reading about it in the novels of the old Klan days, like The Leopard's Spots [the first of Dixon's Reconstruction trilogy]." Similarly, the Klan costume, revealed in the initial hand-drawn advertisement and emblazoned with a cross on the front, mirrors the image featured in Dixon's novel and play. This costume, which Griffith admitted was created "solely from the viewpoint of theatrical effectiveness," would become the distinctive uniform for the modern group, celebrated and advertised through *The Birth of a Nation*.[43]

The film displays this modern costume – both on-screen and through its promotional campaigns – and positions it within an imagined Klan history. It achieves this first by revealing the "inspiration" behind the costume in the 1860s, showing two white children hiding under a white sheet and scaring four African American children (a sequence that would be repeated in comedies of the 1920s, such as *Lodge Night*). In showing "the result" – an establishing shot of two Klansmen on horseback (one facing the camera, one in profile) – the film introduces and historicizes this fictional costume. The sequence also assigns an inherent power to the costume, as the African Americans (both children and then adults) respond in exaggerated terror to the image of largely motionless Klansmen rather than to any specific action or violence.

At other points in the film, the unworn costume is held up to reveal the details of its design. First, Silas Lynch presents the captured regalia to Austin Stoneman and then, shortly afterward, Ben Cameron displays the costume to his sister, asking her and his mother to produce more these outfits. In showing the manufacture of the costume, the film both imagines a traditional role for women and the family within the Klan and highlights the process of making this Klan image. Perhaps ironically, given the Klan's subsequent antisemitism, the costumes were most likely manufactured for the screen by a Jewish immigrant, Robert Goldstein, whose company invested $4,500 in the picture, which comprised $1,500 of his own money and $3,000 in lieu of payment for costume rental.[44]

In celebrating the costume's manufacture, the film champions what would become an integral part of the Klan's business empire. From the outset, members paid $10 to join the Klan and $6.50 for a Klan costume. By 1920, the costumes and other Klan memorabilia would be mass-produced by the Gate City Manufacturing Company in Atlanta, churning out substantial profits for the Klan hierarchy.[45] Promotional strategies for the film, which included ushers dressed in Klan regalia, commodified the on-screen image. These Klan images permeated fashion and social life during the film's Northern run, from KKK kitchen aprons to improvised Klan costumes worn at society balls.[46] Yet the influence of these images would have their greatest impact with the establishment of a new Klan.

The costume was both financially and symbolically integral to the growth of the Klan, a material object that transformed the fictional image of a historical group into a modern, socially active, commercial reality. Critics of the group often present and discuss the costume as a form of disguise, but in the film the costume repeatedly functions not to conceal but to expose the Klansmen. First, Elsie ends her engagement with Ben Cameron after he drops his costume and is thus revealed as an "outlaw," while his father is later arrested after his daughter is spotted hiding a Klan costume within their house. Thus the Klansmen are recognized and exposed not through their actions, deeds, or physiological characteristics but rather by their costume. Similarly, this costume, derived from fiction and popularized through *Birth,* would define the Klan and serve to differentiate it from the many other fraternal groups operating in Atlanta.

A brief consideration of Simmons's background reveals how important the costume was in the success of the Klan. Simmons described himself as a fraternalist by profession and at any time claimed membership in as many as a dozen fraternal organizations. Before establishing the Klan he traveled around local lodges, enjoying access to the rituals, conventions, commercial operations, and personnel of these groups. Indeed, when he first called together his prospective Klansmen on 26 October 1915, the group comprised thirty-four men from existing lodges, including a couple of veterans from the original Reconstruction Klan. Simmons's background thus deemphasizes the singularity of the Klan, as it was merely one of a number of fraternal societies operating in Atlanta in the 1910s.[47] It also helps us to understand the initial motivations behind the new group. For example, Simmons's experiences from April 1913 as "Head Advisor" for the Georgian branch of the Woodmen of the World, a noted beneficiary order, clearly influenced his commercial plans for the Klan. He initially sought to make money through the Klan by selling life insurance, hawking $53,000 worth to forty-two new members within the first few weeks.[48] In its ideology and practices, Simmons's Klan was barely distinguishable from these many other fraternal groups, yet it was through the Klan image – and his opportunistic promotional tie-ins with the film – that he was able to distinguish his new group. Perhaps unsurprisingly, Simmons was not alone in using the release of *Birth* to launch a modern fraternal group. In San Francisco, "The American Order of Clansman" was established during the film's travels as a "patriotic, social and benevolent secret society." Yet Simmons's incarnation succeeded where others failed not only because of the location and receptive audience in Atlanta but also, as Melvyn Stokes has argued, by presenting itself as *the* successor to the original Klan.[49] He achieved this to a large extent through association with *The Birth of a Nation,* even if, as the example of the fiery cross shows, certain details were ahistorical visual fantasies evoked from popular culture.

The accounts of the elaborately staged initiation ceremony, organized on Thanksgiving night, demonstrate Simmons's attempts to engineer this historical context for his new "Knights of the Ku Klux Klan." Meeting the men at the Piedmont Hotel (coincidentally, given that the name of the town in *Birth* is Piedmont, South Carolina), he announced his plan to administer the oath at midnight at the top of Stone Mountain. The reactions were not universally positive – one member reportedly complained, "I can't climb Stone Mountain in the daytime. Can't you revive the ancient glories in the flatlands?" – but Simmons did manage to convince fifteen members to board his hired sightseeing bus. The ceremony itself was awash with references to the Bible, the original Klan, and to American history. The altar contained an American flag carried in the Mexican War, a Bible, a sword from the Civil War, copies of the Constitution of the United States and the Declaration of Independence, and the constitution and laws of the Klan. Inductees drank from the spring of the mountain and lit the fiery cross. It was a suitably elaborate affair notable, the *Atlanta Journal* commented, "for the impressiveness of its setting and detail." The ritual scene would be visualized for locals attending the Atlanta Theater over the next month, although in *The Birth of a Nation* it is Ben Cameron, rather than William Simmons, who raises the fiery cross of "old Scotland's hills" and unveils a flag bearing the "red stain of the life of a Southern woman."[50]

Simmons recounted the story of his group's initiation to the press but, as the *Collier's* article noted, it was unclear at the time whether this story was simply "a press-agent stunt" for the forthcoming release of *The Birth of a Nation.*[51] This reaction hints again at the symbiotic relationship between film and the Klan, and also between the film and other reactionary, patriotic groups. A week after the film's opening, more than a hundred veterans from the Old Soldiers Home were invited to a matinee screening of *Birth*. Newspaper reports wrote of a picture enhanced "almost to reality itself" as the "rebel yell" ascended over the orchestra. As earlier seen with *The Clansman,* the performance provided a local connection and validation to the history presented on-screen, encouraging audience members to recall and attach themselves to the historical cause depicted. "This audience LIVED the picture. This audience KNEW," the *Atlanta Constitution* wrote, quoting former Klan members in attendance. A week later, the matinee was organized as a benefit for The United Daughters of the Confederacy, with Confederate flags on sale before the show. Recognizing the popular interest generated by the film's appearance in the city, The United Daughters of the Confederacy exhibited Klan memorabilia and read Klan stories at their December meeting.[52] These organized screenings, which were mirrored in events arranged for veterans, children, and charities across the country, provide a forerunner to the Klan's use of the film during the 1920s. They also highlight again the close parallels between the emerging Klan and other "patriotic fraternal beneficiary" orders.

The *Birth of a Nation* enjoyed the greatest box office in Atlanta's history and was the first theatrical attraction ever held over for a second (and third) week in the city. Reports and posters claimed that 19,759 people attended within the first week, with thousands turned away and lines running from 9 AM to 6 PM each day. In trying to account for the enormous success of the film, reviews emphasized the emotional responses of local audiences. After describing the Klan sequences in intricate detail, Ned Macintosh in the *Atlanta Constitution* recalled the film's climax: "The awful restraint of the audience is thrown to the winds. Many rise from their seats. With the roar of thunder a shout goes up. Freedom is here. Justice is at hand! Retribution has arrived."[53] Ward Greene, a journalist on the *Atlanta Journal* who would later write the short story on which Disney's film *Lady and The Tramp* was based, stated in his review that "loathing, hate, disgust envelop you, hot blood cries for vengeance," until the Klansmen "roar down to the rescue, and that's when you are lifted by the hair and go crazy."[54]

The reactions generated within the theater filtered out onto the streets, as the numerous accounts of NAACP protests, race riots, and individual incidents of violence testify. In one noted example in Lafayette, Indiana, Henry Brock fired three bullets into the body of Edward Mason, a fifteen-year-old African American high school student, "after witnessing The Birth of a Nation."[55] Yet while reports noted the "frenzied" and "blood stirring" applause during the Klan sequences, and by extension their impact beyond the theater, they did not explain how the film elicited these responses. Similar reactions had been noted for the stage play of *The Clansman,* but Griffith now formalized decidedly cinematic processes to encourage audiences to identify with the Klansmen. One particular sequence is pivotal here. Griffith deploys a tracking shot as the Klansmen ride to the rescue. On the one hand, the shot evokes the "sensation" of the onrushing train found in the earliest days of cinema (for example, *L'arrivée d'un train en gare de La Ciotat,* 1895). The camera is pointing backward in order to face the Klansmen front on, and so the Klansmen may appear to ride "at," rather than with, the spectator. Yet on the other hand, this is a moving shot so that the spectator is no longer fixed and static but rather viscerally propelled by the onrushing Klansmen. Significantly, at the height of this sequence – what Linda Williams would refer to as the "flushing of blackness from the screen" and contemporary reports called the "white Anglo Saxon Niagara" – the leader of the Klan, Ben Cameron, lowers his mask (fig. 1.1). In so doing, he reveals the individual protagonist within this collective mass, retaining his identity as a Klansman (through the costume) while simultaneously allowing audiences to recognize and identify with a central, white male protagonist.[56]

Griffith uses this device on a number of occasions. After showing a procession of indistinguishable horsemen riding past the camera – cut before all the Klansmen have passed to exaggerate the scale of this procession – he shows an unmasked Cameron in close-up and, as he prepares to lead the Klan riders, through an iris shot. Earlier, as the Klan members conduct the "trial" of Gus, Ben removes his mask to give the orders, and when he conducts the rituals of the Klan shortly afterward, his mask is

1.1. Ben Cameron (Henry B. Walthall) beneath the mask in *The Birth of a Nation*, David W. Griffith Corporation, 1915.

again removed. Recent extensive formal analysis has shown how Griffith intensified these Klan riding sequences, particularly through editing and the use of music, but the emphasis on the individual within the costume indicates a particular way in which Griffith used the medium to humanize, and empathize with, the largely anonymous collective group.

While the direct influence of Griffith's film on transforming cinemagoers into Klansmen remains conjecture, by the end of the film's initial run in Atlanta Simmons had recruited ninety-two members for his new organization.[57] For Simmons, the timing of *Birth's* release allowed him to exploit a massive wave of publicity, to provide historical legitimacy to his new group, and to ride alongside other fraternal organizations. Yet the film would also help Simmons in unimagined ways as he launched his new group within a major city. In particular, I argue that the movement of the text and its audiences to major urban centers enacts the movements of the Klan depicted on-screen.

A few days before *The Birth of a Nation* arrived in Atlanta, a poster proclaimed, "The Conqueror is coming!" The poster hints at a correlation between the images on-screen – the ride of the Klan – and the colonization by the film, and its racial ideology, of national urban centers.[58] In the film, the death of Flora, leaping from a cliff to avoid the advances of Gus, had marked the African American "capture" of the public South. Flora transgressed beyond the safe space, crossing the picket fence and moving beyond the clearly demarcated boundary of her traditional Southern home. The final ride of the Klan is ultimately a quest to regain both public and private spaces. Griffith cuts between a locked room in the Southern house (in which Elsie Stoneman is trapped), the interior of the log cabin (occupied by Phil Stoneman and Margaret Cameron), and two outdoor spaces. At the periphery, the Klansmen gather in a rural abyss, while at the urban center African Americans cover the streets. The town is marked here by modern disorder – the pavements are not visible, African Americans are drinking and waving hats – while the Klan rides in orderly rows through the traditional tree-lined landscape. On reaching the town, the onrushing Klansmen force the African Americans to scatter, while also reclaiming the Southern home as they free Elsie, who is dressed all in white and is immediately aligned with her rescuers. In the next sequence – "Disarming the blacks" – the armed Klansmen line up on either side of the street as the African Americans in the middle disperse off-screen. The path is now cleared for the parade of the Klansmen, which celebrates this reclamation of the urban space and, beyond this, the clearance of the African American from mainstream screens.

This imagery and rhetoric is reinforced through the film's exhibition, as the film traveled to major urban centers. Throughout its run, special train services were arranged to bring people into these cities. The *Atlanta Constitution* claimed that no attraction "outside grand opera" had ever attracted so many people from out of town. "Every railroad and every merchant, as well as every hotel, reaped a harvest," it noted, adding that "hundreds came from as far as 200 miles away."[59] The film's exhibition thus brought crowds to the city in a movement reminiscent of the film's finale. The modern Klan would hold a strong urban presence, as Kenneth Jackson highlighted, and Simmons's initial membership drive brought people from neighboring towns (such as Rome, Bowman, Athens, Rutledge, and Decatur) into Atlanta. Seen in this context, the opening night appearance of his new Klan – and the acted performances outside other screenings across the country – becomes emblematic of the Klan's urban centrality.[60]

The Birth of a Nation would, advertisements explained, "positively never be presented except at the important theatres at regular prices."[61] The centrality of the selected theaters, both in their location and cultural importance, now confirmed the position of African Americans at the periphery. For all the African American opposition to the film, there are only a handful of accounts of African Americans attending public screenings. In Atlanta, segregation policies had notably tightened since the race riots of 1906. In 1910 both restaurants and streetcars were segregated, and in 1913 official boundaries were created for white and black residential areas. This segregation extended to the theater where African Americans, if they wanted to attend, were either confined to the balcony or excluded entirely. The high pricing structure and close policing of the theaters (for fear of unrest) further prohibited or restricted the African American presence within the cinema building. This is not to suggest that *Birth* changed theater segregation policy, but rather that it highlighted and consolidated these changes as film increasingly spread to major urban movie palaces.[62]

Charlene Regester suggests that the film's release, which "ignited the passion and sentiments of disgruntled black spectators," coincided not only with the proliferation of urban movie palaces but also with an increase in "black theaters." This raises three points. First, the definition of "black theaters" was not as clear as that of other theaters. For example, in Atlanta, as Jan Olsson notes, the city electrician could not legally license an African American projectionist, which thus ensured that all black picture houses were legally compelled to employ white operators. Second, these largely white-owned theaters were for the most part confined to the urban periphery and, in their formation, indicate a lack of African American presence within the central urban theaters.[63] Finally, the movement of *The Birth of a Nation* helped to create political communities. This is true not only for the Klan but also, as recent scholarship has indicated, for an imagined African American community. Stephen Weinberger argues that through its national campaign against the film, the NAACP mobilized and politicized local chapters and was transformed into a national organization.[64] *Birth* becomes a formative text then, not only for the Klan, but also for some of the groups it would criticize most: the NAACP and, to an extent, the modern film industry, which the Klan defined as Jewish, as we shall see in chapter 2.

The film traveled across borders, moving throughout the country at a moment when African Americans were trying to do the same. The U.S Department of Commerce noted that 454,000 blacks left the South between 1910 and 1920 in search of jobs and social opportunities. In dragging many existing racial tensions and fears out of a purely Southern context, the movement of the film confronted and obstructed the literal movement of African Americans.[65] In the high profile example of Jack Johnson, the black heavyweight boxing champion of the world, the state regulated his movements, both in person and through film. Johnson came to represent a very particular threat to the white establishment, both inside the ring, where he repeatedly defeated every "Great White Hope," and outside, where he enjoyed a series of relationships with white women. Significantly, by 1915, the manufactured threat of Johnson had already been contained and battered by the federal authorities. First, in 1912, the federal government made its first intervention in the policing of cinema with the passage of the Sims Act. The law was introduced specifically to regulate and restrict the movement across state boundaries of films depicting Johnson's fights, which recorded his victories over white boxers. In the same year, Johnson was arrested, under a tenuous interpretation of the Mann Act, for transporting a white woman across state lines for "immoral purposes." Again, the terms of these restrictions, whether of his image or his person, focused on movement and social migration, the literal and figurative crossing of boundaries. Johnson fled the country so that he was, as Lee Grieveson noted, "effectively pushed outside the nation space," like his films. He would finally lose his heavyweight title to Jess Willard in Cuba in April 1915 shortly after the release of *The Birth of a Nation*. Griffith's film provided a response to the defeated Johnson, not only through its violent racial cleansing on-screen, but also through its circulation across state boundaries, which helped to transform a carefully manufactured Southern myth into a national history.[66]

Thomas Dixon claimed in 1915 that *The Birth of a Nation* was "transforming the entire population of the North and West into sympathetic Southern voters," and suggested to President Wilson's personal secretary, Joseph Tumulty, that "every man who comes out of one of our theatres is a southern partisan for life."[67] Yet while noting the national spread of the film, and to an extent its racial ideology, the modern Klan would not immediately, or inevitably, follow. Nineteen fifteen is regularly cited as the date of the Klan's rebirth, but by 1920 the Klan had only a few thousand members and was largely consigned to pockets of Georgia and Alabama. In examining the initial growth of the Klan, the film's travels around the North are perhaps less significant than its regular returns to Atlanta.

The Birth of a Nation would reappear on Atlanta's screens virtually each year, playing on at least nine separate occasions over the next decade. At the end of November 1916, it returned for a two-week engagement, bringing with it electricians, mechanics, and a thirty-piece symphony orchestra from New York. Press reports now emphasized the film's global success – in "the various cities of South America, Europe, Australia and Japan" – while its popularity in Atlanta remained undimmed with a thousand people turned away at its first matinee. Amidst reports that Griffith was intending to withdraw the film from the road, the run was widely discussed as the "farewell visit of the spectacle to Atlanta."[68] However, a year later in January 1918 the film was back "after a sensational tour of the country" at the 900-seat Criterion, now playing four times a day at "popular prices."[69] It would return again less than three months later at the Rialto Theatre, and a year later, in March 1919, it enjoyed "a farewell visit" to the Criterion with four shows a day to "capacity houses" now charging 25 cents a ticket.[70] In October 1921, after its contested but profitable presentation to 150,000 people at New York's Central Theatre, *Birth* returned to the city at the Forsyth, selling out the theater for a week and prompting the box office to close half an hour before performances. After "a tremendous amount of pressure," the film revisited the Forsyth in February 1922 for what was billed, not for the first time, as "positively the last time." It was now advertised in the national Klan newspaper, *Searchlight*, as modern and topical, "The True Story of the Klansman." A year later, in April 1923, it was back where it all began, playing for a week at the Atlanta Theater.[71]

The regular reappearance of *Birth* within Atlanta, coupled with the Klan's delayed expansion, encourages us to look at the film beyond 1915. The returning film would become an open, ongoing dialogue with the Atlanta public, providing Simmons's Knights of the Ku Klux Klan with repeated opportunities to promote itself within the city. Beyond Atlanta, with the emergence of new Klan-like groups in Kentucky in 1917, Oklahoma in 1918, and Virginia in 1919, the film continued to travel and resonate within fresh social and political contexts.[72]

The most prominent appearances of Simmons's Klan occurred in neighboring Alabama in 1918. In May, one hundred Klansmen rode through the streets of Birmingham, and, a few weeks later, up to a dozen cars carried Klansmen in full regalia further south through Mobile. The Klan signed prominent warnings outside the Scottsboro Court House "against pro-German speech" and threatened critics of the government in June. Further notices appeared in Montgomery, where *The Birth of a Nation* had played to capacity crowds in February. The first of these read "Notice: Warning! Women of the streets and hotel-strumpets go to work – keep away from soldiers." By September, the Klan's presence in Montgomery was more publicly acknowledged with a parade through the streets. "Resurrected, the order appeared on the streets of the city in the old garb," the *Montgomery Advertiser* noted, "but used the modern convenience of the automobile instead of the dashing horses which David Wark Griffith showed in 'The Birth of a Nation.'" The Klan advertised its targets here as "All Slackers and Kaiserites." The Klan's reappearance across Alabama reveals a modernization of Griffith's Klan, parading with cars as well as horses, and fixing warnings to prominent locations that now related directly to the war and the present social situation.[73]

The Klan's initial public appearances in Alabama further illustrate the need to look beyond 1915 to evaluate the causative effect of the film on the spread of the organization. Robert Alan Goldberg has suggested that by 1920 there were only 4,000 or 5,000 Klansmen, but that between June 1920 and October 1921 another 85,000 men joined the group. It was in June 1920 that Simmons enlisted two publicists from the Southern Publicity Association for the Klan, Mary Elizabeth Tyler and Edward

Young Clarke. Given the rapid growth in the modern Klan that followed, the marketing tools used by the Klan at this point warrant closer consideration.[74]

Clarke and Tyler helped bring modern marketing and mass mobilization techniques into the Klan, most significantly by setting up a "Propagation Department" and hiring professional salesmen throughout the country to operate as Klan recruiters (Kleagles). The introduction of Kleagles transformed the financial and organizational structure of the Klan by incentivizing local salesmen (who would receive $4 for each new member) while controlling and embracing these local chapters within the national organization ($2.50 from each new member would go to Clarke and Tyler's propagation department, while $1 would go to the King Kleagle within the state, who would oversee the local Kleagles). There were soon more than a thousand Kleagles, and in their attempts to attract and recruit new members, many of them would increasingly turn to film.

As one example, Klan historian Kenneth Jackson notes that Luther Ivan Powell, a King Kleagle prominent in Washington State, commonly used the Fox film *The Face at Your Window* to recruit new members.[75] Powell set up Klan chapters in at least five other states, including California and Oregon, as well as organizing the largely unsuccessful Junior Knights of the Invisible Empire. His interest in media extended to the founding and editing of a Klan newspaper, *The Watcher on the Tower,* and an enormous range of entertainment and educational live events, a number of which featured *The Face at Your Window.*[76] *The Face at Your Window* is emblematic of what (and how) the Klan would look to achieve through film as the organization grew from a few thousand members to its estimated mid-decade peak of five million. Here was a government-supported film reappropriated by a modern Klan, a film that circulated through both theatrical and non-theatrical sites, adopted both through the Klan's institutional center and by emerging local groups, a film that responded to a fresh contemporary enemy and, through the Klan's engagement, would help to define the modern Klan to contemporary American audiences. Most of all, here was a film that would help to complete the transformation imagined by William Simmons in Atlanta

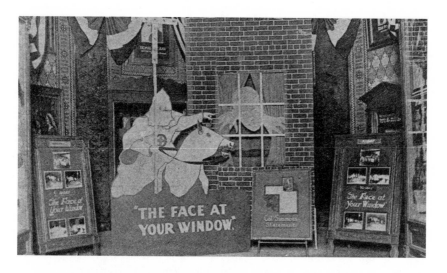

1.2. Promoting *The Face at Your Window* at The Strand in
Atlanta, *Exhibitors Trade Review*, 1 October 1921, 1264.

in December 1915, taking the Klan from its historical model presented in
The Birth of a Nation to a relevant contemporary organization.

1921: UNCOVERING *THE FACE AT YOUR WINDOW*

In August 1921, *The Face at Your Window* arrived in Atlanta for a week's
run at the Strand. Proclaiming the film as "The Picture that all Atlanta
will be talking about," posters featured a Klansman on a rearing horse in
an image that closely recalled the original advertisements for both *The
Birth of a Nation* and Simmons's Knights of the Ku Klux Klan. The front
of the Strand was filled with these pictures and with a large cutout of
the horseman, while theater manager George Schmidt sent out six men
in Klan robes onto the streets to promote the picture (fig. 1.2). Over the
next month the film traveled throughout Georgia, playing, for example,
for two nights at the Springer Opera House in Columbus on 21 and 22
August. Advertisements for this screening again evoked *Birth*, promoting the film as "really and truly another Birth of a Nation." Audiences,
the poster explained, could see "an entire town burned by an angry mob"

and "white crusaders rush in and save the town from the radicals." While the film recalled *Birth* – in form, content, and promotion – it was in the modern Klan's appropriation of the film that this comparison was most apparent.[77]

The Face at Your Window was, as advertisements noted, "Endorsed by the United States Government." Yet a further endorsement was also noted in posters and at theater displays, not from the government but from William Simmons himself. Written beneath an advertisement for a screening at the Springer Opera House (fig. 1.3) was a letter from Simmons to film producer William Fox, the founder of the Fox Film Corporation, in which he outlined his support and aspirations for the picture:

> I have just witnessed a run of your wonderful picture entitled "The Face at Your Window," and, I think the American people who love America, owe you quite a debt of gratitude and my only hope is that this picture may have the widest possible showing throughout the Nation.
>
> In my opinion, this is the psychological moment for the release of this picture and I feel assured that the people of our country will profit greatly by the lesson it teaches and the thought it leaves in the mind will be of great value to America.[78]

Simmons's widely visible endorsement reveals the multifaceted ways in which the Klan looked to engage with film during this moment of initial expansion. Significantly, this campaign was not confined to Georgia but rather served as part of an institutional, nationwide recruitment drive. A month later the *New York World* ran a widely syndicated, twenty-one-day exposé of the modern Klan, which included a letter written by the King Kleagle in Tennessee, J. M. McArthur. On stationery from the Department of Propaganda at the Imperial Palace, the Klan's headquarters in Atlanta, McArthur explained that he would be meeting a state representative of the Fox Film Company to arrange a screening of *The Face at Your Window*. He now urged other Kleagles to follow suit by showing the film, in particular to members of other local fraternal organizations:

> Please let me know immediately when you wish this picture shown in your territory, and if there are any particular dates, such as the Shrine meeting at Kingsport, on which you want [it] in any of your towns.
>
> The system is to have each of your Klansmen take with them at least one man to see the show and then at the finish produce an application and say: "Sign here." If they won't come they are not the kind of people we want anyway.[79]

WM. FOX
Presents

The colossal spectacle of an American community's supreme trial.

THE FACE AT YOUR WINDOW

Springer Opera House
Monday and Tuesday

Atlanta, Ga., April 22nd, 1921

Mr. William Fox, President,
Fox Film Corporation,
New York, N. Y.

My Dear Sir:

    I have just witnessed a run of your wonderful picture entitled "THE FACE AT YOUR WINDOW," and, I think, the American people who love America, owe you quite a debt of gratitude and my only hope is that this picture may have the widest possible showing throughout the Nation.

    In my opinion, this is the psychological moment for the release of this picture and I feel assured that the people of our country will profit greatly by the lesson it teaches and the thought it leaves in the mind will be of great value to America.

            Yours very truly,

                WILLIAM JOSEPH SIMMONS,

                    Imperial Wizard,
                      of the Ku Klux Klan.

1.3. Advertising *The Face at Your Window* in Georgia, August 1921. William Simmons's statement endorsing the picture also appeared at theater displays, as seen in figure 1.2. Records of the NAACP, box 1, C 312, Library of Congress, Washington, DC.

The *Jewish Criterion* published a similar missive from the King Kleagle in Nebraska, announcing that the film would be screened at the annual meeting at Stone Mountain, Georgia, in May 1921 before playing throughout the country. "This picture will be shown in any city where the request comes from the local Cyclops," the letter explained. The hierarchical relationship between institutional center (Imperial Wizard Simmons and the Propagation Department), state organization (King Kleagle), and local chapters (over which the "Cyclops" would preside) was now clearly and commercially organized. The King Kleagle further noted that upon instruction from the local Cyclops, the head of the local chapter, the Propagation Department would contact the film company and ensure that the film is placed in "one of the leading theatres in your community."[80]

Throughout the second half of 1921, Kleagles followed this advice, using *The Face at Your Window* as part of their recruitment drives in a number of ways. In Denver in July, the local Klan launched itself by demanding that the Rivoli Theatre reengage *The Face at Your Window*. In a characteristically dramatic display, Klansmen sped through downtown Denver at midnight and "holding red torchlights, affixed notices to the theater." Their protest persuaded the exhibitor to bring back the film, but, more significantly, the publicity generated heightened awareness of the Klan in Denver. The film was now advertised as being shown "by request of the Ku Klux Klan."[81] This stunt, initially believed to have emanated from the film's press agents, not only shows local Klan groups adopting *The Face at Your Window,* but also shows the Klan's broader recognition of film events as a means of generating publicity for the group.[82]

In addition, the promotion and exhibition of the film also helped to define and legitimize the group within the local community. A week after its appearance in Denver, *The Face at Your Window* was screened at the Lyric Theatre in Anniston, Alabama, "under the auspices of the Knights of the Ku Klux Klan." In arranging free screenings, staging an afternoon performance for "ladies and children of the city" and using "leading citizens" as ushers, the local group positioned itself as a valid, established, and inclusive presence within the town.[83] In Portland, Oregon, in December 1921, the film was screened as part of a launching program entitled "The Truth about the Ku Klux Klan," which included

The Truth About the Ku Klux Klan

Told by a Representative of the Imperial Wizard

Exposing a Colossal Conspiracy Against American Ideals, American
Institutions and American Womanhood

WILLIAM FOX
presents
THE FACE
AT YOUR
WINDOW
BY MAX MARCIN
Authors of "Believe Me Xantippe"
The of Young The House of Glass"
and "Cheating Cheaters" etc etc

"The Face at Your Window"

and

The Knights of the Ku Klux Klan Ride Again

Eight Reels of Thrilling Pictures, With a
Message of Warning to American
Manhood and Womanhood

Municipal Auditorium

ONE NIGHT ONLY

Thurs. Eve., December 22, 1921

Under the Auspices of the Knights of the
Ku Klux Klan

Admission 50c, Including War Tax

1.4. Using film to launch the Klan in Portland, Oregon.
Sunday Oregonian (Portland), 18 December 1921.

a lengthy lecture by local minister Dr. Reuben H. Sawyer (fig. 1.4). The
Portland News claimed that "for the first time since President Wilson
made his memorable tour of the United States, the Portland auditorium
was filled to capacity," with an estimated 6,000 people in attendance.
When a month later the same program was offered in nearby Eugene,
the announcement was presaged by a public demonstration, as two
robed Klansmen rode through the streets while a flaming cross stood
on the overlooking hill of Skinners Butte.[84] In April, the Roseburg Klan
brought both the film and Sawyer back to town, and now invited local
ministers as its special guests. In this way, the Klan looked to use the film
event to define itself, in this case in religious terms, by aligning itself with
the Protestant Church.[85]

The methods that Simmons used on a local level with *The Birth of
a Nation* in 1915 may appear to be replicated on a national and institutional scale by Kleagles with *The Face at Your Window* in 1921. Certainly

the NAACP, which was still picketing and protesting against ongoing screenings of *Birth,* recognized a parallel when speaking out against *The Face at Your Window.* On seeing Simmons's endorsement, the NAACP wrote to William Fox, asking "the extent to which, through such apparent co-operation with William Simmons, you are ready to endorse the Ku Klux Klan," an organization directing propaganda "not only against Negroes, but against Jews and Catholics." The NAACP gestured here toward a hypocritical alliance between an antisemitic Klan and a film company with a strong Jewish presence. Fox's response denied any association with the Klan, explaining that his company had "no sympathy with such intolerance." He explained that the advertisement "did not emanate from this company" and further stated that the film "does not deal with the Ku Klux Klan." There was no intention on the part of the producers, he explained, to "assist the Klan or to spread its teachings through the film." Yet clearly, as we see with *The Birth of a Nation* during the 1920s, *The Face at Your Window* was now reimagined and radically altered through the Klan's engagement with the film.[86]

When *The Face at Your Window* showed at the Modjeska Theater in August, at the exact moment of the NAACP's objections, the theater's management felt the need to print a lengthy "Notice to Misinformed Public." Appearing a few days after Simmons's endorsement was publicized, the notice sought to "correct [a] false rumor" by stating that the film has "absolutely nothing to do with any 'RELIGION.'"[87] The "false rumors," exploited both by the Klan and by exhibitors, had reconfigured the text as "a dramatic tale of the Ku Klux Klan," and "the picture with a 1921 Ku Klux Klan."[88] Yet, as we shall see, *The Face at Your Window* actually depicted the American Legion, and the film itself makes no mention of the Klan. The protagonist is a member of the American Legion, and in the final denouement it is the American Legion that rides into town to overturn a workers' revolt. While producers had transformed the Klan into the American Legion, most notably reworking the costume and the ride to the rescue from *The Birth of a Nation,* the Klan and exhibitors now reversed this process, reimagining the modern Klan within the film both through promotional materials and at the site of exhibition.[89]

Filmed in the manufacturing center of Boonton, New Jersey, *The Face at Your Window* confronted the very contemporary issue of labor agitation in a modern industrial town. Frank Maxwell, the head of the local American Legion who works in his father's factory mill, falls for Ruth, the "pretty daughter of an immigrant worker." Frank is literally stabbed in the back by Ivan, an immigrant worker jealous of his relationship with Ruth and critical of his family's "humane" treatment of the workers. The personal confrontation between American employer (Frank) and foreign employee (Ivan) is magnified by the arrival in town of Comrade Kelvin, "a tall foreign looking stranger" who looks to mobilize the workers. In response, Frank summons the American Legion, whose members, wearing "the garb of the Ku Klux Klan," as a number of reviews noted, gather on the outskirts of the city. By this stage the city streets are awash with wild scenes of chaos and disorder, descending further as Ivan proclaims the nationalization of all women. One of the first victims of this decree is Frank's little sister, Dot, who, in an echo of Flora's jump in *Birth*, leaps from a cliff to her death to escape her pursuer. The breakdown of the social, political, and economic order of the city gathers pace as the "rebels" cut the phone wires connecting the city, take over the town hall, kill the mayor, and burn down Maxwell's mill. Beacons on the hilltops then summon the American Legion, which races into the city, both mounted and on foot. After a lengthy clash at the barricades, Comrade Kelvin shoots Ivan and is exposed as both a coward and fraud. Frank, cheered by all, now takes the opportunity to deliver a patriotic speech before embracing Ruth.[90]

A brief synopsis of *The Face at Your Window* clearly reveals the film's debt to *The Birth of a Nation*, noticeable not only in the visual design but also thematically in its articulation of space. *The Face at Your Window* presents a battle over both the domestic and nation space. The threat to the American home is personalized in the film's title and gendered as a threat to traditional womanhood by the familiar saintly death of Frank's sister. The Legion/Klan is again summoned from outside the city walls, descending from high ground down and toward the screen to reclaim a city that is "captured" by a foreign threat. There are, however, significant deviations from *Birth*, which are largely indicative of the changing social situation into which the Klan emerged after the war. First, the "face" in the title belongs not to an African American, but rather to a Russian Jewish immigrant. Popular anxieties surrounding the immigrant threat – inherently tied to social, political, and economic fears around socialism and unionism – erupted with the Red Scare of 1919, which led to the rapid prosecution and deportation of thousands of innocent "aliens." These fears surrounding immigration, which had brought approximately 14.5 million "foreigners" into the country between 1900 and 1920, fanned postwar debates on national identity, debates that the Klan would channel in its opposition to the "hyphenated American" and "the traitor within."

The shifts from *The Birth of a Nation* in 1915 to the new social cause of 1919 are further revealed in another adaptation of Thomas Dixon's works, the anti-radical film *Bolshevism on Trial* (1919), which was based on his 1909 book *Comrades*. The film exposes the idealism of socialism in familiar terms – equating Bolshevism with "free love" and providing, as Ben Singer notes, the "obligatory attempted rape scene." It explicitly reveals the transformation of the contemporary enemy, as the central villain – known throughout the film as the German-sounding Wolff – is finally exposed as the Russian-sounding Androvitch. Dixon's historical model of the Klan is also now transformed for a contemporary audience. The film concludes with "white-garbed forces of righteousness [that] race to the rescue." These forces, carrying the American flag and overpowering the Bolshevik threat, appear in 1919 as the U.S. Navy rather than the Klan.[91]

While the Klan did not adopt *Bolshevism on Trial*, the film's exploitation provides a productive link with both *The Birth of a Nation* and *The Face at Your Window*. On this occasion, *Moving Picture World* published a lengthy editorial in which it urged the government to use *Bolshevism on Trial* as propaganda, suggesting that exhibitors should "put up red flags about town and hire soldiers to tear them down." This would not only generate further publicity for the film, it claimed, but also future business for the venue, which would now be recognized and defined by these patriotic acts. The editorial encouraged exhibitors to exploit and extend the social tensions beyond the frame – the equivalent of hiring modern Klansmen to parade outside screenings of *The Birth of a Nation* – an act that prompted Secretary of Labor William Wilson to confront both *Moving Picture World* and the film's producers. "Never in all my life have

I seen more dangerous editorial advice," he stated. "It is calculated to produce violent disorder."[92]

The examples of *Bolshevism on Trial* and *The Face at Your Window* show producers reusing and reimagining the Klan imagery from *The Birth of a Nation* at a moment when Americanism was becoming a dominant ideology. The Klan's adoption of *The Face at Your Window* serves to position the modern Klan as a justified response to a contemporary problem. In doing this, it also affiliates the group with the respected American Legion. Just as the Klan in Atlanta had sought to recruit from the clutch of fraternal, patriotic orders that existed locally in 1915, so now the modern Klan, with its militaristic language and structure, looked to respond to the postwar situation by aligning with this emerging patriotic group and by recruiting from its membership. Founded in May 1919, the American Legion had over a million members by the end of the year and not only featured in *The Face at Your Window* but also preceded the Klan in organizing screenings of the film, albeit ones that noted (unwanted) associations with the Klan. After a screening of the film in St. Augustine, Florida, to raise funds for the local Legion post, a letter to a local newspaper complained that "the Klan is glorified and everyone goes away with the impression that the Legion and the Klan are affiliated."[93]

The Face at Your Window listed endorsements on its posters not only from the American Legion but also from the government's Americanism Committee, the Brotherhood of Railway Trainmen, and "men prominent in all walks of life." These affiliations first helped to ensure that this film was widely exhibited within legitimate theatrical circuits. Secretary of the Interior Franklin K. Lane, who was also head of the Americanism Committee, wanted *The Face at Your Window* "exhibited in every city, town and hamlet in the United States."[94] As we shall see, the Klan would struggle to exhibit its own productions within theatrical sites during the 1920s, so transposing its modern incarnation onto popular, widely circulating films (whether *Birth* or *Face*) allowed it to reach a wider audience and to exploit existing distribution and exhibition circuits.

The affiliations also suggest and promote a close ideological confluence between the Legion, the American government, and now the

Klan. The government had offered its patriotic war films to the American Legion in 1919 and in December established the Americanism Committee, which, in direct response to the Red Scare, was set up to educate "immigrants in the ideals of America." Colonel Arthur Woods, who succeeded Franklin Lane as head of the Americanism Committee, argued in 1920 that "there should be injected into every picture some ideas that would make better Americans," requesting that this patriotic propaganda should run throughout all industry output.[95] The Klan was certainly not a minority group and, as we also see with *The Birth of a Nation* in 1915, positioned itself as a defender and supporter of threatened government values. Indeed, the Klan's adoption of *The Face at Your Window* highlights problems that the emerging industry faced in producing patriotic pictures. Seeking legitimacy and under increasing pressure to regulate, the industry had little option but to support the Americanism Committee. It produced patriotic films like *The Face at Your Window* as a defense of its modernity, but, in highlighting the dangers of modern life and immigration, it ultimately contributed to a reactionary, conservative discourse and legitimized the values of these conservative groups. It would appear an uncomfortable irony that the industry, in a bid to boost its own reputation, produced films that would ultimately benefit the Klan and undermine itself.

The postwar social climate ripened America for a myriad of patriotic, fraternal organizations, but it does not explain either how or why the Klan was able to exploit this situation. The Klan was not an inevitable product of, or outlet for, these postwar anxieties; rather, Klan leaders manufactured a demand and role for this new organization within society in part through their use of film and modern media. The arrival of publicists Tyler and Clarke in June 1920 is most timely, then, not simply because this is a socially and politically receptive moment for a modern Klan, but also because it marks a point at which both the state and industry are increasingly invested in using film to inculcate, define, and create modern citizens. In *The Face at Your Window* the assimilation narrative of *Birth* – a union of North and South – is replaced by a romantic union, which ostensibly suggests an assimilation of American and foreigner. Such a message is qualified within this government film, both within the text and through the promotional materials. In Maxwell's final speech, he talks specifically of immigrants having a "duty to the country they are living in" – suggesting that American citizenship remains outside their domain – while promotional materials for the film defined the audiences in terms later used by the Klan (and which are deliberately vague but with the illusion of specificity) as "red-blooded American" and "100% American."

The state was not alone in investing in these questions of citizenship. Henry Ford established a Motion Picture Department within his company in 1914 that produced films during the Red Scare, such as *Uncle Sam and the Bolshevik* (1919), and explicitly sought to teach "Americanization" through film. By 1919 Ford imagined film not only as a means of instructing modern workers in industry and work but also, as Lee Grieveson has noted, of "visualising citizenship" to young working class and immigrant audiences.[96] Philanthropic agencies, like the Rockefeller Foundation and Carnegie Corporation, extended this message overseas, circulating health and educational films like *Unhooking the Hookworm* (1920) to colonial audiences across the British Empire.[97] The establishment of the American Legion Film Service in 1921, which produced pictures, provided projection machines, and distributed films to Legion posts throughout the country, shows patriotic, fraternal organizations investing in film as a means of shaping postwar American national identity. For the Klan, film provides a way of engaging in these debates over national identity and of ingratiating itself within the nation. As the example of *The Face at Your Window* shows, the Klan sought to influence and renegotiate the categories within national citizenship debates – what it means to be "American" – and, in so doing, sought to expand, define, and promote its own membership (as "100% American" or "Red Blooded American"). In this way, the Klan's interest in citizenship also has a direct commercial agenda as it aligns "American" with the interchangeable category of "Klansman."

The example of *The Face at Your Window* positions *The Birth of a Nation* as a generative text for a modern Klan that would exploit both specific films and, more broadly, the film event to mobilize, recruit, and legitimize itself within American society. While Simmons had utilized film on a local level in 1915, Kleagles and the emerging Klan extended and institutionalized these practices with *The Face at Your Window* in 1921.

It provides one significant example of how film as mass media was used by political groups at a moment when propaganda and public relations were being theorized more widely and when the direction of the postwar nation was being contested on a national stage.

At a moment when Kleagles were first organizing the widespread adoption of *The Face at Your Window* in May 1921, the Department of Propagation wrote to D. W. Griffith, asking him to direct a new photo play "which will portray the activities of the present day Klan, and the things for which the organization stands." Griffith was, the letter explained, the "only logical director ... not merely due to your splendid work in the past, but also because of your known sentiments regarding the work of the Ku Klux Klan." The letter – the first of a number of requests submitted to Griffith – is testament to the Klan's heightened engagement with film in 1921; more specifically, it now attempted to use Griffith's earlier work as evidence of his support for the modern Klan.[98]

Despite requests from Kleagles, Griffith did not produce a film about the modern Klan during the 1920s. He didn't need to. Instead, *The Birth of a Nation* enjoyed (or endured) an effective rebirth, remade by and for the modern Klan and becoming perhaps the single most prominent propagandist tool for the reemergent group. As the film's regular returns to Atlanta highlight, *The Birth of a Nation* continued to circulate throughout this period. At the time of the *New York World*'s exposé on the modern Klan in September 1921, there were four companies touring *The Birth of a Nation*. One of these productions was stopped – the mayor of Detroit prohibited the film's exhibition – while elsewhere the agents for the picture were instructed, presumably against their better commercial judgment, to avoid making any connection between the film and the modern Klan.[99] Yet even if national agents and exhibitors did follow these instructions, local Klan groups increasingly aligned themselves with the picture as a means of launching, publicizing, and historicizing their modern group.

By the start of 1922 reports began noting the appearance of modern Klansmen at screenings of *The Birth of a Nation*. In January, the Klan in

Corsicana, Texas, made its first public appearance at a local screening of *Birth,* while eighteen members "marched solemnly" into the theater and sat in the front row at a screening in McAlester, Oklahoma. Forty-two members of the Klan, "mysterious and silent in their robes and hoods of white," attended the final performance of *The Birth of a Nation* at the Academy of Music in Richmond, Virginia, in February 1922. The Klansmen appeared shortly before the performance, occupying five of the six boxes across both sides of the theater, and were greeted by a "burst of applause." In a carefully choreographed move, the hooded figures rose "as one" on three occasions during the performance and "stood motionless with their left arms pointing to the screen." As with the earlier staged productions of *The Clansman,* the crowds watched the audience as much as the screen, as the attending Klansmen now helped to transpose the historical activities off the screen and into the auditorium. The traveling manager of the film, Walter Cox, had noted further staged appearances of Klan members in Columbus, Georgia, and at the final performance in Rocky Mount, North Carolina. A week later at the opening screening in Greensboro, North Carolina, a hundred "robed and helmeted" Klansmen provided a "touch of reality and a breath of romance." In silently marching from the station to the theater, they replicated the methods used by Simmons in 1915.[100]

As with *The Face at Your Window,* the appearance of modern Klansmen at screenings redefined the film for a contemporary audience and also, crucially, in public discourse. On its original release in 1915, criticisms against *The Birth of a Nation* largely concerned the representation of race within the film. The NAACP made no mention of the Klan when giving five reasons why the film should be banned in February 1915. Six years later in 1921, when five people were arrested in New York for distributing leaflets signed by the NAACP outside the Capital Theatre where *Birth* was showing, the Klan issue had come to the fore. The offending leaflet was entitled, "Stop the Ku Klux Klan Propaganda in New York," and it began by claiming that "The Birth of a Nation exalts the infamous KKK which has been publicly accused of voting to blow up or burn Negro school houses in 1921." A closer look at the leaflet (which included observations such as "Do you know that the KKK is not only anti-Negro but anti-Jewish and anti-Catholic?") supports Nickieann Fleener-Marzec's observation that "the pamphlet dealt more with arguments against the Klan than with arguments against the film per se." The screening of *Birth* now provided an opportunity for Klansmen, censors, and social reformers to debate, promote, or denigrate the merits of this modern group.[101]

When *Birth* was banned in Boston in May 1921, protests came not only from the NAACP but also from the Catholic group the Knights of Columbus. *Variety* noted that the film, now barred for tending to provoke rioting, had played without disruption six years earlier for sixteen consecutive weeks. The synthesis between *The Birth of a Nation* and the modern Klan – engineered for differing reasons by Klansmen, publicists, and opposition groups – redefined the film and the parameters of public discourse that surrounded it. The public hearing in Boston, attended by "600 Negroes," now presented the film as part of a "southern campaign of propaganda of nationwide scope." This was designed, the hearing argued, "to stimulate the popularity of the Ku Klux Klan idea and to establish branches of gang-assassins throughout the country." The picture was now credited not only with legitimizing, popularizing, and spreading the ideology of a modern Klan but also, through the involvement of Kleagles, with helping in the establishment of local Klan groups throughout the country.[102]

In examining the NAACP protests and censorial hearings that traveled with the film in 1921, Melvyn Stokes noted that the NAACP saw the benefits of "hitching up the film with the Ku Klux Klan." However, by the end of 1922 it also acknowledged that such an approach could be counterproductive, providing valuable publicity for both the film and the Klan.[103] Indeed, reports noted that on occasion exhibitors hired protestors – as well as Klansmen – to generate publicity for the screenings.

When the film returned to New York at the end of 1922, the NAACP did confront the film's producers. In filing a formal protest to the Motion Picture Commission, the NAACP complained that *The Birth of a Nation* was being screened in the city "as part of a campaign of the Ku Klux Klan to recruit members." This view was endorsed by press reports which announced that the Reverend Oscar Haywood, a prominent national Klan lecturer, recruiter, and future treasurer of a Klan film company, was initiating a drive for Klan membership in New York during the same week as the film's screening.[104] While the NAACP sought to strengthen its case by emphasizing a direct association between the film and the modern Klan, Dixon, Griffith, and their lawyers argued that any connection between the on-screen image and the modern group existed only in name. In response, a few cuts were made and an introductory title added – explaining that after Reconstruction "the originators of the Klan put away their uniforms and disbanded the organization forever" – while a local minister would often provide a "standard speech" before the screening to say that the Klan depicted on-screen bore no relation to the modern incarnation. These responses reveal once more a film reworked, both on-screen and at the site of exhibition, literally edited and changed in a process of complex political negotiation. Yet even within New York, this response was countered by the continued public appearances of the Klan.[105] To reinforce this point, the *New York World* complained a few days later that "the audience seemed to be composed largely of modern Klansman," while *Variety* reported that "every early appearance of a Klansman on the screen was a signal for half the audience to burst into applause along with minor hissing."[106] Another exhibitor in New York in 1924 reported that "from the applause when the KKK appeared I think my audience consisted chiefly of them (Klansmen)," explaining that on account of the popularity among new Klan members, the film had fared better than on its previous release five years earlier.[107] The film was now reimagined in relation to the modern Klan, with audience responses representative not simply of the film's quality, but rather of the viewer's attitudes toward the modern group.

This moment at the end of 1922 marks a pivotal and largely overlooked moment in the film's history. In his hugely valuable and detailed history of *The Birth of a Nation*, Melvyn Stokes claims that the peak earning power of the film was from 1915 to 1922 and that "the decline of the Klan probably also accelerated the decline of the film with which it had become most closely associated." While I agree that the association with the Klan transformed the film, this is not so clearly a tale of decline (for a film that was already seven years old) as one of regeneration into a Klan text within smaller regional venues. As Stokes notes, at the end of December 1922 Griffith's Epoch Producing Company granted Hiram

Abrams, president of United Artists, the rights to distribute the film to cheaper theaters, a move that was questioned within the press given "the sensation created by the Ku Klux Klan."[108]

I argued earlier that the initial screenings of *Birth* in 1915, shown only at leading theaters in prominent urban centers, contributed to the legitimization of an urban Klan and helped, at least ideologically, to transform a local historical group into a national institution. From 1922, however, the reverse process started to take place as this idealized national Klan reconnected with smaller local groups, removed from the urban center. In particular, the film was now staged and sponsored by local Klan groups that, rather than simply attaching themselves to the touring production, actively organized and brought the film to a local audience.

The shifts in the distribution of *Birth,* announced at the end of 1922, coincide with the most pronounced media activity in the history of the Klan. Over the next couple of years – from 1922 to 1924 – the Klan would publish newspapers and magazines, stage theatrical and radio shows, produce feature films and begin controlling exhibition sites. Within this context, *The Birth of a Nation* made frequent appearances at Klan-run theaters and at Klan events. When the Klan-owned American Theatre in Noblesville, Indiana, showed the film in September 1923, advertisements hinted at the film's changed reception as a Klan text. "All Klansmen and all interested in the Ku Klux Klan are urged to see this picture," an advertisement stated, adding, "You may have seen it before but never as you will see it now." Not only was the film shown at lower prices – 10 cents for children, 25 cents for adults – but it was also now reimagined as a Klan production. Described as "The First 100% American Photoplay ever produced" it was, the advertisement reported, "endorsed by all Klansmen, Ministers, Schools etc." (fig. 1.5). The local Klan defined and positioned itself through these screenings alongside established religious and pedagogical institutions. Within these strong Klan areas, the film reappeared regularly. Having played a month earlier at the neighboring rival Opera House, it moved to nearby Tipton at the Martz Theatre in November, where it appeared as a "real 100 Per Cent. Picture . . . put on by a Klan band." The involvement of the Klan band highlights the regeneration of this text through both its performance and exhibition, as screenings were often specifically tailored for Klansmen.

AMERICAN THEATRE
"Pick O' The Pictures"

TO-DAY AND TO-MORROW

The First 100% American Photoplay Ever Produced

The One and Only—D. W. GRIFFITH'S

"THE BIRTH of a NATION"

Endorsed by all Klansmen, Ministers, Schools, etc.

All Klansmen and all interested in the Ku Klux Klan are urged to see this picture. You may have seen it before but never as you will see it now.

Positively never shown on any Screen at our low prices before.

Children 10c———Adults 25c

3—SHOWS DAILY——2:30—6:30—9:00 P. M.

Some theatre managements, for reasons unknown, do not show this picture complete. It will positively be shown here as originally released.

All Civil War Veterans—FREE

NOTE—Owing to the length of the program the night shows will Start at 6:30 P. M.

Come Early and Avoid the Rush

Figure 1.5. *The Birth of a Nation* at the Klan-owned American Theatre, *Noblesville Daily Ledger*, 5 September 1923, 3.

RIALTO THEATRE
——NOW——
FIFTH BIG WEEK

STARTING SUNDAY, AUGUST 12th
THE ONLY 100% PICTURE

D. W. GRIFFITH AMERICAN INSTITUTION

BIRTH OF A NATION

Good Old One Hundred Percenters

One More Chance to See the Most Wonderful Production That Ever Was Produced

KLANSMEN

DON'T MISS THIS PICTURE

5th——BIG WEEK——5th

SHOW 11 a. m.,   1:35 p. m.,   4:10 p. m.,   7 p. m.,   9:30 p. m.

1.6. Attracting Klansmen to *The Birth of a Nation*, *Fiery Cross*, 10 August 1923.

"Good old one hundred percenters – one more chance to see the most wonderful production that ever was produced," wrote one Klan newspaper in advertising a screening: "KLANSMEN Don't miss this picture" (fig. 1.6).[109]

In his study of the Klan in Michigan, Craig Fox notes the film's regular appearances during this period in Newaygo County. *Birth* played at the Ideal Theatre in Fremont and at Newaygo's Park Theatre, both of which were owned by Klansmen. These venues adopted *Birth* as a Klan text and in so doing helped to transform and "modernize" Griffith's Klan. They achieved this in part by supplementing the screenings of *Birth* with Klan lectures and with contemporary Klan pictures, such as *The Toll of Justice*.[110] These contemporary Klan-made pictures, discussed in chapter 3, would use *Birth*'s visual and narrative form to establish a particular brand of racial nationalism, and both closely referenced and were promoted in relation to *The Birth of a Nation*.

The shifts in distribution practice after 1922 ensured that the Klan was able to use *Birth* more extensively as part of its propaganda activities. Maxim Simcovitch offers examples of modern Klan groups using *Birth* for recruitment purposes in areas as geographically distant as Oregon and Virginia.[111] Organizers of the Grand Junction Klan in Colorado launched their membership drive in 1924 with a short engagement of the film, advertised with the claim, "It will make a better American of you." As we saw with *The Face at Your Window,* local Klan groups now used the film and its exhibition as a way of defining American national identity (and by extension its membership). In Jackson, Mississippi, the *Daily Clarion Ledger* included a "three quarters page high endorsement" of *Birth* by the Jackson Klan, in which a local Klan leader wrote, "I feel sure that all good Americans in our city and surrounding territory, both men and women will come to see this wonderful picture."[112] When the Vidalia Unit of the Klan in Georgia arranged a two-day screening in October 1924, Klansmen reverted to familiar tactics by parading through the streets on opening night, "making a big impression upon the citizens." Yet the local Klan was not merely positioning itself at the site of exhibition but rather defining itself to the community through its organization and presentation of the film. In this instance, the group presented itself as a charitable, religious organization, by announcing that all the proceeds from the screening would benefit the local churches. Furthermore, the Klan announced that "both white and colored churches" would receive a portion of the profits, as the Klan now sought to redefine itself publicly in religious rather than specifically racial terms. Exhibitors also now recognized the benefit of using and incorporating the Klan. One exhibitor from Indiana, for example, noted the healthy profits he had generated from a short run of the film. "Get the Klan with you on this picture," he wrote, "and you will need no advertising."[113]

By 1924, the film's renegotiation as a Klan text was virtually complete. Two cartoons from the African American *Chicago Defender* illustrate this transformation. The first, from 1915, shows Thomas Dixon dressed as the devil stirring a cauldron of race hatred ("Chicago") with a stick labeled "The Birth of a Nation." Here it is Dixon rather than Griffith or indeed the film itself that is deemed responsible for this race hatred, using the film to "stir up" these tensions. The second cartoon, from 1924, entitled "Stirring up Hell," shows a hooded Klansman with *The Birth of a Nation* emblazoned on his robe, stirring the cauldron. *The Birth of a Nation* was now, through its costume, literally stitched onto the modern Klan. Furthermore, it was the modern Klan that was actively using this film, highlighting the transformation of *The Birth of a Nation* from the work of Dixon and Griffith to a text of the modern Knights of the Ku Klux Klan.[114] Both cartoons suggest that power lay not with the film, but more specifically with those who controlled and used it. *Birth* was now completely transformed not simply by the emergence of a new modern Klan, but more specifically by the ways in which this new Klan utilized the film.

AMERICA, 1924: REVISITING THE PAST

When W. N. Kramer, the publisher of *Spotlight,* wrote to Griffith in January 1923, he challenged the filmmaker to "cooperate with all good American citizens to stamp out this growing evil [the Klan]." Kramer's claim that this was a "growing evil" acknowledges the increasing prominence of the Klan within American society, and comes less than a month after shifts in the distribution of *Birth,* which would open up the film for regional Klan-sponsored screenings. The film was now seen as topical rather than historical, already transformed not simply by the emergence of a new modern Klan but more specifically by the ways in which this new Klan was using the film.[115] Furthermore, Kramer's designation of the "good American citizen" hints at the extended parameters of the debates between the Klan and its opponents, as *The Birth of a Nation* became a battleground on which these opposing forces now contested and grappled with shifting definitions of American national identity. *The Birth of a Nation* was now an integral part of these citizenship debates; its very title and assimilationist narrative foregrounded the Klan as a founding arbiter of the modern nation.

The origins of the film's regeneration as a Klan text can be traced back to Dixon. In 1905 Dixon had taken to the stage in Atlanta at the opening performance of *The Clansman,* localizing and making contemporary this tale of a Reconstruction Klan for a modern, racially divided city. Ten years later, Simmons introduced his modern Klan at the film's opening in Atlanta, again reimagining the text through live performance. Simmons's motivation was not to promote and commercially exploit the play or film but his new fraternal organization. Almost a decade later, both film and play were reworked and appropriated by modern Klan groups. When *The Clansman* played in Arkansas in 1924, the Klansmen of Eldorado No. 92 took over during the third act, bringing the authentic modern Klan ceremony into the drama's historical fiction. "A class of aliens was naturalized upon the stage before a huge audience," wrote *Imperial Night-Hawk,* adding that "the play was a very good drawing card" and musing that the local Klan made "a thousand new friends in one night."[116]

Certainly, Dixon and Griffith's work was often, like the Klan, Janus-faced, reactionary, and historical in content, yet through its promotion made to appear socially and politically relevant for contemporary audiences. The pair were still employing and reworking these incendiary promotional techniques, developed in 1905 and 1915, during the 1920s. When seeking to finance another Reconstruction-era novel, *The Traitor,* in 1923, Dixon argued that this historical work would again provide a "two edged sword cutting into the present."[117] In speaking out against the modern Klan, Dixon adopted familiar methods from 1905, albeit from a different ideological standpoint. His opposition to the Klan – which one official

Klan publication evocatively described as a plan to "market a little hatred" – recalled his opportunistic interventions in 1905 and 1915, once more looking to exploit social and racial division for his own financial gain.[118]

For Griffith, this same moment would present him with a fresh opportunity to use the historical film to influence and engage with contemporary conservative discourse. While ignoring calls from Klan groups to make a new film highlighting the virtues and values of Americanism today, he did respond to a request in 1923 from another conservative social group, the Daughters of the American Revolution (DAR). The DAR contacted Griffith – via Will Hays, the president of the Motion Picture Producers and Distributors of America (MPPDA), the trade association for the American film industry – proposing a historical picture on the American Revolution that would celebrate the birth of the American nation. The DAR was concerned, in its own words, "not only for [the] preservation of history, but for the inculcation of 'true patriotism and love of country' and for an enlightened citizenship through educational mediums." With a department for "Americanization" and "Motion Pictures," the DAR was now imagining its proposed film as a "lesson in values" and as part of the citizenship process.[119] The DAR was an active social reform group challenging the film industry, campaigning against "immorality" on-screen and, like the Klan during this period, issuing calls for "better" American films. Just as the Klan attached itself to Griffith's work, produced motion pictures, and distributed films to local chapters, so too did the DAR look to use cinema as a response to what it perceived as the failings of the film industry, as a way of boosting and defining its membership and of shaping postwar American identity.

Publicity for *America,* the resulting film that Griffith directed, emphasized that the filmmaker had also worked with a plethora of other respected American institutions – such as the Army, the Boston Historical Society, and the New York Public Library – and included letters of endorsement from ministers, educators, and senators. Just as they did with *Birth* a decade earlier, the film's producers even claimed presidential support, with publicity materials labeling *America,* somewhat speculatively, as "the one motion picture" of interest to President Coolidge.[120] What we see here are familiar promotional discourses and devices, used by Griffith not only to promote his film but also to legitimize his own position within American social, political, and cultural life. Griffith's stated engagement with these authorities serves to institutionalize his version of history, as a way of participating in and even shaping popular debates on the dominant ideology of the day, Americanism. Griffith's reported if clearly overstated partnership with the DAR is a significant part of this process.

In producing *America*, Griffith sought to use the historical film to create a vision of modern America and, through its exhibition, to help define modern American citizens. In effect, he was trying to do what he could no longer do with *Birth*. There are obvious parallels here between the Klan and DAR, both conservative, fraternal, patriotic groups enacting change through the media. As the Klan continued to use his most famous work in ways that directly damaged his reputation, Griffith's production of *America* – endorsed by the DAR, with industrial support from Will Hays and supporting statements from senators, ministers, and presidents – may be understood as an attempt to reclaim his position within American social, cultural, and political life by maneuvering his conservative politics onto another less divisive and contentious group. The modest critical and commercial success of *America*, coupled with *Birth*'s consolidation as a Klan text, ensured that he was largely unsuccessful in this process.

America can be understood as an attempt to reclaim or ideologically remake *Birth*. Yet while Dixon and Griffith might publicly have sought to relocate their politics and the promotional and instructional devices developed through *Birth*, there is also some evidence that the pair were complicit in the film's regeneration as a Klan text. The chief of staff and Grand Dragon of the Klan in Ohio wrote to Harry Aitken, a producer of *Birth*, and to C. N. Conway, Griffith's secretary, in December 1925, in apparent response to separate requests from them both: "Some time ago an attorney, presumably representing Mr. Griffith's interests, called at our office, asking us to use our influence toward having the Censor Board of the State of Ohio rescind its action prohibiting the showing of The Birth of a Nation in Ohio."[121] This response challenges Griffith's claims, in Paul McEwan's words, to "political and artistic neutrality," suggesting instead that this relationship between film and Klan was mutually beneficial and supported.[122] This is not to suggest that Griffith was either ideologically consistent or universally championed by the Klan. One Klan group condemned the "filth promoting Griffith" for his "vilely suggestive and abominable" 1923 film *The White Rose,* which it described as an "anti-Protestant play." The Klan paper *Searchlight* further criticized Griffith's heroic depiction of Danton, a famous character of the French Revolution, in *Orphans of the Storm* (1921). Without a hint of irony, *Searchlight* suggested that "if he [Griffith] is going to make a practice of portraying historical events, he had better go back to school again."[123] Despite Kramer's desire to hear his "personal opinion" on the subject, Griffith's attitude toward the modern Klan is largely irrelevant. What we do see is the Klan somewhat paradoxically and inconsistently attaching itself to the high-profile figures of Griffith and Dixon as a means of negotiating Klan identity.

The response in Ohio also illustrates the Klan's increasing presence within film discourse, asked here to exercise its "influence" within censorial debates in one of the strongest Klan states. The white riders depicted on-screen racing into Piedmont would, the Klan proposed, now race to the rescue of *Birth's* producers. S. W. Lawrence, the chief of staff for the Ohio Klan, further suggested that the local group might be able to secure "special dispensation" to show the film under its auspices. "In a number of places over the state, we either own or control large auditoriums or halls," Lawrence wrote, proposing that the Klan could show the film through "a percentage basis" or some form of "kindred arrangement." Lawrence was suggesting here a partnership between the local, modern Klan and the producers of *Birth,* a partnership that would formalize the film's position as a "Klan text" within non-theatrical and Klan-run exhibition sites. A film that had helped generate a modern Klan would now in turn be regenerated by the Klan.[124]

In March 1926, the Ohio attorney general rejected the Klan's request to show the film "privately" as part of the "educational and entertainment program for the Klan in the state."[125] This is hardly surprising given that much of the recent controversy and censorial opposition to the film had centered on *Birth's* connection to the modern group. However, the Klan's widely circulated request indicates the group's desire to exploit the film through its own exhibition circuits and attests to its involvement in, and manipulation of, film discourses. *Birth* presented an opportunity for the modern Klan to extend its message, not only through the representation on-screen but also through the discourses generated off-screen.

As a final example, when the Klan publication *Dawn* reported the banning of *Birth* in Chicago in 1924, it stated that the "Roman Catholic municipal Police administration" had stopped a packed screening of the film for fear that "it might engender racial and religious hatred." Despite *Dawn* claiming that the film was concerned with the original Klan and "was produced before the modern patriotic organization was developed," the film was contemporized both by the hundreds of Klansmen in attendance and by the Klan's participation in the disputes. The modern Klan now used the film's exhibition as an opportunity to attack its depicted target, the African American, and its new manufactured enemies, the Jews and Catholics. In this example, *Dawn* complained that the police did not interfere in "Roman propaganda plays, such as 'The Hunchback of Notre Dame,' [Griffith's] 'The White Rose,' nor such degrading spectacles as Pola Negri's 'Sheik' picture, in which she, portraying a white woman, made love to an African." In reporting the arrest of the two projectionists working at the theater, *Dawn* pointed out that all the arresting officers and indeed the judge involved in the case had Irish names. The incident was presented as a very personal confrontation between the Klan and Catholics.[126]

There were further disputes throughout the 1920s, yet it was not merely *Birth* that triggered these clashes, as the Klan embraced and redefined conservative criticisms against film representation, Hollywood, and film theaters. In attacking the perceived foreign influences operating within the industry, the Klan not only promoted and defined itself within American society but also positioned itself as a significant and hitherto overlooked pressure group. While rejecting the notion that a single film "made" the Klan, we can start to see how the Klan "made" itself through film, not simply through its exploitation of particular films, such as *The Birth of a Nation* or *The Face at Your Window,* but also through its highly publicized criticisms and protests against film in general. This is the subject of the next chapter.

TWO

The Battle

CENSORSHIP, REFORM, AND THE KLAN'S
CAMPAIGN AGAINST THE FILM INDUSTRY

IN AUGUST 1937, ATTORNEYS FOR THE KU KLUX KLAN FILED suit against Warner Bros. The Klan objected to the alleged use of its insignia in the Humphrey Bogart film *Black Legion* and sought $113,500 in a "patent infringement" suit.[1] The notion of a secret organization suing a high-profile Hollywood company may appear curious, but in the context of the Klan's media dealings, it is indicative of both the group's commercial opportunism and its concurrent desire to promote and publicize itself through film. By 1937 the Klan was an increasingly marginalized, spluttering, and insignificant presence within American society – far removed from its 1920s heyday – but the case marks the culmination of a fierce battle, fought between the wars, between the Klan and the modern film industry. For the Klan, this was a battle over American national identity, a battle between "tradition" and the corrosive forces of modernity, between its own ideals of Protestant Americanism and a destabilizing modern decadence, propagated by a "foreign" film industry that it regarded as predominantly Jewish. Throughout this period, the Klan imagined the film industry as a public antithesis against which it could attack and define itself. The legal case against Warner Bros. was merely the latest example of this.

The case ostensibly concerned the on-screen representation of the Klan and more specifically the (mis)use of its costume. Discussing the case, under the somewhat unlikely heading "Kluxers Sue WB on 'Black Legion' Insignia," *Variety* explained that a petition had been filed in the name of the KKK, asking for $250 each time the picture had been shown, with a further $100,000 for "damages."[2] For the Klan, the legal case attested to the continued importance of the Klan costume in establishing and defining its identity. This image, manufactured and popularized by film twenty-two years earlier, was now being desecrated by the same medium. The Klan response to this "misrepresentation" was to send in the lawyers.

Yet, while evidently aware and protective of its representation on-screen, the Klan appeared more interested in how it could use this legal dispute to "represent" and define itself in public discourse. In writing about the *Black Legion* case, *Variety* spoke of "this legal move on [the] part of [the] bed sheet boys."[3] The press discussed the case largely in relation to the Klan, and Warner Bros. similarly appeared far less interested in the claim than in the claimant, initially seeking to defend itself not over the intricacies of the patent laws but rather by attacking the Klan as a group. Morris Ebenstein, overseeing the case for Warners, wrote, "We will of course claim that it [the Klan] is an illegal organization and has no rights to ascertain a claim, but it may not be easy to prove this."[4] In attempting to expose this long-held foe, Warners also corresponded with a staunch opponent of the Klan, Captain Ramsay, who claimed to have evidence of Klan raids.[5]

Ebenstein admitted that initially he was "not taking [the case] too seriously." He wrote of the action as a "nice legal question," one that "I am inclined to think that we will win."[6] Yet for the Klan the probable failure of this case was of less significance than the publicity generated through the action. Just as a critical engagement with film nourished and mobilized an embryonic NAACP after 1915, so too would the Klan look to confront individual films, Hollywood and the movie theater as a social space, in order to define itself to a wider American public. Its staged protests outside film venues would now evoke the parades at screenings of *Birth*, with which the Klan had initially launched itself. These public displays would serve to establish local Klan groups not through a celebration of film, but through its condemnation. Through these protests, and in particular through their coordination within an emerging Klan media, the group sought to position itself as a legitimate and moral social force.

At the end of the previous chapter, we saw how the Klan redefined the censorship of *The Birth of a Nation*, presenting it as part of a broader attack on Protestantism. In reworking the parameters of public discourse around the film, the Klan sought to emphasize its own religious values. In this way, the film became a battleground for the Klan and its predominantly Jewish and Catholic opponents, a way for the Klan to publicize and articulate its modern ideology. During the 1920s these ideological disputes stretched beyond *Birth* and beyond Klan representation. Beginning with the Klan's opposition to Charlie Chaplin's *The Pilgrim* – a film condemned ostensibly for its representation of religion – the chapter, through an examination of the Klan's print media, examines how Klan groups campaigned against certain on-screen images, the perceived excesses of Hollywood, and individual film theaters.

These disputes have significant repercussions for both Klan and film historians. As the Klan emerged as a social and political force in the early 1920s, it directed and supported conservative calls for industry reform. The Klan worked here with local police authorities and established social, educational, religious, and political reform groups, rearticulating and redefining conservative discourse. At a moment of heightened patriotic fervor, at what we can now recognize as a formative moment in the history of the American film industry, the Klan aligned its criticisms of film to mounting conservative anxieties surrounding immigration, race, religion, and national identity. In so doing, it emerged as an influential and critically overlooked social reform group, using its own media to challenge an emergent dominant media industry that, in its "foreign" construction, the Klan perceived as a direct threat to America's social and political future.

RELIGION ON-SCREEN: CHAPLIN, FORD, AND THE PROTESTANT CHURCH

A vulgar little ape of the screen at present is busily pocketing dollars as a reward for caricaturing the Protestant ministry. In ministerial garb the guttersnipe comedian drinks booze, waves a pistol and in general behaves like a moron.

"Screen Ridicule of Protestant Ministry," *Imperial Night-Hawk*, 4 April 1923, 3

In 1923, the Ku Klux Klan launched a series of protests against Charlie Chaplin's latest film, *The Pilgrim*. The Klan's objections, clearly outlined in its newspapers, ostensibly concerned the representation of Protestantism within the film, but this was aligned to anxieties surrounding Prohibition, violence, and social behavior. The on-screen "ridicule" of its purported values was, for the Klan, borne of the financial and commercial demands of those involved in the production. On this occasion it was Chaplin "busily pocketing dollars," but more often it was the Jewish producers whom the Klan held responsible for film's on-screen immorality.

The protests against *The Pilgrim,* which were organized by local Klan groups and then reported and circulated through an emerging Klan press, ensured that the film was banned in areas of Pennsylvania, West Virginia, and Kansas, which prompted the Klan in Pittsburgh to claim triumphantly that "The Pilgrim has been driven off the screen in several states by the Klan."[7] At the same moment, Klan groups throughout the country were protesting against *Bella Donna,* starring Chaplin's fiancée Pola Negri. Screenings of *Bella Donna* were blocked in Texas, while Klan newspaper advertisements opposing the film in Hickory, North Carolina, led *Moving Picture World* to announce that "the Ku Klux Klan has at last invaded the precinct of motion picture censors."[8]

As the Klan was protesting against these two films in April 1923, Klan leaders in Indiana were launching the Cavalier Motion Picture Company. Outlining the motivations behind this new film enterprise, Roscoe Carpenter, the company's secretary, explained that Cavalier was "organized to produce pictures which would counteract the influence of certain productions which have been found objectionable to the Klan."[9] Cavalier represented a further attempt by the Klan to mobilize against these "immoral" film productions and, more broadly, against the film industry.

The example of *The Pilgrim* illustrates the ways in which the Klan used its own media both to invigorate its local chapters and to position these local incidents as part of a broader nationwide campaign. The specific details of the campaign against *The Pilgrim* – what local Klan groups chose to prioritize and oppose – would come to inform and direct the terms in which the Klan campaigned against film for much of this period, and also borrowed heavily from existing conservative discourses, particularly those propagated by Henry Ford's weekly *Dearborn Independent.*

The first reference I have found to *The Pilgrim* appeared at the end of 1922, when a letter was sent to a Klan newspaper, *Searchlight,* objecting strongly to Chaplin's forthcoming appearance. "It is a well known fact," the writer argued, "that when a Protestant minister is shown in any manner on the screen, it is always in a ridiculous manner, and that if a Catholic priest or rabbi is shown it is in a dignified manner." The writer enclosed a clipping about *The Pilgrim* and urged the paper to "launch a fight" against this representation of Protestantism. This suggestion was quickly picked up a week later in an editorial in *Searchlight*.[10] Over the next few months, an array of regional Klan papers restated the group's stance, directing the terms in which local Klan groups would oppose the film. For example, in April 1923, a few weeks after the Klan newspaper *Imperial Night-Hawk* had condemned the film under the headline "Screen Ridicule of Protestant Ministry," the Daniel Morgan chapter of the Klan in South Carolina stopped a screening on the grounds that it "ridiculed the Protestant ministry."[11] The criticisms, fueled by the Klan press, later extended into both film and popular press. In July 1923, the Pittsburgh Klan wrote to *Movie Weekly* complaining about the "bigoted, sacrilegious, untrue and disgraceful portrayal of the Protestant Church as is shown in The Pilgrim." The letter warned that "no man, no movie house, no actor and no corporation can insult the Christian religion and get away with it."[12] The Klan was responding to the negative representation not of its own groups, but rather of its values, defining itself through these discourses primarily in religious terms.

The Klan's campaign against *The Pilgrim* directly coincided with the rise of its own print media. In May 1923, *Dawn*, an official Klan publication, listed twenty-four newspapers published in sixteen states "which are devoted to the furtherance of Klan principles."[13] This number would escalate further over the next year, while the manner in which these papers circulated – papers emphasized that once read, a copy should be left for (other) non-members – ensured that these accounts moved beyond existing subscribers. Through these papers, which contained nationally syndicated stories alongside reports of local incidents, the Klan was able to organize disparate local chapters within a shared national identity. The campaign against *The Pilgrim* is an eloquent example. Specific local actions became immersed within the national movement, while the Klan press both directed the terms of the debate and also encouraged local action. In discussing *The Pilgrim*, *Searchlight* presented the on-screen "ridicule" by "certain Jew picture-show magnates" as a "willful, deliberate, cunning piece of propaganda that is going on daily." It was not merely objecting to *The Pilgrim*, but also positively urging readers to protest, to "raise a storm of unrest that will sweep the country."[14] In this, it enjoyed some success. In April 1924, a few weeks after the paper had again urged "100% Americans" to "open your eyes," the Fort Pierce Klan No. 85 in Florida launched its own official protest. This protest, widely reported in a number of Klan newspapers, attacked producers for "portraying our Protestant ministers and places of worship in a laughable, undignified way," and promised to "wage a relentless war" to stop such depictions.[15]

These continued complaints prioritized the modern group's religious credentials. The Klan defined itself in its press as "pro-America, pro-Protestantism" and as a group that was "'for' Protestant Christianity, first, last and all the time." Every week in Klan papers there was a section listing local churches entitled "Go to Church Sunday," alongside provocative headings like "Protestant church in danger: Klan only hope says Pastor" as the group presented itself as defenders of the Protestant faith.[16] Klan papers would regularly note public Klan appearances in church, reporting donations made by local groups during services, and quoting sermons. One sermon from Rev. James Hardin Smith in St. Louis, reprinted in *Dawn* in 1922, speculated on what Jesus would think of the Klan. "I think Jesus would have worn a robe such as they use," the sermon concluded, "but because He did not wear a robe the mob came and took Him and crucified Him."[17] The suggestion that Jesus would have joined the Klan, and that he may not have been crucified if he had, may appear fanciful, but it reiterates both the Klan's tendency to piggyback on respected authorities and to foreground religion within its modern identity. Indeed, the Klan's protests against *The Pilgrim* often partnered Klan groups with local religious authorities. For example, when almost a quarter of the film was cut in Mason City, Iowa, newspaper reports explained that the complaints came from "the Protestant Preachers' association and a man who said he was a representative of the Ku Klux Klan." In Atlanta the protests were supported by the Evangelical Ministers' Association, who labeled the film "an insult to the gospel and an attempt to ridicule the Christian religion."[18]

While the Klan led the way in its protests against *The Pilgrim*, its broader criticisms on the representation of Protestantism echoed existing calls. For example, when the Board of Religious Organizations, which represented the "religious women of St Louis," threatened the local movie managers with a boycott in 1921, it asked, "How can we expect our children to respect the clergy and the cause for which it stands if they constantly see ministers caricatured on screen?"[19] The General Assembly of the Presbyterian Church – endorsed by almost 900 commissioners in Iowa in May 1922 – passed a resolution urging its members to boycott any theater that showed pictures that were "suggestive and unclean." The assembly referred here to the "moral blight . . . striking at the vitals of the nation" when "certain interests" in the industry make light of marriage, women's virtue, the sabbath, and, in particular, the Eighteenth Amendment (the prohibition of alcohol).[20]

The assembly referred to familiar Klan concerns – in terms of the subjects depicted on-screen, their effect on American identity, and the "certain" powerful interests controlling the industry – and also called for legislation at the point of production. Speaking on the subject, the assembly's chairman, the Rev. Dr. Breigleb of Los Angeles, reserved particular condemnation for the industry's depiction of Protestant ministers as "weak-kneed, lady-like men" and asked why producers do not take a Jewish rabbi or Catholic priest and "hold him up to ridicule." In answering his own question, Breigleb concluded it was "because their people would not stand for it."[21] A couple of years later, the council announced a plan to petition Congress demanding federal censorship at the point of production. The details of its new crusade – which contained the slogan "Clean up the Movies!" – were widely published in the national and trade press and were also picked up by Klan newspapers. In response to the committee's claim that it wanted all reform, civic, religious, and patriotic organizations to join the campaign, *Dawn* announced that, having been "most active in the fight for cleaner pictures," the Klan would certainly "aid in the proposed crusade."[22] As we will see, Protestant voices were clamoring for industrial reform during the early 1920s. William D. Romanowski highlights the influence of Protestant churches and organizations in introducing almost one hundred movie-related measures in thirty-five states in 1921, while also noting that they were rarely unified and centrally organized.[23] Thus the Klan positioned itself as part of a significant Protestant movement, directing the terms in which film reform was discussed and, in so doing, seeking to establish its own position within American society.

Henry Ford was perhaps the most significant conservative influence in this arena. In February 1921, Ford's *Dearborn Independent* ran a piece entitled "Jewish Supremacy in Motion Picture World," complaining that the motion picture was "exclusively under the control, moral and financial, of the Jewish manipulators of the public mind."[24] In looking at the "ill-concealed propaganda" of these "manipulators," the article noted that "non-Jewish religions" often came under attack. "You never saw a Jewish Rabbi depicted on the screen in any but the most honorable attitude," the article claimed, "but the Protestant Clergy is still the elongated, sniveling, bilious hypocrite from anti-Christian caricature." It further noted that while reformers complained of and recognized the dangers of showing crime and seduction on-screen (what it referred to as an "evil schooling which bears bitter fruits in society"), the representation of religion was not closely monitored. The article also quoted Benjamin Hampton's influential 1921 article "Too Much Sex Stuff in the Movies?" in which Hampton commented on a poster he had seen showing a Protestant clergyman leaving his wife for his "free lover." The film in question was *One Woman* (1918), based on a 1903 Thomas Dixon novel in which the socialist ideals of the "churchless clergyman" are exposed and ultimately reformed. Significantly, the *Dearborn* article presented this caricature of the ministry as part of a calculated "campaign of subversion," a "rehearsal" for a revolution, and as emblematic of a far wider threat to national identity.[25]

The reference to this on-screen representation of a Protestant minister appeared in a series of agenda-setting articles produced in Ford's newspaper, under the heading "The International Jew: The World's Problem," which ran for two years beginning in 1920, the year of the Klan's effective reemergence. There are two points to note here. First, Ford's media empire provides a neat point of comparison to the Klan's nascent operations. Alongside his newspaper, printing press, and workplace indoctrination (his factories were said to contain signs saying, "Jews produce filthy movies"), Ford was also, as Lee Grieveson has shown, a significant producer and exhibitor of non-theatrical "useful" cinema.

He imagined film in much the same way the Klan did, as a tool for citizenship, as a way of inculcating workers within his model of the nation. Grieveson argues that Ford's production of film was recast in light of his criticisms of "money-grabbing" Jewish producers, now providing a direct challenge to the "commercial and nonuseful, or nonpurposeful, Hollywood cinema."[26] As we see in the next chapter, the Klan's own film operations, while often seeking to work within commercial channels, were also promoted as a direct response to the "un-American" pictures produced by the industry.

Second, Ford's antisemitic writing foreshadowed the terminology and focus of the Klan's writing. Ford's connections with the Klan may have been merely ideological – despite claims from Jewish groups that Ford helped fund the Klan – but the Klan would embrace Ford's writings, commenting on, quoting from, and indeed reprinting pieces from *Dearborn* in its own papers. Klan papers praised Ford's stance on Prohibition in 1925 and celebrating his efforts to "keep this country American."[27] Some Klan papers, such as the *Fiery Cross,* even carried advertisements for the *Dearborn Independent* (with the tagline "It prints plain facts"), and years later, in 1941, the relaunched *Fiery Cross* would describe Ford's advertisements as "literary masterpieces." The Klan recognized the broader pedagogical value of Ford's advertising materials, which "aim not so much at selling Ford products (which sell anyway), but rather at putting across, in simple, though beautiful language, some worthwhile lesson in citizenship or Americanism."[28] For its part, the *Dearborn Independent* appeared largely sympathetic to the Klan, despite suggesting that its "secrecy policy [was] a mistake." It recognized the shared problems to which both itself and the Klan were responding, writing in 1921 that "these movements, when they are spontaneous and virile, are natural reactions to the abused of their times."[29]

The anti-Klan paper *Tolerance* also noted the close parallels between Ford and the Klan in a series of articles. One front cover (fig. 2.1) depicted Ford leading a group of Klansmen over the edge of a cliff labeled "National Disunion," while a 1924 Hebrew book, *The Truth about Henry Ford,* had on its cover a drawing of a Klansman standing next to Ford with his arm draped over his shoulder.[30] Upton Sinclair's 1937 novel *The Flivver King* fictionalized this close relationship between the values of the Klan

2.1. Henry Ford and the Klan, *Tolerance,* 5 August 1923.

and Henry Ford. In Sinclair's novel, Abner Shutt, a loyal Ford worker, subscribes to his boss's paper and absorbs all of Ford's ideals. Schutt is then approached by the Klan, who took his name from the subscription list of the *Dearborn Independent*.[31]

There are, however, important distinctions between the motivations of Henry Ford and those of the Klan. For Ford, antisemitism served in part as a defense of his own technological modernity. As a symbol of industry, of new wealth and class movement, Ford emphasized that the perceived problems with modern America were triggered not by industry, class, or urbanization but specifically by race and religion. For the Klan, aligning criticisms of modernity with fears about Jewish immigration helped the group to promote its role in society and to define itself against a manufactured foreign threat. There are also distinctions between Klan publications and the *Dearborn Independent*, most notably Ford's more tolerant attitude toward Catholics, which was the subject of criticism in Klan newspapers.[32] However, Ford's antisemitism, and the manner in which he connected issues of film representation and reform to the far larger issue of national identity and media control, clearly shaped the Klan's film discourses.

The initial letter condemning *The Pilgrim*, for instance, connected the on-screen representation of Protestantism directly to the ethnic makeup of the film industry, noting that "the movies are controlled by the Jews and Catholics."[33] The *Fiery Cross*, when discussing a ban of *The Pilgrim*, similarly blamed "the Jewish control of the movie industry and the highly organized Catholic pressure," while an earlier article commented that Chaplin "should be hilariously funny to the Jews and Catholics whose capital controls this form of amusement."[34] The American Catholic Church also condemned the Jewish influence in the industry and assumed a prominent role in calls for film reform, but for the Klan the Catholic and Jewish forces were more often presented in conjunction, collectively seeking to use "this great medium to ridicule American beliefs, creeds, and customs."[35] The Klan was certainly not opposed to film as a medium, but rather aligned criticisms of modernity with fears about Jewish and Catholic immigration. "Jewish money controls the movies, and the baleful influence of the papal hand is consequently felt throughout moviedom," a 1924 article stated, further arguing that "with the active co-operation of the Jewish element the Roman Catholics are working their propaganda to a fine finish."[36]

Through its media, the Klan picked up the campaign that Ford was now abandoning. It presented itself in a battle against controlling Jewish and Catholic influences, describing the barring of *The Pilgrim* as "one more victory to the credit of the Klan."[37] The Klan was clearly fighting here for media control, using its own media – whether the printed press or its independent film productions – to confront what it presented as an organized, industrial threat to American national identity. The Klan's idealized national identity (its oft-quoted "100% Americanism") was inherently tied to notions of Protestantism, prompting the Klan to complain that Catholicism "is clearly screened in preference to American ideals" or that these films strike "at the very basis of American right-mindedness, the Protestant church."[38]

On occasion, the Klan aligned its criticisms of *The Pilgrim* to discourses surrounding Chaplin. *Imperial Night-Hawk* described him as a "vulgar Jewish comedian in the role of a Protestant minister," while *Searchlight* wrote that the film was "produced by Jews and starring a Jew ridiculing [the] Protestant ministry."[39] Although Chaplin was not Jewish, he regularly avoided questions about his ethnicity and, in light of his recent engagement to the exotic foreign actress Pola Negri, he was an obvious target for the Klan. The Pittsburgh Klan referred disparagingly to Chaplin as "Bella Donna's side partner," and certainly the Klan's protests against Chaplin complemented its concurrent criticisms of Negri.[40] A report in the *Fresno Bee* in 1927 further suggested that the Klan's objections concerned Chaplin himself. Two theaters cancelled screenings of *The Pilgrim* in Queens that year after theater programs signed "K.K.K." and with a picture of a Klansman on horseback were handed to the doormen.[41]

The Klan's objection to the film was ostensibly related to Chaplin's messy, expensive, and very public divorce from his second wife, Lita Grey, for which he was seen to transgress the strict moral code advocated, but certainly not always followed, by the Klan's leadership. This protest may have been directly related to Chaplin as a star, whether to the anxieties around his ethnicity or, in particular, the moral failings of Hollywood that were exposed in his divorce proceedings, but it is significant that it was *The Pilgrim* that was targeted; *The Pilgrim* was replaced by another Chaplin picture at the two theaters in Queens, and there is little evidence of the Klan responding to any other Chaplin film. The Klan was not chasing Chaplin off the screen but was responding only to *The Pilgrim,* which, it outlined in its notes to the theater, served as "an affront to the Presbyterian ministry." For the most part, Klan newspapers preferred to blame the larger, faceless figures of the film industry for the perceived anti-Protestantism within *The Pilgrim.* Under this reading, Chaplin was a tool, a scapegoat, a product of a greater problem; as *Dawn* commented in 1923, "Jewish producers recently prostituted the ability of Charlie Chaplin, the English comedian, who has been so well received in the United States."[42]

Although the industry was perceived as having a stronger Jewish influence during the 1920s, the Klan used debates around film representation to attack its other staunch opponents, the Catholics and Bolsheviks. In October 1923, *Dawn* warned about the spread of "Roman Catholic propaganda" through the Catholic Motion Picture Actors' Guild. The Klan presented the Guild as an organized, deliberate threat to Klan ideals, influencing "hundreds of thousands of Protestant children" who will be subjected to "sugar coated doses of Catholicism." In its attempts to evoke panic and action amongst its readership, the paper reported that five hundred movie stars had attended the last Guild meeting and that "Protestants will do well to keep their eyes open for the effects of their work on the screen."[43] The Klan presented the industry as a microcosm of the nation, fractured by foreign, "un-American" influences. Indeed, the calculated move against Protestant actors, according to the Klan press, marked an attempt to "Roman Catholicize the whole United States." The West Texas *Fiery Cross,* in an article syndicated throughout the country, went further still, adding that "an actor who would profess to be a Klansman might just as well cut his own throat, because Rome would see that he starved to death."[44] This growing Catholic influence would, a *Fiery Cross* editorial warned, lead to a strengthening of Catholic propaganda on-screen. The editorial labeled the 1923 Norma Talmadge picture *Ashes of Vengeance* "a direct insult to the intelligence of every Protestant; a distorter of history and merely a part of the gigantic system of Catholic propaganda now flooding this country."[45]

The Klan's criticisms prompted a picture house in the west to invite a local committee of Klansmen to a screening of the Lillian Gish film *The White Sister* before its public release. The on-screen transformation of Gish from the Southern heroine in *Birth* to a Catholic nun – still defined somewhat provocatively for the Klan as "white" – may have supported the Klan's fears that traditional Protestant values were being marginalized and replaced within American cinema. The direct involvement of the Catholic Church in facilitating the filming in Rome further fueled the Klan's fears of a monopolizing Catholic and Jewish influence within the film industry. On this occasion, the watching Klansmen "pronounced it [*The White Sister*] the most insidious piece of Roman Catholic propaganda that has been shown in this country." As a result, the manager decided not to show the picture, which encouraged further action, most notably in Dallas, where the Klan was credited with the film's initial ban in 1924. "The time is ripe for all good Protestants to stand together on this thing if they would put a stop to the Roman practice," wrote the *Fiery Cross*. "Now is the time to strike, while the iron is hot."[46] The example reveals the extension of Klan protests beyond *The Pilgrim*, its desire to work with existing Protestant groups, and its authority within specific local strongholds.[47] Indeed, a brief look at the trade journal *Exhibitors Herald* suggests that local exhibitors gave some consideration to Klan reactions when screening films, whether noting that the Our Gang comedy *Lodge Night* "is funny if the K. K. K. does not object" or that the anti-Klan picture *Prodigal Judge* should only be booked "if you want to lose your patrons who think the Klan is alright." In Texas, the Jewish-themed comedy *Potash and Perlmutter* did well, we learn, "even in a Ku Klux neighborhood."[48]

By 1924 the Klan was primarily exploiting and generating fears around Jewish and Catholic influences within society, but the earlier anxieties surrounding the mysterious Bolsheviks, evident in the promotion of *The Face at Your Window*, did on occasion resurface. In 1924 *Imperial Night-Hawk* reported, in a typically vague piece, that a recent attempt had been made to "penetrate the American moving picture industry as a means of red propaganda in this country."[49] *Searchlight* went a step further and named Charles Recht as an apparent Bolshevik agent, who it claimed was planning to invest eight million dollars on "anti-religious, anti-capitalistic" pictures. *Searchlight* claimed that Recht had consulted with Will Hays and had also met with the actress Norma Talmadge and her husband, the Russian-born Jew Joseph Schenck, as the Klan sought to manufacture a foreign threat infiltrating America through its media. The Klan's related battles over on-screen representation and the control of the mainstream media engineered a need for the Klan within modern America, while simultaneously acknowledging the integral role of the media in shaping contemporary American society.[50]

The Klan's interest in the popular representation of both itself and the values it cherished stretched beyond the cinema to radio and the stage. *Dawn* complained about the "constant propaganda in favor of Roman Catholicism and against Protestantism" on the New York stage in 1923, reserving the most vitriolic condemnation for the 1923 play *The Miracle*.[51] The *American Standard* dismissed the play as a "desperate effort 'to make America Roman Catholic,'" and as a "colossal effort on the part of the popery, with the connivance of the Jewry, to advance the papal cause in America and other Protestant countries."[52] For the Klan, the representation onstage was again indicative of a broader threat to Protestant Americanism, witnessed through the production of this "Jew-Jesuit propaganda." The Klan (along with other groups such as the Lord's Day Alliance) also protested against *Rain*, a play in which "a Protestant minister is cast in such a disgraceful role." The Klan's press coverage of the play sought to explain its reception in relation to its religious position. The *Fiery Cross* credited the Klan press for a fall in attendance in Indiana after it had labeled the play as Catholic propaganda. However, an earlier article suggested that the Klan remained powerless to influence the production in New York. "So long as Sam Harris, the Jew owner, can get enough Irish and Jews to see the play," the article suggested, "he will probably continue it for another 500 times."[53] What we see throughout this period is the Klan using these debates on religious representation to criticize its opponents collectively, writing again in 1925 of the Jews that "unite with Roman Catholics to censor the press."[54]

At the beginning of 1923 a play was staged at the Aryan Grotto Theatre in Chicago that aroused considerable interest in the Klan press. A full-page advertisement in *Dawn* for *The Invisible Empire* celebrated this new work as "a sequel to The Clansman" and suggested that it was "to the speaking stage what The Birth of a Nation has been to the screen."[55] The role of the Klan within the play – a protective law enforcement group countering the threat of bootlegging – offered a contemporary reworking of the Klan's role in *Birth* and one that, as reviewers noted, was especially pertinent to Chicago. Yet while the Klan was not defined on stage in religious terms, it again reinserted these terms within the play's reception. A lengthy review in *Dawn* barely spoke of the text, instead focusing on the censorship that this Klan-sponsored show faced, and offering a single reason for the "onslaught" faced at the hands of the censors. "It is a PROTESTANT show, financed, and produced by Protestants for the purpose of promoting Protestantism," *Dawn* explained, adding that this was the third time in eight months that "the Protestants have been double crossed by an element that can stage anything from a gambling house to a Chinese smoke shop and through corrupt politics get away with."[56]

The Klan, a powerful force onstage, used these censorship debates to present itself as a victimized minority group off stage. Reviews talked mysteriously of "forces that are foreign to a free press" and of "certain elements" fighting the Klan, presenting the Klan as the victim rather than the exponent of religious persecution, just as it would in 1924 when noting the "rabid discrimination" it faced after *Birth* was banned in the city.[57] The Klan deployed the tactics and discourses of other minority groups and avoided presenting the Catholic and Jewish groups as minorities in order to reveal itself as an overpowered victim of their on-screen propaganda. What is striking here is that the Klan again used this manufactured sense of injustice as a means of recruitment, reworking the politics articulated on the stage or screen beyond the auditorium. The reviewer now encouraged Protestants to respond to these apparent injustices by "joining the greatest organization in the world, THE KU KLUX KLAN." This sense of injustice was used as a dual commercial selling point, both for the Klan and also for this Klan-sponsored show. The review concluded with a call to arms, urging "Protestants and Members of the Ku Klux Klan" to see the show. "Be one hundred per cent American," the review urged. "Let us make it run a year instead of three weeks – come on. Let's go!!"[58]

The Klan's call responded to the scathing condemnation offered by anti-Klan publications, such as the *Evening Post* in Chicago. In suggesting that the play should be used to "torture" the Klan's enemies, the *Post* concluded that "no punishments for crimes, treasons and misdemeanors could be more dire than to abduct the guilty wretch and take him on a joy ride to a performance of this show." While the review was unlikely to be featured on any posters for the show, such a direct critical engagement from an anti-Klan press was useful for the Klan. The Klan not only used the play's release as a forum to discuss and promote the merits of the Klan, but also now reimagined its reception as an indication of the Klan's position within society. The success or failure of the play now served either as evidence of the Klan's strength within Chicago or of the continuing dominance of "foreign" influences within the entertainment and media industries.[59]

SEX ON-SCREEN: "JEW MOVIES URGING SEX VICE"

The Klan's criticisms of *The Pilgrim* had focused on religious representation, but its concurrent opposition to *Bella Donna* centered ostensibly on the depiction of racial relations. A lengthy editorial published in the *Fiery Cross* in April 1923, entitled "'Bella Donna' – Bah!" described the film as "coarse, degrading and insulting," "a disgrace to the white race" and "open propaganda for social equality." The Klan publicly opposed a film in which "a white woman submits herself to an Egyptian Negro only to be spurned by him," while *Dawn* complained that "the Polish actress is made to say 'WHITE SKINNED LADIES WILL FLIRT WITH BLACK SKINNED MEN WHEN THEIR HUSBANDS ARE AWAY.'" The *Fiery Cross* noted that this line was used on an electric bulletin advertising the film in Houston.[60]

The Klan's opposition to *Bella Donna* appeared to share much in common with its criticisms of Eugene O'Neill's interracial play *All God's Chillun Got Wings* a year later. Klan newspapers emphasized the social threat, beyond the auditorium, carried by the play's display of physical interaction, but they suggested that it would be African Americans rather than Klansmen responding violently. After condemning the closing scene in which a white woman must kiss the hand of her African American husband ("Can you imagine anything more repulsive than that?"), *Searchlight* concluded that "there is enough racial trouble in

America without manufacturing more of it through the drama which is calculated to stir the negroes of the country to violence towards the white race." This claim was somewhat undermined by the death threats that O'Neill received, printed on Klan stationery.[61]

Yet on closer inspection, the Klan's campaign against *Bella Donna* was once more motivated by the group's antisemitism. First, the Klan aligned Pola Negri's ethnicity to issues of film morality. After criticizing the "low ideals of womanhood" portrayed in *Bella Donna,* the Pittsburgh Klan urged films to "produce he-men and patriotic womanly women, not cigarette smoking devils who love poodle dogs more than they do babies."[62] Negri's ethnicity made her a destabilizing presence on film, and Klan groups viewed her depiction of the "loose woman" as a threat to domesticity and traditional womanhood. The Klan responded in part here to the flurry of reports littering the film press. By 1920 *Photoplay* commented on the clutch of film divorces by reprinting the popular line, "Are you married or do you live in Los Angeles?" while *Movie Weekly* published articles entitled "Marriages are not made in Heaven" and "What evil influence wrecks the happy homes of moviedom?"[63] The Imperial Wizard spoke frequently of the need for a "happy, wholesome family life for our nation's development," further arguing that the Klan should "feel free to take whatever action may be necessary" to curb the growing practice of divorce. In California in 1921, this action reportedly included dragging a doctor from his house, hanging him until unconscious, reviving him, and flogging him back into unconsciousness after he carried out divorce proceedings.[64] *Bella Donna* represented the modern, destabilizing, independent woman, and, with the development of the star system, the Klan also increasingly recognized this figure off-screen within Hollywood.

Second, the Klan again blamed the apparently insidious morality displayed within *Bella Donna* on the more powerful "Jewish" industry: "Lacking that inborn feeling of supremacy toward the black races that is peculiar to the better born Americans, Jewish producers starred Pola Negri in a revolting play called 'Bella Donna.'"[65] The suggestion was that the Jewish immigrants were unable to understand American customs and the "de facto" segregation that dominated American race relations at this time. In blaming the Jewish producers for this on-screen representation, the Klan's criticisms of *Bella Donna* were closely aligned to its simultaneous attacks on *The Pilgrim*. An editorial in the *Fiery Cross* suggested that "Pola Negri, Europe's alleged star, must have received her inspiration from the same interests that inspired Charlie Chaplin in *The Pilgrim*." The Klan presented the film as a deliberate, personal attack on the group, with the *Fiery Cross* even suggesting that "hate for the Knights of the Ku Klux Klan could have inspired this picture."[66]

The Klan's criticisms of *The Pilgrim* and *Bella Donna* formed part of a broader attack on the film industry, which intensified during 1924 as the Klan launched a fresh assault on the "sex plays" produced by Paramount Pictures. This began with an article in the *American Standard,* a New York–based Klan publication edited by Charles Lewis Fowler, who was also president of the Klan's Cavalier Motion Picture Company. The article, which was subsequently repackaged as a pamphlet, objected to titles such as *Manhandled, The Enemy Sex,* and *Changing Husbands,* while also condemning Paramount's promotion of *The Female,* which promised to show Betty Compson "more nearly nude than she has yet appeared on screen."[67] The Klan's criticisms, although ostensibly concerned with on-screen representation, were shaped in part by its attitude toward Paramount. First, among the prominent names on Paramount's roster were the director William Desmond Taylor and the actors Mary Miles Minter, Wallace Reid, and Fatty Arbuckle, all of whom had been involved in high-profile scandals in recent years. In reference to the Klan's criticisms of Paramount, *Variety* commented that "the more divorces, separations and scandals cropping up in Hollywood, that much more dangerous do mothers know pictures will become."[68] In a period of off-screen excess and increased tabloid journalism, the issue of on-screen morality was closely related to the activities of the stars off-screen. Furthermore, Paramount was the first and most powerful example of a vertically integrated film company, described by the Klan as "the biggest movie trust in the world." This "movie trust" was defined by its religious construction. The Klan noted that the studio was headed "by the former Jewish furrier" Adolph Zukor, again building on a rhetoric served up in the *Dearborn Independent,* which had described Zukor in 1921 as an "ambitious foreigner" and presented his company as emblematic of Jewish control of the film industry. "A gentile has no chance to advance in his organization," the paper had written; "as soon as they are squeezed dry they are supplanted with young Jews whom he has had in training."[69] The Klan's criticisms of the Paramount films were likewise used to attack Jewish control of the industry, which it repeatedly defined in economic terms. *American Standard* quoted a Paramount advertisement, which was sent to exhibitors, promoting Gloria Swanson's appearance in *Manhandled:* "Imagine the punch, the gowns and best of all the profits." The Klan response to this was simple: "They [Jews] are willing to despoil a nation for a pot of gold."[70] As we have seen, the Klan also looked to incorporate the Catholic threat into film discourse. This is perhaps best evidenced by the title of the *American Standard* article, and subsequent pamphlet, which was advertised for sale through the Klan press: "Jew Movies urging sex vice: Rome and Judah at work to pollute young America."[71]

The title also illustrates a prominent feature of the Klan's film rhetoric, which built on popular conservative anxieties by emphasizing the influence of film on children. *Searchlight* claimed that the movies were as important as school textbooks and suggested that "with its eight million students daily, the moving picture ought to be the greatest university in the world."[72] In launching its own film companies in 1923, the Klan emphasized the pedagogical function of film. Indeed, as we will see, both *The Toll of Justice* and *The Traitor Within*, two Klan-made films, were exhibited within schools during 1924. It was this pedagogical function that made film at once appealing and appalling to the Klan. For Charles Lewis Fowler, who also founded the Klan's first short-lived university in Atlanta, the desire to control "young America," whether through the printed press, film, or in the classroom, was directly challenged by the "Jew-Jesuit motion picture producers [who] persist in making the screen a school for teaching seduction."[73] In this way, Hollywood represented not only an ideological opponent to the Klan but also a commercial competitor in the business of educating American youth.

Film's effect on young minds, which had been used to mobilize and justify film reform since its first decade, remained the most quoted argument in support of censorship and was further noted and nurtured by the Klan. The *American Standard* article positioned on-screen images "hand in hand" with a series of wild parties that had recently occurred at schools, and further implied that the rape of a fifteen-year-old girl in Kalamazoo, Michigan, was a direct result of the "base tendencies" stimulated by "certain motion pictures."[74] When the *American Standard* complained in 1925 about an advertisement for *A Thief in Paradise* presented in New York by "Samuel Goldstein (Jew)," its complaint again concerned the "poison . . . that the anti-Christian Jews are ladling out to the children of America." The article then offered three lengthy quotes from "eminent jurists" emphasizing the "salacious and vicious" influence of films on children.[75]

The Klan sought to position itself as a moral guardian "on behalf of the children." In doing this, it effectively reached out beyond its existing membership for support, as it suggested that the issue of film morality was relevant to "every parent-teacher's organization, every educational association, every women's club, every minister, every friend of decency." The Klan then carefully posited its own values within these familiar discourses, as it urged these groups to unite against the "flood of oriental and papal debauchery which floods the country through Jew-Jesuit motion pictures."[76] In many respects the Klan was merely opportunistic, exploiting the popular debates over censorship and film morality that littered the papers after the war. As an example from the national press, the *New York Times* in 1921 reported that two boys in Michigan had confessed to an attempt to wreck a train "like they had seen on screen," while another boy, fifteen years old, shot a man, apparently "inspired by movies." The Klan similarly claimed that "the commercialized movie is America's biggest school of crime," adding that "as a result [of movies] the city of New York is literally filled with boy thieves and criminals and degenerate girls." It further stated that "the biggest menace to Sunday school work and organized religion in general in the United States today is the commercialized motion picture industry," suggesting, with a hint of overstatement, that this propaganda, if unchecked, "will eventually destroy civilization."[77]

The Klan recognized the publicity generated by film discourses and embraced the criticisms offered by reputable religious and educational groups. For example, in 1925, *Kourier* published an address given by the former president of the American Bar Association before the Arkansas Educational Association, which highlighted the influence of film in educating the nation's youth and complained about the popular films of the last year, "which dealt altogether too much with the sex problem."[78] A year earlier, *Searchlight* had quoted at length Mrs. Howell, counselor of the New York Civic league, who suggested that movies were one of the principal reasons why "immorality has been made popular," and further crediting them for the popular increase in kissing, hugging, and "petting." Once more, when the Klan reported this address, it referred to the "moving pictures, most of which are controlled by Jews."[79]

In embracing and extending existing antisemitic writing, the Klan related the problems within the film industry to some of its other, well-established social campaigns. The Klan wrote of the "white slave dealers in motion pictures" – white slave dealers were, as we have seen, widely perceived as being Jewish – and as late as 1933 it was claiming that the "white slave business is respectable" in comparison to the "Jew controlled moving picture industry."[80] The comparison with white slavery was a provocative one, particularly given the widely circulating fears around Hollywood's impact on young, aspiring actresses. A sample issue of *Photoplay* from 1927, a regular source of exploitative warnings, highlights the perceived dangers for young women, whether in its regular columns ("Friendly Advice on Girls' Problems"), its series of sensational true stories' of girls who disappeared from Hollywood ("The Port of Missing Girls"), or in Ruth Waterbury's piece ("Don't go to Hollywood"), which begins "Don't go to Hollywood! Don't go! Don't go, no matter what beauty, talent or youth you have." *Movie Weekly* offered a fresh tale every week, from "No Girl should come to Hollywood without money warns Mary Pickford" to "Should a girl be chaperoned in Hollywood?" Pickford's warnings were reported in the *Fiery Cross* in December 1923, as she urged girls to "take mamma along. You'll need her."[81]

The Klan also compared the situation to Prohibition, which with its supercharged feelings of nationalism and Protestantism had been widely adopted as a Klan cause. Christopher Cocolchos, in his study of the Klan in Anaheim, California, suggested that the Klan enjoyed success there, as in many other areas, primarily as enforcers of the Prohibition laws.[82] In the aforementioned 1924 Klan pamphlet, the writer urged the Klan (and concerned moral guardians) to crush the film industry as they had previously destroyed the liquor industry. In arguing that the film producers "occupy the position which the brewers and distillers did ten years

ago," the Klan presented film reform as a modern crusade, allowing it
to relocate popular fears surrounding Jewish bootleggers to a modern
target. In discussing the pamphlet, *Variety* appeared to recognize the
value of the film industry to the Klan, stating that "since the war has
ended and a violation of the liquor law is a crime, there remains moving
pictures for the target, with Paramount as well as others becoming the
targets for their own bullets."[83] *Variety* suggested that the Klan attacked
the film industry because it offered the only remaining explanation for
the problems of modern society, but this was also a target the Klan could
use to justify its ongoing role within society and through which it could
promote its religious identity.

The Klan's criticisms of the industry were not only articulated in its
writings and speeches, but also evident in Klan cartoons. A brief look
at the work of Reverend Branford Clarke, a minister with the Pillar of
Fire movement, shows these discourses incorporated into the Klan's
visual materials. Clarke provided illustrations for the writings of Bishop
Alma White, a prolific fundamentalist minister, who was credited with
establishing forty-nine branches of her Pillar of Fire churches, setting
up two radio stations, founding three colleges, editing six magazines,
and writing over thirty-five books.[84] White forged extremely close links
with the Klan, championing its cause in her monthly periodical, *Good
Citizen,* and in edited collections of her work, such as *Heroes of the Fiery
Cross.* The cartoons depict the Klansmen in classical, biblical scenes, as
defenders and heroes of the Protestant cause and then, by extension, of
the nation, as they present Klansmen defending the White House, the
American flag, and public schools. They show the Statue of Liberty as a
Klanswoman, Uncle Sam as a Klansman, and further Klansmen ringing
the Liberty Bell, often flanked by former presidents. Two cartoons are
particularly noteworthy here. The first, "On the Run" (fig. 2.2), shows a
single Klansman in full regalia, with baseball bat and clenched fist warning off three fleeing figures that represent the related Jewish and Catholic
targets. Alongside "Rome" and "Rum," the Jewish figure has two labels
attached to him – "immodest fashions" and "corrupting movies" – as the
cartoon defines "the Jew" by his influence on the movies. The cartoon is
largely typical of Clarke's work, showing the Klan as a successful aggres-

2.2. "On the Run" by Rev. Branford Clarke, originally published in Bishop Alma White, *Heroes of the Fiery Cross* (Zarephath, NJ: The Good Citizen, 1928), 74.

2.3. "In Proper Hands" by Rev. Branford Clarke, originally published in Bishop Alma White, *Heroes of the Fiery Cross* (Zarephath, NJ: The Good Citizen, 1928), 37.

sor forcing these foreign threats away from the country, and contrasting with some Klan writings that presented the group as a threatened underdog. "In Proper Hands" (fig. 2.3) depicts a large arm emblazoned with "KKK" grabbing hold of two figures, "The Jew" and "Rome." The Klan arm featured regularly in these images, whether the "protective hand of true Americanism" or a fist emerging from the ground as the "defender of the 18th amendment" rushing drinking revelers. While Rome is defined in this cartoon by three terms – "Politics," "World Domination," and "Parochial Schools" – "The Jew" is represented by money and the twin labels of "Indecent fashions" and "Corrupting Movies." The Klan used film as a vehicle to attack "the Jew" so that an opposition to the perceived Jewish control of film becomes an important propaganda tool for the modern Klan.[85]

The cartoons condemn "The Jew" for his role in "corrupting movies," yet during the 1920s these anxieties extended beyond the screen. As Mark Lynn Anderson has argued, most movie reform efforts of the late teens targeted film content, and in particular the "so-called sex picture," but in the early 1920s "the demand for cleaner pictures was soon joined by the demand for cleaner stars." This is an important shift within the context of the Klan's reemergence. Anderson notes that the "identity of the performer" became a principal focus of external regulatory bodies in the eighteen months following the arrest of Roscoe "Fatty" Arbuckle in September 1921. Arbuckle, one of the most successful and recognizable film stars of the period, was arrested on charges of manslaughter after aspiring actress Virginia Rappe died from peritonitis shortly after attending a party in Arbuckle's hotel room. Ever more sensational stories circulated, claiming that Arbuckle had raped and crushed an intoxicated Rappe, causing her bladder to rupture.[86] Arbuckle was acquitted seven months later at his third trial, but his film career was, in effect, ended by the scandal. While film was perceived as a threat to the Klan because it represented the advances, social mobility, and media control of an immigrant society, Hollywood as the new conceptual center for the film industry now served as a microcosm of these social shifts, an area with fluid social, class, and racial boundaries. Reformers and church groups discussed "Hollywood" as an area of wild living, short marriages, excessive drinking, and instant fame, positioning it as the antithesis of the Klan's idealized image of the nation.

THE KLAN IN HOLLYWOOD

A year after the much publicized murder of film director William Desmond Taylor, *Movie Weekly* offered a possible solution to this unsolved
crime. On the front cover of the 24 March 1923 edition was the question "Did Movie Ku Klux slay Wm D. Taylor?" Inside, a lengthy article
asked, "Is there a Ku Klux Klan in the movies?" The article stopped short
of directly accusing the Klan of Taylor's murder, but it did present the
principles and practices of the Klan as a direct threat to the film industry.
"If it [the industry] is to succeed in accomplishing the high objectives of
picturedom," the article concluded, "[the industry] must work toward its
goal unhindered by the machinations of any invisible power."[87]

The article linked this "invisible power," which was "shrouded in all
the foreboding secrecy of the Ku Klux Klan," with a succession of crimes,
including the recent murder of "pretty" Fritzi Mann, a dancer and oc-
casional movie player. The writer, T. Howard Kelly, even suggested that
the surprise retirement of a "certain well-known girl star" (possibly Pearl
White) might be the result of a "force which held her in thrall – a force
which she had offended in some unknown way." The evidence offered
was inevitably inferred ("impossible to disclose") rather than revealed,
but it does raise the interesting possibility of a Klan group operating in
Hollywood targeting not only the conceptual notion, but also the literal
space. The Klan's function and identity, its position as a moral guardian
and social reformer, was exemplified, consolidated, and publicly circulated through this high-profile engagement with Hollywood.

By 1923, California was recognized as "a strong Klan state," and a
particularly violent one. David Chalmers argued that Klan violence here
was "as brutal as anywhere in the South." Tales of well-attended events,
growing membership, and, in particular, confrontation were widely reported in the Klan papers. For example, *Imperial Night-Hawk* reported
the cancellation of a state convention in Oakland in 1924 after news
of an assassination plot on one of the Klansmen due to attend.[88] The
infamous 1922 Inglewood raid saw thirty-seven suspected Klansmen
brought to trial (and acquitted) after a fatal attack on a suspected Spanish bootlegger and his family in southwest Los Angeles. Three of the
suspected Klansmen were listed as working in motion pictures.[89] Tales

of Klan groups operating within the studios soon began to appear in the film press. In 1925 *Variety* claimed that two directors were involved in recruiting members from the "film colony" and that over 200 actors and more than 400 technical staff had already been enrolled by the Klan. The report also claimed that a large independent studio had removed a significant proportion of its staff after discovering a strong Klan clique. The report followed earlier claims of a theatrical branch of the group opening in Chicago, predominantly comprising stage actors, which was reportedly intended as an organized response to "the Jew and Catholic" control of show business.[90]

Certainly California as the manifestation of an immigrant land, filled with outsiders who since the Gold Rush had moved west in search of riches, would appear an apposite target for the modern Klan. Yet despite the group's prominence in California and its noted antagonism toward the excesses of the industry, the Klan's movements in Hollywood would not always follow the expected course, according to the *Afro-American,* a Baltimore newspaper. Under the heading "Hollywood Klan to Welcome All Races," the paper suggested as late as 1926 that a new local group would maintain the principles of the national Klan, but would be "unique" in being open to all and would "not attempt to run religious creeds or races from Hollywood." The article again noted the transitory, cosmopolitan nature of the "colony" – "there are representatives of most every nation on earth resident" – but stated that the Klan's main function would be to protect women and to make the studios "a better place to live in."[91]

The Klan's influence within the Hollywood industry as a self-appointed moral guardian was already noted by the local and film press before 1926 and has since been recalled by director Lewis Milestone. In an interview with Kevin Brownlow, Milestone claimed that "the Ku Klux Klan got so strong in Culver City that you know you would drive to the studio and in the middle of the road you see a white paint, the initials – Klansmen I greet you – KIGY." *Variety* also noted that "K.I.G.Y." would appear on some roads in California "every 20 to 25 feet" and even, according to Milestone, on the light screens on set. Milestone recalled Kleagles (Klan recruiters) openly signing up members and recounted the story of a young bachelor at the studio who received a letter with a silver bullet in it from the Klan, which carried the warning, "Mend your ways or we will call on you." According to Milestone, the man in question prepared for the Klan visit, so that when they arrived "he came out blasting." The next day in the studio "the chief electrician came in with his arm in a sling, somebody else was limping. . . . All these guys were from the studio and they were members of the Klan."[92]

Yet despite the apparent Klan presence within Hollywood, the group's reported involvement in William Desmond Taylor's death serves as something of a smokescreen for the industry. This piece of sensationalist journalism exploits the popular fascination with the Klan, while also allowing the industry (as represented by the trade press) to extrapolate itself from the scandal by shifting focus onto the Klan. Discourse surrounding Taylor's death had speculated on his sexuality, his tempestuous relationship with female film stars (most notably Mabel Normand, who, aside from the killer, was the last person to see him alive), and his opium and drink parties. *Movie Weekly* now transferred the negative publicity generated by these scandals into a lengthy critique of the Klan, recounting tales of a midnight flogging and of recent violence in Louisiana. This dual function – sensationalist exploitation and defensive riposte – is neatly encapsulated in a cartoon featured in the article, which features a Klansman shooting at a picture of Taylor. The cartoon also highlights the simple, monolithic division presented between the Klan and "Hollywood," a contrast further evidenced by child star Jackie Coogan's comments in *Movie Weekly*. Eight-year-old Coogan was guest editor for one issue of *Movie Weekly* and offered his own views on this serious and sensitive subject. "I don't know what all this means," Coogan stated, "but Daddy says if it's true, it's certainly 'bad dope.' I hope the Ku Klux won't get Mother or Daddy."[93]

A closer look at the film scandals of the early 1920s reveals the restrictive social environment, along with a perfect storm of conservative anxieties, from which the Klan would enjoy its most robust period of growth. The popular response after the events in Arbuckle's hotel room in September 1921 highlights the value of these scandals to both the Klan and conservative reformers. It was not the moral indiscretions that were products of their time, but rather the responses to these events and the eagerness of conservatives to create a "scandal." It took very little imagination for outraged reformers to reassess Arbuckle's profitable persona in light of the events of September 1921, presenting this funny, overweight ladies man as a threatening, morally bankrupt rapist. We can see his fatness becoming "polluted and obscene," a symbol not of fun but of excess, of a loss of sexual and moral control, manifested most outrageously in the claims that he effectively crushed his victim to death during sex. Arbuckle, known for his frequent appearances in drag and as a baby, blurred and disfigured traditional gender categories, at a moment when voting rights and new fashions were destabilizing clearly defined gender roles. The press and conservative groups alike also now leaped on the playful image of a womanizer, apparent in comedies such as *Crazy to Marry* (1921), which contained the tagline "Pinched and on his wedding day. Just because he was running away with another girl." Publicity materials for Arbuckle's recent films, many still circulating in the press in September 1921, now problematized his fun-loving persona. A few months before his arrest, advertisements had featured the figure of Arbuckle surrounded by nine playful girls for the inopportunely titled "The Life of the Party."[94]

Arbuckle's financial rise and moral decline were also used to illustrate the dangers of new wealth and fame, a theme articulated and lampooned on-screen in *Brewster's Millions* (1921), in which Arbuckle's character had to blow an inherited million dollars within a year. The erosion of traditional financial responsibility and, in particular, the popular desire for fame without achievement remained a constant source of criticism in the Klan press. A favorite example from *Kourier* recounted the tale of an Ohio woman who, "admitting she was moved by the desire to have her picture appear in the newspapers, was recently arrested for having set her house on fire."[95]

The Arbuckle scandal remains an enormously significant moment in the history of American cinema, but, despite its apparent usefulness to the Klan, there is very little evidence of the Klan initially responding to Arbuckle, as women's groups, church leaders, and even Congress did.[96] Protests against Arbuckle led to the withdrawal of his films in areas throughout the country, including Pittsburgh, Detroit, Los Angeles, and Memphis, all within a week of the scandal breaking, yet there were only isolated reports of Klan groups directly protesting against Arbuckle or his films, and many of these came years later. For example, in 1924 the women's Klan "marched in on the Council" in Long Beach, California, presenting a petition demanding the cancellation of Arbuckle's planned public appearances.[97] Local Klan groups did, on occasion, respond to the on-screen appearances of other scandalized figures, most notably Clara Smith Hamon, a secretary acquitted of murdering her employer and purported lover, the millionaire Republican committeeman Jake Hamon. Smith Hamon's picture *Fate,* in which she played herself in the sensationalized story of her life, was refused a license by the New York State Motion Picture Commission and condemned by church and reform groups. In January 1922, the Cisco Klan No.170 in Texas wrote to the local theater manager protesting against the exhibition of the film. "We stand for protecting our homes from corrupting influences and guarding the morals of our youths," the statement began. "We believe the portrayal of this woman's life in moving pictures is calculated to corrupt the morals of our boys and girls." A few months later, a newspaper in Oklahoma reported a phone call made to the local press from a representative of the Klan, which commended the local mayor for prohibiting the film's exhibition.[98] These examples, while local isolated incidents, reveal Klan groups already using film criticism – and in particular anxieties around the effect of film on American youth – as a means of defining what they "stand for," of generating publicity (in specifically phoning a newspaper), and of aligning emerging Klan groups with high-profile conservative campaigns and respected authority figures.

It may therefore appear surprising that the Klan was not more actively involved in condemning Arbuckle and opposing his films after his arrest. Perhaps the explanation for this, and the most significant aspect of the scandal for the Klan, is its timing. The local and national Klan press was not yet established by September 1921, restricting any unified Klan response here, while the Klan also had its own problems to confront at this juncture. For three weeks that month, the Klan was sharing front-page space with Arbuckle during a twenty-one-day exposé of Klan activities, launched by the *New York World* and syndicated throughout the country. This had two immediate and unexpected effects. First, alongside the congressional hearings that followed in October and were intended as an investigation into the actions and motives of the group, the exposé brought publicity and legitimacy to the emerging group, fanning news of the Klan's widespread growth across the country. As William Simmons later famously remarked, "Congress gave us the best advertising we ever got. Congress made us," a claim supported by the reported two hundred new chapters chartered in the following four months.[99] Second, juxtaposing the motives and activities of the Klan with increasingly sensationalized, sordid tales from Arbuckle's hotel room helped to justify the Klan's existence while simultaneously positioning the Klan as a response to the excesses of Hollywood and modern society. Hilary Hallett noted the coverage of these "mutually reinforcing melodramas" across the Hearst papers in September 1921, arguing that these accounts of the mob spirit "offered readers a virtual experience of its frenzied pleasures."[100] What we see on the front pages is both the problem and a potential solution for conservative America.

A closer look at another famous scandal of the period, involving the 1919 Chicago White Sox baseball team (which was not brought to trial until the summer of 1921), provides further context for the Klan's religious attacks on Hollywood. In his comparative study of the White Sox and Arbuckle scandals, Sam Stoloff argues that both were presented as the work of Jewish corruptors undermining American life, yet there are crucial distinctions between how they were received.[101] The baseball scandal, which involved eight players conspiring to throw the World Series at the behest of gambling interests, highlighted the traditions and values of America being undermined by an outside foreign influence, while the film scandals involved a new industry run from within by the very forces that undermined baseball. Thus, while contemporary newspapers presented Hollywood as a product of the Klan's immigrant opponents, baseball was embraced and adopted by the Klan as emblematic of traditional American identity.

Klan festivals usually featured baseball, while Klan papers would report the scores of these games – "Palace Department 32, Accounting Department 0. Believe it or not as you like" – and comment on the number of new Klan teams "flying thick and fast." *Imperial Night-Hawk* proudly noted the number of Klan players in this most American of sports, with one major league baseball team from a town heralded as being very anti-Klan said to "boast nine one hundred percenters in the line up."[102] As we saw earlier, Klan cartoons frequently featured hooded figures protecting the country with a baseball bat from these outside (often Jewish and Catholic) enemies. In turn, the Klan also characterized threats to baseball, the national sport, as very personal attacks on itself. For example, when vandals damaged Wrigley Baseball Park in 1923, the Klan press viewed the vandalism as a racially motivated, personal attack on William Wrigley Jr., the owner of the Chicago Cubs, who was reported to be a Klan member. According to *Dawn*, the police admitted that they were investigating this incident from the "anti-Ku Klux angle."[103] By presenting itself as a supporter and protector of baseball – the "national game" and the "pastime of America" – the Klan elevated its role as a guardian of popular, traditional American values, and then positioned the foreign influences undermining the sport as direct enemies of itself and the nation.

It is hardly surprising that baseball should also feature so prominently in emerging star discourse, used by studios as a means to outline a movie star's all-American credentials. Charles Ray "plays baseball, drives his own car and loves his wife," *Photoplay* reported, while Florence Deshon "still believes in baseball and babies and continues to hate free verse and futurist art."[104] Arbuckle went a step further in 1919, acquiring a majority interest in the Vernon Tigers, a minor league team from Los Angeles. Arbuckle was a regular visitor to the team's ballpark, performing there alongside Buster Keaton, Tom Mix, and other Hollywood stars. It is probably no coincidence that Vernon was one of only two "wet" towns around Los Angeles, or that the ballpark adjoined Doyle's Tavern, which billed itself as "longest bar in the world." Yet Arbuckle's tenure as a team owner was both short-lived and troubled. In a move that presaged Arbuckle's own fall and exclusion from American society, a number of players were implicated in a match-fixing scandal and thrown out of the league for conspiring to fix games in the Tigers' favor. Arbuckle would sell the team soon afterward.[105]

The explanations for corruption within baseball would shape the terms in which the Klan would come to define the film industry. Responsibility for the scandal was placed not on the white American ballplayers but on the Jewish gamblers who bribed them. As early as 1919, the *Sporting News*, a famous weekly baseball magazine, responded to the rumors of a fix by blaming "a lot of dirty, long nosed, thick-lipped and strong-smelling gamblers [who] butted into the World Series – an American event, by the way."[106] This less-than-subtle rhetoric was embraced by Henry Ford's *Dearborn Independent,* which served up a host of antisemitic polemics on the subject during 1921 in articles with titles like "Jewish Gamblers Corrupt American Baseball." The paper wrote about Grover Cleveland Alexander, the American pitcher called up to play in a controversial game for Chicago, hurling "his heart out to beat Philadelphia and thwart the Jew gamblers." "If fans wish to know the trouble with American baseball," the paper surmised, "they have it in three words – too much Jew." The Klan would exploit these established antisemitic attitudes, claiming that betting and a lust for money were threatening the sport, and that the vast majority of those involved either as gamblers or bookmakers were "of foreign birth" with "no interest in Athletics except to bet on the contests."[107]

The baseball scandal cemented the image of the Jewish scapegoat and emphasized the threat of "aliens" both on American identity and within the entertainment industry. Given the discourses surrounding the modern, immigrant nature of the film industry, Hollywood would appear ripe for a scandal after the "Black Sox" tale. Harold Brackman argues that the "rise of Hollywood's Jewish mogul was coincidental rather than causative" to the film scandals, yet while the morals and actions of stars were obviously not connected to the Jewish involvement within the industry, it is no coincidence that the scandals arrived at a moment when Jewish involvement in the industry was consolidated.[108] The scandals were only scandals because of their reception, and the desire to condemn the industry was, at least in part, fueled by the perceived Jewish control of Hollywood. As late as 1933, when *Kourier* wrote of "the orgies which have become nationally infamous," it related these activities to the "greasy hawked nosed merchants of Hollywood." The Klan may not have been responsible for the wild image of Hollywood, yet it did reinforce the Jewish responsibility for this. "This is the type of man," *Kourier* wrote of Jewish film producers in 1933, "to whom the unthinking American public confides the educational amusement of the nation's youth. Hollywood certainly needs a Hitler!"[109]

A decade earlier, *Movie Weekly* had envisaged that the Klan might assume this "Hitler" role, exercising a level of influence over supposedly

2.4. *Movie Weekly* speculating on the Klan's involvement in Hollywood, 5 May 1923, 4–5.

"immoral" film stars. The discussion over the death of William Desmond Taylor presented a forum through which the Klan could engage with the industry and present its views to non-Klan audiences. The initial response instead reinforced the division between these two parties as *Movie Weekly* reported a series of Klan threats against one of its writers, T. Howard Kelly (fig. 2.4). Kelly explained that he had received a letter from Washington, followed by telephone calls warning, "Are you going to keep your mouth shut about the K.K.K. in the movies? If not you go the way of William Desmond Taylor and Fritzi Mann." Clearly, *Movie Weekly* was not unduly worried about these threats – as the cartoon of the writer chased by riding Klansmen suggests – rather using the Klan to boost its own profile by standing up strongly and writing of its "crusade against these people." The magazine did acknowledge that this unofficial, poorly written letter might not have come from the Klan, but still presented the group as an "avowed enemy." The piece also alluded to the terms of this dispute, when describing the threatened Kelly in racial terms as a "fighting Irishman."[110]

A couple of months later, *Movie Weekly* published an official response, in the form of a letter from the Pittsburgh Klan. The letter denied any connection with the previous unofficial correspondences, but made no mention at all either of the Taylor murder or of any Klan involvement within Hollywood. The letter instead outlined the group's concerns about film representation ("This organization is opposed to the mixture of white women and Sheiks"), moving the discussion within the magazine away from the subject of Hollywood and scandal, and toward a discussion of censorship and film morality.[111] Certainly the issue of film representation would appear to be of most significance to the Klan throughout this period, but what is noticeable here is the Klan's mode of address when corresponding directly to film fans: it adopted a more conciliatory approach. The Klan presented the issue of film representation in largely moral terms and avoided directly criticizing the Jewish and Catholic influences within the industry. The letter clarified that the Klan "does not oppose the movies – AS SUCH" and instead concluded, "We are not antagonistic, but wish to co-operate in the good work you fellows are capable of, if you only wake up."[112]

Movie Weekly could scarcely avoid aligning itself with the Klan's moral stand, acknowledging that "it is indeed laudable for the Ku Klux Klan to go on record as being officially opposed to indecency of any kind." The Klan's moral objections invited and indeed demanded support from broad sections of society. The Klan had reclaimed the moral high ground here, with *Movie Weekly* admitting that "right-minded citizens of this country in all levels of life will applaud the order for such a stand." The magazine revealed a willingness to work "shoulder to shoulder with Ku Kluxers" to produce "good, clean screen entertainment," while the Klan claimed that it was "not antagonistic" and wished to "co-operate" with the film industry. Yet, given the ideological tensions between the two, such a partnership was unlikely.

For *Movie Weekly*, the Klan's removal of Chaplin's *The Pilgrim* from a number of states represented a dangerous precedent, an attempt to "impose its own censorship upon the motion picture industry."[113] The Klan was the latest addition to a postwar conservative protest movement that, in the words of *Motion Picture Magazine* in 1921, used "cooked up evidence and hysterical screaming" to enforce industry regulation. This writer offered a thinly veiled attack on Klan-like organizations, claiming that these groups demanding censorship appeared "with a bible in one hand and a knife in the other. . . . They meet and whisper." By 1923 *Movie Weekly* acknowledged but also warned of the Klan's potential role within the film industry. "Given the range of power which this organization claims for itself," it wrote, "there is no limitation to be placed upon the influence it might exert as a censorial factor in picturedom."[114] The discussion, spread over a number of issues, illustrated the Klan's involvement within debates over film reform and highlighted the group's tactics in maneuvering itself into a position of political influence. At a formative moment for the industry, under intense pressure from a battery of church, reform, and social groups, the Klan emerged as a further player, attempting to exploit and direct the moves toward industry regulation and, in the process, cementing its own position within American society.

THE INFLUENCE OF THE KLAN ON FILM REFORM

When *Photoplay* described censorship as "the hooded Ku Klux Klan of art" in 1922, it disparagingly presented what it saw as a restrictive, conservative, and somewhat violent act, as a manifestation of Klan ideals and practices.[115] However, the Klan's attitude toward censorship was more complex and was motivated once more by its religious sensibilities. An editorial published in *Searchlight* in February 1922 compared censorship to "witch-burning in old Salem" and argued that "in this free, clean thinking country there is no place for artistic overlords and literary censors." The editorial labeled film censorship, and specifically politically designated censorship, as "dangerous in the extreme" and as a "step in the direction of further curtailments of our liberties." The Klan distanced itself from the "hue and cry for censorship" and spoke out against these restrictions when it trampled on presentations of its own values. For example, *Dawn* referred to the censorship of *The Invisible Empire,* a play positively featuring the Klan, as "this cruel deed," opposing censorship when it perceived it to be Jewish- or Catholic-controlled.[116]

After the protests against *The Pilgrim* and *Bella Donna,* the Klan appeared much more active in supporting industrial regulation. *Dawn* stressed the need for censorship in October 1923 "when certain moving picture theatres, catering to many thousands of men, women and children daily are permitted to exhibit films that strike at the very basis of American right-mindedness, the Protestant church."[117] The Klan still claimed to oppose official censorship – an "idea obnoxious to American principles" – but its leadership also now spoke publicly of the "strict censorship needed to keep the Jew-controlled stage and movies within even gunshot of decency."[118] The Klan positioned itself as a necessary Protestant regulatory force. "If film houses flash before the family degrading, depraving or disgusting moving pictures," *Kourier* warned in 1925, "there is, likewise, no authority to check them." The Klan would often assume this role, with the film press claiming that in certain cities, such as Dallas, censorship activities were by 1924 "largely sponsored" by the Klan.[119]

This shift may highlight, in part, the opportunism of the Klan as it redefined the debates on film reform to promote and justify its own antisemitism. In January 1925, *The American Standard* reported the establishment of the Federal Motion Picture Council of America, under the headline "Patriots Make War on Jew Movies." As a predominantly Protestant group lobbying congress and seeking the federal regulation of film, the council is a testament to the endurance of the Klan's ideals and rhetoric within conservative film discourse. Yet the article also reinterpreted the council's role, infusing the proposals with the more extreme and activist language of the Klan. "The poisonous flood of filthy Jewish suggestion, which has been paralyzing the moral sense of America's children is going to be swept into the ocean," the *American Standard* surmised, along with "the rat-like anti-Christians who are responsible for this condition."[120] The council was fronted by noted Klan sympathizer Canon William Chase, whose justification for film reform, based on fears of Jewish agency and control, was, as Steven Carr has observed, "highly compatible with Klan anti-Semitism."[121] One of the council's first moves was to support a bill proposed in 1926 by Senator William D. Upshaw of Georgia for federal censorship, which the *New York Herald Tribune* described as "a supreme example of extreme bigotry." Upshaw was an "outspoken friend" of the Klan, having written articles for *Searchlight* and, according to Klan officials, worked for the Klan in Congress.[122] In addressing the House of Representatives during hearings on his bill, he complained about film's propensity to encourage "illicit drinking"; he could almost have been reading from the *Fiery Cross* when he stated that "the god-fearing, law-abiding masses of America are getting righteously tired also of the insidious reflections on Christian ministers. . . . For the sake of our children and our country's purity, security, and perpetuity we want it cleaned up."[123] This example is not unusual and shows the Klan's film protests – adapted from existing Protestant groups and circulated through Klan newspapers – now adopted by national reform groups and offered up as official public policy. In this way, it encapsulates the Klan's own movement into the political landscape of America.

As early as 1923 the National Board of Review had recognized the increasing influence of the Klan in film discourse. Turner Jones, the Board's director of public relations, warned that "there is brewing in Texas one of the worst fights that the industry will ever face, and the leaders will be the ministers, backed by the Ku Klux Klan."[124] Jones suggested that, in opposing the industry, the Klan would align itself with established religious figures and regulatory groups. In this, he was proved correct. The *Hawkeye Independent,* which billed itself as "The Klansman's Newspaper" in Des Moines, Iowa, corresponded with the National Committee for Better Films in 1923, asking for literature "that would aid us in intelligently fighting the battle" against "the indecent motion pictures that infest the picture theatres of Iowa."[125] The Klan press offered both praise and criticism of the National Board of Review, but local Klan groups recognized the value of aligning with this estab-lished educative board. When the Women of the Ku Klux Klan wrote to the Board in 1925 asking for information about the pictures that were due to be shown in Elkhart, Indiana, they noted that the Board "gave this information to churches." "We [WKKK] appreciate what your board has meant to the public in general," the letter continued, "and are very eager to co-operate with you in any manner."[126] The Klan would often have no direct contact or affiliation with the groups it was endorsing, but in reporting on their activities in its press, it would appropriate their policies for itself. An example from the pages of the *Fiery Cross* in 1923 shows the paper endorsing the establishment of a women's committee that endeavored to "place wholesome and entertaining films before pub-lic schools, churches, Young Men's Christian Associations, community centers etc." The committee explained that by showing religious and geographical pictures, children "will grow up predisposed against the low-brow, moron type of film."[127]

The Klan launched its own protests against film, aligned itself with established campaigns, and also supported and bolstered those figures that it deemed sympathetic to the Klan cause. Most notably, the Klan endorsed Will Hays, a Protestant Republican from the Klan heartland of Indiana, as president of the Motion Picture Producers and Distributors of America (MPPDA) in 1922. The author and journalist Edward G. Lowry described Hays in language that was reminiscent of the Klan: "the one hundred percent American we have all heard so much talk about," someone who is "the most characteristic native product" and a "national institution."[128] The Klan itself predicted that Hays would "clean house in the movies, if an awakened, intelligent public opinion gets behind him and stays behind him."[129]

As the Klan spoke out against Paramount's films in July 1924, Hays offered his own critique of the studio's salacious titles and ordered sixteen of the forty titles changed. Hays would appear to endorse the Klan message: he was particularly critical of *Manhandled,* a film that the Klan had also singled out. However, the Klan's criticisms of the industry would intensify after the appointment of Hays in 1922. As early as April 1923 an editorial in the *Fiery Cross* declared that "the greatest service that Will Hays could do to mankind" would be to resign and "declare to the world his impotency and his utter inability to cope with such a powerful and damnable situation."[130] By February 1925, the Klan was publishing statements from the Federal Motion Picture Council which argued that the "coming of Will Hays to the films had resulted in no improvement" in the quality of pictures. The *American Standard* now dismissed Hays's appointment as "merely another Jewish smoke-screen," complaining that he "was bought by the Jews." Indeed, the Klan characterized Hays as part of the Jewish film industry, making reference to "Will Hays' Jewish group of movie magnates." In now presenting Hays not as a manipulated gentile but rather as a corrupt controlling force, the Klan suggested that "Mr. Hays is a figurehead" for the Jewish trust and argued that Jews "operate through Mr. Hays."[131]

The Klan's antagonistic attitude toward Hays highlights the challenges that he faced in negotiating with disparate religious groups. William Romanowski has recently argued that the Protestant churches and women's organizations represented "Hays's natural constituencies," providing him with both a moral compass and a massive communication network.[132] One of Hays's first moves with the MPPDA was to establish the Committee on Public Relations, which sought to offer a "channel of communication between the public and industry," relaying comments, criticisms, and suggestions to the industry. The Committee claimed to represent seventy-eight members from sixty-two national organizations, as Hays sought to appease, negotiate, and provide an outlet for the concerns of religious, educational, labor, and fraternal groups.[133] Amongst the organizations well represented was the American Legion, which had two members on the executive committee. As a patriotic veterans group, the Hollywood post of the American Legion had organized and led opposition to imported German films in 1921. This included a large-scale protest parade and rioting – or at least some egg throwing – in front of Miller's Theatre in Los Angeles where *The Cabinet of Dr. Caligari* was scheduled to appear.[134] The post would also seek to suppress Erich von Stroheim's *Foolish Wives,* which it claimed (incorrectly) was being made by a German director with German money "as German propaganda." In addition, the Legion, along with other veterans groups, forced the cancellation of screenings of *The Fifth Year* in early 1924, claiming that the film's purpose was to "disseminate Soviet propaganda."[135]

Writing that year, Earle Mayer, the head of the American Legion Film Service, explained that the Legion had been running a campaign over the preceding two years "for cleaner and more truly American films." He criticized producers for making pictures that would appeal to the "'thirteen year old' intelligence of the average motion picture audience" and spoke disparagingly of the continued presence on film of "flappers, custard pies and triangles."[136] While expressing these broader concerns, also articulated by the Klan, the Legion responded to the more specific representation of its values and image on-screen. Later in the year, it wrote to Hays urging "drastic measures" to "stamp out a practice which brings nothing but ridicule to the different branches of the United States Service by indiscriminate use of the United States Service Uniform." Just as the Klan had protested against the depiction of Protestant ministers, now the Legion claimed that whenever a director wishes to make a scene "look tough, obscene and rough" or to show men under the influence of liquor, "all that needs to be done is to place a few hard boiled extras in the uniform" of the armed services. The complaint was motivated by the Pathe film *Dynamite Smith* (1924); Hays responded to the Legion by promising to get in touch at once with the distributor, to look more closely at the picture, and to see "what can be done about eliminations." The correspondence reveals Hays's role in liaising between these influential American groups and the industry. He had worked hard to foster a spirit of collaboration and to ensure that the complaints came first to him. Shortly after his appointment, he wrote to the leader of the Legion praising a recent article, "The Movies Discover America," published in the *American Legion Weekly*. Hays endorsed this "constructive effort, which typifies in my mind the spirit of your organization," and corresponded regularly with Legion representatives, even advising on production and distribution queries.[137]

Yet the Klan remained largely outside this system, not directly represented on the Committee on Public Relations, in contrast to religious organizations such as the National Catholic Welfare Council. Frank Walsh has argued that Protestant ministers actually constituted the core of Hays's opposition in the 1920s, as Hays embraced and incorporated other religious and civic groups and recognized Catholic groups amongst his most dependable allies.[138] By aligning his reforms with these Klan opponents, Hays began to isolate himself from the Protestant church and the work of the Klan; at least, the Protestant position within these debates became less dominant, culminating, as we will see, with the emergence of the Catholic Legion of Decency. For the Klan, of course, it was also productive to criticize Hays. The Klan justified its own necessary role within society by presenting the industry as a corrupt Jewish institution, with Hays now positioned as part of this larger Jewish conspiracy.

While much of the Klan's engagement with film focused on issues of representation and the external regulation of film, it also immersed itself in debates over film exhibition and, more specifically, the closure of movie theaters on Sunday. The Klan's criticisms of movie theaters had followed a well-worn path, noting the cinema's perceived effects on social behavior, as a space for young men and women to interact. *Imperial Night-Hawk* reported children stealing money in order to visit their local cinema, while the Corsicana Klan in Texas wrote to each local theater in

April 1922 explaining that "through personal investigation and observation we are aware of considerable improper conduct in some of the theatres." Exhibitors were encouraged to display this letter in their foyer.[139]

The morals of children were corrupted not only by the images on-
screen but also by the very process of visiting the cinema. Again this
problem was credited more broadly to the "commercialized motion picture industry," which *Imperial Night-Hawk* labeled as "a promoter of
crime, a wrecker of religion and a destroyer of civilization."[140] The Klan
would now look to adapt and use this campaign to promote its own
agenda. In Indiana, Klan historian Kathleen Blee has noted the Klan's
efforts to "make a public issue" of dance halls and other "vile places of
amusement." She cites the example of the Hammond Klan, which announced that it would monitor all picture shows and other places of
amusement, after receiving complaints about "impassioned 'love grips'
in the 'cheaper movie houses' of the town." Again, Blee suggests that the
Klan's objections to the cinema were fueled by the group's antisemitism
as the Klan highlighted the perceived financial benefits for Jewish proprietors in fostering these promiscuous spaces.[141] When the *American
Standard* complained in 1925 that "the 15,000 motion picture theatres in
the United States are nearly all owned by Jews and Roman Catholics,"
it emphasized the moral influence that these exhibitors exercised over
society and suggested that many were formerly gamblers, pawnbrokers,
peddlers, or "keepers of unsavory resorts." The exhibitors were defined
racially, having the same "instincts and characteristics" as the "morally
lawless" Jews deemed responsible for the bootlegging trade.[142]

The Klan's attitude toward the film theater as a social space was
perhaps most clearly articulated by the Reverend Oscar Haywood. In
his capacity as the treasurer of the Klan film company Cavalier Motion
Pictures, Haywood clarified in 1923 that he did not urge Klansmen to
stay away from the motion picture houses, nor did he wish to criticize
any local theater manager. Instead, his criticism was with "the motion
pictures as an industry, which he said was 90% owned by Jews."[143] Haywood's comments served to justify the Klan's own use of film, showing
the Klan's objection to cinema on an institutional level. Even when the
Klan targeted individual picture houses, its objections were motivated
by those running the site. It complained in one town that it couldn't

deliver a lecture because "it is impossible to rent a hall on account of the influence of the Jews," while the official monthly bulletin of the Klan in Mississippi complained strongly against the "indecent movement and nudity" presented by an "un-Christian Jew manager."[144] These complaints went further in Tulsa in 1923, when the local Klan was held responsible for whipping a Jewish projectionist. James Hirsch noted that the mayor, James Walton, imposed martial law, but within a year he was impeached and removed from office in "a move orchestrated by the Klan."[145]

The Klan criticized film exhibition in religious terms ("un-Christian manager"), but its broader criticisms of modernity connected to related anxieties around race and national identity. When discussing the effects of urban modernity in 1925, *Kourier* noted that "the site of the first public library in America is now a theatre; the laboratory of S. F. B. Morse, is an Italian movie [theater]. Both sites are in Boston." *Kourier* chose an example within Boston, a cosmopolitan city with a large Catholic population, and singled out the scientific laboratory of telegraphy pioneer Samuel Morse, a Calvinist noted for his staunchly nativist, anti-Catholic views. The cinema building thus appeared as a foreign import (in this case Italian) undermining the traditional, Protestant educational "culture" of the country.[146] For the Klan, the cinema now served to represent both the foreign control of media and the related destabilizing effects of urban modernity. Steven Ross has presented silent film as an assimilationist tool, breaking down language barriers with "a dozen different nationalities being represented in the audience."[147] For the Klan, the cinema created what Ben Singer refers to as "cultural discontinuity," by moving women and children into a threatening interethnic public space, a melting pot of races, nationalities, and religions, controlled by "foreign," "Un-American" influences.[148] As we will see, when the Klan bought and ran its own theaters during the 1920s, they were, in contrast, often positively promoted as "100% American."

The Klan's anxieties around on-screen images, moviegoing, foreign ownership, and the cinema's collective effects on American youth found a perfect outlet in the long-running campaign against the Sunday opening of movie theaters.[149] Bishop Alma White, a staunch Klan supporter, discussed this issue in her 1925 book *The Ku Klux Klan in*

Prophecy, complaining that "in many states the Jews are running the theatres and the motion picture shows on Sunday, thus undermining Christianity by luring the multitudes away from the Protestant churches into these vile places of amusement."[150] The Klan considered the cinema to be in competition with the Protestant church, and its public stance on the issue reinvigorated calls for closing theaters on Sundays. This campaign, led by Protestant ministerial groups such as the Lord's Day Alliance, challenged the perceived Jewish interests that were either ignoring or attempting to overturn existing laws regarding Sunday exhibition. By early 1919, ministers were virulently confronting bills proposed by exhibitors that would allow Sunday exhibition in areas within such states as New York, Pennsylvania, Ohio, Indiana and Missouri. In February 1921, the leading Protestant magazine *Christian Century* outlined what it saw as the root of the problem. "As is well known, the moving picture film corporations are largely in the hands of wealthy Jews in New York," it stated. "They have long since forsaken the prophets for profits." While producers and exhibitors – for example, the Philadelphia Theatrical League – argued that it was the "duty" of the state to allow recreation during these "depressive times" and that films could complement the work of the pulpit by providing moral education, a largely Protestant opposition argued against what they saw as a further commercialization of the sabbath, a lust for profits that threatened the moral and religious fiber of the nation.[151]

For the Klan, the campaign provided an opportunity for its leadership to muscle onto the national stage and to spread its influence in sympathetic local communities. When the Nathan Hale chapter of the Klan in Kokomo, Indiana, passed resolutions calling on the city council to close local theaters on Sundays, it explained in a letter to the mayor that "as an organization that believes in the tenets of the Christian religion," it wanted this ordinance passed immediately. In this way the Klan presented itself as a legitimate religious group, as seen in the *Kokomo Daily Dispatch*'s headline ("Klansmen vote to aid churches in movie fight") and in the group's work alongside the Kokomo Ministerial Association. The prominent evangelist Bob Jones gave a sermon at the local Klavern in which he discussed the Sunday closure of movie theaters and received "rousing applause."[152] These local demands appeared soon afterward in 1924 in a bill proposed to the Indiana General Assembly by the recently elected state senator Earl W. Payne. Payne had the backing of the Klan, and in particular that of Roscoe Carpenter, instigator of various Klan film initiatives, and D. C. Stephenson, the former Grand Dragon of Indiana. The pair was tasked with generating support for Payne's bill, particularly from Protestant preachers and church groups.[153]

The Klan was also involved in various initiatives to restrict Sunday openings in neighboring Ohio. Both *Moving Picture World* and *Variety* reported the Klan's boycott of the Lyceum Theatre in Canton after it was taken over by Sam Bernstein, a Jewish entrepreneur from New York City. According to *Variety,* the theater's attendance had slumped "since the sheet wearers said thumbs down on Bernstein." Klan pressure forced Bernstein to close his theater on Sundays, and members of the Klan reportedly attempted to buy it from him.[154] The Klan also cooperated with prominent figures from the church to enforce the closure of theaters on Sundays in nearby Youngstown. In this instance, it publicly supported Charles Scheible's campaign for mayor in 1923 on the condition that he would enforce the blue laws in the area. When Scheible subsequently failed to fulfill this promise, Colonel E. A. Watkins, the head of the local Klan, called together local ministers and threatened a recall. Under pressure, the mayor partially enforced the blue laws at the start of 1924, restricting vaudeville shows and certain businesses, but still allowed movie theaters to operate after 1 PM on Sundays. *Moving Picture World* spoke of a "Ku Klux Klan political victory" and presented Scheible as a Klan puppet, but this did not stop ministers pushing for complete Sunday closure. One minister, quoted in *Kourier,* remarked that Scheible "is a creation of that organization [the Klan] and I cannot see why they should not be called to use their influence in bringing about a better law enforcement in the city."[155] While the response testifies to the Klan's significant political influence within much of the Midwest, not all officials were so responsive to the Klan's demands. When the Klan served notice on the mayor and chief of police in Buffalo, accusing them of violating the blue laws, the mayor staunchly refused to meet the demands of the Klansmen, dismissing them as "damn fools looking for notoriety."[156]

FROM THE SIDELINE: CRUMBLING INFLUENCE IN THE 1930S

The widespread growth of the Klan's media empire from 1923, which included a series of local and nationally syndicated newspapers, film companies, printing presses, and radio stations, coincided with the Klan's most active and volatile engagement with the mainstream popular media. This is no coincidence. The Klan's consolidated media outlets enabled local and national groups to promote and define themselves to existing and potential members. One of the ways they achieved this was by targeting the most modern, expansive, and influential axis in media: film. Its motives here were predominantly twofold. First, in film the Klan recognized and manufactured the dangers of modernity, from the representation of sex and the desecration of Protestant values on-screen to the social excesses of Hollywood and the impact of moviegoing on American youth. The Klan followed existing reform groups here, but appeared most influenced by the writings of Henry Ford in attributing these failings to the Jewish and Catholic influences that it determined were dominating the movie business. The issue was one of media control, one that became all the more important to the Klan as its own media interests grew. Second, the Klan was, to a great extent, opportunistic, leeching on respected Protestant "Americanism" campaigns and reworking them as a means to position itself as a legitimate moral authority within American society. This postwar period represented the apex for the modern Klan, a moment of unparalleled growth, but it was also a decisive, formative moment for a burgeoning film industry under intense pressure from conservative reformers. In a postwar moment – specifically between the Red Scare of 1919 and the introduction of the Johnson-Reed Immigration Act of 1924 – when the makeup of American social, cultural, and political life was as fiercely contested as at any other point in its history, the Klan's criticism of the film industry served to successfully justify and enforce its conservative agenda.

For all their avowed ideological differences, Protestant, Catholic, and Jewish criticisms of film were often remarkably similar during this period, both in language and intent. As Alexander McGregor has recently illustrated, the American Catholic Church campaigned strongly against both film content and Hollywood, "a sleazy fiefdom controlled, as far as the American Catholic Church was concerned, by immigrant Jews."[157] For its part, the Jewish press outlined the need to fight Catholic control of the industry, which it argued was responsible for the "insidious lowering of moral and religious standards in this country."[158] The Jewish press was also notably critical of religious representation, as when it widely condemned Cecil B. DeMille's *King of Kings* for reviving anti-Jewish prejudice in 1927. In criticizing DeMille, who the Jewish press reported was, despite his denials, born to a Jewish mother, Rabbi Newman in *The Scribe* inadvertently aligned DeMille's repressed Jewishness to a lust for profits, writing that DeMille's motives "appear to be blatantly commercial." Newman positioned the Jews as a victimized minority, unable to counter this media representation. He claimed that a proposal to produce a picture exposing the "excesses" to which the Klan has gone "in persecuting Jews, Catholics and Negroes" had been rejected: film writers would be more likely to "bring in a stick of dynamite to our studios" than "a scenario exposing the Ku Klux Klan," but an on-screen attack on the Jews, he lamented, was entirely different.[159] The battle over religious representation and, more broadly, film reform was contested from all sides. These moral, social, and religious groups, often using similar language and shared motives, were all jockeying for position in an attempt to present themselves as the arbiters of American popular culture.

By 1934, when reformers campaigned strongly against "objectionable motion pictures," it was not the Klan but its Catholic rivals that directed and dictated these reforms, establishing the Catholic Legion of Decency as a crucial arbiter of morality. Established with $35,000 from the American Catholic Church, the Legion of Decency sought not only to arbitrate media images and film morality, but also, in a notable parallel with the Klan, to define and unite American Catholic citizens through this campaign. The Legion of Decency even initiated a pledge, in which church members – an estimated seven to nine million by 1934 – vowed to "condemn those salacious motion pictures" which serve as a "grave menace to youth, to home life, to country and religion." Those taking the pledge vowed to "remain away" from theaters that "offend decency and Christian morality" and, in an effort to use the campaign to grow its membership, promised to "secure as many members as possible" for the Legion.[160] By the early 1930s, Catholic groups had clearly usurped the Klan by working with church and educational authorities in leading the church boycott of so-called "indecent films." We can understand this shift in various ways. On the one hand, the rise of Catholic pressure groups has been linked to shifts in state policy during the Depression, as the government attempted to integrate predominantly urban-based Catholic groups within society as a way of staving off perceived unrest amongst working-class ethnic groups.[161] On the other, divisions amongst Protestant reform groups made the more centralized Catholic Legion of Decency the most viable partner for effecting change in the film industry and, in its emphasis on monitoring film production rather than dismantling the profitable studio system, the one most appealing to Hays. With the Klan a fading force, its earlier efforts in reforming this moral vacuum were now superseded by those of Catholic reformers.[162]

While Catholic reformers' policy preferences and the antisemitic terminology used to articulate them were barely distinguishable from earlier Klan campaigns, the Klan was still quick to criticize them.[163] The Klan's criticisms of policies that it had earlier supported may suggest an ideological shift, but its motivation for these protests remained unchanged. It still sought to use its criticisms of film reform to promote and define itself as a Protestant group, to strike at its religious adversaries, and to draw attention to an apparent "foreign" threat within American social and political life. As late as 1940, the *Fiery Cross,* the recently reestablished Klan newspaper, presented the Legion of Decency as part of a larger Catholic conspiracy, claiming that "the Catholic church has set up a dictator of the motion picture industry in the person of Joseph I. Breen, who travels to Rome every year to receive orders straight from the Pope." The article, written by a California Klansman, still focused on the representation of religious figures on-screen, but with responsibility for this now placed on Breen, as censor and moral arbiter, rather than exclusively on producers and financiers.[164] Clearly much of the Klan's frustration here stemmed from its extraneous position, and, more broadly, that of Protestant groups: the article complained that Protestant church groups have only ever been invited to contribute from the "sideline."

These anxieties are similarly articulated in Klan protests against the Legion of Decency. Gregory Black suggests that the Legion campaign was destroyed in Jacksonville, Florida, because Klansmen presented these reforms as a "papal plot to take over the movies." One Klansman "foamed at the mouth" as he spoke at length about the pope hatching a new plot to take over the world. Frank Walsh told of two ministers who ripped up sermons supportive of the Legion after a Klan colleague "denounced the campaign as a Popish propaganda plot."[165] The Klan attacked these regulatory policies because they were presented as Catholic initiatives, again presenting film reform as a religious issue. However, these were local incidents, with the Klan no longer able to influence or impact national policy.

The Klan's decline was also evident in its own press. *Kourier,* a monthly newspaper that represented the surviving facet of this once thriving media empire, became ever more extreme in its views and increasingly regurgitated material from the group's heyday. When condemning the "Jew controlled moving picture industry" in 1933, it again referred back to the familiar examples of *The Pilgrim* and *Bella Donna.* "One Jewish actor based a whole show on [the] ridicule of the Protestant ministry," it complained. "Millions of people saw this supposedly 'comic' picture."[166] The fact that these same films were repeatedly referenced suggests that the Klan was no longer looking to influence film representation or policy directly, but instead was using these examples to attack its Jewish and Catholic opponents.

The Klan's presence in Hollywood also testifies to its increasingly marginalized social position and to the challenges it faced as its media influence crumbled. One incident worth noting here involved the openly gay former movie star William Haines. In June 1936, more than a hundred men and women attacked Haines as he was driving in the Manhattan Beach area with his "companion" Jimmy Shields. The *Modesto Bee* reported Haines's comments on the attack: "'Some wild untrue rumor must have stirred them up,' said Haines at his antique and interior decorating shop. 'It was a lynch mob, all right. It might have been some sort of klan or secret organization.'"[167] The attack was subsequently credited to the White Legion, which promised to "clean up this town." The White Legion was closely linked to the Klan in California and directly affiliated and headed by Klan members in Alabama.[168] The White Legion was just one of a number of conservative and terrorist groups emerging throughout America in the mid-1930s, often as products of the Depres-

sion, opposing the state management of political and social life and react-
ing against New Deal liberalism. These groups were now predominantly
anticommunist, and the Klan often struggled to differentiate itself from
their violent actions. Only a few weeks earlier, Charles Poole, a Catholic
man falsely accused of beating his wife, had been brutally murdered by
a mob in Michigan, a crime that resulted in the conviction for murder of
eleven members of a local group, the Black Legion. A subsequent grand
jury investigation of these events, which Warner Bros. would later depict
in *Black Legion,* drew damning comparisons between the Legion and the
Klan. Judge Hartrick, reporting his findings, described the Black Legion
as a "Black Klan," while the State Police Captain in Detroit termed the
Black Legion "the strong arm agency for the Ku Klux Klan."[169]

While the Klan had previously sought to entangle itself with other
fraternal, patriotic, and religious organizations, it now sought to dis-
credit the parallels, both on film and in public discourse, between itself
and the murderous Black Legion group. One of the Klan's main objections, noted in its legal action against Warner Bros., concerned a specific
line in *Black Legion* in which a character asked, "Are we in for yet another
reign of terror from the Ku Klux Klan?"[170] It is perhaps ironic that given
the Klan's own historical tendency to feed off other groups it should be
so eager to extricate itself from the Black Legion. There are, of course,
financial motivations for this. Its legal action against Warners, as a patent
infringement case, ultimately centered on the Klan image and the unso-
licited exploitation of its enormously lucrative costume, which had been
introduced to the public and commercialized through film. In its legal
moves to reclaim its regalia and to disrobe the Black Legion, the Klan
followed a familiar defensive rhetoric. In literature and indeed its own
films, it regularly depicted its avowed enemies dressing up in the Klan
costume to commit their heinous crimes, highlighting a widespread misuse of the Klan costume.

Despite its dwindling influence, it is notable that the Klan still
looked to film when presenting itself on the public stage, promoting
itself not simply through film but through its criticisms of film.[171] The
Black Legion case now offered the possibility of a large financial boost,
of free publicity and of legitimacy through the court's response, but the
Klan appeared to use the case fundamentally to defend and renegotiate

its reputation. The Black Legion also involved itself in these debates, albeit less publicly, writing to Warners through its attorney, Bernard Cruse. After complaining that the film was "far lacking in portraying the Black Legion as it really is," Cruse suggested a meeting with Warners to discuss another picture that "would bring the largest box office receipts ever known and portray the Black Legion as it really is."[172] The Black Legion, like the Klan, was seeking to control its own representation, to gain an improbable foothold within the media.

For the Klan, the control of the media became integral to its expansion into mainstream America. In its criticisms of the "Jewish" film industry, the Klan recognized film as a "school" for American youth and as a tool through which it could create and define citizens. Yet, given its well-publicized criticisms of the American film industry, the Klan would increasingly look beyond the established industrial parameters to achieve this. In short, if the Klan couldn't infiltrate or control the "Jewish" industry, it would have to produce its own films, and if it couldn't control what exhibitors screened, it would have to find its own theatrical spaces.

THREE

Klan Cinema

THE KLAN AS PRODUCER AND EXHIBITOR

AS PART OF ITS PULITZER PRIZE–WINNING EXPOSÉ OF THE Klan in September 1921, the *New York World* ran a story headlined, "Klux Closes Deal for $400,000 Film to Advertise Klan," detailing plans for an "elaborate and costly" propaganda film. Taking its title from a pamphlet by Imperial Wizard William Simmons, *Yesterday, Today and Forever* was to be produced by Clifford Slater Wheeler, an army veteran, a Kleagle in New York, and now the self-appointed president of Wheeler Productions, Inc. According to Wheeler, "The idea of the moving picture scheme met with the approval of [Imperial Kleagle Edward] Clarke and Imperial Wizard Simmons." Clarke had discussed plans for the project as early as March 1921 with a King Kleagle in New Jersey, Arthur Donald Bate. At a moment when Clarke was mobilizing the Klan and encouraging Kleagles to use existing films such as *The Face at Your Window* for recruitment, he was also, the reports claimed, working with Wheeler on a piece of "up-to-date Ku Klux advertising." Less than a year after joining and effectively relaunching the Klan, Clarke was already looking to branch out into film production.[1]

The nature of the Klan's involvement within the picture industry was, however, still to be determined. While reports claimed that the Klan was "going into picture production on a large scale," Simmons argued, in a rhetoric reused throughout the decade, that the films would not serve directly as Klan propaganda but would rather address "patriotic subjects." Wheeler explained that he had found a wealthy backer and proposed producing pictures that show the value of "one flag, one language, one country, one allegiance – in other words, Americanism." The first of these films would focus on "the beauty of old-fashioned home life." What Wheeler was proposing, at least in public, was the kind of patriotic fare sponsored by the government's Americanism Committee and by independent producers like the American Legion Film Service. Wheeler welcomed Klan involvement, but he imagined this as an endorsement along with other "patriotic and religious organizations," similar to the model adopted with *The Face at Your Window*. However, the Klan was also now looking to invest funds in "clean, desirable entertainment." This was, as always with Clarke, commercially motivated, as he sought direct income from the sale and exhibition of film while also imagining more indirect economic benefits in using the films as part of Klan recruitment. Film could serve here as a further means of promoting Klan values, of recruiting and molding Klan citizens and legitimizing the Klan's position within national debates on Americanism and immigration.[2]

These initial plans for a Klan film enterprise were soon undermined by a succession of personal scandals, which went some way to discrediting those involved and also foreshadowed many of the Klan's film experiences over the next decade. A week before the *New York World* announced plans for *Yesterday, Today and Forever*, it published a damning report claiming that Edward Clarke and fellow Kleagle Elizabeth Tyler had been arrested in 1919, reportedly drunk and half-naked after a police raid on a house of ill repute. Their reputations were irreparably damaged, and their position within a group that portrayed itself as a defender of domestic values and supporter of Prohibition was inevitably called into question. Amongst those who called for Clarke's immediate dismissal were Arthur Bate and Lloyd P. Hooper who, according to the *New York World*, had originally received the contract from Clarke for the film. Hooper went to Atlanta in December 1921 and spoke out strongly against both Clarke and the Klan, an action that resulted in him being fired from the group.[3] Clifford Wheeler had also left his position as the "King Kleagle of the realm of Connecticut" shortly before the *World* story was published. His departure was the result of a mix-up at the local post office, in which his mail was misplaced in a neighboring box.[4] The *New Haven Register* wrote of the "unfortunate publicity, in the eyes of [the] organization." It noted that Simmons himself had ordered the removal of Wheeler, explaining that "once the identity of a King Kleagle becomes known he must be shifted to other territory." Wheeler eventually moved to Hollywood, where he changed his name to Alexis Thurn-Taxis and produced a number of films, but not, it would appear, *Yesterday, Today and Forever.*[5]

Despite the apparent failure of this initial foray into film production, Klan leaders and local Klansmen would increasingly look to film as the group's membership and profile grew after the *New York World* exposé. In the month of the exposé, the Marlowe Hippodrome in Illinois had exploited the topical curiosity engineered by the revelations, exhibiting *The White Riders* and Ku Klux Klan Pictures, which offered to show "the latest of the mysterious actions of this mysterious organization."[6] This interest in the "mysterious actions" of the Klan prompted Bernard Mc-Comb, an operator for the Liberty Theatre in Oklahoma City, to spend three months filming the Oklahoma Klan No. 1 at the start of 1922. In publicizing the completed film, *The Mysterious Eyes of the Ku Klux Klan*, newspapers highlighted the dangers involved in securing the pictures. One night in February – "the night was chill and a hazy pall spread over the moon" – McComb was picked up by a car from Broadway Circle and, the papers claimed, taken blindfolded to a "lonely spot in the woods." Once the bandages were removed he saw, in his own words, "what appeared to be fully a thousand sheeted Klansmen" on a vast expanse of prairie. "At a signal, the white, human cloud started towards a ravine," he explained, the "spooks" formed a circle and the "weird rites of the original initiation began." While McComb was allowed to film the initiation ceremony, he was warned against showing the pictures publicly until he had received "permission from the proper sources." The process for this was a typically elaborate and dramatic affair, which involved taking the film to "a certain theater at midnight" where a group of white robed figures watched the picture before giving it official approval.[7] Regardless of the questionable veracity of this account, the filming reports served to emphasize the excitement, authenticity, and contemporary significance of the film, by connecting on-screen and off-screen Klan activities. While *The Mysterious Eyes of the Ku Klux Klan* was not presented as a Klan production, it sought and, for the most part, gained Klan approval,

3.1. Presenting the Klan in Fort Wayne. *News-Sentinel,* 25 October 1922, 17.

whether through the national Klan press or, more notably, the local responses of Klansmen who attended screenings in full regalia as the film
traveled across the country.[8]

The participation of local Klansmen was a notable feature of the film
in Klan strongholds like Indiana, where the film played extensively in
the second half of 1922. Local newspaper advertisements for a screening

at the Lyric Theatre in Fort Wayne (fig. 3.1) showed crowds gathering around a hooded Klansman outside the theater and noted the "hundreds turned away."[9] A month later, when it played at another Lyric, this time a hundred miles away in Connersville, the image was reused. The local paper again noted the "record-breaking crowds," while also reporting on the film's current screening in neighboring Richmond and its recent week-long run in Indianapolis, where it played to "capacity business." The Rialto Theatre in Indianapolis was said to resemble a "Klan Klavern," with the majority of the audience, it was speculated, comprising the city's estimated 30,000 Klan members.[10] At a moment when Klansmen were publicly flocking to screenings of *Birth,* the response of local Klan groups to *The Mysterious Eyes of the Ku Klux Klan* shows a wider infiltration of public theatrical venues by the modern Klan. This movement into local theaters would continue over the next few years, as venues became contested sites, often either associated with, or directly controlled, by Klan interests.

The Mysterious Eyes of the Ku Klux Klan sought, through its publicity, to both reach out to and define local audiences. For example, advertisements stated that *The Mysterious Eyes of the Ku Klux Klan* was a picture that "every man, woman and child should see," positioning the film and, by extension, the Klan itself as a moral force for educating not only menfolk but also America's women and youth.[11] Promotional descriptions of the film both exploited and responded to the *New York World* exposé, addressing a subject that "has been read about in every newspaper" but now offering to show "the real inside dope." It also now sought to reach beyond the standard Klan audience, to provide outsiders with a chance to see "who they are, what they are, what they do and how they do it."[12] Allied to these claims of "truth" was an emphasis on mystery and spectacle, inherent in a title that also suggested glimpsing behind the costume ("eyes") to reveal the individual within the collective group.

The film offered to unveil the modern Klan but, crucially, on the Klan's terms. This is clearly articulated in widely adopted advertisements:

> The Inner Workings of the Klan.
> The Genuine Initiation Ceremonies.
> The True Belief of the Klan.
> The Uprising of the Klansman [*sic*] in Oklahoma when they marched through the streets of Tulsa and Oklahoma City.[13]

The language used here – "true," "genuine," "inner workings" – positioned the film as a document of modern Klan activities. The advertisements provided a historical specificity, noting particular events and locations, and in this example referencing the march "through the streets of Tulsa." This most likely refers to a parade on the evening of 1 April 1922, which began with an airplane unveiling a "fiery cross" of lights underneath.[14] On that April evening in Tulsa, an estimated 2,000 Klansmen, three to a row, marched out of Convention Hall in full regalia and preceded behind fully covered mounted horsemen and, in a more modern twist, a Ford truck carrying an eight-foot cross. Some carried bright red flames, which added a "picturesqueness to the marchers as the rays shone on their snow white robes," while, at one point, the marchers disappeared into colored clouds created by smoke machines that were more commonly used in the theater. The *Tribune* suggested that Oklahoma had likely never seen "a march so spectacular," noting the absolute "awe" that gripped the crowd as the "long white line swept through the city."[15] The crowd, which reportedly included Imperial Wizard Simmons, outnumbered the participants, with the sidewalks said to be overflowing and all available vantage points taken.

While this crowd, along with the parading Klansmen, provided a potential audience for the film within the state, it also attests to a popular fascination in what was, in effect, a Klan performance. In its use of costume, mounted horsemen, the fiery cross, and particularly the parade "sweeping" through the main street, the performance owed a considerable debt to *Birth*. Yet this was not a theatrical event or reenactment detached from contemporary politics, but a significant part of the town's continuing and dramatic racial breakdown. The "uprising" of the Klan and the symbolic reclamation of the streets, as witnessed at the conclusion of *Birth*, assumed particular significance in Tulsa, an area beset with race riots the previous year. Greenwood, in North Tulsa, which was recognized as one of the most successful and affluent black communities in America, had been besieged on 1 June 1921 with looting, machine gun fire, and even, it was claimed, airplane attacks from the town's white residents. Greenwood was desecrated – even its two African American theaters were destroyed by fire (fig. 3.2) – and over the next year, the Klan would emerge and prosper in this environment. Film was part of this

3.2. Williams Dreamland Theatre on Greenwood in the aftermath of the Tulsa race riots, June 1921. *Image courtesy of the Tulsa Historical Society and Museum.*

story. *Birth* played for five days to open the season at Convention Hall only a few weeks after the Klan was relaunched in town. Indeed, there were public parades at screenings of *Birth,* as when a hundred hooded Klansmen marched through the theater in nearby Drumright in February 1922. Finally, at this moment of Klan growth, McComb's film played across the state.[16]

James S. Hirsch cited an initiation ceremony in July 1922 in which more than a thousand Klansmen were inducted; he claimed that, within a year, the state had an estimated 150,000 members, with three of the county's five members of the Oklahoma House of Representatives said to be Klansmen.[17] The parades and their repeated appearances on film helped to relive this moment for local audiences and also, given the resonating tensions behind the riots, encouraged viewers to connect the Klan's ceremonial work on-screen with racially motivated violence, which was now very rarely presented in film. It is not only the social context in Tulsa that encourages such extratextual readings. For example, the most enduring and renowned on-screen Klan appearance in *The Birth of a Nation* concludes with the clearance of African Americans from a town, similar to the process now reported but not shown in Tulsa. The on-screen appearance of the modern Klan parading in Tulsa thus invites audiences to relate the recent "reclamation" of Tulsa and the horrific violence behind it to the modern Klan.

Within a week of the Tulsa parade, the local Broadway Theatre was advertising *The Ku Klux Klan featuring the Tulsa Parade* as a coming attraction. At the same moment, the Tulsa Anti-Klan No. 4 "Knights of the Visible Empire," which offered "Just plain unmasked Americanism," was advertising its own meeting in the District Court Room.[18] The film was embedded within these debates. Some exhibitors urged viewers to come along "whether for or against" the Klan, attempting to present the film as part of the debate rather than as the useful Klan tool that it had become.[19] The film was evidently connecting to local, contemporary politics, which was engineered in part through the film's publicity. In one syndicated campaign, small advertisements appeared throughout local newspapers shortly before the film's arrival. In stating, "Look out for The Mysterious Eyes of the Ku Klux Klan," the advertisement offered no indication that this was referring to a film – no venue, time, or additional details were given – serving again to blur the boundaries between screen appearance and real-life activities.[20]

Exhibitors sought to connect the film to local Klan activities; indeed, screenings in Oklahoma sometimes referred to the film as "The Mysterious Eyes of the Ku Klux Klan of Oklahoma." As the film traveled across state borders – also playing in, amongst other places, Arizona, Illinois, California, and Texas – it manufactured and exploited fresh local connections. The film, or at least a version of it, incorporated footage from Texas, where it played extensively in 1922.[21] After appearing for two nights at the Majestic Theatre in Wichita in May, *The Mysterious Eyes of the Ku Klux Klan* played over the summer in Bonham, Houston, and Port Arthur, where it was advertised again as "the most talked about picture ever made."[22] When it played in San Antonio in October, posters adopted a picture of a hooded Klansman on a horse and again highlighted the revelatory function of the film: "Their secrets exposed, initiation and inside workings of the Klan."[23] The film utilized the familiar Klan iconography by which the national group was identified (offering, for example, the chance to see "Klansmen in full regalia"), but it was also adapted for local audiences, appearing in various forms and under different titles.[24] When the film was shown in Lincoln, Nebraska, years later in 1925, it now appeared as *The White Rider,* and while it was still advertised as the "original and only genuine Klan moving picture ever produced," the poster now added that the film featured "an exterior view of the Lincoln Klavern," as the exhibitors sought to emphasize additional local sequences.[25]

The film sought to connect directly with local audiences in its promotion, through the involvement of Klansmen at the site of exhibition and through the inclusion of local sequences or references within the film. While this harks back to the earliest traditions of local filmmaking – filming the audience – the film's fractured history was also, to an extent, a result of state censorship. For example, the Ohio Board of Censorship rejected the film in December 1922 "on account of [it] being harmful" and classed the film as "propaganda." When the board passed a barely recognizable version of the film two months later, it had been completely reconstructed and cut from three reels to two.[26] In Kansas, where *The Birth of a Nation* was still banned, the film was rejected entirely, a decision that was upheld in May 1922. A member of the appeal board, E. L. Miller, explained the reasoning. "We could see nothing objectionable in the film," he stated, "nor could we find any reasons why it should be run. The name is sensational. It would undoubtedly induce many persons to spend 45 minutes to see it, but it would be an entire waste of time, for they would gain no information, learn nothing." In effect, Miller supported the decision not because the film was sensational or shocking, but rather because it wasn't.[27]

In addition to *Mysterious Eyes,* state censors blocked other short films depicting local Klan ceremonies in 1922. Charles Fitzmorris, Chicago's chief of police and a former record holder for around-the-world travel, refused a permit for a film depicting a Klan ceremony held near Joliet, Illinois, on 4 June 1922. According to *Searchlight,* Reverend Alonzo Bowling, "a dark skinned Methodist preacher," was the only member of the board of censors to oppose the film; his concerns, reportedly that the picture would "excite his people," evidently responded to the furor that had surrounded screenings of *Birth* in Chicago earlier in the year. *Searchlight* presented the banning of the film once more as evidence of religious persecution against the Klan, complaining that "the colored minister appealed to Chief of Police Fitzmorris, a Roman Catholic, and the Klan picture was barred."[28] The incident highlights not only the sensitivity surrounding depictions of the Klan (particularly in areas where screenings of *Birth* had been challenged), but also a related commercial interest in bringing topical scenes of Klan parades and ceremonies to the screen. Indeed William J. Voss, who bought the rights to show *Mysterious Eyes* in Modesto, California, claimed that he paid "a price greater than any ever paid for a single reel by any Modesto theatre."[29]

After *Mysterious Eyes,* further independent productions brought Klan parades to the paying public. These films, prioritizing the imagery rather than the motivations and ideologies of the group, further muddied the waters between audience and subject by presenting these displays directly to the local audiences depicted on-screen. In September 1923, theaters in Shreveport, the Klan's headquarters in Louisiana, showed pictures of a recent downtown Klan parade. The Klan newspaper the *Fiery Cross* noted that the theaters "were crowded with patrons eager to see the pictures of the Klan marchers," but again highlighted the failure of the Klan to control the media: the local theaters at which these films played "are all owned and controlled by Jewish interests." A month later, the American Theatre in Noblesville, Indiana, showed 1,000 feet of original night scenes from Klan activities in Shelbyville and Rushville as well as at the Indiana State Fair. These films, harking back to the appeal of early pre-industry films, offered the brief chance to "see yourself as others see you."[30]

Such films, in gaining access to the Klan, were often carefully stage-managed pieces of Klan propaganda. Describing a screening of *Mysterious Eyes* in Florala, Alabama, in 1924, the cinema manager referred to "three reels of very clever advertising matter for the Ku Klux Klan with practically no entertainment value."[31] Yet while widely promoted as actualities, as "genuine" pictures purporting to reveal the "truth" behind the Klan, these "genuine" sequences were often incorporated within a narrative. A Kansas censor report for *Mysterious Eyes* noted that the initiation ceremonies appeared alongside "posed activities of Klansmen apprehending robbers, pickpockets and bootleggers," while advertisements claimed that the sequences were "interwoven into a strong story."[32] Where Griffith had sought to authenticate his fiction, local exhibitors often looked to rework the actuality footage within the parameters of popular fiction. This blurring of "actuality" and fiction strengthened as Klan groups moved into feature production in the latter half of 1923.

We now turn to the Klan's more systematic and ambitious attempts to produce and exhibit film. In 1923, two Klan groups from Indiana and Ohio branched out into film production, attempting to realize the ambitions set forth by Clarke and Wheeler in 1921. The Indiana-based Cavalier Motion Picture Company produced the propaganda film *The Traitor Within,* while the Ohio Klan was involved in the production of *The Toll of Justice,* a film endeavoring to rival *The Birth of a Nation* and spread Klan propaganda throughout the country. Taken together, these films reveal the ways in which the Klan sought to represent and define itself, not only on-screen but also through the promotion and exhibition of film. Traversing cinemas and non-theatrical spaces, appearing alongside Klan stage shows and entertainment acts, these films illustrate the Klan's political use of film, while also revealing the inherent challenges it faced as an independent player working outside the industry.

MAKING MOVIES

In October 1923, *Movie Weekly* ran a three-page article explaining that "the Ku Klux Klan have made a movie that presents for the first time, as the K.K.K. sees it, the truth about the Klan." The article, written by T. Howard Kelly, who a few months earlier had speculated about the Klan's involvement in the death and retirement of a number of film stars, was somewhat light on details, but it did reveal that a "ten-reel picture had been made under the strict auspices of the Ku Klux Klan." The article confirmed that news of the picture "produced by the hooded organization" had come from an official announcement by the Klan, but suggested that a familiar "veil of secrecy" had "camouflaged the production of the picture."[33]

Moving Picture World revealed that *The Toll of Justice* was produced by the "C. & S. Pictures Company," described elsewhere as the Stanley and Cook Company, a short-lived enterprise in Columbus, Ohio, run by Corey G. Cook, the film's writer and director, and Earl Stanley, a local actor who appeared in the film.[34] Although C. & S. submitted the picture to the Ohio censor board and was originally credited as the film's maker, the film was widely discussed as "the first to be produced under the auspices of the Klan organization." Publicity materials emphasized that the film was made with the "co-operation of the Columbus Klan" and that more than a thousand members had volunteered to appear in full regalia on-screen.[35] Furthermore, while presented as a feature film, reports invariably noted the "authentic" footage of a Konklave at nearby Buckeye Lake and claimed that this was the first time a director had "worked a Klan meeting into a photoplay." The footage dated from 12 July 1923, when an estimated 40,000 Klansmen gathered to hear Dr. Evans and David Stephenson speak at the Klan meeting ground prior to a spectacular night-time initiation ceremony involving, according to the *Fiery Cross*, fifteen hundred male candidates and a thousand women. After describing the elaborate displays, which included choreographed Klansmen forming a human cross, a sixty-foot burning cross, and a fireworks display featuring "a little red school house" on fire, the *Fiery Cross* noted that "many moving picture scenes of the assembling of the Klan and the ritual were taken."[36] The completed film included these ceremonial displays but also incorporated scripted sequences, showing, for example, the film's heroine interacting with and addressing the assembling group.

On the one hand, the film's production clearly follows the example of *The Mysterious Eyes of the Ku Klux Klan*, both in its production – working with the local Klan and incorporating and displaying "actual" footage of Klan ceremonials – and in its promotion: it was, for example, presented as a "first" and offered to show "the truth." Press reports for *The Toll of Justice* even emphasized the inherent dangers and mystery involved in securing these images. Two cameramen were said to have been crushed when filming the onrushing horsemen in Columbus, bed-ridden for a year, and, in one case, "crippled for life."[37] On the other hand, these Klan productions moved beyond *Mysterious Eyes,* now responding to a very specific moment in Klan, cinema, and American social history.

At the same moment that the Klan in Ohio was announcing *The Toll of Justice,* Cavalier Motion Picture Company was attempting to produce *The Traitor Within.* Incorporated in Delaware in March 1923, Cavalier was, from the outset, defined by its strong Klan links. The *New York World* noted, under the headline "Friends of Klan Aspire to the Screen," that the president of the company was Dr. Charles Lewis Fowler.[38] Fowler was a Klokard (a paid lecturer of the Klan), a writer of Klan literature, and the founder and president of Lanier University, the first university owned and controlled by the Klan. After the university was declared bankrupt in the summer of 1922, Fowler became "one of the most widely travelled and best known Klan organizers" and, despite having no discernable experience with film, assumed the presidency of Cavalier. He was supported within the organization not by film personnel but instead by fellow lecturers, educators, organizers, and publicity men.[39]

The Kleagle of Buffalo, Major J. E. D. Smith, became vice president, while the treasurer was the Reverend Oscar Haywood, who had delivered a series of pro-Klan lectures in New York on the week of *Birth*'s re-release there a few months earlier. Haywood evidently recognized the potential of film as a recruiting tool for the Klan and, as an extremely prominent Klan lecturer, gave a succession of talks outlining the aims of this new film enterprise during the summer of 1923. He spoke at Mooresville in July 1923 before an estimated audience of 50,000 at a meeting of the Women of the Ku Klux Klan, a group said to be active in supporting the development of this "clean" motion picture company.[40] In August 1923, Haywood also gave a talk at Foster Park in Kokomo, Indiana. The *Kokomo Daily Dispatch* reported that Haywood devoted the "principal part of his address" to the motion picture industry.[41]

Haywood's address broadly outlined the Klan's attitude toward film and, as discussed in the previous chapter, justified the Klan's own use of film by making a distinct qualification between film as a medium and what he saw as the foreign-controlled film industry. For Haywood, the film "problem" was connected to the broader issue of press control – in a subsequent talk he also complained that "ninety percent of the newspaper proprietors of the country" were Jews – and these views were widely articulated by other members of the company. Roscoe Carpenter, the secretary of Cavalier and another Klan lecturer in Indiana, explained that Cavalier had been organized "to release pictures of a real American nature to counteract some of the anti-Klan pictures that are now being made and exhibited by the opposition." In a similar vein, the *Fiery Cross* explained that *The Toll of Justice* was "designed to counteract the poisonous propaganda circulated by alien enemies who have declared their determination to wipe out the Klan."[42] It is no coincidence that these Klan film companies were established at the exact moment that Klan groups were launching their protests against *The Pilgrim, Bella Donna,* and the Jewish film industry. This was also a moment when public relations was being taken more seriously, with Walter Lippmann's seminal 1922 book *Public Opinion* emphasizing the prominent role of mass communication in shaping popular opinion.[43] Within this context, it is significant that Cavalier was using educators, publicity men, and Klan recruiters in its efforts to challenge what it saw as foreign control of the media.

These Klan production companies responded to anxieties around the media and a growing awareness of film's potential as a pedagogical tool. They also reveal the rapid changes, insecurities, and tensions threatening the Klan at its point of greatest strength. First, there were significant distinctions between the officially endorsed *The Toll of Justice* and Cavalier's *The Traitor Within.* Cavalier had as its major shareholder David Stephenson, the head of the extremely powerful Klan in Indiana. After helping Hiram Evans to assume power from the organization's founder, William Simmons, at the end of 1922, Stephenson was handed responsibility for multiple states, but this was an uncomfortable and short-lived alliance between Evans and Stephenson, the two powerhouses of the expanding Klan. After Stephenson tried to extricate the Klans of Indiana from the national organ in May 1924, a succession of disputes and lawsuits saw Stephenson further removed from the established Klan. These two Klan film companies thus appear to represent, at least in part, different factions. If *The Toll of Justice* adopted the support of the established official Klan, *The Traitor Within* seems to be the product of the ambitious factions – particularly publicists, lecturers, and Kleagles – looking to exploit and develop the Klan themselves.

Second, the film companies themselves underwent significant restructuring even before their films were released. Under the headline "Klan Film a Fizzle," *Moving Picture World* reported in December 1923 that the Ohio Klan had "encountered difficulties" on *The Toll of Justice* "which spell failure for the proposition." In the final week of production, after the film's director, Corey Cook, had quite literally distanced himself from the film by moving to Egypt, the Klan had become "sole owner and producer," with the film now listed as a Miafa Pictures production.[44] "Miafa," which stood for "My Interests are for America," was a popular Klan slogan, and the film was now widely promoted as a Klan-made picture. This is a significant shift, as initially producers had claimed that *Toll* was "not strictly a Klan picture, and that it will be offered as a regular photoplay, and not as Klan propaganda." The Ohio Board of Censors evidently agreed, as it classed the film as a drama and passed it in November 1923 with no eliminations. However, a month later, when the film had its premiere at the Rex Theatre in Newark, the local press was reporting that "the picture [was] directed by the Ku Klux Klan and taken by Klansmen." A poster for this screening advertised the film as "a Ku Klux Klan picture."[45]

The film would regularly change ownership over the next two years. By the second half of 1924, the Columbus-based "Wilbert Pictures Company" had assumed responsibility for its distribution, and no longer advertised a "Klan production" but rather "a powerful story of the Ku Klux Klan" that was "not a Klan propaganda picture."[46] The shifts in description, a partial product of changes in ownership, attest to the distributor's attempts to negotiate a position for the film within various exhibition spaces and to different audiences. Roscoe Carpenter had initially claimed that he was "not identified with the Klan" and that he had for the last year been promoting films "glorifying Americanism." Carpenter further claimed that the pictures Cavalier intended to produce "will be on Americanism and not touch the Ku Klux Klan at all." Such claims were somewhat undermined by Oscar Haywood's approach to Thomas Dixon, scribe of *The Clansman*, asking him to write the first scenario for the company. Dixon, who had recently been challenged to a debate by Haywood after criticizing the modern Klan, declined, prompting the group to announce instead that the title writer, Joseph W. Farnham, would direct its films. Farnham described the situation as "entirely tentative and very hazy," and, in the end, it was Haywood who assumed the role of writer.[47] The selection of Haywood is symptomatic of a lack of professional film expertise – a byproduct of the Klan's position outside the industry – that would undermine both films. The *Ohio State Journal* observed the "rather crude" production techniques on *The Toll of Justice*, while *Moving Picture World* noted that the interiors had to be reshot after a problem with the lighting was discovered when the film reached the lab.[48]

By the time both companies came to release their films, their initial ambitions were somewhat diluted. While producers had claimed in September 1923 that *The Toll of Justice* would be released in at least twenty-one states, it arrived three months later with a handful of screenings in local halls, school auditoriums, and Klan-supported theaters, predominantly in Indiana and Ohio. Cavalier had maintained, as late as August 1923, that its first film would be a pictorialization of Lincoln's assassination called *A Portrayal of the Life of Abraham Lincoln*. However, when it finally released its first (and only) film in January 1924, it was *The Traitor Within*, a film now advertised as "The True Story of the Ku Klux Klan."[49]

While both companies had previously resisted the Klan label, by the end of 1923 when their films were ready for release, Klan involvement was emphasized in order to authenticate the films' representation. The *Fiery Cross* explained that *The Toll of Justice* would "acquaint the uninformed public with the true principles of the organization," extending a rhetoric adopted by producers and exhibitors with *The Mysterious Eyes of the Ku Klux Klan*.[50] These films were now presented as documents of Klan ideology, showing how the secretive Klan wished to present itself on a national level to Klansmen and (as the phrase "uninformed public" suggested) non-Klansmen alike.

REPRESENTING THE KLAN

While produced by different companies in different states, *The Toll of Justice* and *The Traitor Within* articulate a broadly consistent view of the modern Klan and, moreover, use an identical narrative device to do so.

Both films sought to redefine the Klan by directly confronting popular misrepresentations of the group. In *The Toll of Justice,* the central villain, Haskell, concocts a plan to frame the Klan for a murder that he has committed. Haskell, whose drinking den and "underworld" activities are condemned by the Klan, forces two of his desperate customers to get him two Klan costumes in exchange for drink and drugs. In a series of flashbacks, the audience discovers that Haskell, with his weak-willed and desperate accomplice Saunders, dressed up in the Klan costume and carried out the killing. Haskell shifts the blame onto the "real" Klansmen, telling the policeman, "I saw Tom Grant leave the Dale home on the night of the murder and hide this [Klan costume] in a bush." Haskell then points to the badge on the costume.[51]

This emphasis on the costume – a cinematic construction, which was by now one of the most emotive and identifiable visuals in American society – challenges audience and media responses to the costume and, in so doing, highlights inherent, paradoxical tensions with its use. In recognizing a costume that conceals the individual but instantly identifies the collective group, Haskell finds a way to undermine the Klan. In one scene Haskell, in costume, scares an African American character and then laughs. The film presents this as a misuse of the Klan costume, and responds not only to the apparent false representation of the group within society (by villains like Haskell), but also to the misrepresentation of the group by the media. The film illustrates the need for the Klan to control its own representation, and shows the dangers of allowing opponents or outsiders to represent the group.

The Traitor Within addresses a remarkably similar theme, showing "how crooks disguise themselves as Klansmen and commit robberies and murder," an argument that the Klan would revive when distancing itself from the Black Legion murders in 1936. A further report explained that *The Traitor Within* reveals "the methods of Klan enemies in their unscrupulous attacks on Klansmen and Klan principles." The film's attempts to "tear away the mask" served as a defensive riposte to popular criticisms and were also a feature of Klan stage plays.[52] For example, in *The Invisible Empire,* which played in Chicago at the beginning of 1923, "night riders, using the Klan as an unwilling shield, go about committing misdemeanors." The play, according to one review, "voices the chronic alibi" that a rival organization is "stealing the Kluck stuff," defending the widespread criticisms of Klan violence by suggesting that the Klan's enemies, adopting the Klan costume, were deliberately undermining the group.[53] The play did deviate from the film in one significant way, as it presented a racial enemy who, according to the *Chicago Evening Post,* was depicted as a "yellow devil of a Jap but also a foul field of a Russian."[54] For the most part, the Klan publicly underplayed its racist values and avoided presenting racial enemies or extreme violence on-screen. This was, in part, a result of the restrictions imposed by censors that condemned films depicting Japanese enemies, such as *Shadows of the West.* Industrial regulation, as I argue in the next chapter, inadvertently helped legitimize the group by manufacturing a more sympathetic and less divisive model of the Klan.

The Klan within *The Toll of Justice* is not a violent racist group, but rather a moral force, protecting threatened womanhood and administering Prohibition. An advertisement for *The Toll of Justice* succinctly explains the Klan's role within the film: "Do away with the underworld – Protect clean womanhood."[55] These two issues are linked together within the film as the heroine, Billie, who is hunting her father's killer, is captured and tied up in Haskell's drinking den. In one scene, a lecherous drinker puts his hands on Billie, effectively assuming the role of Gus from *Birth,* as the film highlights the threat drink poses to women, while also showing more broadly the dangers faced by independent women within modern society.

The Toll of Justice closely follows dominant industrial narrative and thematic conventions, attempting here to re-create the excitement of the earlier hugely popular female serials. The motherless Billie, with her masculine name and modern clothes (she wears trousers and a tie), undertakes the role of investigator for her father's death, racing around in a car and climbing out of a plane in mid-air. Yet while those serials produced by the industry may, as Stamp and Singer speculate, be viewed as liberating and empowering to the female spectator, *The Toll of Justice* would appear to serve more clearly as a warning. Billie is helpless as she is captured and tied up by the villainous men, and she is ultimately reliant on male protection.[56]

Yet Billie's role is, as with the female serials, more nuanced and, in this case, indicative of the burgeoning female presence within the modern Klan. The WKKK, which was officially formed in June 1923, quickly established itself as powerful institution, particularly in Indiana, where its 250,000 members represented half of the Klan's total membership for the state.[57] Women's Klan groups were notably active in the moves for cleaner pictures, and they supported the Klan's ventures into film production. Given the perception that females represented a majority of the film audience, catering to them was widely recognized as commercially prudent. Billie's independence may be medium-specific, following the popular conventions of the industry, but within this context the independent modern woman becomes reformed as an exciting, attractive, and unconventional example to the modern Klanswoman. While not depicted as a Klanswoman, Billie ultimately recognizes and reconciles traditional, clearly defined gender roles, investigating her father's death and then calling for the male night riders to resolve the situation. The Klan responds, as an intertitle states, to "the appeal which stirs every man to vow allegiance to this brave little girl and help bring the criminals to JUSTICE." The independent modern woman is now presented as a "brave little girl." She does not ride with the Klan herself, as the Klan appears to qualify the definition of modern womanhood put forward by the female serials.

The Toll of Justice, as with the earlier serials, presents Billie's actions as a direct response to her father's death, but it also positions the criminal activities as a failure of the family unit. The crimes of Saunders, a captured villain recovering in hospital, are presented in relation to his mother. Saunders's mother sobs as the intertitle notes, "Love best must suffer most." She represents a traditional, threatened form of womanhood, depicted in flashback baking a cake while described as "lavender and old lace." Earlier in the film when Tom Grant is falsely arrested, his mother is shown crying as her son is led away. In emphasizing the importance of family order, the Klan presents itself as a necessary protector of family values.

The Traitor Within was more overtly political and direct in its propaganda, as it presented the Klan, which was an increasingly powerful force politically in Indiana, within "an American city on the verge of a mayoralty election."[58] The Ohio Board of Censors rejected the film outright in April 1924. The same censor had rejected a Selznick newsreel showing Klan ceremonies in Dallas in 1922, but passed *The Toll of Justice*

3.3. The capture of Gus in *The Birth of a Nation,* David W. Griffith Corporation, 1915.

after concluding that, while it did have "a distinctly Klan atmosphere," this was not what would "ordinarily be termed Klan propaganda."[59] The role of the Klan in *The Toll of Justice,* as an early review in the *Ohio State Journal* admitted, is not as prominent as "one might be led to expect." In keeping with the growing band of contemporary patriotic pictures, the film sought to promote and define Americanism on-screen, opening with a one-reel prologue presenting the history of the American flag or, as the *Fiery Cross* imperiously termed it, "a lesson in flag etiquette."[60] This is not to say that the film is totally apolitical; it does reference contemporary Klan anxieties around labor and immigration. In attempting to vilify the film's wronged hero, Tom Grant, Haskell forges a letter in which Grant supposedly decides to replace "native-born" labor with a "class" that will "work longer hours for less wages," while Haskell also blames Grant for a workers' strike that he himself instigated. Yet, for the most part, the Klan features as a barely updated model of Griffith's picturesque band of Civil War veterans.

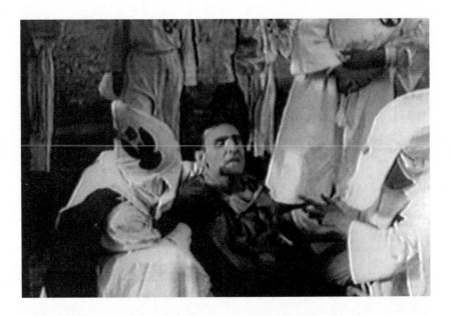

3.4. Reimagining the capture of Gus within *The Toll of Justice*, Miafa Pictures, 1923.

The first appearance of the Klan in *The Toll of Justice* shows the transformation of the individual Klansman into a collective mass, as the robed figures join hands in a circle under the American flag and envelop the screen in white. It is here that Billie first interacts with the Klan, making a speech in front of the flag while flanked by two Klansmen. Inspired by Billie's words – or, more accurately, by *The Birth of a Nation* – the Klansmen run to their waiting covered horses and ride. There follows a series of unashamedly derivative shots of Klansmen riding and running toward the screen and across the rural landscape. The visuals of *Birth* are referenced elsewhere as well. A tussle in the cabin between captured girl and villain, also reworked in Oscar Micheaux's *Within Our Gates,* replays Elsie's struggle with Silas, while a shot of an apprehended villain updates the capture of Gus (figs. 3.3 and 3.4). The film's evident channeling of *Birth* was reinforced in the press publicity book produced for the film in 1924. Suggested taglines included "The greatest attraction since The Birth of a Nation," while the film was also described as "the first great picture since The Birth of a Nation," one that "raises one's American blood to the boiling point."[61] Yet, for all its attempts to remake *Birth,* with references to modern technology and transport (which the Klan entirely bypass), the film is a formally dated presentation of the modern Klan, one that fails to capture the scale, tension, or any sense of narrative space found in Griffith's work. Furthermore, a modern remake of *Birth* is to an extent superfluous, given the modern Klan's "textual poaching" of the original film at this moment.

The influence and legacy of *The Birth of a Nation* permeates these Klan-produced films. A report on *The Traitor Within* remarked that "while it will not be shown at movie houses, it is claimed to be in a class with 'The Birth of a Nation.'" The *New York World* reported that *Yesterday, Today and Forever* was intended as "a screen spectacle to imitate and outrival 'The Birth of a Nation,'" while *The White Rider* was, according to the *Lincoln Sunday Star,* "destined to grip the hearts of Americans as completely and become as popular as 'The Birth of a Nation.'"[62] Yet for all their similarities, these later reinterpretations also incorporated actual footage of the Klan within their fictional world. Posters for *The Toll of Justice*'s first extended showing in Newark contained a large picture from the Klan meeting at Buckeye Lake, while an advertisement for *The Traitor Within* in Indiana emphasized that the film featured "the world's greatest night parade at Fort Wayne," filmed during the armistice celebration in November 1923.[63]

The Klan's stage plays, like its films, also promised an inside view of the organization. For *The Flaming Cross,* a "play accurately depicting the principles" of the Klan, the audience was "permitted to 'sit in' on a modern Klan meeting," while in *The Mysterious Way,* "the big scene is with the Klavern in full regalia."[64] Even a seemingly negative depiction of the Klan, like *Behind the Mask,* offered to show the inner workings of the Klan, featuring a scene in a Klavern with a glowing fiery cross and "many startling revelations."[65] These plays reiterated the theatricality of the Klan's rituals and performances and, in articulating a reality within a fictional framework, reaffirmed their pedagogical function for both the Klan and its opponents. The emphasis on Klan authenticity would also direct the films' distribution and sites of exhibition. *The Toll of Justice* and *The Traitor Within* were evidently intended for widespread distribution and heavily influenced by mainstream cinema, but, given the Klan's repeated criticism of perceived Jewish influences in the industry, these films were often presented as distinct from, indeed in opposition to, mainstream films. This tension, like the difficulties facing all independent films, ensured that independent Klan films struggled to exceed short-run local screenings. In so doing, they developed and exploited a burgeoning but critically overlooked model of sponsored screenings and non-theatrical performances, through which local Klan groups promoted and defined themselves within their communities.

PROMOTING THE KLAN

In the summer of 1924, Wilbert Pictures Company, which was now responsible for distributing *The Toll of Justice,* produced an "exploitation advertising campaign book" for the film, providing a series of posters, materials, and suggested publicity devices for exhibitors (fig. 3.5). The materials highlight the complex identity of the film, which was defined by and exploitable for its Klan connection, but at the same time the distributors sought audiences in established venues, not just those for Klan supporters. The booklet still prioritized the Klan involvement in familiar terms – "the most talked of organization in the world in a thrilling drama of the underworld," "the first picture ever made with the Klan" – and noted that "never before" had a director infiltrated the "inner circle." Yet it also noted the "stirring scenes, gripping story, beautiful pathos and tremendous human interest," the airplane and car chases, the appearance of "America's new girl star, Mildred Melrose," and "the wonderful love of an American school girl and her beautiful deeds." Wilbert Pictures was looking beyond Klan membership, providing stories and taglines to appeal to "every class of theatre goer in your community." It also looked beyond the Klan to other familiar groups. Mirroring the Klan's own reworking of *The Face at Your Window,* it suggested soliciting the support of local American Legion posts by writing and offering complimentary tickets to its aviator members: the "mere reading of this letter at the meeting is worth a lot of money to your box office." This would not only generate valuable advertising for the Klan but also, by extension, further serve to legitimize the local group.[66]

The booklet recognized a need to reach beyond Klan territories, noting that "if your town is strong for the Klan, you can play up the Klan

3.5. Wilbert Pictures presented posters and suggested promotional devices for *The Toll of Justice* in its extensive "Press Matter Exploitation Advertising Campaign Book."

angle," but, if not, "go after the romance, [and] thrilling dramatic story angles." Suggested taglines highlighted this balancing act, presenting the film not as a Klan work but as a privileged insight into the group, and increasingly part of an ongoing debate. "One of the greatest questions of today – 'is the Ku Klux Klan a menace to the country,'" was one proposed tagline; another was "What is the Ku Klux Klan about? What is the idea of the K.K.K.?"[67] This partly reflected a shift in the film's distribution, with the film no longer controlled by the Klansmen of Miafa but by the "group of Columbus Businessmen" that constituted Wilbert Pictures. Yet this shift was also evident with *The Traitor Within*. By the summer of 1925, advertisements asked, "What do you know about Ku Klux Klan? Is it Guilty?" and "Is the Ku Klux Klan Guilty or Not Guilty of all the crimes and vices laid at their door?" For this latter screening, "anti-Klansmen and families [are] especially invited."[68]

Promotional strategies inevitably varied according to location, particularly as the film moved beyond Klan strongholds, but there was also a temporal shift as the Klan's reputation was increasingly eroded by scandal. What exhibitors recognized was the topicality and notoriety of the Klan. In this case, the booklet saw an opportunity to "cash in on a real NATIONAL ADVERTISED topic," one found "on front pages every day." This confrontational approach, imagining film as a part of social debate, was potentially problematic for censors and now contrary to industry convention. However, in many respects this was nothing new and merely replicated promotional activities used for *Birth*. Proposed promotional strategies for *The Toll of Justice* included dressing up two horsemen in Klan robes to ride along the street advertising the film, while two robed Klansmen in the lobby would "create atmosphere." The publicity book explained that robes for both men and horses "can be rented from our publicity department" and also suggested a more direct Klan involvement, noting that in strong Klan areas "you can enlist the aid of the entire local organization."[69]

The extent to which the Klan was used to define and promote *The Toll of Justice* shifted as the film traveled and as new distributors assumed responsibility for the film. The film was initially imagined as a direct part of the Klan's publicity and recruitment drive within Ohio. Its first screening, in Columbus at the Apollo Theatre on 9 December 1923, took place before a select audience of Kleagles and Cyclops from local Klan groups who had gathered to discuss plans for the next year's Klan activities.[70] When Wilbert Pictures later assumed control of the film, it recognized the need to target a wider audience. "'The Toll of Justice' is not a Klan propaganda picture," Wilbert explained, "but it has the endorsement of the Ku Klux Klan." Posters for a four-day run at the Windsor Theatre in Canton, Ohio, in August 1924, clarified that the "public is invited. Is not a Propaganda Picture!" When the film went on to the McKinley Theatre directly afterward, posters reaffirmed, "We shout loud and clear – No, not a propaganda picture," emphasizing instead the "powerful story of love and mystery." The film's credentials as a piece of Klan propaganda were barely concealed – a poster declared this "one of the greatest 100% American Photoplays since *The Birth of a Nation*" – but the film was reaching out beyond Klan membership, to potential members and also to critics. A poster for the run in Canton asked boldly at the top, "Why do you condemn the K.K.K.?" before offering the succinct reply, "Because you don't know what you're talking about." The poster suggested the film would "educate"; viewers' "blood will fairly boil with a desire to obliterate lawlessness." "If you can sit through the show without a thrill," the poster concluded, "you must be either anti-American or sick."[71]

By the time the film reached Canton in August 1924, it had already "thrilled" audiences all over the state, according to the posters. Twelve thousand were said to have witnessed the film in Columbus alone, while a telegram from the theater manager in Canton labeled the picture the "biggest money getter we ever had."[72] While such claims are dubious – the film evidently wasn't profitable – any level of success was due to Klan support which, despite conflicting claims, Wilbert continued to target. An advertisement for a screening at the Reel Theatre in Charleston in September 1924 was headed "Notice K.K.K.," while even in Columbus in October when posters showed the romantic leads and noted the "stupendous, thrilling, amazing drama of love," a tagline emblazoned across the top toted the film as something "every Klansmen should see."[73]

Promotional materials for the film were every bit as significant as the film itself. In particular, posters in the local press or in public spaces enabled the Klan to reach beyond its existing membership. At its first public appearance at the Rex Theatre in Newark in December 1923, *The Toll of Justice* was advertised as "a show that interests every American man, woman or child." Posters went a step further a few weeks later in Dayton, presenting "the picture that every red blooded American should see."[74] This line appeared frequently in advertisements for *Toll* but also for *The Traitor Within,* which the *Protestant Home Journal* described as "a drama of American life, personified by American characters familiar to everyone of us. Every AMERICAN should see this picture."[75] These advertisements attempted to attract non-Klansmen to screenings but, more strikingly, were also part of a process that sought to legitimize and consolidate the Klan's position as a Protestant and American group within local communities.

The promotion of these films thus served not only to advertise the pictures, but also to project the values of the modern Klan to local communities. When *The Toll of Justice* was shown in Columbus in January 1924, advertisements contained two boxes, one stating "Clean up crime and filth" and the other "Protect our women." A further advertisement in

Mansfield in February urged the viewer to "rid your city of crime," while in Ashland, where the film played at the Palace Theatre, "Do away with the divorce evil" appeared in large, bold, capitalized letters above the film's title.[76] The Klan emphasized and extended the performative role of film, seeking to influence social behavior not only through the film but also the publicity surrounding it. This constant, dogged emphasis on addressing social and political problems challenged the dominant conventions of a film industry that often presented films as a form of escapism.

These advertisements also served to differentiate Klan-made films from the supposedly "foreign" industry films that it so often opposed. *The Traitor Within* described itself as "The Greatest of all American Pictures," while other advertisements noted that "It's all American" and that "It is a clean American picture."[77] Advertising a screening of *The Traitor Within* in Tipton in 1925, a poster declared, "Let us prove to you that real entertainment may be obtained without lowering the ideals of the home, the virtue of our women and without fun at the expense of religion." When *The White Rider* was shown in 1925, advertisements pointedly emphasized that the film was "morally clean."[78]

The Klan used film posters and advertisements as an attractive strand of media – one traditionally reaching a younger reader – and placed these posters in local papers and also throughout communities, whether in shops sympathetic to the Klan cause or in public spaces deemed likely to attract Klan sympathizers. The waiting room of the traction station in Anderson, Indiana, was said to be "plastered all over with bills and illustrated placards" advertising *The Traitor Within* at the local Starland Theatre. "The picture was stupid," the anti-Klan newspaper *Muncie Post-Democrat* determined, "but the Klan boobs went in their droves and paid out good money to see a moving picture of amateurs draped in sheets."[79]

From the outset, local Klan groups supported and adopted these films, either by very publicly attending screenings as a group, as occurred in Columbus in January 1924, or by sponsoring the shows.[80] For example, the Junior Klan organized a three-day run (with five screenings a day) at the Exhibit Theatre in Portsmouth in March, which reportedly broke attendance records, while the Women of the Ku Klux Klan of Putnam County sponsored a screening of *The Traitor Within* at Cook's Opera

House in Greencastle, Indiana, in February 1924.[81] In recognizing film's reputed appeal to women and children, the Klan exploited a medium that could specifically reach these fresh, targeted audiences.

For the most part *The Traitor Within* was presented by, and for, local Klan groups. Hoosier Distributors made little attempt to distribute the film through established (industrial) channels, but instead advertised it directly to Klan groups in the local Klan press.[82] As a result, the film was often staged as a Klan event and fundraiser. When *The Traitor Within* was shown "under the auspices of the Ku Klux Klan" at the Jefferson Theatre in Decatur in July 1924, electric crosses were placed on each side of the stage, "members of the Klan in full regalia acted as ushers," and a woman in full regalia sang.[83]

Although *The Toll of Justice* played at established theaters in Ohio throughout 1924, in many cases the local Klan group had hired the venue. Above posters for a screening at the Rex Theatre were further advertisements explaining that "the Rex Theatre has been leased to the Miafa Picture Co. during this week." The Palace Theatre in Ashland was also "rented to outside parties" for *The Toll of Justice,* as was the Exhibit Theatre in Portsmouth and the Strand in Ohio, while the Klan leased the Lincoln in Iowa to show *The Traitor Within* in November 1924.[84] Yet many owners were reluctant to hire out their venues to the Klan; those that did could find themselves at the center of a local storm. For example, when a Klan representative hired out the Mecca Theatre in Decatur, Illinois, for a two-day screening of *The Traitor Within* in January 1924, parts of the motion picture machine were stolen. A note was left explaining that "these parts will be returned by Saturday providing no more K. K. K. pictures are shown in Decatur." The Klan reported this theft as a direct attack on the organization – adopting a phrase used extensively in Klan literature to describe the thief as "the enemy within" – and the theater manager, L. J. McCormick, immediately aligned himself with the protestor, refusing to provide a portable machine and refunding the money paid for the lease. While the Klan complained that the manager had been "frightened" into canceling the engagement, McCormick announced that he had no plans to prosecute and assumed that the parts had been taken by "some friend" of the theater. McCormick appeared particularly concerned about the effect associating with the Klan would have on his reputation, stating that "it has been rumored that I am a member of the Klan. This is untrue."[85]

While theaters were often quick to note that they had been hired for the occasion, the screening of Klan films still often implied a theater's support for the organization. This would provide a further obstacle for independent producers, already operating outside industrial distribution channels, as they sought suitable venues for these Klan films. As a result, the Klan would often look beyond the cinema building to non-theatrical venues, such as churches, community halls, and schools. In so doing, they not only brought the film to very specific, targeted audiences, but also found new ways to define and position themselves within the local community.

The Toll of Justice was often screened in schools. When it played in Homer, Michigan, in October 1924, before an audience "that packed the building to overflowing," *Searchlight* reported that "Mrs. Squires, the teacher, was greatly pleased at the results." The film had featured at Bowman School auditorium earlier in the year, where local churchmen monitored films, showing only those that "may be seen by the children without any harmful results whatever."[86] It also appeared at the High School Auditorium in Elyria, Ohio, in March 1925. The school board originally turned down the request "made by a representative of the Ku Klux Klan" because the school would not allow "any entertainment that might cause racial or religious dissension." It was eventually shown after a member of the board, at the Klan's suggestion, went to view the film in Cleveland and decided that there was "nothing objectionable about the picture." In the same month, the Junior Klan in Akron arranged a two-day screening where, according to the *Youngstown Citizen*, "the lessons learnt will leave a lasting impression."[87] The screenings aligned the Klan with local schools, foregrounding and legitimizing its role within local communities and presenting a group positively influencing and educating young Americans.

Through these screenings the Klan also highlighted the educational role that it believed film should play within society. The *Decatur Review* described *The Traitor Within* as "an educational motion picture," while the film was advertised at one of its earliest screenings at a high school in

Kokomo in January 1924 as a "picture full of instruction for both old and young."[88] *Movie Weekly* drew a parallel between the Klan's production of *The Toll of Justice* and its proposed purchase of Valparaiso University, noting that the acquisition of an entire educational institution was "a move on the Klan's part to take a hand in educating American youth along certain principles."[89] Cavalier presented film as an educational device within a school setting and directly sought to attract children to *The Traitor Within*. A special free showing was arranged at 9:30 in the morning for school children in Muncie in February 1924 before a further screening was arranged for the children of the Delaware County Children's Home. When *The Toll of Justice* played in Ashland, an afternoon screening was organized for local school children. The price was reduced so that "each and every boy and girl may see this production before it leaves town."[90]

The Klan presented these films within a myriad of non-theatrical venues – *The Traitor Within* played in baseball parks, county clubs, and even Knights of the Pythias lodges – and, in particular, in churches and religious venues. *The Traitor Within* played at the Scoville Tabernacle in Muncie, at the First Christian Church in Hammond, and the Universalist Church in Logansport.[91] In March 1924, it enjoyed an extended run at the Cadle Tabernacle, an established Klan center in Indianapolis, where it was presented "under the auspices of the Lawrence Community Brotherhood of the Lawrence M. E. Church" and served as a fundraiser for the church's community building (fig. 3.6).[92] The screenings foregrounded the Klan's Protestant values, its position within the religious fabric of the local community, but also the church's own support for the Klan. The *Indiana Catholic and Record* responded to the established Klan presence at the Tabernacle, commenting on this "anti-Catholic Picture show." Noting the "very appropriate" sign outside the building – "The Traitors Within" – it commented that "the Cadle Tabernacle, being a Klan headquarters is the natural home of traitors."[93]

The Tabernacle often showed educational religious pictures and demanded a high moral tone from its selected films. Within a few months of the screening, Tabernacle founder E. Howard Cadle would face legal action from Epic Film Attractions after describing *After Six Days,* Epic's film version of the Old Testament, as "lewd, lascivious and immoral."[94]

DON'T FAIL TO SEE

The Greatest of All American Pictures

"The Traitor Within"

at the

CADLE TABERNACLE

Ohio and New Jersey Sts., Indianapolis

March 24, 25, 26, 27, 28 and 29

Music
Furnished
by the
Pollard
Orchestra

Hear
the Cadle
Choir
of 500
Voices

Absolutely the First Showing of This Wonderful Photoplay in Indianapolis

A Picture That Every Red-Blooded American Should See

Featuring

THE World's Greatest Night Parade at Ft. Wayne
True Ideals of Americans
American Drama of Life and Action

**A Well-Sustained Love Romance Around Which
Are Builded the Features Interesting to Klansmen**

Special Music by the Cadle Choir of 500 Voices

*Given by the Lawrence Community Brotherhood
for the Benefit of the Lawrence M. E. Church*

Doors Open 6:30--Program Starts 7:40 P.M.--Admission 50c

Tickets on Sale at { BROOKS' DRUG STORE, Ohio and Pennsylvania St.
CADLE TABERNACLE, Ohio Street Office

Get Your Tickets in Advance If You Want to Be Sure of a Seat

3.6. *The Traitor Within* at the Cadle Tabernacle, *Fiery Cross*, 21 March 1924.

The Traitor Within, like the Klan itself, was positioned in this religious context as the antithesis of the un-American, immoral productions that the Klan condemned. The group's Protestant identity, propagated within the film and, in particular, through the film's promotion and exhibition, was further enhanced by a series of lectures offered each night during the film's run. On opening night, the evangelist Dr. E. J. Bulgin, described by the Catholic publication *Tolerance* as a "foul-mouthed sensationalist," spoke before the film.[95] The Klan used the exhibition of film to legitimize its religious values, often positively appealing to churchmen. As an example, when *The White Rider* was shown in Lincoln in 1925, posters stated that "ministers are especially invited to attend."[96]

There were further Klan productions during this period that, for the most part, also circulated outside first-run theaters within educational, civic, and religious centers. A notable example is *The Fifth Horseman,* produced in Texas in 1924 and written and directed by E. M. McMahon. McMahon was no stranger to Klan entertainment propaganda and wrote the lyrics to the popular Klan song "Why I Am a Klansman" in 1922 ("That's why I'm a Klansman and wear a Klansman's mask") and the music to "We Are All Loyal Klansmen" in 1923. While less clearly positioned as a Klan production – particularly as it did not appear to have the institutional support of either *The Toll of Justice* or *The Traitor Within* – *The Fifth Horseman* was advertised as a Klan feature within the Klan and film press.[97] The *Fiery Cross* used the familiar tagline "A picture every American should see," and later stated that "no real American can afford to miss it. A picture of America – for America."[98] The language adopted in promoting other Klan features again resurfaced, whether describing *The Fifth Horseman* as a film that "every red blooded American regardless of creed and color should see," or as "the most mysterious, best and most talked of picture of modern times."[99]

The Fifth Horseman was often presented by and for the Klan, benefiting the local group when it played at the Community Hall in Sugarcreek and playing "under the auspices of women's organization, Marion Co." at the Lincoln Square Theatre in Indianapolis.[100] The film was shown at Klan venues, such as the Klan Tabernacle in Xenia, Ohio, in April 1925, and again served to position the local Klan as a useful and charitable group positively shaping American citizens (fig. 3.7). A screening orga-

The Most Mysterious, Best And Most Talked of Picture of Modern Times

THE

FIFTH

HORSEMAN

THE GREAT AMERICAN PICTURE

IF you were thrilled by "The Four Horsemen of the Apocalypse" and "The Birth of a Nation"; your heart was touched by "Over The Hill" and "The Old Nest."

THEN BE SURE TO SEE THIS GREAT PICTURE — GREATER YET THAN ANY OF THE ABOVE PICTURES

FIRST TIME SHOWN AT THIS POPULAR PRICE

—AT—

KLAN TABERNACLE

East Third Street

Tuesday and Wednesday, April 14 and 15

At 8 O'Clock p. m.

Adults 25c; Children 15c

Every man, woman and child in Greene County should avail themselves of the opportunity to see this truly wonderful picture.

3.7. *The Fifth Horseman* played at Klan venues, in this instance in Xenia, Ohio. *Evening Gazette,* 13 April 1925, 3.

nized by the Klan at Convention Hall in Hutchinson served as a hospital fundraiser for the Grace Hospital, with promotional materials promising that the film would teach a moral "lesson that will never be forgotten."[101] When the film moved to the Hiawatha Auditorium in Kansas, it played with "actuality" footage of the Klan parade in Washington in order to contemporize the fictional film. Now described as "America's Greatest American Picture," a film "produced by Klansmen for the uplift" of the American nation, it again reached out beyond a Klan audience, targeting "Every Father and Mother: Every High School Student."[102]

Advertisements prioritized the picture's "American" credentials, often stipulating that this was "not a religious picture" but that the "key note" of the picture was "patriotism."[103] Producers and exhibitors were increasingly sensitive to religious depictions on-screen, but the film certainly defined the Klan primarily in religious terms. The synopsis explained that the film was "inspired by St. John the Divine's vision of the Fifth Horseman of the Apocalypse," the prologue featured a close-up of St. John, while the first location was described merely as "Biblical atmosphere."

The film extends the historical lineage of the Klan, presenting the modern Klansmen not only as successors of the original Reconstruction-era group but also as direct descendants of Christ. In the film, the Confederate veteran Colonel Woodson explains "with deep earnestness" the function of the Klan: "Nearly two thousand years ago, Sonny, a man gave His life that you and I might live. Down through the centuries, Christian men and women have struggled to keep alive His great teachings. I was one of thousands who struggled through reconstruction days, to defend the helpless and preserve the sanctity of the home."[104] Woodson continually emphasizes the links between Christ and the Klansman and, through the American flag, aligns Protestantism directly to Americanism. "We were led by the fifth horseman," Woodson states when passing the flag down to the young Sonny, "for God, our country and our homes!" Religion also serves a narrative function, akin to early social uplift films like *A Drunkard's Reformation* (1909). Sonny's father, Tom, is finally reformed after finding a card placed within a copy of the Bible, pointing out verses pertinent to his struggle. After reading the verses, a stage direction explains that Tom "raises his eyes from [the] Bible and sits back – a picture of desolation."

The Klan appears as an innately mysterious and mythologized band. The Klansmen are never contextualized within society, while the modern hero is referred to throughout as "Young American" and defined entirely by his Klan role. Furthermore, the film concludes by revealing that Colonel Woodson is not a real, living person, but rather the embodiment of the spirit and valor of the modern Klansman. As the "Young American" explains to Sonny, "We have but to seek, and we shall find ... the Christly Spirit of Yesterday, Today and Forever!"[105]

The film's concluding sentiments recall the writings of William Simmons, and indeed the title of Clarke and Wheeler's proposed film in 1921. Yet while *The Fifth Horseman* – and in particular *The Traitor Within* and *The Toll of Justice* – may have partially realized Clarke and Wheeler's plans to produce contemporary Klan propaganda, all were largely unsuccessful in infiltrating mainstream industrial circuits. The exhibition of these films within non-theatrical spaces should not, however, be seen as a failing, but rather as evidence of a form of cinema predicated on educating and instructing its audiences and, in this instance, on usefully molding, defining, and imagining its viewers as part of a local and national polity.

As early as April 1924, barely three months after the release of *The Traitor Within*, Cavalier acknowledged that its productions would, by necessity, play outside traditional cinema spaces. In seeking further investment, Cavalier published and distributed brochures to potential investors, which, according to reports, contained "vituperative attacks on negroes, Catholics and Jews." The brochure outlined the challenges facing Klan productions, explaining that "many theatres owned by non-Protestants decline to show cinematographs depicting the Klan activities." As a result, Cavalier was pursuing a new exhibition and distribution strategy, issuing "special photoplays designed for exhibition in Protestant churches and special theatres."[106] Cavalier was looking to sell stock exclusively to Klansmen through its well-established hierarchical network of Klan agents. Such a network, integral to the spread of the Klan, consisted not only of personnel but also of buildings, affiliate organizations, technologies, and other media. While there were other significant and comparable independent film organizations, such as the Ford Motion Picture Department and the Church Motion Picture Corporation in New York, the most productive comparison is the American Legion Film Service. The Legion sought to educate and create American citizens through film, saw film production and exhibition as part of a broader conservative response to the perceived failings of the film industry, and also systematically used its well-established network of Legion posts to circulate and exhibit its films non-theatrically.[107] It is to the American Legion that I turn briefly now.

KLAN ENTERTAINMENT BUREAUS

At the same moment that Clarke and Wheeler were considering their Klan film scheme in 1921, the American Legion was establishing the "American Legion Film Service," which would operate from Indianapolis as part of the Legion's publicity department, under the leadership of James E. Darst.[108] The film service was particularly active in providing projection machines and films to Legion posts throughout the country, using the Legion's network of 11,000 posts to circulate and incorporate film to and from the national center.[109] An early example of this is the Official US Signal Corps film *Flashes of Action* (1919), which by October 1922 had been exhibited by more than 500 Legion posts. The Legion emphasized the pedagogical function of these screenings – a "forward step in Americanism" – with the national adjunct (effectively the administrative head of the Legion) claiming in a piece in *Visual Education* that its selected films could "inspire a finer appreciation of our government and the country we are privileged to call our own than any other medium of teaching."[110]

The Legion actively recontextualized these films as American Legion texts, useful to the Legion cause. For example, the Speakers Bureau of the National Publicity Division prepared and distributed an explanatory lecture that would be delivered during *Flashes of Action*. In using film in education, the Legion stretched beyond its membership and directly targeted children. Many schools were dismissed early to enable children to attend special afternoon screenings of *Flashes of Action*, which were often held as fundraisers for schools or other local community institutions. The National Commander of the Legion, John R. Quinn, noted the "priceless publicity" generated from these screenings, bolstering the Legion's role and identity within the local community.[111]

From the outset, the Legion recognized film as a "powerful aid in membership drives" with movies serving as "good advertising" for the group and also as an attraction that helped "get everybody out for a meeting."[112] In this respect, the films not only showed publicly in theatrical spaces, but also increasingly after 1923 – when rental prices were further reduced – as free, "good entertainment features for regular meetings."[113] The selected films promoted the broad patriotic notion of Americanism propagated by the Legion, but they were also adopted for specific contemporary campaigns. In the case of *Flashes of Action,* the film was used to support state campaigns for adjusted compensation, and proved particularly successful in Kansas where it was exhibited in more than 150 towns and cities.[114] In this way, the Legion was formalizing a mode of textual poaching through the distribution of these films and their related materials, which not only positioned them as American Legion films, but also directly related the historical footage to contemporary politics.

The Legion also produced some of its own films and made cameras available to Legion posts, allowing local audiences to record and view themselves on-screen and also serving to circulate local activities to the national center and out to other Legion posts. Writing in 1924, the Film Service director, Earl Mayer, not only recognized film as the "most lucrative post activity" and the "easiest way" for a post to make money, but also saw the circulation of Legion-produced films as a chance to see what other posts are doing: "They take you on a trip to France with the Legion delegation, or on a tour of the United States with Marshall Froch." The Klan would also, on occasion, record and relive its own events. Even as late as 1940, a Klansman filmed the annual Klorero (Klan convention) in New York in an effort to "preserve" this moment for future Kloreros, while movies from the previous three sessions were shown, "bringing back memories of previous years."[115]

Earl Mayer had earlier noted the value of "community movies" for the American Legion in advancing a "better appreciation of good citizenship and clean living." The Legion produced its own films to this end. By 1929, its catalogue contained fourteen titles for rental, with the most recent, *Old Glory,* written and directed by the head of the National Emblem Division, E. O. Marquette. All parts in the film were played by Legionnaires – the director of the National Americanism Committee played a judge – and the film itself was said to be "based on the Legion's code of flag etiquette." It was advertised as "an educational classic that every American should see."[116]

Film scholars, magnetized toward the increasingly powerful industry, have often overlooked the plethora of organizations, like the Klan and American Legion, emerging and using film after the war in pedagogical, non-theatrical contexts. Responding in part to the perceived failings of the film industry, these organizations sought to promote "Americanism," visualizing film as an educational tool, through which they could recruit members and promote, define, and formalize their role within local communities. While both groups were involved in production – and not just of feature films, but also of local events and performances – the American Legion functioned primarily as a distributor, adopting suitable films and circulating them along with projection machines and supporting materials. Where a comparison with the Klan is perhaps most instructive is in considering their similar organizational structures as national groups, comprising local posts and chapters, which operated with a chain of national, state, regional, and local officers. The infrastructure of successful fraternal groups provides a useful network for non-theatrical film. In the case of the Legion, it hired out films and equipment to local posts, and presented films in its own buildings. As early as 1921, national and state Klan leaders were helping local Klan groups bring *The Face at Your Window* to their town while, as I have shown, Klan film distributors sought local groups to arrange screenings of their films through the Klan press. Yet, despite the evident interest in film from all levels of Klan leadership, there was not a comparable central film library or facet of the publicity department, providing advice, films, or equipment to Klan groups.

The Klan did work, however, to create entertainment networks. These were not simply production or distribution companies but rather "entertainment bureaus" responsible for booking up suitable lectures and plays. Notes from the Ohio Klan in 1923–24 show how organized the entertainment programs were throughout the state. One of the notes states that "the entertainment bureau will have two dramatic companies for the winter season." These were to be "clean, wholesome comedy-dramas" that must be recommended by the state office. The "actors must be high class and their morals above criticism." The note again responded to these same concerns regarding film morality, as the entertainment bureau differentiated its plays from the perceived foreign and immoral productions regularly presented.[117] While film was not considered within the bureau's official release in Ohio, it operated alongside these other forms of media and was used by the Klan in much the same way.

The entertainment bureau catered for three different types of meeting: open, invitational, and closed. The extent to which local Klan groups used film at invitational and closed meetings varied (and is naturally harder to ascertain), but certainly local Klan groups did present short educational pictures within their Klaverns. This is partly evident through Klan correspondence. The WKKK in Indiana contacted the National Board of Review, which compiled lists of suitable films "for church use, school use etc.," asking for information and for pamphlets such as "the Best Motion Pictures on Americanism" (*The Face at Your Window* received an honorable mention).[118] A telegram from Ross N. Lammott, the Kligripp of Klan Number 60 Richmond, Indiana, to the Indiana University Visual Institution in May 1924 requested that they "send something for Saturday," suggesting that the Klan had an ongoing relationship with the bureau.[119] Klan newspapers also advertised some of the suitable independent producers and film exchanges, such as the Scenic Film Corporation in Atlanta, which produced "scenic, educational and commercial motion pictures." The records of the Fort Wayne Klan contain a catalogue for the Chicago-based Pilgrim Photoplay Exchange, which distributed films to churches, schools, lodges, "and all non-theatrical institutions where clean and highly censored pictures are appreciated."[120] Its records also include a film catalogue from the Bureau of Visual Instruction at Indiana University, which provided one-reel government films and a collection of patriotic shorts.[121] While the engagement of local Klan groups with these libraries and distributors highlights the presence of film at Klan meetings, it also reveals a notable lack of any central film rental body, explicitly serving the numerous Klan groups now using film.

The open meetings included large outdoor Klan picnics, public speeches or Klantauquas, and on occasion included a film program. For example, in June 1924 "The super-Klan film" *The Traitor Within* played as part of a big open-air demonstration at a racetrack in Plainfield, Illinois. The program also included "speaking, music, entertainment, and, of course, the naturalization of scores of this community's best men and women." A month later, the Klans of Wisconsin, Michigan, Indiana, and Illinois organized a screening of *The Traitor Within* at a "monster picnic" in the Klan Park in Racine, Wisconsin. The films were contextualized by live initiations and spectacular displays. On this occasion, the event also included Klan bands, clowns, acrobatic stunts, an aerial circus, and a fireworks display with "floating Klan crosses."[122] The Jackson County Klan in Indiana intended to show *The Fifth Horseman* at a large gathering in Maquoketa in 1925, although the screening was cancelled after the film and apparatus got stuck "somewhere in the Iowa mud" after terrible weather.[123]

In an attempt to organize this traveling circuit of Klan performers and outdoor entertainment, Charles Palmer, the head of the Klan in Illinois, established the Klantauqua in 1924. Palmer explained in *Variety* that "the Klantauquas were originated with the idea of bringing before the public the order of the K.K.K. We discovered early that to do this we had to supply clean and legitimate entertainment." Palmer used popular, established acts to attract people to the event before Klan speakers, often ministers, would attempt to recruit new members by handing out cards at the end of shows.[124] The Klantauqua was an unashamed attempt to exploit the burgeoning market of Chautauquas. Founded in 1874 as a form of adult education, the Chautauquas reached their peak in the early 1920s, bringing lectures, plays, music, and movies to audiences over a few days. By this point, Charlotte Canning estimates that circuit Chautauqua performers and lecturers appeared each year in up to 9,000 communities in forty-five states to audiences totaling between 9 and 20 million. Famously described by Theodore Roosevelt as "the most American thing in America," this form of mass culture, spreading and consolidating American values beyond the major cities, held an inevitable appeal for the Klan.[125]

By July 1924 *Variety* was reporting on the "phenomenal success" of the Klantauquas throughout Illinois, Indiana, and Iowa. These events closely followed the Chautauqua model, but also consolidated the kinds of outdoor spectacles – which invariably concluded with fireworks, Klan displays, and initiation ceremonies – regularly put on by Klan groups. The Klantauquas utilized Klan talent and help – Klansmen even helped set up the tents and put speakers up in their homes – to minimize admission prices and crucially sought to attract the same "patriotic" (but not explicitly Klan) market as the Chautauquas.[126] Palmer's project highlights the Klan's efforts to exploit existing American entertainment networks, using its considerable influence within the traveling show and employing established entertainment acts to attract and instruct potential new members.

Many of the acts or plays booked for Klan events had no discernible connection with the group, but rather followed the bureau's remit of offering "clean wholesome comedy-dramas." An example here is the comedy play for women's clubs, "Clubbing a Husband," which was put on by The Ladies of Foster Memorial Church at a Youngstown Klavern in 1925. Larger Klaverns seated thousands, functioning as major community auditoriums that presented Klan plays, such as *Safety First,* in Akron, as well as popular entertainment acts. Klan groups also used outdoor Klan parks for regular screenings of "suitable" pictures. After the Red Bank and Long Branch Klans bought the Elkwood Klan Park in New Jersey in 1924, they announced plans to put on a picture show twice a week during the summer.[127]

Music formed an integral part of the Klan's entertainment, with the Ohio bureau advising that "at least two musical companies of high class" should be kept on the books. The Chicago Klan claimed in 1924 to have the world's largest band of six hundred pieces as Klan bands emerged all over the country, playing the many Klan songs advertised for sale by "patriotic" publishing houses in the pages of Klan newspapers.[128] These bands would often provide musical accompaniment for meetings, lectures, and, on occasion, film screenings. Minstrel shows were particularly popular, judging by the plethora of advertisements found in the Klan press. These included a big minstrel show presented by the American Glee Club for three nights in Indiana in 1924 "under the auspices of the Ku Klux Klan at the Klan park," which was also staged in Ohio two months later. The Fort Worth Klan was rehearsing for a minstrel show in Texas when their 4,000-seat Klavern burned down in 1924.[129]

Of more direct interest are the numerous plays produced by Klan groups during this period. As with the films, these featured in both theatrical and non-theatrical venues, appearing at Klan gatherings and in Klaverns and also again in local community halls and schools. One of the most widely presented and enduring was James H. Hull's *The Awakening*, set in the Reconstruction era, which reportedly took its direct "inspiration" from Griffith's *The Birth of a Nation*. The play was produced for the Beaumont Klan No. 7 in Texas, where it initially played to capacity for six nights in May 1924, gaining the local Klan a reported net profit of $10,000. Other local Klan groups soon began negotiating with James Hull to bring the play to their community, with the Dick Dowling Klan No. 25 and the Women of the Ku Klux Klan next presenting the play at The Elks Theatre in Port Arthur in June.[130] Reports and photographs from these initial productions attest to both the scale and local involvement within the show, while the local press in Port Arthur reported that the entire cast of three hundred and twenty was selected locally. By the time the play reached Dallas under the auspices of the "women of the Klan and Klan No.66 of Dallas," the cast had swelled to 517, including a dancing chorus of 150 girls and boys.[131]

A photograph from the production in Port Arthur shows a row of young schoolgirls dressed in versions of the Klan costume – white knee-length socks, white skirts, white pointed hats, uncovered faces – flanked on stage by up to 100 local men and women in full regalia (fig. 3.8). The play reportedly played to 25,000 people over twenty nights in Beaumont and Port Arthur; in displaying its audience on the stage, or at least their friends and relatives, the play mirrored commercial devices used in the Klan's film productions.[132] This local involvement also, of course, served to legitimize the Klan and incorporate these targeted populations, such as schoolchildren and women, within the local group. These moves were further strengthened when *The Awakening* played in school venues. For example, the local Klan sponsored the show at the high school auditorium in Charleston in 1927, with rehearsals taking place in the junior high school gymnasium. Similarly, when *The Birth of a Klansmen* was

3.8. Encouraging a next generation of Klansmen and women through a performance of "The Awakening" at Port Arthur in June 1925. Photographic Print, Library of Congress Prints and Photographs Division, LC-USZ62–38118.

presented at Massillon in February 1925, it was sponsored by the junior organ of the Franklin County Klan.[133]

These plays both revealed and furthered the Klan's imbrication within local communities. Craig Fox, in his valuable account of the Klan in Michigan, notes the "remarkably mainstream Klan social scene" within the state, as the entertainment offered under the Klan banner was "barely distinct from already popular and mainstream entertainment forms in the non-Klan world."[134] This was evident in the Klan-sponsored staging of *The Awakening*, which embraced the local variety show and then framed it within the narrative of *The Birth of a Nation*. This was not simply a reconstruction of Griffith's Reconstruction tale; rather, it contained twenty scenes – from blackface comedy to follies-style dance numbers – within what an official program described as "a musical patriotic, dramatic spectacular extravaganza."[135] Later described as the "dramatic version of The Birth of a Nation," the play directly funded ongoing Klan activities. When it played at the Academy Theatre in Richmond in 1926, drawing local talent "from every section of the city" to fill its cast of 500, the proceeds went toward the construction of a new local Klavern.[136]

It is hardly surprising that theatrical producers and Klansmen alike should look to bring the inherently theatrical performance and displays of the modern Klan onto the stage or that they should use local Klansmen to authenticate their productions. A number of plays even incorporated "genuine" Klan ceremonies within the final act. *The Mysterious Way*, "a powerful lesson in Klancraft," concluded with Kleagles in full regalia performing Klan rites onstage. Initially presented at the Lyceum Theatre in St. Joseph, Missouri, by the local Klan in 1923, the play was still appearing in 1925 in theaters in, amongst other places, Nebraska and Kansas. On each occasion it was sponsored by local Klan groups, but, with its theatrical exhibition and tagline "Know the Truth," the play also targeted non-Klansmen.[137] Klan groups adopted a similar tack when showing *The Martyred Klansman,* asking, "Is the Klan friend or Foe? See the answer in The Martyred Klansman."[138] Originally presented by members of the Marion Klan on a farm near Meeker as part of a statewide event, this "thrilling patriotic drama" that taught "the mission of the Klan" also played in theaters and at community venues, such as the McKinley High School auditorium.[139] In reporting a forthcoming staging of the play in 1925, *The Protestant Home Journal* suggested that "not only should Klansmen see this play but every person in the county should be given the opportunity to see it and therefore be made a better citizen."[140] Craig Fox notes that in Michigan, state headquarters offered scripts of Klan plays, such as "The Crucible," to local chapters, which they could then perform in order to educate "the general public" in Klan affairs. These plays circulated around the state and were performed as part of the Klan's citizenship process, whether directly revealing the initiation or conversion of the Klansman or instructing audience members in how to become a Klan-defined "better citizen."[141]

In bringing these plays to local communities and finding an audience for them, the Klan utilized its existing networks. When *The Light,* which was promoted as showing the Klan in its "true light," performed poorly in Detroit, a call for financial aid "through all the Klan chapters" provided a backer to bring the play to Indianapolis. *Variety* noted the publicity measures now used, as two Klan lecturers acted as "advance men," exploiting the show at each meeting and securing support from local Klansmen, while thirty men and women in each town acted as "supers."[142] What is most striking in Indianapolis is that *The Light* played at the Lincoln Square theater, immediately after a run of *The Fifth Horseman*. This theater had very recently come under new management, and both events were advertised in the *Fiery Cross*.[143] The theater certainly appeared to be catering to a Klan audience and, while it is not clear whether the proprietor or exhibitor had any direct Klan affiliation, by now a number of cinemas were either taken over directly by Klan interests or were actively fostering a Klan audience.

"KOOL, KOZY, KLEAN": KLAN CINEMAS

In October 1923, the Urbana, Illinois, Klan completed a deal, worth a reported $60,000, to buy the Illinois Theatre, which would operate as a Klavern and as Klan headquarters. A report in *Imperial Night-Hawk* explained that the theater "will be operated under the management of Protestant Americans and a number of sterling attractions have already been booked." The paper then reiterated that the theater was under Protestant control, a response to the Klan's broad concerns about the foreign control of the entertainment industry, while the operating company, Zenith Amusement Company, explained that only "shows of respectability and sports that are clean will be presented to the public." Amongst the first acts booked was a company of mystics and vaudeville acts, "brim full of amusing klimaxes and klean, klever komedy that you can take your kid sister to see." The theater would house the Klan's entertainment programs, whether showing a "big 100% minstrel show," high school glee clubs, an evangelist by the name of Holzer – described as "the converted Jew" – or national Klan speakers. It would also invite local figures, such as the governor, and would be rented out to other religious and patriotic groups. As a Klan auditorium between October 1923 and April 1927 (when it burned to the ground), the Illinois Theatre provided a venue for

Klan events and meetings but also allowed the Klan to operate locally as a moral purveyor of American entertainment.[144]

The Illinois Theatre is symptomatic of a desire on the part of Klan groups to buy and control legitimate entertainment sites, of which there are numerous examples. The *Indiana Citizens' Post*, an anti-Klan paper, reported in 1924 that "the Grand Theatre on Market Street [in Logansport] is losing a good percentage of its patrons since it has become known as a Kluxer joint."[145] Similarly, there were theaters, like the Alhambra in Decatur, that frequently showed "Klan" films, while others used the Klan press to advertise. The Classic Theatre in Elwood, a site of Klan plays, films, and entertainers, posted regular notices in the *Fiery Cross*, encouraging readers to visit "if you want to see GOOD PICTURES," while *Searchlight* advertised and posted reviews for the Howard Theatre and the Rialto in Atlanta.[146] An advertisement for *When Knighthood Was in Flower*, a Marion Davies film funded by William Hearst with no discernible Klan link, directly targeted Klansmen by adapting its publicity materials for the Klan press. A poster for a two-week screening at the Rialto now proclaimed:

> Knights were bold in days of Old,
> And a man was really a man.
> That spirit is kept alive today
> By Knights of the Ku Klux Klan.[147]

The Klan was embedded in specific local communities, particularly in Indiana, Ohio, and Illinois, and so while national distributors could afford to overlook (if not isolate or upset) Klan audiences in localized pockets of the country, the Klan supporter was an essential part of the film audience. When the secretary of the WKKK in Indiana wrote to the National Board of Review in 1925 asking for information about suitable films, she claimed that "in fact the majority of the picture show attendance [in Indiana] is from our Orders."[148] In an Indiana town such as Noblesville, where, as Allen Safianow has argued, a quarter to a third of all native-born white males of its population of 5,000 were Klansmen, the group provided an influential core audience, moreover, one that defined itself primarily through its Klan affiliations.[149] Exhibitors here chased the Klan audience and established their sites as Klan venues. The history of exhibition in the town in the early 1920s serves as a microcosm of the Klan's own public rise and fall, a fall that would play out most dramatically in a Noblesville courtroom in 1925.

The fortunes of the Klan in Indiana are most closely aligned with one man, David Stephenson. After his arrival in Indianapolis in 1922, Stephenson would coordinate a mass recruitment drive – backed by his own Klan paper, the *Fiery Cross* – bringing the state 100,000 new members within a year. Within this context, Klan pictures appeared more regularly and prominently within the town. In November 1922, the *Noblesville Daily Ledger* contained a large advertisement for *The Mysterious Eyes of the Ku Klux Klan,* showing at the Opera House. Under the heading "Ku Klux Klan Movie Monday Night," the *Ledger* reported that the theater's manager, C. E. McConaughy, had covered the theater with branches and leaves and erected a "fiery cross, neatly arranged with electric lights" on the balcony. The success of the film across three screenings prompted the *Ledger* to conclude that "there must be a large number of the Ku Klux Klan in this locality . . . or crowds must have flocked there through curiosity." The paper further suggested that, while Klansmen did not reveal themselves during the screenings, "the order seems to have an enormous following here."[150]

A couple of months later, in February 1923, the Opera House screened *One Clear Call,* with the words "Night Riders!" and "Knights of the Ku Klux Klan" highlighted alongside large pictures of riding Klansmen. The theater again appeared to be targeting local Klansmen, both in its artwork and its program, which included on the same bill "Fox News – The All American Pictorial Review."[151] Significantly, this was not a small independent picture house, but a three-story building, bought in July 1922 by the prominent Indiana exhibitor Frank Rembusch. The theater was considered a social center within Noblesville, which makes its perceived Klan allegiance all the more significant for the local community.

In June 1923, McConaughy, the former manager of the Opera House, opened a new picture house in Noblesville, and also served as one of three directors for the recently incorporated American Amusement Company, the new theater's parent company. Initial reports described the theater as "owned and controlled by home people," and advertisements noted that it was "Hamilton County's own," aligned with local educational, religious, and patriotic groups. Management announced that there would be no matinees on Wednesday afternoons because local Sunday school organizations played baseball games at that time. Reports further noted the modern seats, excellent ventilation, and careful "accommodation of the ladies," all of which immediately differentiated the theater from the supposedly foreign-controlled, unsafe, and morally suspect ones that the Klan so strongly opposed.[152]

The name for the new venue, the American Theatre, was chosen to emphasize its patriotic ideals. Advertising displayed an American flag draped through the A of "American" and, from the outset, directly targeted its Klan clientele. Only four days after the opening, a poster for that night's screenings noted that "you can see a complete show before or after the K.K.K. parade tonight." The theater's Klan affiliation became even more apparent when it showed *Birth* at the start of September. The film was advertised as "the first 100% American photoplay ever produced," and as a film "endorsed by all Klansmen, ministers, schools, etc." The advertisement also stated that "all Klansmen and all interested in the Ku Klux Klan are urged to see this picture," with Civil War veterans admitted without charge.[153]

The Birth of a Nation had played at the Opera House a few weeks earlier, and a rivalry between McConaughy's present and previous establishments was already evident. The American advertised its forthcoming appearance of *Birth* during the film's run at the Opera House. In response, the Opera House warned viewers: "Don't be deceived for this is the last appearance of the real 'Birth of a Nation,'" before the American Theatre retaliated with an advertisement reaffirming that *Birth* "will positively be shown here." A few days later, the Opera House countered with the warning that "you may be disappointed if you don't see it now." The dialogue between the two theaters in the local press illustrates the unique attraction of *Birth* for theaters in areas with a strong Klan following, and the importance of the Klan audience within the town. As the theaters tussled over the same cinemagoers and looked to nurture a loyal, regular clientele, the venues sought to define more clearly their values to the community.[154]

After gaining new owners in November 1923, the Opera House advertised itself as "Clean! Courteous! Comfortable!" and "the theater of class and tranquility." The American Theatre responded with a large advertisement in which McConaughy listed a series of "facts" about his theater, asking, "Did you know the American Theatre is owned by American citizens only, all over Hamilton County?" McConaughy was again responding to the Klan's criticisms of film and film exhibition, seeking clean pictures in a space owned and controlled by local Americans. The theater presented itself, like the Klan, as an underdog in direct opposition to the controlling Jewish and Catholic influences infiltrating America: "At a time when odds were against us and clean amusement furnished by Americans only was almost improbable, the present American Theatre management worried and worked day and night till the apparently impossible was accomplished for you and yours." McConaughy signed the statement "Americanly yours."[155]

As the dispute between the theaters intensified, the new owners of the Opera House, the Kenworthy brothers, resorted to offering a $1,000 reward in a January edition of the *Ledger* "for the person or persons who are circulating the report, and have any proof what ever that the Wild Opera House still belongs to, or is any way controlled by, F. J. Rembusch."[156] It is unclear who was spreading this rumor (and indeed why), but the direct mode of address adopted by theater managers in the local press highlights the stakes in Noblesville, where local advertisements were not simply promoting individual films but were rather looking to build and inculcate a strong, loyal audience, one defined by its political and religious values. McConaughy often used advertisements to write directly to his patrons. "This is our first opportunity," he wrote in November 1923, "to acknowledge our appreciation of the part you have played in making The American Theatre, 'Hamilton County's own,' the success it is." The success of the theater was clearly not measured in financial terms, as McConaughy himself admitted that it was losing money and would have to raise prices.[157]

The American Theatre sought to target and nurture an audience of Klansmen, yet this remained a problematic approach even in such a strong Klan area. It not only risked isolating other sections of the community, but also potentially compromised the types of popular entertainment that the venue could show. An advertisement for The American in November 1923 had explained the theater's policy in selecting pictures: "Every production is screened in advance of public showing and all improper scenes (if any) are cut out."[158] The American responded to the Klan's criticisms of film morality, often favoring pictures by clean-cut American stars like Hoot Gibson, who provided "Blazing Red-Blooded Double-Barreled Action!" Yet, for all its idealism, the American evidently concluded that paying audiences were still more likely to watch a Paramount drama and Pola Negri than another film about flag etiquette. The theater had screened *Manslaughter*, "the 10 reel De Mille Paramount Special" in October 1923, and followed this with Gloria Swanson in *Her Gilded Cage*. By July 1924 it was showing Negri in *Shadows of Paris* and advertising itself as "the home of Paramount and First National Pictures," despite the Klan's simultaneous, well-publicized criticisms of Paramount. In its quest for audiences, the theater justified its use of Negri by now branding the film "an All-American production with a foreign flavor." Once more, the issue of national identity was inherent in both the Klan's criticism and use of film.[159]

Alongside these productions, The American also increasingly presented Klan pictures and entertainers. In October 1923, it showed "Klan-O-Grams," 1,000 feet of night scenes of recent parades and naturalizations within the state. The advertisements responded and testified to the Klan's embedded legitimacy within the local community, stating, "You owe yourself and your family this treat." Significantly, these pictures were shown alongside footage of the County's centennial celebrations, further consolidating the Klan's position within the county's history.[160]

In the early part of 1924, The American showed both *The Traitor Within* and *The Toll of Justice*. The three-day run of *The Traitor Within* in January served as a fundraiser for the charity fund of the Hamilton County Klan and was featured as part of a broader Klan program, which included Mark Bills singing the Klan anthem, "The Old Rugged Cross," and a two-reel comedy entitled *Uncle Sam*. Advertisements for *The Traitor Within* emphasized that it was "produced for, owned and controlled by Protestants," with "produced for" highlighting that the film, like the American Theatre, was catering exclusively for a Protestant American (Klan) audience.[161] When The American showed *The Toll of Justice*, "the one picture every red blooded American should see" (fig. 3.9), in April, its advertisements positively called out to Klansmen, exclaiming in bold

3.9. *The Toll of Justice* at the Klan-owned American Theatre, *Noblesville Daily Ledger*, 24 April 1924, 6.

capital letters, "Come on – All you Americans. This is Your Picture."[162] Through these films, the theater specifically targeted the local Klan community, but, in noting that "there was always a good program," it sought to present itself as a curator of morally sound, American film, establishing a loyal audience of Klansmen who would return even when the theater did not show the Klan on-screen.

The American Theatre would undergo a series of changes in ownership and management in 1924, but it remained a strongly pro-Klan venue. In the spring, R. E. Thompson bought a controlling interest in the theater, seemingly managing it himself for a few months, before he chose L. G. Heiny, the chairman of the Republican County Central Committee but a man with no apparent experience in film, to take over as manager.[163] The American's Klan affiliations became even more pronounced during the summer. In August, the theater advertised itself as "Unquestionably 100 per cent," and began using its advertisements to present patriotic Klan addresses. One advertisement, appearing across the top of the page, asked, "How Strong is America? Never in World's History, On Foreign Lands or Seas, was Uncle Sam's Glory thrust down by any creed. Although the tide may ruffle, ships may drift astray, we'll carry her to the highest peak and place her there to stay."[164] A further lengthy advertisement began, "To do a thing tomorrow, that should be done today, is not a pure bred Yankee, is what the people say." In bold at the foot of the rhyme were the words "To do a thing and see it through is true Yankee Red, White and Blue – American 100%."[165] The advertisements were presenting an ideology both for the theater and its audience. The theater responded to anxieties around film morality by presenting itself as a moral purveyor of "clean pictures," countered fears of "foreign" controlled exhibition sites by emphasizing that it was an American establishment instructing through film, and addressed concerns about the cinema buildings themselves by rearticulating a space of darkness and moral sin as a light, clean, safe area where "seats are new and comfortable." These related points were most succinctly articulated in advertisements in the *Noblesville Daily Ledger* during the summer of 1924, which used the familiar three Ks to describe the American as "Kool, Kozy and Klean."[166]

Despite the strength of Klan support within Noblesville and Hamilton County as a whole, within a month of adopting its more virulently pro-Klan advertisements the American Theatre closed. The *Ledger* reported that the theater had "not been a paying proposition for some time," and while the theater did reopen a month later as the Palace Theatre, it was only briefly mentioned in a very small advertisement that it was the "previous American."[167] Significantly, its first advertisement promoted a forthcoming screening of *Birth* – still an enormous attraction within Klan heartlands – but the film was now described as the "greatest historical play ever produced" without any direct mention of the Klan. The theater no longer adopted the aggressive and blatantly pro-Klan policy of its predecessor, and by 1926 there was no listing at all in the city directory for 860 Logan Street, the former home of the American Theatre.[168]

THE DEMISE

In August 1924, just a few weeks before The American closed, Miafa Pictures Co., the group responsible for *The Toll of Justice*, was placed in receivership after it was revealed that various people employed in the picture's production were still awaiting payment.[169] Cavalier had, it seems, already met a similar fate, while within six months Charles Palmer was abruptly cancelling his plans for a season of Klantauquas.

On the face of it, the collective failing of these Klan enterprises – production companies, exhibition sites, and entertainment networks – might reveal and respond to a decline in Klan support, most dramatically played out in Noblesville where Klan leader David Stephenson was tried and convicted for the manslaughter of Madge Oberholtzer in 1925. The case against Stephenson – a tale of drink, kidnap, and rape that led to the victim's suicide – provided the single most damning unmasking of the Klan's idealism and leadership, a moment widely recognized as the beginning of the end for the modern Klan. Significantly, the media-savvy Stephenson was directly involved in many of these film enterprises, inviting a more explicit connection between his scandal and the fortunes of the Klan's media operations.

In the Indiana Supreme Court case against Stephenson, it was revealed that he was the major shareholder in Cavalier, while his conviction was pronounced less than a mile from the defunct site of the "Kool, Kozy, Klean" American Theatre.[170] The scandal surrounding Stephenson was also credited as a principal factor behind the cancellation of the Klantauquas in 1925. As late as January 1925, Charles Palmer was planning an ambitious countrywide circuit for the year, but by April the whole project was called off, with Klan sources claiming that the "chief trouble" was the "number of higher-up officials who have become involved in scandal." These scandals not only undermined Klan support, but also often made the group retreat from a public platform.[171]

While scandal had similarly derailed the Klan's initial film enterprise in 1921, and certainly accelerated the Klan's demise in the mid-1920s, most of these Klan operations were already defunct before Stephenson's moral bypass became front-page news. When Roscoe Carpenter was called to testify at Stephenson's trial in 1925, he claimed to be president of Cavalier, yet by this point Cavalier was no longer operating and Carpenter was listed in the city directory as the president of a new company, the Twentieth Century Motion Picture Company of Indiana. The closure of these short-lived Klan companies, in most cases predating the Stephenson scandal, also testify to the wider challenges facing independent film enterprises after the war. What is of more immediate interest here is what happened next, the legacies and afterlives of these Klan companies.[172]

Rather than abandoning film after their somewhat chastening experience with *The Traitor Within,* many of the figures from Cavalier would reconvene with the Twentieth Century Motion Picture Company. Alongside Carpenter was Charles Lewis Fowler, the former president of Cavalier, now serving as vice president of the new company. An article in the *Indianapolis Star* in the summer of 1925 introduced another familiar figure, Edward Young Clarke – a man "credited with obtaining 3,000,000 members" for the Klan – as the "guiding head" of the enterprise. The new enterprise deviated from Cavalier by offering "motion picture training and scenario writing at $16 a membership." The company was not directly affiliated with the Klan, but in bringing together familiar Klan figures – leaders, educators, and lecturers – it attempted once more to exploit commercially the burgeoning film market and to confront the dominant film powers. "I rocked the nation with the reorganization of the Ku Klux Klan," Clarke explained, "and our enterprise will rock the motion picture world. We will be in direct competition with the biggest motion picture companies in the world."[173]

Yet the plans also revealed lessons learned, or at least addressed some of the earlier failings of the Klan film enterprises. While announcing plans to produce "ten master motion pictures," Clarke now considered how and where these pictures would be shown. His plans to set up three hundred clubs – "centers of movie fan groups" – throughout the country, which would provide a foothold into "first-run cities," marked an attempt to create a distribution and exhibition network for its films. With this in mind, Clarke also discussed plans to build a 10,000-seat venue in Indianapolis and to establish a Florida Land Development Company, which would acquire 225,000 acres of West Florida land on which to construct a $5 million studio.[174]

Clarke's interest in film as a pedagogical tool was driven, like the Klan itself, by a heady mix of high idealism and materialism, and, more specifically, by a desire to commercialize this idealism. In this instance, Clarke appeared to use this short-lived film company to boost his own bank balance; a series of lawsuits subsequently alleged that he had "misappropriated $200,000 of the corporation funds."[175]

His next move, announced at the start of 1926, reveals the opportunism of the Klan's leadership and the splintering of Klan policies and personnel. Acknowledging the declining reputation of the Klan, Clarke now formed his own fundamentalist secret society, one that responded to the latest Protestant fear, Darwinism. In attempting to exploit the nationwide publicity generated by the recent Scopes "monkey" trial in Tennessee – Clarke even hired the presiding judge from the trial, John Raulston, to lecture for the group – Clarke planned an elaborate nationwide drive, with chapters in every major city, to cleanse American culture and "rebuild in the minds of our children the religion of our fathers." Clarke's plans generated publicity from the outset, aided no doubt by a window display at the Atlanta headquarters of the Supreme Kingdom (Castle No. 1), which contained a live monkey beneath a sign reading, "He may be your Grandfather – but not ours!"[176]

In setting up this new secret society, Clarke sought to claim members directly from the Klan. "One of the requirements of the membership," he stated in 1926, "will be 100% Americanism," before clarifying that the new order would not be "openly hostile" against any race or creed. Dismissing the possibility of Klan regeneration – "The public doesn't forget the crimes of a convicted murderer" – Clarke pointedly admitted that he was looking to "embody the good points" of the Klan in his new order, but to eliminate all its "mistakes and blunders."[177] With the Klan increasingly discredited and marginalized, Clarke sought to pick off its members, writing in the Supreme Kingdom's official publication, *Dynamite,* of his aims to add four million members to his group and to light bonfires (minus the crosses) throughout the country, "devouring those damnable and detestable books of evolution."[178] Clarke reworked the goals, pedagogical rhetoric, and structure of the Klan, giving himself the title "Supreme Sovereign," and overseeing a governing body of fourteen "senators." A central figure in launching the Kingdom in Atlanta in January 1926 was the veteran of Klan media enterprises, Roscoe Carpenter. One of his immediate tasks was to establish a radio station for the group, at a reported cost of $500,000. This move, to "carry to the world the fight against the Darwin Theory," was reported in the *Oakland Tribune* under the improbable headline, "Secret Society Plans to Fight Apes by Radio."[179]

Klan groups had often used radio before. The Fort Worth Klan group No. 101, for example, had presented a regular Klan radio program in 1923, and radio station KFKB in Kansas offered a "clean and wholesome" program featuring Klan musicians in 1924. Reports in 1925 had suggested that the Klan leadership was seeking broadcasting licenses from the Department of Commerce for a major chain of stations, while the Fellowship Forum contacted Klaverns and received support from Klan groups for its own station, billing itself as "the national voice for Protestant fraternal America."[180] This station was, it explained, built by "Protestant money for broadcasting Protestant and fraternal messages throughout the country."[181] Perhaps in light of his experiences with film, Clarke now foregrounded radio within The Supreme Kingdom, even appointing a "Minister of radio and silent drama." The new radio station would again reveal the dichotomy between reactionary content and modern method, so apparent in the Klan's film enterprises. "There will be no jazz programs," Clarke explained. "We will broadcast the old hymns."[182]

Clarke's foray into religious fundamentalism ended in the same way as many of his other enterprises: in scandal, with Clarke accused of embezzling two-thirds of every $12.50 membership for himself.[183] While Clarke represents the hypocrisy and public failings of the Klan's leadership, his emphasis on publicity and modern media – from his first attempt to produce a Klan film in 1921 to his ambitious radio plans in 1926 – attests to the group's widespread, varied, and often visionary use of modern media. Yet while the Klan looked to use film to recruit new members and, beyond this, to impose its values on American society, so too did those most threatened by the Klan. African American, Jewish, and Catholic groups would also turn to film in their efforts to challenge and discredit this emerging power, attempting to relocate the discursive battle onto the screen. In so doing, they were often confronted by the same restrictions and challenges that stymied the Klan's own short-lived film enterprises.

IN RESPONSE

In late 1921, less than a month after the *New York World* uncovered Clarke's initial proposal for *Yesterday, Today and Forever, Variety* revealed plans for an "anti-Klan" picture, based on the *World's* recent Klan exposé. The film's producer, Mark Dintenfass, sent a postcard to a thousand exhibitors and fifty exchanges "asking the prospective chances for a peaceful presentation of the Ku Klux subject in their territory." The replies contained a "surprising number" of refusals and a notable lack of demand from exhibitors, fearful of the censorship and public agitation that such a production would bring.[184]

The following year, when John W. Noble directed *The Hooded Mob*, a film "that pans the entire Klan," *Variety* again reported that "no-one seems anxious to handle the picture" and that, despite the evident commercial potential of the subject, popular priced theaters were reluctant to take the film on.[185] Noble had previously been credited with the ambitious but ill-fated 1918 African American response to *The Birth of a Nation, The Birth of a Race,* and now found his latest response blocked not only by exhibitor resistance but by state censors. Now titled *After Dark*, the film was denied a license in New York State in May 1923. According to the license record, the film featured a "law abiding, prosperous citizen of a community, [who] for no reason that the story shows is persecuted by an organization of men wearing hoods and masks." Klan violence was now motivated by religion, as the law-abiding citizen is abducted and beaten by the hooded men because "he is of another faith." Despite the addition of an ending declaring that all that had gone before was a dream, there is no evidence that *After Dark* was ever shown publicly.[186]

Emerging Catholic production companies that sought to confront the Klan through film faced similar obstacles. In 1922, Creston Feature Pictures produced *Knight of the Eucharist*. Creston, which advertised itself as "a great Catholic enterprise," set out to combat "forces of evil which aim to destroy our religious liberties," and chief amongst these forces was the Klan. Again, the New York censors intervened, objecting firstly to the language offered – "accusations are made against the characters of members of the Ku Klux Klan and their children, in language that would necessarily be eliminated from screen" – and then, most significantly in light of *Birth*, to a feared public response to the Klan image. "Under certain circumstances, and in certain localities," the report concluded, the film "might 'incite to crime.'" The potential response of the politically active modern Klan made a critical presentation of the group dangerous, as the social impact of *Birth* effectively crushed the possibility of a response on film. When the film was rejected again a few months later, the censors advised the elimination of twenty-two subtitles. These included a number of lines spoken by the Klansmen, such as "You lie. You are a foreigner with a foreign religion and you shall pay the penalty"; "It is up to us to do something before the Jews and Catholics run the earth"; and "I hate you like hell – and all your filthy crew. You are worse than the cursed Jews." Six additional scenes were also cut, but this was still not enough to save the film, which was once again rejected in November 1923 when Hopp Hadley presented it under the new title *The Mask of the Ku Klux Klan*. The censors now determined that "the entire subject is such that it would arouse antagonism against a certain class of people."[187]

The most noted and prolonged response to the Klan came from the African American filmmaker Oscar Micheaux. Micheaux sought to challenge the dominant formal conventions of American cinema in order to question its ruling ideologies. He responded directly to *Birth*, most notably in *Within Our Gates*, which, in showing a white man's attack on African American womanhood, pointedly reversed the racial roles in Griffith's film. His next film, *The Symbol of the Unconquered: A Story of the Ku Klux Klan*, provided his most direct assault on the Klan and confronted *Birth* not only on-screen but also in its publicity. The familiar image of a Klansman on horseback was accompanied by the tagline, "See The ΚΚΚ in action and their annihilation."[188] The Klan reappeared across his work. Charlene Regester has argued that the New York commission's "principal cause" for rejecting his 1924 film, *A Son of Satan*, might have been the film's "uncomplimentary portrayal of the Ku Klux Klan." The commission objected to the scenes of "masked men becoming intoxicated" and the "killing of the leader of the hooded organization."[189] This highlights a significant legacy of *Birth*, with any attempts to respond to Griffith's polemic on-screen, partially as a result of the African American response to *Birth*, rejected either by censors or exhibitors. *Within Our Gates*, for example, was initially banned in Chicago for fear of inciting a "further race riot." After a heavily edited version was released, a Chicago schoolteacher observed in a local African American paper that "had *Within Our Gates* been entirely banned, then should the press and pulpit of our group remain silent on oppression and injustice."[190] Yet, while a version of the film was eventually shown, the racial construction of the industry, and society at large, ensured that the "oppressed" voice remained unheard beyond its own racial group.

This brief mention of the anti-Klan films raises several points. The Klan's opponents often looked to use film in much the same way as the Klan. As noted in the previous chapter, the Knights of Columbus strongly opposed immoral productions, later forming the influential Legion of Decency, and they campaigned against films that they felt ridiculed the Catholic faith. Catholic newspapers advertised theaters or films that were sympathetic to the cause, while the group circulated films to local groups, organized non-theatrical film screenings, and arranged its own outdoor screenings, as when presenting "the great Americanization film" (and a favorite of the American Legion) *The Man without a Country* at Fairview Park in August 1923.[191]

In addition, all these groups responded to what they perceived as a misrepresentation of the Klan. This formed the basis for the narratives of both *The Traitor Within* and *The Toll of Justice*, which was intended to counteract "poisonous propaganda." Oscar Micheaux spent much of his career directly challenging Griffith's depiction of the Klan in *Birth*. *Knight of the Eucharist* sought to expose the violent actions of the modern Klan on the Catholic Church, and even *Armageddon*, a film proposed by a Klan group but never made, was intended as a response to Dixon's anti-Klan film, *The Traitor* (also never made). At one level, these films appear to be in dialogue, attempting to shape public attitudes toward the Klan. Yet by the 1920s these independent presentations appeared less capable of extending their influence beyond their existing supporters. Steven Ross, writing about the labor films produced before the war, presents the movies and mass culture as an "arena of struggle." He suggests that "groups outside the industry recognized the power of this new medium and turned out polemical films that addressed national debates over the domestic values and future direction of American society."[192] This was certainly an intention with these films, but the restrictions on distribution and exhibition ensured that they were rarely in dialogue and were more often isolated polemics, reinforcing the established ideological positions of its audiences.

The Toll of Justice and *The Traitor Within* – the latter advertised for distribution through the Klan press – played predominantly to Klansmen in areas with a strong Klan following, while *Knight of the Eucharist* ultimately played to specialist Catholic audiences in non-theatrical venues, appearing, for example, in March 1923 at the auditorium of the Sacred Heart cathedral school in Iowa.[193] Oscar Micheaux often traveled with his films, drumming up interest on lengthy tours, and he presented them almost exclusively within African American theaters.[194] While the Klan did find ways to connect beyond its existing members – if not through the film itself, then through the publicity surrounding it – the difficulties it faced in distributing and exhibiting its films were largely shared by its opponents. These difficulties were, to an extent, symptomatic of the challenges facing all independent producers after the war, but the topical and divisive subject matter clearly exacerbated this. The subject of the Klan – regardless of the ideological standpoint of the filmmaker – was now problematic for censors and exhibitors, fearful of the social impact of placing the Klan on-screen.

Yet while *Birth* had cemented the Klan's position as a divisive and controversial topic for film, it also simultaneously revealed – and continued to reveal – the almost unparalleled commercial and aesthetic power of the Klan on-screen. The Klan and its opponents may have struggled to negotiate this paradox to the satisfaction of censors, distributors, and exhibitors, but industry producers did work versions of the Klan onto mainstream screens. Between the wars, from the Klan's rebirth to its enforced disbandment, the Klan appeared in various guises, across periods, locations, and genres, from children's comedies to social problem films. The role and representation of the Klan on-screen would shift in response to changes in the film industry and to the Klan's own fluctuating position within American society. Indeed, while industry producers now foregrounded spectacle and largely attempted to eschew, and detach from, the political uses imagined by independent producers, the costume, politics, and function of the night riders would nevertheless be reworked and negotiated in the popular imagination through these screen appearances. As the industry faced mounting pressure from conservative reform groups, including the Klan, and was forced to defend and prove its "American" credentials, its articulation of the Klan on-screen became imbricated in these far wider debates over American national identity. The industry's response to the Klan, across its rise and fall, thus provides both a way of exploring the construction and renegotiation of dominant attitudes toward the group, and also a way of examining the place and function of the film industry within American society.

FOUR

On Mainstream Screens

THE FILM INDUSTRY'S RESPONSE TO THE KLAN

IN AUGUST 1928, LAMAR TROTTI, A FORMER REPORTER FOR THE *Atlanta Georgian* now working in the Public Relations Department of the MPPDA as an assistant to Jason Joy, wrote to MPPDA president Will Hays expressing his concerns about Howard Hughes's new film *The Mating Call*. Trotti's concerns, which centered on the appearance of a thinly disguised version of the Klan labeled "The Order," neatly encapsulated the film industry's conflicted position toward the Klan in the 1920s:

> I have one big thought about "*The Mating Call*" – that whatever we do is dangerous.
>
> As decent people, we can't be allied with a picture which accepts, or at least condones lawlessness as this one certainly does. As business people, we can't, probably, afford to alienate a large group of citizens who thrive on attacks.
>
> The Klan developed, not through its friends, but through its enemies. One Congressional investigation gave it more members than all the pamphlets, speeches and horse whippings ever launched by the order. If we did anything about this picture and it became known, probably they'd be a big increase in the sale of night shirts to guard against this "Catholic-Jew controlled industry." If we don't, we are like a man who while in a mob, protests he isn't of it, and yet stays on and does nothing to prevent its display of passion. . . .
>
> . . . It is too bad that when the backbone of that organization is about broken, that such a theme should be revived.[1]

While "decent people," in Trotti's words, would certainly not want to condone the actions of the Klan, the industry was equally wary (as "business people") of alienating the Klan's substantial and influential membership. Trotti recognized the impotency of the MPPDA on this matter and, through the example of the congressional hearings, highlighted the dangers of criticizing the Klan openly. Such criticism could provide publicity for the group, a platform for debate, and, most crucially, a direct threat that the Klan could use as evidence of the un-American influences dominating American cultural life. Trotti's reference, in quotes, to the "Catholic-Jew controlled industry" attests to an awareness within the filmmaking business of Klan discourses that continued to influence industry policy.

Even as late as 1928, the MPPDA was evidently wary of the Klan's influence, both institutionally and in local communities. Exhibitors were warned of the dangers of offending local Klan groups with *The Mating Call* – "if you are in a Ku Klux Klan territory you should first find out whether you should show it or not" – and still appeared to consider the potential Klan audience (a Texas exhibitor reported that "both Klux and anti-Klux can see this picture").[2] Hays's secretary, Carl Milliken, predicted a "good deal of legislative trouble" from the film, which would provide "very bad publicity" and give "impetus to the movement for censorship." The MPPDA clearly did not want the Klan represented on-screen, but neither did it want the controversy of removing the Klan from the screen. Milliken would warn against opposing the sound version of *The Birth of a Nation* in 1930, arguing that the film would not get much circulation "unless a controversy should develop."[3]

Throughout this period, the industry's response to the Klan sought to negotiate the tension between "decent people" and "business people," with the Klan's appearances on-screen shaped and dictated by the status, fortunes, and practices of both the Klan and the film industry. *The Mating Call* was initially banned in New York and Chicago and received cuts elsewhere. The Motion Picture Commission in New York instructed the producers at Paramount to "eliminate all views of the meeting of [the] hooded order." In particular, it objected to scenes of Klan violence – "men shown tied to [a] cross and beaten with [a] whip by [a] hooded man" – as well as its interrogation and unlawfulness. "Scenes of [a] masked hooded order unlawfully dispensing justice," the commission noted, "will incite to crime and tend to corrupt morals." Industrial regulation limited appearances of the Klan on-screen but also, significantly, determined how it should be featured in the 1920s.[4] Comparing the film to Rex Beach's 1927 source novel also highlights a medium-specific removal of racial targets and of direct references to the motives, morality, and function of the modern Klan. The result on-screen was often, somewhat paradoxically, a sympathetic (or at least uncritical), visually attractive, and morally ambiguous action group. In this process of depoliticizing the Klan, of making it an "acceptable" subject for the screen, producers and regulators often manufactured a more acceptable and moderate organization.

There are, however, significant shifts in the representation of the Klan across the interwar period. In his memorandum to Hays, Trotti lamented the timing of *The Mating Call*'s release, noting that by 1928 the Klan was "about broken." Trotti was fearful of any publicity that could revitalize the organization, but his comments also foresaw a shift in the industry's response to the Klan. This shift was partly a result of the Klan's declining influence but also of changes in the industry, which included the popularization of synchronized sound and the subsequent emergence of more adult-orientated genres in the 1930s.[5]

In the first three chapters, we have seen how the Klan used film and engaged with the industry after reemerging in 1915, whether as "textual poacher," protester, or producer. In this chapter the focus shifts to consider how the mainstream film industry, in turn, responded to the modern Klan across the organization's almost thirty-year history. By considering the industry's articulation of the Klan, on- and off-screen, across different moments – directly before the modern Klan's widespread reemergence in 1919, at the height of its influence in the 1920s, and, finally, in the late 1930s – this chapter explores film's role in the rise and fall of the Klan. In order to understand the ways in which these "mainstream" films revealed and, at times, shaped the history of the Klan, we return once more to Atlanta in 1915.

LOCATING THE KLAN IN THE 1910S: MARY PICKFORD AND THE FEMALE NIGHT RIDERS

In December 1915, as *The Birth of a Nation* continued its record-breaking run in Atlanta, a three-part drama presented by the Gene Gauntier Feature Players entitled *In the Clutches of the Ku Klux Klan* played in the city at the Victoria. Historians have often presented the picture as an edited version of *Birth* – indeed, *Birth's* producers sought an injunction to prevent its exhibition for this reason in 1916 – but Gauntier's version was released two years prior, in 1913.[6] Its reappearance and promotion in 1915 highlights an opportunistic desire on the part of producers and exhibitors to exploit the rising interest in the Klan after the release of Griffith's film. Yet while *Birth* reinvigorated the on-screen Klan – both visually and as a dramatic resolution in the popular chase film – the Klan also became acutely problematic, connected through its reception to contemporary racial politics. As a result, producers initially looked to historicize or relocate the Klan imagery on-screen, concealing Griffith's night riders in a myriad of organizations, including the Navy, American Legion, and even children's clubs.

An early example of this can be found in the 1916 historical epic *Joan the Woman*, which featured as villains "a Catholic bishop and hooded inquisitors resembling Klansmen."[7] The night-riding scenes in *The Flower of Faith* (1916), in which the riders plan to lynch a man wrongly accused of adultery, were widely compared in publicity to scenes in *Birth*, while *A Mormon Maid*, released in 1917 and advertised in Kansas as a "sequel to 'Birth of a Nation,'" featured an antebellum group of Mormon fighters, labeled "the avenging angels," who reviewers noted were dressed in the "mysterious garb of the Ku Klux Klan."[8] While the costume was safely distanced ideologically from Griffith's Klan, producers highlighted parallels in the film's titles, which explained that "this costume, but with a cross substantiated for the 'eye,' was later adopted by the Ku Klux Klan." Indeed, reviews suggested that the reuse of the Klan costume from *Birth* would provide "added interest" and, with "intelligent use" of the costume in advertisements, which often featured a robed rider on top of a horse, exhibitors could do "a lot of business."[9] Producers were clearly trying to feed off the success of *Birth*, with references to Klan groups appearing in ever more unusual contexts. In 1919, notices advertising *For the Freedom of the East* promoted "the sensational uprising of the Ku-Klux-Klan of the far east."[10]

Prior to 1920 the Klan remained, in all but a few areas, a long-deceased historical phenomenon. The costume and actions of the Klan in *Birth* were therefore relocated to other contemporary American institutions, in a process that the modern Klan would subsequently look to reverse. In the examples of Thomas Dixon's *Bolshevism on Trial* (1919) and *The Face at Your Window* (1920), the night riders appeared as the US Navy and the American Legion and responded to the latest social fear, Bolshevism.[11] On other occasions, night riders appeared as an archaic, localized, and non-specific group on-screen. Alice Joyce donned the Klan costume of the "White Riders" in Tom Terris's 1919 picture *The Cambric Mask*. Exploiting the popular imagery and excitement generated by *Birth*, *Wid's Daily* wrote that the White Riders "take the law into their own hands after the manner of the famous Ku Klux Klan."[12] While *Moving Picture World* suggested that the appearance of the masked riders would give the production "popular appeal," the riders were viewed as a reproduction of an outdated group, with an advertisement in the *Kansas City Star* describing the film as a "story of Ku Klux Klan days."[13]

In the same year, the biggest star of all, Mary Pickford, "America's Sweetheart," dressed up as a Klanswoman in an adaptation of John Fox Jr.'s 1913 novel *Heart o' the Hills*. Pickford's appearance suggested an existing legitimacy and social acceptance in popular fiction for vigilante violence. Her studio bosses, Jesse Lasky and Adolph Zukor, had earlier warned Pickford against appearing in the topical war story *The Little American* (1917), arguing that "it is best for us to keep away from anything bearing on the conditions – past, present or future in connection with the European conflict. This is particularly true with Pickford as the star."[14] Yet a night rider was seemingly not viewed as a topical, controversial, or potentially damaging role for Pickford in 1919, nor did Pickford recognize its violence as problematic. She later turned down the role of Norma Desmond in *Sunset Blvd.* (1950), saying, "I wouldn't do that kind of picture, why, she kills a man," somehow overlooking her murderous actions in *Heart o' the Hills*.[15]

Pickford's response can be explained, in part, by the setting and genre in which she rides, with the vigilante actions of the Klan group in *Heart o' the Hills* dislocated from contemporary urban life and featured as part of an action sequence in a female-centered comic melodrama. Yet while the film may espouse a distant model of the Klan, the appearance of Mary Pickford "dressed in the garb of the Night-riding Ku Klux Klan" would help to position and legitimize the actions of these regional Klan groups as an American response to "outsiders."[16] Released on the cusp of the Klan's national expansion, the film both reveals the broad currency of Klan values in American society and circulates and romanticizes, through its star, a cinematic model of vigilante action.

Heart o' the Hills centers on the "primitive and picturesque people" of the Kentucky hills, with Pickford appearing as Mavis, a twelve-year-old girl out to avenge her father's death ("I promised Pap, I'd Git him"). The girl also opposes planned developments on her land and leads a group of night riders who murder Sanders, a "northern capitalist." These activities are justified in the film through their remote regional settings. The opening intertitle explains that these people "operate with a stern code of justice," while a later title remarks that the "mountaineer is often a law unto himself."

This dislocation, particularly from urban and northern sites, is entirely typical of the industry's placement of the Klan. The locale of John Stahl's *One Clear Call* (1922) is a small Alabama town. A fictionalized account of the film published in *Photoplay* dismissively referred to the "Clan, which flourishes here and there in the South."[17] *The Cambric Mask* was widely described as "an exciting and thrilling tale of the South and of the 'Ku Klux Klan,'" the "avenging angels" in *A Mormon Maid* were positioned in the far west "beyond the furthest outpost of civilization," while the Klan group in the Franklyn Farnum western *The White Masks* (1921) worked "in the wilderness of a Western town."[18] Even in the Harold Lloyd short *An Eastern Westerner* (1920), the "masked angels" operated in "the Little Town of Piute Pass," where "it's considered bad form to shoot the same man twice on the same day." The regional setting was presented in direct contrast to the dance halls of Brooklyn, where Lloyd's character originated. *Lodge Night,* a Hal Roach comedy from 1923, might appear an exception, since it was based on a children's Klan group in Sayville, New York, yet this fact was not referenced in the film. Despite the Klan's established presence in Sayville, producers continued to reposition the group in distinct and remote regional settings.

The presentation of the Klan as a localized Southern group was, of course, a myth, but one that would crucially allow producers, reviewers, and censors to distance the on-screen model from modern organizations emerging in the North and Midwest. In contrast, independent productions, whether produced by the Klan or its opponents, challenged this regional myth. *The Toll of Justice* and *The Traitor Within* emphasized their authentic footage from Ohio and Indiana, while Oscar Micheaux positioned his dramatic scenes of Klan violence in New England and the Midwest in *The Symbol of the Unconquered*. Jacqueline Stewart has argued that Micheaux "exposes the fact that night riding is not limited to the seemingly more repressive southern districts," suggesting that this was intended to "increase political awareness and his [Micheaux's] box office receipts."[19] Micheaux confronted the modern Klan on-screen, but film industry anxieties ensured that mainstream producers underplayed the topicality and divided the country along regional lines. This repressed topicality was often restored, as we will see, at the site of exhibition, while film, particularly through the use of stars, articulated a rejoining of regional difference in support of a united national space. *The Birth of a Nation*, with its twin love stories, provides the classic example and prompted Thomas Dixon to claim to Woodrow Wilson that his film was "transforming the entire population of the North and West into sympathetic Southern voters."[20] *Heart o' the Hills*, like the majority of mainstream films featuring the Klan, presented a distinctly Southern setting and even offered a Northern aggressor. The film justified the vigilante activities in the film by suggesting they were specific to that local community, yet through the appearance of Mary Pickford the values of this community could be embraced on a national level.

By 1919 Pickford was the world's biggest screen star, established as the pictorial embodiment of American national identity. Her transformation from the Canadian actress Gladys Smith to "Our Mary" and "America's Sweetheart" (a term widely adopted by 1914) is striking testament to the development of the American star system. Furthermore, her position as a constructed manifestation of American ideals was consolidated during the war, when she sold war bonds, delivered ambulances for the Red Cross, and "stirred the hearts of the nation" in her patriotic picture *The Little American* (1917). Posters even circulated of "little Mary" knocking out the Kaiser. The *Chicago Tribune* stated that "in the hearts and minds of her countrymen [Americans!] she ranks second to none," claiming that there was more "universal interest" in Pickford than President Wilson.[21] An examination of her evolving star persona – the ideals celebrated and foregrounded through her image – reveals a particular set of conservative values that would come to define Americanism at this moment. *Heart o' the Hills* was released in December 1919 in the midst of the Palmer Raids, the most public response to the Red Scare. Overseen by Wilson's attorney general, A. Mitchell Palmer, this series of raids would see more than five hundred "foreigners" deported from the country and many more arrested. While *Heart o' the Hills* premiered shortly before the Klan rose to national prominence, Pickford's manufactured brand of Americanism and her costumed response to "outside" threats appeared against the backdrop of the same social panics that would fuel the modern Klan.

Picturegoer outlined the appeal of Pickford succinctly when it presented her in 1919 as "the big sister to the family of picturegoers," appearing as a positive influence over the nation and as a moral force for good.[22] Her persona as a big sister to the moviegoing public was reinforced by reports of her own (lost) childhood. The film press reported that Pickford had been thrust on the stage to become the family breadwinner at the age of five after the death of her father. *Heart o' the Hills* portrayed Pickford's latest attempts to reclaim her lost innocence, on this occasion by joining the Klan. Pickford's moral purity as a big sister to the nation, seemingly uncompromised by the violence in the film, ensured that she was for the most part desexualized in public discourse, preserving traditional gender identities at a moment of sexual liberation, rising consumerism, and female emancipation. Her feisty "girl-child" was in stark contrast to the sexualized and foreign flappers that the Klan would come to oppose, such as Pola Negri.

Star discourse established Pickford as the shining embodiment of purity, whether acting as a model for paper dolls or advertising Pompeian Beauty Powder products, which promised to add a "pearly clearness to the skin."[23] This notion of moral purity was aligned to ideals of whiteness. Pickford's ethnicity was constructed and glamourized on film – much like Lillian Gish in *Birth*, who was shot from above with a white sheet – and her whiteness was reinforced in *Heart o' the Hills* through the night riders' costume. The appearance of Pickford in white robes thus racializes the activities on-screen and helps to present the

4.1. Mary Pickford putting on her costume in *Heart o'*
the Hills, Mary Pickford Company, 1919.

costume and activities of vigilante groups as a significant and legitimate
response to a threatened strand of American national identity.

The casting of Mary Pickford greatly shaped the film's treatment of
the night riders and indeed the reception of their actions. At the film's
conclusion, Mavis is convicted of having murdered the northern capitalist, but a sympathetic jury cannot, in the words of one reviewer, "bear to
see Mary hanged" and so each juror, in turn, claims responsibility for the
killing until the judge decides to release her.[24] Pickford's all-pervading
stardom ensured that audiences saw Mary, not Mavis on-screen. Promotional materials proclaimed "Mary Pickford as a Night Rider, whirls over
the mountains with the clansmen at her heels" and that "Mary Pickford
can shoot and she shoots to kill," transposing the actions of the character onto Pickford.[25] The transformation of Pickford into a night rider is
enacted on screen. Pickford emerges from her cabin dressed in a full-
length white robe and looks around for a few seconds before putting the

hood over her head and riding off (fig. 4.1). This transformation mirrors some of the processes used by Griffith in *Birth*, and allows audiences to identify with the night-riding protagonist within the collective group.

Pickford's casting also ensured that the film offered a far more sympathetic presentation of the night riders than Fox's original novel. In the novel it was Steve Hawn, the central villain, who, "reddened by drink," rode with the night riders, stealing and abusing power. Fox wrote that "the night riders had been at their lawless work," and when the honorable Colonel Pendleton spoke out against them, noting that "men had been threatened, whipped and shot," he received threats "that the night-riders would burn his house and take his life."[26] In contrast, the film presents the night riders as a just and necessary group, maintaining law and order in the community.

Furthermore, the night riders feature much more prominently on-screen than in Fox's novel, a testament both to a popular interest in representing night riders after *Birth* and to the cinematic potency of this image.[27] The film also does not directly reference or contemporize the original Klan, whereas the book draws a direct parallel between that group and the lawless night riders, noting that "the dormant spirit of the Ku-Klux awakened, the night-rider was born again." Of course, any screen depiction of night riders in 1919 would evoke an association with the Klan through the popular memory of *Birth*, but the 1913 novel more explicitly positioned the original Klan as part of an ongoing lineage of night riders, who upheld traditional notions of masculinity and operated in opposition to the law: "The Ku Klux, the burning of toll gates, the Goebel troubles, and the night rider are all links in the same chain of lawlessness, and but for the first the others might not have been. But we are, in spite of all this, a law abiding people and the old manhood of the state is still here."[28]

The transfer of the Klan from page to screen often reveals the dominant practices, conventions, and, in particular, anxieties of industry producers, in determining what could and could not be presented on-screen. In this instance, the representation, function, and popular reception of the night riders was most clearly shaped by the film's star. The image of Mary Pickford killing her father's murderer was part of a widespread legitimization of these conservative protective groups, just at the moment in December 1919 when the federal government was establishing its Americanism Committee to teach immigrants the "ideals of America." It also, through a process of star identification, encouraged audience sympathy for the activities of the night riders. In *Heart o' the Hills*, Mavis is not punished for her actions, and after the murder of her father's killer an intertitle states, "Tragedies are quickly forgotten in the mountains." The sheet music for an accompanying song called "Heart o' the Hills," advertised extensively, concludes with the lines, "Everything came about just as they planned, and they lived happily ever after in the Heart of the Hills." There are no repercussions for Klan actions, unlike the 1937 Humphrey Bogart film *Black Legion,* in which Bogart is sentenced to life imprisonment even after repenting and revealing the identity of other night riders. In further contrast, *Heart o' the Hills* crucially presents the courtroom scene as a comic moment. One reviewer remarked that while *Heart o' the Hills* was "seemingly a heavy drama," there was enough comedy to "keep the house in a chuckling humor all through the performance."[29] The use of comedy, common to Klan appearances in the 1920s, and the presence of Pickford contributed to the presentation of an attractive, largely non-threatening organization. However, Pickford's appearance also complicated and undermined attitudes toward the Klan, most notably concerning the group's gender politics.

The character played by Mary Pickford in *Heart o' the Hills* was a young boy both in Fox's novel and in a 1924 remake, *The Hill Billy,* which cast Pickford's brother Jack in the central role. Certainly the appearance of a male protagonist in both novel and remake complicated the popular reception of vigilante violence. For example, the release without punishment of a strong male character, rather than the schoolgirl Mary Pickford, completely transforms the aforementioned trial scene, in which all of the jurors (and even the judge in *The Hill Billy*) confessed to the murder in order to see the heroic central character released. Yet while Pickford's presence as a night-riding schoolgirl encourages audience empathy with these vigilante activities, her appearance at the front of the riders destabilizes the Klan's traditional gender boundaries. Pickford assumes the missing paternal role in her household – when her mother attempts to beat her, she grabs the Hickory Cane stick and snaps it before shouting, "Be My Dinner ready, Mammy" – while her claims that "I air a Lady" are immediately undermined as she finds herself in a fight with a man who claims that she isn't. She talks of "raisin' h—l ginerally!," while she dismisses one man with "I ain't answerin' no questions from a fella that wears gal's socks." The gender boundaries become increasingly blurred, and this has strong repercussions for the presentation of the Klan.

The dual appearance of female night riders in 1919 – Pickford in *Heart o' the Hills* and Alice Joyce in *The Cambric Mask* – positions the Klan beyond the confines of a strict male preserve and foreshadows the enormously prominent role of women in the Klan after the establishment of the WKKK in 1923. The role of the WKKK was, publicly at least, largely confined to less dangerous pursuits, such as organizing events or consumer boycotts, but the night riders in 1919 were empowered to resolve their problems themselves.[30] The attitude toward the night riders may differ across these films – Joyce's character, Rose, dons the white costume in order to infiltrate the night riders and save her beau from them – but in presenting independent, empowered women, the films complicate the Klan's protectionist role, which was dependent on clearly defined gender boundaries. In *The Birth of a Nation*, Lillian Gish, seen kissing a dove and dancing gleefully, had "served to reempower the white man."[31] Griffith intercut shots of the family and then the army, panning from a crying mother to a battle in order to highlight the distinct gender roles. Yet in these two films from 1919, the night riders are not protecting the threatened women (as we see in earlier films like *The White Caps* and *Birth*) but are able to use the disguise (which allows them to conceal their gender as well) to undertake the role themselves.

The female night rider was partly a product of film convention, an extension of the popular women's serials and an attempt to cater for the lucrative female market. While Pickford's appearance in *Heart o' the Hills* unified, legitimized, and desensitized perceptions of the night riders on-screen, Pickford's appearance as a young independent woman who stands and fights her own battles also contributed to shifts in her star persona at a turning point in her career. Her next film, *Pollyanna*, was her first produced for United Artists, the company she co-founded in 1919 with Chaplin, Griffith, and Douglas Fairbanks. Pickford was an increasingly powerful figure within the industry, exercising creative control over her films. Advertisements for *Heart o' the Hills* had emphasized that this was Pickford's third picture from "her own studios," prompting the film's director Sidney Franklin to describe Pickford as "the boss; she was her own producer."[32] It was Pickford herself, under the name Gladys Mary Moore, who had purchased the exclusive motion picture rights to the novel in June 1919. The contract between Pickford and Fox confirmed that, for $11,000, Pickford had complete control over the material.[33] She was the driving force behind the film, and her activities as a modern, independent producer and, in particular, her divorce from Owen Moore and subsequent remarriage to Douglas Fairbanks in March 1920 threatened both her image as the innocent yet feisty schoolgirl and the cherished traditional American values that she was seen to represent.[34]

While still able to play a twelve-year-old girl, Pickford was now twenty-seven, empowered in business and in her personal life. Pickford's actions both on- and off-screen would appear to challenge, modernize, and renegotiate her star persona – now as much a modern, independent woman as a traditional "big sister" – yet importantly, star discourse largely preserved Pickford as the feisty schoolgirl, upholding and reinforcing traditional values. *Variety*, in its review of *Heart o' the Hills*, focused on Pickford's femininity, writing of the "pretty little dresses that become her" and observing that "in close-up it is evident that she is making up her upper lip too heavily." *Wid's Daily* celebrated a "real old fashioned Pickford picture," looking to preserve Pickford as a symbol of traditional American values at a moment when the preservation of these values was emerging at the center of social and political discourse.[35]

After 1919, as a new Klan spread across the nation and into public life, representations of the night riders were seen in relation to this modern incarnation. At the end of 1920, the *New York Age* noted that Micheaux's *The Symbol of the Unconquered* confronted "the viciousness and un-Americanism of the Ku Klux Klan, an organization that is beginning to manifest itself again in certain sections of the United States." Micheaux sought to "capture and capitalize on" a subject that reviews recognized was "most timely."[36] While "timely" for both activist filmmakers and audiences, this topicality presented a challenge in an industry that largely avoided controversial and divisive material. Klan sequences were now singled out by censors and reporters. When *The Nation* attacked censorship in an editorial in December 1920, it complained, in reference to *The*

Symbol of the Unconquered, that "even Ku Klux Klan pictures were barred by the Kansas board."[37] The *New York Times* commented on a ban of *The Birth of a Nation* in September 1921, at the exact moment of the *New York World's* high-profile exposé of the modern Klan, by reporting that police had prohibited the showing of a film "dealing with the activities of the Ku Klux Klan of Civil War days." In distinguishing between the original and the modern group, the paper implied that it was the appearance of the Klan that was now particularly problematic and noteworthy.[38]

Over the next few years Klan groups would appear in many guises, but those films that directly addressed the modern Klan could be counted on one hand. One early example from 1921 was the Snub Pollard short comedy *Law and Order,* produced by Hal Roach and described in *Wid's Daily* as "novel and timely." The copyright material for the film emphasized the relevance of the film's subject. "With the newspapers revealing alleged stupendous grafting on the part of 'Ku Klux' potentates," the report began, "Pathe announces for release a comedy featuring 'Snub' Pollard called 'Law and Order' in which a local group of the 'Klan' figure in wholesale automobile burglary." Even in this relatively minor comedy, *Wid's Daily* recognized a potential problem with this topical subject matter, suggesting that "this one should do well before any audience, excepting perhaps in certain sections of the South."[39]

The emergence of a modern Klan would inevitably affect the reception of films featuring night riders. When *One Clear Call* played in Louisiana in 1922, an exhibitor noted that the appearance of Klansmen on-screen was "hissed by the audience" in an area where the Klan "would stand much show as a snowball in hell." The critical and regulatory responses to the re-release of *Birth* in 1922 also recognized and responded to the emergence of the modern group. The *New York Times* complained that the "treatment of the story is such as to inflame passions today," adding that the "social value of its revival at the present time is open to question – to say the least." *Variety* further noted that "the recent and present publicity regarding the Klan situation made it [*Birth*] problematic."[40]

As the Klan became ever more active and visible in mainstream America, the ways in which the industry represented Klan activities became all the more closely monitored, both by censors and by the conservative reformers that questioned the industry's American credentials. For the most part, producers avoided directly representing the modern Klan as the subject of their films, yet characteristics that made the Klan so problematic on-screen – its topicality, the associations with *Birth* – also made it exciting and potentially lucrative. As a result, producers negotiated versions of the Klan on-screen, often rebranding or concealing the Klansman in brief action sequences.

RACE OFF-SCREEN IN THE 1920S

In October 1921, William Simmons, the Imperial Wizard of the Klan, testified before a congressional hearing and offered a powerful defense of his organization. Simmons claimed that the Klan was "purely a fraternal and patriotic organization and is in no sense a regulative or corrective organization." He said the group was "opposed to a profiteering in race prejudice and religious bigotry," but admitted that the Klan occasionally assumed "the role of regulators of public morals and the enforcement of law."[41]

While Simmons's model of the Klan was dismissed by large swaths of the media and public – John Mecklin denounced it in his influential 1924 exposé of the Klan as "pure idealization and to all extents and purposes non-existent" – it often closely resembled the vision proffered by the film industry.[42] In November 1921, Franklyn Farnum appeared in the comedy western *The White Masks*, which, according to advertisements, showed "a modern version of the once famous Ku Klux Klan." Described as "unusually timely," the film depicted a secret band known as the 601, and along with other westerns such as *Cotton and Cattle* (1921) and *Big Stakes* (1922), it depicted a group disguised as the Ku Klux Klan.[43] Jean Paige appeared in *The Prodigal Judge* in February 1922, which was set before the Civil War and featured a Klan group appearing as law enforcers helping to resolve a land dispute, while eighteen months later, in July 1923, the Our Gang comedy *Lodge Night* presented the Klan as a fun fraternal group, unconcerned by race or religion, and serving only to protect the law. Most strikingly, John M. Stahl's *One Clear Call* was released in May 1922. Newspapers recognized the contemporary relevance of the picture, "owing to the present uncertain feeling regarding the Ku Klux Klan," and added that it should be "doubly interesting" as perhaps the first film to portray "this night riding organization" since *Birth*.[44] The film featured a largely honorable Klan, once more serving to maintain law and order in the seedy world of bootlegging and crime. The night riders in the film do not target any religious groups, and ultimately show compassion toward their repenting target. At the end, it is not the Klan but their victim who sees the error of his ways and repents his sins. The Klan appears as moral leaders; one review emphasized that the film had a moral "so exquisitely coated and presented that you're grateful for it."[45]

In order to explain why the film industry, battered and threatened by the Klan, would offer a largely uncritical take on its activities across a corpus of films, it is necessary to return once more to Lamar Trotti's dichotomy involving "decent people" and "business people." More specifically, industry anxieties, which are, in part, another legacy of *Birth*, greatly shaped and restricted the possible representation of the Klan. I have already suggested that the industry largely avoided topical references to the Klan and positioned the group in distant, rural locations, but there are three further areas that I wish to explore now. First, there was the restriction on racial and religious targets, which ensured that the Klan was more often presented as a moral force targeting wife beaters or liquor outlets. Second, there were restrictions on the level of violence shown on-screen, and third, the function of the Klan in the narrative, more often as part of an action sequence, was shaped by the genres of the films in question.

At the end of *The Birth of a Nation*, in a sequence titled "Disarming the Blacks," armed Klansmen line both sides of the streets as African Americans drop their weapons in the center and disappear off-screen. This provides an apposite visualization of *Birth's* impact, as African Americans are rendered impotent, and largely eradicated from the cinema screen. One consequence of this is that the Klan could no longer be defined on-screen in relation to race. Independent productions that offered racial or religious targets, such as Micheaux's *The Symbol of the Unconquered* (1920) and *A Son of Satan* (1924) and Hopp Hadley's *The Knight of the Eucharist* (1922), were all heavily censored. The Motion Picture Commission in New York refused a license to *The Knight of the Eucharist*, noting that the film was "sacrilegious" for showing the Klan "announcing their intention of desecrating the altar of a Roman Catholic Church."[46] The censorship of *Shadows of the West* in 1920 further highlights the difficulties in representing an ethnic Klan target. In the film, the night riders (claiming to be the American Legion and riding horses in casual clothing) rescue a kidnapped girl from Japanese captors. The film presents the Japanese as "profiteers, wife-beaters and would be murderers," a directly confrontational piece of cinema that reviewers acknowledged "will increase the difficulties between the country and the island empire."[47] This eight-reel film was rejected on two occasions by the Board of Censorship in Ohio, and was prohibited in many areas because of its inflammatory characterization of the Japanese. It was eventually released in some areas in 1921 as a five-reel film.[48] The film industry's restriction on racial and religious targets was supplemented by a financial reluctance to antagonize any segment of the cinemagoing public or, more importantly in a period of enormous industrial pressure, to invite an organized response from any group against the industry.

There are still plenty of examples of African American characters featuring in the industry's "Klan" films, but, significantly, they were now largely removed from the Klan's direct attentions. In its review of *One Clear Call, Moving Picture World* reported that a scene involving the Klan "is broken at two intervals by a happy little colored boy's melon feast." An advertisement for the film described the two African American characters as "Toby, the quaint old southern darky," and "Smoke, whose heart was as big as a water melon."[49] Now consciously removed from the film's narrative, the African Americans appear as contented, non-threatening figures. A mulatto character also appears in *One Clear Call* but, rather than as a rapist or wild schemer, she was a maid played by Annette de Foe (in blackface) in a minor supporting role.

In *Lodge Night*, released a year later in 1923, two African Americans join the Cluck Cluck Klams, a children's fraternal group based on the Klan. The film willfully ignores the Klan's prohibitive membership policies – the group is open to African American children – and is notably sketchy on the details and values of the group. The younger African American character is introduced with the title "Farina – Doesn't know what the lodge is all about – But is in favor of anything." The film reworks traditional assumptions about the Klan, as the two African American children run *to*, not *from*, the Klan, escaping their guardians in order to go to a Clam meeting: "We gotta melt outta here – the Kluxers is waiting." The film's comedy, however, is partly generated by challenging audience expectations. For example, in showing black faces in familiar white hoods, the producers draw attention to the Klan's well-publicized racial values. Furthermore, the white robes of the Klan still generate fear and panic. The adult African Americans all run frantically for cover when an African American child appears in his white costume. *Kid Speed* (1924), a Larry Semon film best remembered for an early appearance of Oliver Hardy, also reveals the paradoxical nature of the Klan costume, visually potent but, through its use in comedy, somewhat desensitized. In one sequence Semon is racing in his car with an African American, when a white sheet (complete with face markings) falls on him. On seeing this white robed figure, the African American is petrified and leaps from the car. These sequences were obviously played for comic effect, with the African Americans invariably frightened by a misused costume, one that is not worn by an actual Klansman.

Even in Klan-made films, like *The Fifth Horseman* (1924), an African American character appears only to stare in "amazement with eyes wide" when a Klansman appears. In this instance, the African American appeared as a subsidiary character bearing no relation to the main narrative of the film, yet the Ohio censor board still insisted that producers "cut out [the] entire episode of [a] boy talking with [a] young Negro on [the] street." The censorship certainly highlights the difficulties or presenting the Klan in relation to race even in a small scene, and indeed of depicting African American characters on-screen.[50]

Adult African Americans also feature in *Lodge Night* but, as with *One Clear Call*, they serve in an incidental comic sequence. Lightly mocked and lampooned, they appear as illiterate fools unable to resist the urge to gamble. These "Klan" films testify not to shifting attitudes toward race – historical work has suggested that attitudes were not significantly reconfigured in this period – but to the removal from film of any discourse about racial hierarchies.[51] Nervous non-confrontational film bosses were unwilling to present the African American as a villain, regardless of their racial prejudices, but positive redefining and empowering depictions of the African American were equally scarce.

A further examination of *The Mating Call* highlights the impact of industry regulation and commercial pressures on the Klan's screen appearances. In the film's source novel, the central hero Leslie Hatton discusses at length the motives, morality, and function of the Klan, but the film, released a year later, instead presents a group of night riders known as "The Order."[52] The novel featured Double R, an African American who credits the Klan with the sudden departure of farm workers and who moved to the area himself after "the Ku Klux riz up an' burned a cross." The film, in contrast, does not feature any African American characters and also largely overlooks the Klan's other modern racial opponents. In one lengthy exchange in the novel, the deputy sheriff compares the modern racial enemies with the carpetbaggers of the Reconstruction era. "The carpet baggers ran things in those days," he states. "Now it's the Jews, the Catholics, and the niggers."[53]

The removal of racial targets shifts the motivation behind the Klan's attacks onto the film's protagonist, Leslie Hatton. This is illustrated in a warning letter posted on his door, which appears racially motivated in the book:

TAR AND FEATHERS!
This is a decent community. The woman who is living with you is not wanted here any longer.
First and last warning.
K.K.K.[54]

The woman referred to was a Russian immigrant, but in the film "The Order" appears ostensibly as a moral group protecting traditional family values. The note responds to his perceived relationship with the married Rose Henderson:

It is the duty of this organization to protect the honor of our homes.
Your relation with a certain married woman must cease.
The Order.

The removal of "foreign" enemies from the screen inadvertently aligns the on-screen Klan with the model promoted by Imperial Wizard Simmons. Simmons claimed in 1921 that the Klan was not an anti-Catholic organization, arguing that only once was anti-Catholic literature circulated, and that the man responsible was banished from the organization forever. The Klan's other modern targets were equally avoided on-screen. Strong Jewish influence in the industry ensured, as Lester Friedman has argued, that all films featuring Jewish characters "historically faced a gauntlet of highly placed Jewish executives."[55] While Jewish screen villains appeared in films at the height of the Red Scare in 1919 and 1920, they were more specifically presented as Bolsheviks and screen connections between "Bolsheviks" and "Jews" remained closely monitored. Steven Ross has shown how pressure from the Jewish press and the Catholic Al Smith (a subsequent Klan target as governor of New York and Democratic nominee for president) forced the producers of *The Volcano* (1919) "to alter its blatantly anti-Semitic plot." The hero's name was changed from Garland to Nathan Levison and the "hook-nosed" villain was given the line, "I am not a Jew; I am a Bolshevik."[56]

In 1923, a *New York Times* editorial, entitled "None but the Native Villains," suggested that in film the "only safe villain is an atheist American."[57] The removal of the "foreign" villain encouraged an often nostalgic and romantic presentation of a non-racist Klan, one that more often targeted moral transgressors and, more specifically, drinkers. In *One Clear Call* the Klan targets Henry Garnett, the owner of The Owl, a disreputable "gambling dance and drinking place" (fig. 4.2). Garnett is attacked because of his profession, with his character defined by a social cause; he serves purely as an obstructer of Prohibition. The intention of the Klan in this film is the "virtuous one of closing his [Garnett's] den," which has "so incensed the citizens."[58] The Klan group in *The Fifth Horseman* (1924) also attacks bootleggers as the enemies of Prohibition. The villainous father, Tom, is introduced in a seedy saloon "shuffling cards. Bleary-eyed and stupid with liquor." The script explains that there is a "close up of [a] quarter filled whiskey bottle on the table," used as a well-established visual signifier of his moral character and as a cause and motivation for his criminal activity. When Tom's son, Sonny, finally reacts against his father, he does so by throwing the "whiskey bottle down savagely." Similarly, when his father is eventually reformed, the script explains that "with an oath, he sends the half-filled whiskey glass crashing to the floor and stalks out" of the saloon.[59]

4.2. Gathering outside The Owl in *One Clear Call*. *Image courtesy George Eastman House, International Museum of Photography and Film.*

The Klan's role in *The Fifth Horseman* is almost identical to that in *One Clear Call*. In *The Fifth Horseman*, the heroic "Young American" warns Gorman, the proprietor of the saloon, "You'll either close this place in forty-eight hours or it will be closed for you!" In *One Clear Call*, Dr. Hamilton is given thirty days to arrange the closure of The Owl before the Klan takes action. There is a consistency here across industry and Klan features – the villain in *The Toll of Justice* is always viewed in relation to drink and introduced in a saloon – and even in the anti-Klan Catholic production *The Knight of the Eucharist*, the Klan targets not only Catholics but a "band of radicals who are involved in bootlegging and city politics."[60]

The Klan's appearances fit into a broader history of American narrative cinema, which links villainy with anti-temperance. While social commentators and historians have widely noted how Griffith used color in *Birth* to define his villains and to explain their villainous actions, the characters were also defined by drink. Silas was "drunk with wine and power," while the African Americans in Congress were shown swigging from bottles to indicate their lack of moral order and self-control. From Griffith's earlier films, most notably *A Drunkard's Reformation* (1909), drink represented a threat to domesticity, and the Klan would come to operate as a protective force in this established narrative tradition. Drink was used as a defining feature of the villains, as the explanation for and signifier of their corrupt character.

Yet even these immoral villains were closely monitored on-screen. *Photoplay,* in criticizing the "self-righteous, self-appointed, ignorant, holier-than-thou" censors in 1922, reported that "screen comedies touching upon prohibition get hit hard."[61] The Motion Picture Commission in New York ordered two cuts to *One Clear Call* in 1922, after complaining that the intertitles were "immoral" and "would tend to corrupt morals." One line that had begun "If there is one among you who one time or another hasn't patronized a place like this [a saloon] . . ." was changed to "If any of you has the courage to go in unmasked, and take him single-handed – man to man – not by mob violence – go get him." The commission objected to the implication that Prohibition was widely violated, and appeared wary of showing the moral degradation to which the Klan responded. In altering this line, it also urged the night riders to take off their masks, aligning these groups with "mob violence." While questioning the methods of these groups, the reworked script did not challenge their reasons or right to act.[62]

Film was often unable to depict the acts that the Klan responded to, and when it did present Prohibition it was in subtly reconfigured terms. *Kourier* in 1925 paraphrased the words of Henry Ford, writing that "if the opposition to prohibition were analyzed, it would be found that it was mainly alien – every true American's heart and soul is for it."[63] The Klan still associated Prohibition with ethnicity (as *Birth* had done by showing the African American characters drinking), but films now largely avoided such associations. The villains appeared to be defined purely by their moral failings, and the Klan was depicted as indiscriminating extensions of the police force. In *Lodge Night,* the young Klansmen catch car thieves, who are described as "prejudicial against the Police." The on-screen Klan was motivated not by race but by a moral code, prompting *Moving Picture World* to describe the murder by the night riders in *The Hill Billy* (1924) as a "grand act of courage and sacrifice."[64]

Such representations cannot be credited entirely to industry anxieties. The use of vigilante violence as a response to moral transgression in rural communities was an integral, founding principle of American narrative cinema. This is evident in the 1905 Edison film *The White Caps*, which offered an easily comprehensible narrative based around a chase sequence. The night riders operated in the rural border states, not as a racist group but as a moral force, in this case targeting a husband shown beating his wife and daughter. Advertised on occasion as "The Ku Klux Klan or White Caps. The Greatest of all sensational pictures," the film presented the vigilantes as "law abiding citizens [that] were compelled to secretly organize themselves for their own self-protection . . . [and] to rid the community of undesirable citizens."[65] As a precursor to *Birth*, playing as Dixon's *The Clansman* toured the country, the film constructed a cinematic identification with the hooded vigilante "rescuers," visualizing Dixon's response for the screen. Furthermore, contemporary reports endorsed the film's morality. The *Portsmouth Daily Herald*, for example, explained that "the White Caps were not law breakers at heart" but instead comprised "reputable citizens" punishing "wife beaters, habitual drunkards etc."[66] The *Altoona Mirror* headlined its review "Warning to Wifebeaters," and when the film showed at the local Pastime Theatre, it was listed as "Punishing a wife-beater or The White Caps."[67]

The White Caps may indicate a pervading social acceptance of vigilante justice in early cinema as a justified response to moral failure. This is best understood in the broader historical tradition of the "unwritten law," which provided a code of moral conduct extraneous of existing legal forces. The legacies of these early forms of vigilante violence would, Michelle Wallace argued, be "memorialized" subsequently in cowboy movies.[68] Furthermore, the Klan's chase and parade sequences in *The White Caps* are remarkably similar to the group's later appearances, with two notable distinctions. First, the film aspires to relate in a most "realistic and vivid way" directly to recent events in Ohio and Indiana, and, most notably, the film displays graphic levels of violence, depicting its victim tied up and covered in tar and feathers.[69]

Such levels of Klan violence were not found on-screen in the 1920s. A review for *One Clear Call* explained that the "Klansman sidle off on their horses without having done much but wave their guns."[70] The Klan does nothing on the condition that the local bar, The Owl, shuts itself down within thirty days. In *Shadows of the West,* the American Legion works with existing legal forces, resisting the urge to lynch the Japanese villain. "Men listen – you have done your work well. Now let the law take its course," the hero urges after rescuing the female victim; "He'll get all that's coming to him I promise you." The riders then cheer and embrace, with the retribution never actually shown.

During his appearance at the congressional hearing, Simmons dissociated the Klan from reports of violence by claiming that these incidents were carried out by non-Klansmen misusing the Klan costume. Producers would also offer up this explanation for Klan violence. For example, in *Cotton and Cattle* the villainous leader of the night riders is exposed as an opportunistic local businessman, who wishes to scare Al Hart's character, Bill Carson, off his valuable land. The Klan costume is again adopted, not by genuine Klansmen, but by immoral figures using it for their own personal gain. This narrative device, through which producers could dissociate the actions of the night riders from the modern group, was also widely adopted in Klan productions and Klan literature. Ultimately, by removing the violent actions of the night riders from the genuine Klan, the films endorsed Simmons's defensive rhetoric and presented the Klan as a legitimate moral group, misrepresented by villainous outsiders.

In *The Mating Call,* the Klan group is not depicted as inherently evil but, once more, as the victim of a corrupt leader. For the most part, it listens to the cases of those brought before it, such as the "shiftless, drunken reprobate" who goes out to get drunk while his "mother hasn't enough to eat." In its responses – telling the shirtless reprobate, "You're dismissed – but improve your ways. We'll be watching you" – the Klan appears as a paternalistic group, only resorting to violence when a man unashamedly admits to beating his wife. Even at the film's conclusion, the Klan is not punished or brought down, but uses its influence to correct what it sees as an earlier wrong. In this instance, the falsely accused hero, Hatton, appears to accept the Klan's role as a moral force in society even after being whipped on the cross repeatedly. This serves as part of the film (and book's) wider acceptance of vigilante violence. After the murder of The Order's adulterous leader, Henderson, the Klan group works to ensure that the murder looks like suicide, so that, as in earlier films such as *Heart o' the Hills* (1919), no one is convicted of this apparently justified murder. The acting head of The Order further illustrates the common acceptance of vigilante justice when he says to the suspected assassin, "If you didn't kill him, you should have."[71]

In many ways, then, *The Mating Call* follows earlier depictions of the "moral" Klan, but the representation of American values – and the Klan's position as the upholder of these values – had become far more nuanced and complex by 1928. The American woman in the film, Rose, embodied the dangerous modern woman, sexually driven, adulterous, and constantly moving outside of the home. Previously married to Hatton, before her parents had her marriage annulled, Rose subsequently married Lon Henderson. Upon Hatton's return from war, Rose throws herself at him, and, apparently disgusted by the immorality of this modern American woman, he decides that he needs a hard-working, domesticated, appreciative wife ("a real woman who wants a home – and is willing to work for it"). Hatton decides that such a woman can only be found at Ellis Island, and in a curious scene (even in the context of this film) he prevents a European woman and her family from being deported in exchange for marriage. This foreign woman proceeds to run his household, cooking, cleaning, and assuming the traditional American matriarchal role. She appears vulnerable and in need of her husband's protection when she is drawn outside the domestic space, and her feminine character appears to reinforce the clear gender boundaries threatened by modern society. Strikingly, it is this immigrant character who embodies the values so cherished by the Klan, while the threatening vamp character is reimagined as an American.[72]

A more thorough reading of the film would therefore suggest that the film addresses and seemingly challenges popular attitudes toward race. The removal of the racial target on-screen may ensure that the Klan in the film appears to target Hatton because of his perceived adultery, but Hatton's marriage to a foreigner encourages viewers to see him (and the Klan's attacks) in a racial context. For example, the *Kansas City Star,*

having explained that Hatton "goes to Ellis Island and marries a peas-
ant girl," suggested that "such un-American conduct" (the marriage of
an immigrant) "arouses the ire of the local Kleagles" in the film.[73] Furthermore, Thomas Meighan, the actor playing Hatton, was a prominent
Catholic figure who had served as the first president of the Catholic
Motion Picture Actors Guild in 1923. The Klan's attacks on Hatton therefore circumnavigate film industry restrictions, but can still be viewed
in the context of the modern Klan's very public attacks on Catholics in
America, exemplified by its highly publicized and virulent criticisms of
Al Smith.

The Mating Call arrived at a transitional moment in Klan and film
history. With the Klan's influence rapidly crumbling, it offered a glimpse
of a reconfigured Klan and tentatively looked forward to the more adult,
critical exposés that would follow in the 1930s. It was at this point no
more than a glimpse, still largely eschewing the direct, confrontational
approach adopted later.[74]

THE KLAN IN ACTION

At the release of *One Clear Call* in the summer of 1922, a syndicated article considered the film in relation to the Klan's most famous on-screen
appearance seven years earlier. "Were D. W. Griffith to remake *The Birth
of a Nation*," the article asked, "to what extent would he change the spectacular clansmen scenes in view of recent progress in photography and
the technical details of picture making?"[75] In prioritizing technical
rather than ideological shifts and in foregrounding the scenes of "spectacular clansmen," the article exemplifies the industry's emphasis on the
display of the Klan rather than its politics, on action rather than motive.

Klan appearances during the 1920s rarely reveal signs of technical
or aesthetic "progress" but, at first glance, *One Clear Call* may suggest
a recent ideological shift in the representation of the Klan. The Klan
target, Henry Garnett, is played by Henry Walthall, who played the role
of the colonel leading the charge of the Klan in *Birth*. Walthall had also
appeared as a Catholic priest in *The Confession*, a pro-Catholic film in
1920, moving on-screen from Klan leader to Catholic priest and finally
to victim of the Klan. While Walthall's presence places a greater focus
on the "victim" and wrongdoer in *One Clear Call*, the Klan's function,

4.3. The onrushing night riders in *One Clear Call* (1922). *Image courtesy George Eastman House, International Museum of Photography and Film.*

though morally justified, is obfuscated by its visually striking appearance in an exciting action sequence (fig. 4.3). *Variety* wrote that *One Clear Call* had "everything that goes to make a successful screen production," including "wandering boy and blind mother bit, comedy and a touch of Ku Klux Klan that serves as a thrill."[76] The Klansmen, posters noted, brought "drama, action, tingling sensation," while a review for the film in Texas appeared under the headline "Ku Klux Klansmen provide screen thrills."[77]

In other areas *One Clear Call* was promoted as a story of "night riders [of the] Knights of the Ku Klux Klan," with a picture of riding Klansmen and the tagline, "Whoop! What a thrill when they [night riders] come roaring down for Vengeance!"[78] Posters for the film emphasized the "hundreds of mystic midnight riders," while an advertisement in the *New York Times* featured a picture of a Klansman on a horse with a caption urging the reader to "See the Night-Riders." The advertisement offered little insight into the plot, characters, or setting – nor into the function or ideology of the modern group – instead foregrounding the visual presence of the Klan in order to sell the picture. An advertisement for the film in Chicago did not mention the Klan, but underneath a small picture of a night rider were three words: "Mystery-Thrill-Love."[79] There are two points to note here. First, in seeking to appeal to every potential cinemagoer, mainstream film producers used the familiar white Klan costume in the 1920s as a source of action and excitement in these comic, romantic, and dramatic tales. Second, the publicity for *One Clear Call* suggests that what was avoided or underplayed on-screen, in light of censorship concerns, was often positively emphasized off-screen.

The Klan sequences in *One Clear Call* were not part of the 1914 source novel of the same name, but author Frances Nimmo Greene "outlined a new plot" for the 1922 film adaptation with references to "that mysterious organization, the Clan." A novelization of the film in *Photoplay* in 1922 highlighted the excitement generated by the Klan costume: "And one night the white-robed, masked body gathered outside the city, and swept through the streets. Somewhere the cry started, 'The Clan is raiding the Owl,' and spread on the wings of feverish excitement."[80] Similarly, Clifford S. Elfelt's 1922 film *Big Stakes* added Klan sequences that were not in the original source, Earl Wayland Bowman's 1920 short story "High Stakes." The adaptation included an entirely new subplot and a lengthy end sequence involving the Klan, with the central hero changed from Senor Skinny to Jim Gregory. Bowman was certainly not impressed by the changes. Having sold the story for "practically nothing," he soon broke off all dealings with the "indescribable" producers, complaining that "of course it [his original story] will be butchered." His mood was hardly improved on seeing the finished film: "It was not as bad as it might have been but it was bad enough to make me swear. I told the producer that no other bunch would ever put another of my stories on the screen unless it had been shot under my direction. They simply have not sense enough to see the really big things in the story."[81]

One sequence added to the film warrants closer scrutiny. Near the end a woman dressed all in white runs frantically over the rocks. As she nears the edge of the cliff, she turns to face her pursuer and warns him, "If you come near me – I'll jump." The man takes a step closer, forcing the innocent woman to take one final step backward. Though she crashes to the ground, her "purity" has been preserved. The sequence invites an immediate comparison with *The Birth of a Nation,* in which Flora, pursued by the evil African American Gus, jumps to her death to avoid his advances. Flora, the intertitle explained, "learned the stern lesson of honor." However, while in *The Birth of a Nation* Flora was chased by an African American, in *Big Stakes* the young woman, Mary Moore, is pursued by Bully Brand, a repulsive outlaw who is the leader of the Klan. In Griffith's film, the Klan had served to protect womanhood and avenge Flora's dramatic death, yet seven years later it was presented as a direct threat to female innocence. The traditional Southern values of honor and the protection of women, so carefully aligned to the Klan in *Birth,* are here portrayed as fraudulent.

Yet on closer inspection *Big Stakes* is neither an anti-Klan critique nor indicative of a significant shift in screen articulations of the Klan. While its negative presentation is explained – it shows a localized Klan group, misdirected by a corrupt leader – the representation of the Klan also appears subsidiary to the spectacle of the Klan costume. *Moving Picture World* did not comment on the representation of the Klan in *Big Stakes,* but it did report that "the scenes involving the white riders add to the spectacular value."[82] The ideology of the Klan was overlooked in reviews of similar films of the era, so that even in seemingly critical presentations (such as *The White Masks* or *Cotton and Cattle*) advertisements noted only the appearance of the Klan and the excitement that this generated. As one example of many, advertisements for *The Cambric Mask* described the film as "a thrilling Ku Klux Klan story" and a "thrilling play of Ku Klux Klansmen," with the "band of white robed night riders" providing "thrills, action and suspense."[83]

The Klan's function in the narrative – providing an exciting climax or action sequence – deflected discussions away from Klan representation, its ideology and role in modern society. In June 1923, the hardboiled detective magazine *Black Mask* ran a special issue in which all stories took as their theme the Ku Klux Klan. Describing this hugely popular issue a few months later, the editor explained that it "was issued as a purely literary experiment – to see if the Klan idea would make a good background for stories and articles. We did not pick the writers for their affiliations of any kind; we simply selected the authors we thought would turn out the best stories on short notice."[84] While constantly reiterating that the magazine was "absolutely neutral" on the Klan issue, to publicly avoid dividing or isolating potential readers, the editor also recognized the particular appeal of the Klan as "the most picturesque element that has appeared in American life since the War." *The Black Mask,* he explained, was less interested in the political arguments or critical responses to the group, but rather recognized a potentially interesting "background for fiction stories."[85]

On film, the appearance of the night riders served to generate excitement irrespective of the sympathies displayed toward them. "The whole horde of night riders in pursuit makes a succession of dramatic climaxes," wrote one reviewer of *A Mormon Maid,* "which for sheer excitement have rarely been equaled on the screen."[86] In prioritizing the image, exhibitors and publicists eschewed any criticism attached to the hooded riders, while attitudes toward the night riders were further muddied by the frequent misuse of the Klan costume on-screen. The final shot of *A Mormon's Maid's* showed a man in the Klan costume embracing the heroine. In this case it was the heroine's father, John Hogue, who adopted the appearance of his enemies in order to protect his daughter, but the image of the tall robed man (with hood removed) embracing the heroine is unmistakably similar to the triumphant conclusion in *Birth.*[87]

The emphasis on spectacle might further suggest an industry reluctance to use the films to initiate debate about the modern Klan. In the aftermath of *The Black Mask's* special issue, the magazine ran "Our Ku Klux Klan forum," described as the "only open, free, absolutely unbiased discussion, for and against the Invisible Empire, published anywhere in America." The response saw a "large majority of letters" in favor of the Klan and indeed a number from local Klan groups, but also a few selected critical letters and articles ("A Catholic's View of the Ku Klux Klan").[88] The magazine certainly exploited this topical issue in a quest for publicity and readership, using the Klan appearances to generate a lively debate on the role of the organization in modern America. Yet the qualified representation of the Klan on-screen – whether renamed, historicized, or localized – largely stifled a similar level of discussion, particularly as the night riders were positioned in youth-oriented genres that critics tended to overlooked, most commonly appearing in comedy shorts and westerns.

The Klan's appearance in these genres was a further response to industry conventions and anxieties – the proliferation of female and youth-orientated pictures and a fear of censorship or unrest – and further contributed to a non-threatening, accessible presentation of the group. Certainly, genre helped determine the aspects of the Klan that would be prioritized. In comedy shorts, the humor is often generated through the exaggerated rituals of the group, as for example in the 1921 Buster Keaton comedy *The High Sign,* in which the hero inadvertently meets up with the Blinking Blizzards, a group described as a "murderous secret society." A year earlier, Harold Lloyd had battled a "western version of the Ku Klux Klan" in *An Eastern Westerner.* The "masked angels" were introduced as "men who have broken eight commandments and twisted the other two" but, as with *Big Stakes,* the film presented a central villain, in this case "Tiger Lip" Tomkins, who used the group for his own gain. His motives worked directly against the ideals of the Klan – he grabs the innocent heroine and says "I want that girl – and what I generally want I generally get" – supporting the notion that opportunists and enemies of the Klan were adopting the Klan costume for their own personal gain.

Even in literature that was critical of the Klan – for example some of the short stories in *The Black Mask* – it was the Klan's methods rather than its values and ideals that were questioned. "He realized that while the ideals of the Klan might be right," concluded Whetland, the rich manufacturer in Neuton A. Fuessle's "Hoodwinked (A Story of the Klan)," "certainly their practices that he had been able to observe at close quarters were wrong."[89] Dr. Hamilton, the hero in *One Clear Call,* reached a similar conclusion, supporting the values and role of the Klan in administering justice, but criticizing their secret methods and labeling them a "gang of cowards" for appearing in masks. In Rex Beach's 1927 novel *The Mating Call,* Hatton clarifies his position: "I don't object to the principles the Klan advocates, but I don't favor the enforcement of these principles by secret influence or mob violence. It's too dangerous, too hard to control." It was not the morality or ideals of the Klan that were criticized but the inherent problems caused by self-appointed regulators, with Rose also remarking that "that's my only objection to the Klan – its altogether too secret."[90]

An Eastern Westerner is one of a number of Hal Roach comedies to feature a Klan group, in addition to two of his "Our Gang" comedies that exploited the Klan costume and rituals on-screen. In *Young Sherlocks* (1922), the gang works as detectives and forms a secret society called the J. J. J.'s (Jesse James Juniors). At one point as the costumes are donned, an intertitle reads, "We gotta put on disguises – an act creepy." In *Lodge Night,* the children dress up in white robes and take part in a high-speed car chase, but huge emphasis is again placed on the childish rules, rituals, and names in the club. The initiation ceremony centers on an overweight child being kicked and punched. This glorified bullying appears as an extension of childish playground games, with the group presented as a fun, male fraternal group.

The Klan can be presented in a modern context, precisely because these are comedies aimed at children. It may appear curious that the Klan features predominantly in films aimed at the very audience that censors and reformers sought most vehemently to protect, yet these films are not subject to the same levels of critical scrutiny. While the Klan tracks down car thieves in *Lodge Night,* a couple of years earlier in another Hal Roach comedy short, *Law and Order,* a group of car thieves, in order "to protect themselves, 'desert the poolrooms' and form a Klan." The representation of the secret society – whether supportive or antagonistic, whether catching or acting as car thieves – is motivated by the comedy that can be generated from these secret societies, their rituals and costume, and the high-speed chases. In *Law and Order,* "Snub" Pollard's character, the district attorney, accidentally finds the costume of the "Chief Ku Klux" and rides out in disguise to collect evidence. Pollard has a "thrilling time avoiding the noose of a rope," as the Klan costume becomes a visual shorthand for a form of mystery and excitement that these comedies relied upon.[91]

The Klan costume was also used in Disney cartoons. In *Alice and the Dog Catcher* (1924), a film that combined live action with animated footage, the figures wear grocery bags over their heads. Alice presides over a secret club, again exploiting their rituals, and dons the costume in order to free the captured dogs. In *Alice's Mysterious Mystery* (1926), Alice and her accomplice Julius save the imprisoned dogs from a ghoulish character robed like a member of the Klan. The costume was used both by the heroine and the enemy to free and capture the dogs. In desensitizing the Klan, these films avoid serious scrutiny but also support the industry's dominant representation of an exciting, mysterious, but largely non-violent group.

The other main genre in which the Klan was featured in the 1920s was the western, which, according to a survey in 1923, was the most popular genre among young boys.[92] B-movie westerns and serials again largely bypassed close scrutiny or serious discussion, enabling producers to position the night riders in action sequences, reassuringly removed from modern urban America. The western provided an apposite, ideologically complex setting for the Klan, one that was founded on a code of ethics – vigilante justice and the unwritten law – and that responded to contemporary populist fears concerning immigration and urbanization. While this connection between the Klan and western figures is rarely considered by film scholars, Peter Stanfield points out parallels both in appearance (a "strong visual parallel to the Ku Klux Klan") and moral code ("the use of extrajudicial means to right perceived wrongs"). Referring specifically to westerns of the late thirties, Stanfield described this ideological and visual comparison as "an uneasy symbolic relationship."[93]

The ways in which the Klan was featured in the popular western invites comparison with the Klan's concurrent appearance in ephemeral, "low brow" formats exemplified by *The Black Mask*. Scholars have often linked these forms of popular fiction – dime novels, hardboiled detective fiction – to the kinds of working-class populations that are also often seen to constitute core Klan support.[94] For example, in the emergence of hard-boiled crime fiction, Sean McCann sees an anti-elitist literary genre that visualized the Klan's "nonfictional variety of nativist populism" on the page. Pulp fiction and the western B-movie seemingly offered a popular outlet for the nativist anxieties that motivated the Klan, damning the failings of contemporary society and, in their own ways, propagating a largely conservative form of Americanism. Beyond the ideological crossovers here, the pulp magazine's model of "fraternal intimacy" – for example, passing the magazine around friends – also aligned this form of literature with the communal idealism of the Klan.[95]

When tracking the representation of the Klan in popular fiction, across media and history, it is not a stretch to see how the vigilante activities of the modern Klan might be projected onto the narratives of the western. These narratives often involved the "spectacular" rescue of white women, threatened or taken captive by "foreign" races, and a central villain located in the saloon. Yet the neat resolutions found in the Klan's nativist fantasies, in its restoration of a social and racial order, were often challenged in these cinematic and literary genres.[96] While producers would position Klan-like groups in the western, by the early 1920s the night riders more often appear not as rescuers but as enemy assailants, carrying out the orders of the central villain. In *Cotton and Cattle*, the corrupt leader of the night-riding group, Buck Garrett, attempts to assault the innocent female, Ethel, while also frightening the "colored pickers" and burning their huts to the ground. The film constructs a clear contrast between the cowboys, representing the western plains, and the night riders, who are products of the South. "*Cotton and Cattle* might also be entitled *When West Meets South*," began *Exhibitors Trade Review*, while elsewhere it was presented as "Night-riders of the South vs. cowboys of the West."[97]

In *The White Masks*, Franklyn Farnum played the western hero Jack Bray, "a wanderer" who is confronted by Jim Dougherty and the "crooked work of the gang." Filmed in Tulsa, Oklahoma, in the summer of 1921 – a time of the most destructive race riots in the city's history – the film's battle between "South" and "West," between individual hero and collective group, indirectly questions the Klan's position in American society. As Farnum noted, "I have had occasion to portray many characters that were of the red-blooded American type, but Jack Bray in *The White Masks* has them all outdone."[98] These red-blooded American characters are not riding with the Klan but are the (misdirected) subjects of the Klan's attacks. In *Big Stakes*, a film advertised as a "wholesome, clean, American comedy drama," J. B. Warner's character embodies these patriotic values and yet directly opposes the night-riding group.[99]

Certainly the individualism of the western hero often countered the collective mass – evident also in Harry Carey's *The Night Riders,* which presented the lone western hero fighting "a gang of night-riding bandits" – but the hooded night riders also become a part of the economic subtexts that would inform so many low-budget westerns.[100] In *The Midnight Riders* (1920), for example, the masked and heavily armed members of a secret society that "only venture forth at night . . . take the law into their own hands without regards to the rights of property owners and spread terror throughout the country."[101] The night riders become imbricated with a set of issues, specific to the genre, such as property ownership, land rights, financial corruption, and private enterprise. In so doing, the films create a more complex economic model of the night riders, one that ultimately reinforces the presentation of a group that is widely misused for personal and economic ends.[102]

It is ultimately this misuse of the Klan costume that provides both the central source of criticism for Klan opponents and also its most enduring form of defense. In testifying to the misuse of the Klan costume, the films remain ideologically elusive and acceptable to both sides of the Klan divide. This is one of the ways in which producers sought to circumvent the ideological complexities and tensions in presenting this modern social group on-screen. Another is through their use of genre, repackaging and relocating Klan groups in youth-oriented genres, often as a source of action and excitement. What is striking here is that while producers attempted, at least ostensibly, to detach the night riders on-screen from the modern Klan, exhibitors appeared much keener to emphasize the links between screen and society. In reinserting and foregrounding the Klan image at the site of exhibition, promoters would work directly with modern Klan groups. They recognized the powerful, topical value of the Klan image and looked to use it to draw audiences into the theaters.

EXPLOITING THE KLAN

The social relevance of the now-topical Klan, a source of tension for censors and studios, presented a peculiar set of challenges for exhibitors and promoters. In advance of the New York premiere of *Birth* in 1915, horsemen had been hired to dress up in Klan regalia and restage the film's ride of the Klan through a New York park. Seven years later, a "troop of gowned knights" paraded outside the Strand Theatre on Broadway for the release of *One Clear Call* (fig. 4.4).[103] By 1922, the appearance of Klansmen with film banners draped over their horses was no longer a historical reenactment. *Kinematograph Weekly* noted this, stating that the introduction of the Klan would have an "appeal to many now that the party is again prominent in the daily news," while an exhibitor in Tennessee acknowledged that the popular interest in the Klan was boosting the film's success. "We played it while the newspapers were full of K.K.K. stuff," he stated, "and the Ku Klux end of the picture drew them in fine."[104] Exhibitors across the country extended these established exploitation practices, connecting them more directly with contemporary events. For A. P. Desormeaux, the manager of the Strand Theatre in Madison, Wisconsin, these stunts generated front-page coverage and local and national exposure for the theater. Desormeaux began by sending a picture of a Klansman to a number of local officials and businessmen and then hired a "lone horseman, masked, wearing white robes" to ride around the capital square. The horseman was taken to the police station for questioning before Desormeaux revealed that it was all a publicity campaign for *One Clear Call*, opening at the Strand Theatre the following night.[105]

Certainly some theater managers recognized potential dangers in associating with the modern Klan. In Winston-Salem, North Carolina, the manager of the Auditorium Theatre "got over the Ku Klux Klan effect" without the use of night riders, instead adopting large displays when "it becomes impossible or inadvisable to use the street ballyhoo."[106] A theater manager in Bellingham, Washington, "used the Ku Klux Klan rider on the streets," adopting this now-popular publicity device, but according to *Motion Picture News*, he "took care to have the rider dressed in a garb that did not resemble the costume of any known organization." *Exhibitors Herald* noted that such a stunt "carried a certain element of danger" and suggested that the man on horseback should carry a sign reading, "I am not a real Klansman. I am only answering One Clear Call to go to . . . theater." The paper argued that friends of the Klan might resent an impersonator, while opponents might send the actor back to

4.4. Promoting *One Clear Call* on Broadway. *Exhibitors Trade Review,* 9 September 1922, 984.

the theater as a "corpus delictu." The neutral costume may have been a curious compromise but, while theaters were keen to exploit the image of the night rider, some managers were more reluctant to align their theater directly with the local, modern Klan.[107]

In regions with a strong Klan following, the Klan elements were often emphasized more prominently. In Amarillo, Texas, for example, the manager at the Fair Theatre arranged a promotional campaign with the local Klan, which incorporated a large photograph of the local group as part of an elaborate but "inexpensive" lobby front. The display highlighted the words "One Clear Call," "Ku Klux Klan," and "1,000 riders" in bold lettering, while cutouts of masked riders stood at each side of the entrance and on the sidewalks. The Amarillo Klan generated even more publicity for the film (and for itself) by using six of its men to ride around the streets on horses in Klan robes prior to the film's release.[108]

The appearance of the masked horseman remained a most enduring, albeit adaptable, exploitation device. In Des Moines, Iowa, a masked bugler on horseback brought forward a Saturday night parade of night riders, marking "the first time night riders ever appeared on local streets." While local dispensation had been granted from the mayor and council, neither police nor public were seemingly aware of this, resulting in 120 telephone complaints about the parade. *Film Daily* reported only positives in this exploitation – "the trouble necessitated in reassuring these anxious ones gave added publicity to the picture" – but the publicity was not merely exploiting audience fears but also engineering and imagining a social impact and response in the town (in the form of a modern-day parade of night riders). There was, in the short term, mutual benefit for the theater and the Klan, the former for having sought publicity and exposure through this association, and the latter for gaining a level of legitimacy and advertising through the film.[109]

Exhibitors worked with local Klansmen in support of *One Clear Call*, even though the Klan appeared only fleetingly in the film. When the film played in Jackson, Mississippi, in September 1922, coinciding with a Klan convocation, the theater management offered five hundred Klansmen free admission to the balcony on the condition that they attended in "regular Klan regalia."[110] In Tulsa, a letter was posted in a "secret" letter box and read to an estimated 5,000 Klansmen, urging them to attend the local performance. The film played at the Isis Theatre in New Market, Iowa, in 1924 directly after *The Toll of Justice*. "Every real American should see both these pictures," the local advertisement stated.[111]

Such was the impact of using the image of night riders – in window displays, parades, and in other more elaborate promotional stunts – that promoters looked to use these devices even when the Klan was not featured on-screen. The manager of the Bijou Theatre in Racine, Wisconsin, "used the masked riders," previously associated with *One Clear Call* to promote the Norma Talmadge film *Smilin' Through* in 1922. The masked men traveled the streets in cars "ready to jump out at any moment" and take photos, which were then included in a "Best Smile" competition.

This particularly curious piece of exploitation may suggest that the Klan costume was commodified and desensitized, but, according to the theater manager, the Klan costume "aroused tremendous interest" and provided "about 200 inches of free publicity space" for his establishment.[112] The Klan image featured in a range of other exploitation contexts. The display for *Connecticut Yankee* (1921) showed a horse covered up in white, while the posters for *I Am the Law* (1922) depicted men on horseback, looking distinctly like night riders. For the Mack Sennett one-reeler *One Spooky Night* (1924), performances were staged outside the theater involving "ghosts," all dressed in white sheets.

As well as using the Klan costume, exhibitors found ever more ingenious ways to exploit the popular fascination in the modern Klan. In Washington, Indiana, the manager of the Liberty Theatre was particularly proud of his advertising campaign for *The Midnight Riders* late in 1921. He explained in *Exhibitors Herald* how he exploited the escalating local discussion of the Klan – in editorials, on the street, and "from the pulpit" – which had been fueled by a rumored visit to the city from a Klan organizer. A week before the film's arrival, the theater began distributing leaflets around the town with phrases like "Clansman. Let this be a solemn warning." Only later did the theater follow up with posters for *The Midnight Riders*. The posters introduced "the picture that stirred up the whole town" and, despite being set in the 1890s, reimagined and foregrounded the presence on-screen of "mysterious Klansmen."[113]

Similar campaigns followed in states like Ohio, a well-established center for Klan activity in the early 1920s. In one example, exhibitor George J. Schade had signs painted all over the town of Sandusky, which read, "Look out, bootleggers. K.K.K." Newspapers speculated on the forthcoming Klan activity, but the sign was merely a publicity stunt for a new film that bore no connection to the Klan. The full sign a few days later read, "Look out, bootleggers. Every K.K.K. will see Within the Law. Schade Theatre, Sun., Mon., Tues." Schade recognized the publicity and notoriety that could be generated through the Klan and used this to his advantage once more when promoting *The Christian* in 1923. The local Klan built a fiery cross on the ice on a lake and set a second cross ablaze on a neighboring hill. Schade produced his own thirty-foot cross, electrically lit, which he placed on top of his theater. In doing so, he claimed cheap yet valuable publicity, with the discussions and excitement generated from the Klan's original displays leading to conversation about Schade and his new film.[114] The Klan was the basis for another stunt in Ohio in 1923 when the Dome Theatre in Youngstown placed an advertisement in a Klan paper "inviting the Knights of the Invisible Empire to meet the two best known Jews in the world face to face." It is unclear what happened at this meeting and indeed who was involved, but *Moving Picture World* recognized that, although "it was a daring stunt, the gag worked."[115]

These elaborate publicity stunts were not exclusively the domain of local, independent theater owners; the larger studios also utilized the Klan in promotions. One such campaign began when a hundred leading citizens in San Francisco received warning letters from the KKK, which, according to *Moving Picture World,* they promptly showed to friends and police. A week later the first of a set of three large, twenty-four-sheet stands appeared, reading, "Prepare! K.K.K. is coming!!" Later posts provided the name of a theater and a date. According to reports, speculation mounted in the local press that the Klan was preparing to rent out the theater for a demonstration, and on the specified date locals flocked to the venue. On arrival, they saw no evidence of the Klan but found instead *Three Ages,* a new Buster Keaton comedy. The exhibitors explained that KKK had actually stood for "Keaton's Kolossal Komedy" and that the whole campaign had been a stunt to attract audiences to the film.[116]

This was not an isolated incident. Indeed, the studio's own press book for *Three Ages* had suggested the idea. *Film Daily* reported the same campaign in Nashville, Tennessee, "based on the K.K.K. stunt mentioned in the Metro press book," and noted that the most effective aspect of the publicity was the mail campaign. Citizens received a letter, with "Prepare K.K.K. Is Coming!" written in bold red letters over the entire page, followed the next day by another stating that "Nashville Will Soon Know The Power of K.K.K." "By this stage curiosity had turned to the keenest anticipation not unmixed with a little anxiety," wrote *Film Daily;* "wherever two people got together the conversation immediately turned to the K.K.K."[117] This attempt to control and contain the Klan image, while simultaneously exploiting it, highlights the industry's paradoxical relationship with the Klan. Though the Klan was somewhat taboo on film, studios (and independent exhibitors) were more willing to use the group's distinctive imagery to promote films, many of which had no discernible link with it. In doing so, they drew attention to or inserted Klan elements that were often concealed by producers. It is a contradiction that underscores the appearances of the Klan throughout the 1920s. In the case of *The Mating Call,* promotional materials emphasized the excitement and spectacle generated by the hooded group. "Terrorists furnish climax," was the headline of one Paramount publicity report; "the activities of a band of hooded terrorists provide a spectacular climax to Thomas Meighan's latest photodrama." This exploitation suggests once more that it was industrial as well as economic factors (censorship, controversy after *Birth,* and the need to attract young audiences) that guided presentations of the group, given the evident demand to use this Klan material. By the 1930s, with Klan groups back in the news, these factors would largely dissipate, and the industry found new ways, settings, and genres in which to address and respond to the Klan on-screen.

1930S: THE SOCIAL PROBLEM FILM

In a pivotal sequence in Fritz Lang's 1936 film *Fury,* the district attorney brings a movie projector into the courtroom (fig. 4.5). After a succession of witnesses have refused to testify against members of the mob accused of lynching the innocent working-class victim, Joe Wilson, newsreel footage is projected into the darkened courtroom. Pausing over shots of the accused men – pouring kerosene and lighting torches – the film exposes the individual members of the lynch mob and, more broadly, makes visible the concealed practices of sections of American society.

Beyond its narrative function, the scene also, as Amy Louise Wood argues, transforms the footage from a form of tabloid sensationalism into a political and moral tool.[118] This transformation is not without its problems. *Fury* also illustrates the unreliable nature of film as an indexical medium since, despite what the sensational images lead courtroom viewers to conclude, Joe is not actually killed by the mob. Yet in using film to expose vigilante violence – both in the narrative and beyond – the scene extolls the pedagogical function of film as an aid to social change. "More than I have ever seen it done before," wrote Walter White, execu-

4.5. Using film to bring vigilante groups to justice in Fritz Lang's *Fury*, MGM, 1936.

tive secretary of the NAACP after viewing *Fury* in 1936, "has the medium of the moving picture been used to bring home to America what mob violence really means." White hoped that the film would encourage congressional action in support of the Costigan-Wagner anti-lynching bill, and he wrote to all branches of the NAACP urging members to see the film. MGM suggested special screenings for law enforcement officers and city officials, while extracts from both *Fury* and *Black Legion* were adopted by the Progressive Education Association in New York as part of its "Human Relations Series" in schools and colleges.[119] Film was now employed to expose the illegal vigilante acts of Klan-like groups.

In the final sequence of Mervyn LeRoy's *They Won't Forget*, released a year after *Fury*, a young woman, widowed by the mob, places the blame for her husband's murder not on the men who dragged him from a train but on a politically ambitious and opportunistic district attorney and also a newspaper reporter. "You're the ones who really killed him. You're the ones who stirred up all the hatred and prejudice," she concludes, "for no other reason than it suited your ambition and it made a good story." Based on Ward Greene's novelization of the Leo Frank case, *They Won't Forget* focuses less on the intricacies of the murder – the film never does reveal the culprit – and more on the public response, revealing a media-made mob. The culpability of press and law enforcement was more explicitly outlined in a 1938 radio episode of *The Shadow,* featuring Orson Welles, which concluded with the newspaper editor and judge being disrobed as the leaders of the White Legion (a Klan-like vigilante group) and led away from the courtroom.

This narrative focus on the press's responses to (and culpability for) vigilante violence is supplemented by the aesthetics in these films. At LeRoy's suggestion the trailer for *They Won't Forget* adopted the format of a newsreel, while the use of sensational newspaper headlines was a narrative device common to a number of "exploitation" B-movies, such as *Nation Aflame,* and also Warner's social problem films, such as *Fury, Black Legion,* and *Mountain Justice.* The trailer for the latter film, directed by Michael Curtiz, opens with a succession of newspaper headlines ("Mob seizes prisoner in mountain jail") and shots of the machinery of the printed press ("It's hot news . . . And Warner Bros. score another daring screen scoop"). In constantly incorporating and referencing different media, the films foreground the media responses to these forms of violence. In contrast to the concealed depictions of the Klan in the westerns and children's comedies of the 1920s, social problem films of the 1930s not only presented contemporary vigilante and Klan violence as a subject but also addressed the function and responsibility of film itself, as part of the media, in responding to these events and shaping popular attitudes toward them. In *Nation Aflame,* the Klan is finally exposed by a newspaperman through the pages of his paper. In effect, these self-reflexive films, like *Fury* and *They Won't Forget,* offer a call to arms for the medium at a moment when a cycle of industry films, for the first time, sought to confront and make visible the activities of the Klan and Klan-like groups.

Between November 1936 and March 1937, three films were released that took as their subject the recent murder of Charles Poole in Detroit by the Black Legion group. In November 1936, Columbia released *Legion of Terror,* which was followed a couple of months later by Warners' *Black*

Legion, before *Nation Aflame* appeared in March 1937. Taken together, these three films reveal a significant shift in the on-screen representation of the Klan, one that responds both to the Klan's marginalized position in political and film discourse and also to industrial changes, in particular the emergence of the social problem film that was addressing and confronting contemporary news stories. These two factors, the fortunes of the Klan and industry, altered the ways in which the subject could be articulated on-screen.

The emergence of this short-lived "Klan cycle" coincides with a renewed press interest in these Klan-like groups. On the back of the Poole murder and the revelation in 1937 that President Roosevelt's nominee for the Supreme Court, Hugo Black, was a former Klansman who had used the Klan in the 1920s to further his political ambitions, editorials speculated about the rise of a new Klan. *Liberty* magazine ran a special edition in 1937 with the heading, "Is the Ku Klux Klan coming back?" while a month later, *Look* asked if the Klan was "rising to power again."[120] While these questions attest to a renewed interest in the Klan, ultimately the "Klan cycle" confirms the displacement of the group in American popular culture. Indeed, these films suggest that the Klan had lost the ideological war that it had fought, both on and through the media, over the previous twenty years. By 1936, the Klan was not simply the product of a corrupt leader or dubious "secretive" methods, but was also presented as fundamentally "un-American," a direct threat to the ideals that it earlier claimed to uphold.

Nation Aflame depicts a group of "un-American" murdering opportunists who, as the film explains, decide to "capitalize on jealousy, intolerance and patriotism." Written by Thomas Dixon, the film presents a villainous mastermind, Sands, who, in his own words, seeks to establish a secret lodge "with plenty of mystery, secret meetings, secret oaths, mysterious robes and phoney rituals. Boy the suckers will eat it up." The film opens with a quote from Lincoln, but while *Birth* had presented the Klan upholding and administering Lincoln's ideals as part of the rebirth of a nation, *Nation Aflame* now presented the Klan as a direct threat to these ideals. A poster for the film read, "Save a nation from shame and slavery," with the Klan no longer representing freedom and national pride but enforcing "shame" and "slavery."[121]

They Won't Forget opens with a different quote from Lincoln, inscribed beneath his memorial, and then introduces a group of six Confederate veterans as they prepare to march on Confederates Day. Ostensibly set in Atlanta and based on historical events from the mid-1910s, the parade appears almost as a sequel to that in *Birth*. The same music is used in both films, and while there may only be a few surviving veterans in *They Won't Forget*, the legacy of violence, racism, and sectarian differences celebrated and memorialized in *Birth* is not forgotten but continues in modern society. *They Won't Forget* recalls the context in which *Birth* flourished and shows the dangers that come with memorializing the "lost cause." In looking back at the teens from the perspective of 1937, the film challenges Griffith's processes of memorialization and history making, while also revealing the impact that film can exercise on social behavior.

The publicity for this "Klan cycle" also illustrates and contributes to the repositioning of the Klan in patriotic discourse. Where previously the Klan was established as the embodiment of Americanism, which in turn protected it from industry condemnation, by the 1930s the industry was able to promote and define its own patriotism by criticizing these "Un-American masked mob gangs." A publicity expert in *Independent Exhibitors Film Bulletin* urged theater managers exhibiting *Legion of Terror* to tell their patrons that these groups "preach '100% Americanism,' but would destroy the very fabric of our country if they had their way."[122] Promotional campaigns for *Legion of Terror* included a newspaper contest to find "the 'real American family' in your town," while another contest asked readers to name "the greatest living American." For *Black Legion*, Warners proposed sending people out with sandwich boards declaring, "Learn how to protect the American ideals – Life, Liberty and the Pursuit of Happiness," while another suggested public notice for *Legion of Terror* stated, "If you're an American[,] if you stand for democracy[,] if you despise secrecy and racketeering[,] attend mass meeting Friday night, Rialto Theatre!" Such publicity sought to politicize the film, with these proposed campaigns presenting these Klan-like groups as direct threats to traditional American values. Columbia even suggested special screenings of *Legion of Terror* for "local American Legionnaires, and other patriotic organizations which stand for American democracy and Liberty."[123] Producers aligned themselves with genuine patriotic organizations, which they now contrasted with discredited Klan-like groups. The on-screen criticisms of these Klan-like groups no longer called into question the studios' patriotism, but served to establish their true patriotic values.

The film industry's changing response to the Klan can also be understood by looking at the films in relation to genre. In the 1920s the Klan featured predominantly in westerns and comedies intended for youthful audiences, but synchronized sound and the emergence of the social problem film provided a framework for more critical exposés of the group. In a notable shift, the "Klan cycle" of the 1930s sought to address the Klan directly and with claims of authenticity. Promotions for *Black Legion* included large cut-outs for theater lobbies exclaiming, "It really happened," while other posters displayed the menacing hooded murderer saying, "I may be standing next to you" and "Beware of these brothers of Butchery."[124] Further advertisements declared that "the screen brings America's INVISIBLE TERROR right out into the open!" while newspaper reports of the Poole killing were used as publicity for all these films, in the case of *Black Legion* sent out to schools by the Progressive Education Association. The industry was emphasizing the social relevance of these pictures – albeit with some disclaimers – by presenting a direct link between the Klan on- and off-screen. "Are dramatic pictures competing with newsreels?" asked one report on *Legion of Terror*, a film that was, according to publicity, "daring in its exposé of the racket behind hooded organizations that are infesting sections of America." Advertisements explained that this was the "first breath-taking exposé of the hooded hoodlums who menace the nation," and further labeled the film the "year's most timely picture!"[125]

The position of the Klan in these more adult genres may have enabled producers to depict a modern, violent Klan, but such a representation was still dictated by industry regulation. Matthew Bernstein has shown the elaborate process of negotiation that took *They Won't Forget* from page to screen. On viewing the first draft, Joseph Breen, the head of the Production Code Administration, ordered the removal of all scenes of drunkenness and police brutality and emphasized the need to show justice administered by the "processes of law."[126] The PCA objected to

The Birth of a Nation in 1938, complaining that the film "creates sympathy for those who take the law into their own hands . . . and tends to inspire in others a desire for imitation."[127] The Klan also remained a problem. Breen noted that all scenes of "masked men" would need to be cut from *They Won't Forget,* while as early as November 1936 the Maryland State Board of Motion Picture Censorship had written to the MPPDA "to complain about the cycle of films dealing with the Ku Klux Klan organizations." Morris Ebenstein at Warners admitted that he was unsure "whether to make a Black Legion picture at all," aware of the extreme reactions that the subject might generate.[128] These reactions were partially defined by geography. *They Won't Forget* was refused a permit in Atlanta and performed less well in the South, suggesting that Trotti's "business" concerns about depictions of the Klan still applied, although as Bernstein suggests, the paucity of first-run theaters in the South alleviated some of these concerns for Warners.[129]

Furthermore, censors still closely monitored the presentation of "foreign" characters on film. Breen only agreed to the premise of *Nation Aflame* on the condition that the victims of the Avenging Angels "would definitely not be characterized as Jews, Catholics or Negroes." Breen had also told Warners that an early script for *Black Legion* was "unacceptable" because it addressed the "provocative and inflammatory subjects of racial and religious prejudice." Censors may have restricted the presentation of specific foreign targets, but producers worked around this by presenting unspecified foreign and immigrant groups on-screen. Gregory Black notes that in the case of *Black Legion,* "once the script had been changed to straightforward hatred of foreigners, Breen had issued a seal."[130] During the 1920s, the removal of racial and religious figures on-screen had ensured that the Klan was presented in relation to moral enemies. The appearance by 1936 of non-specific "immigrants" and "foreigners" certainly helped to distinguish the motives of the Klan from those of the idealized group of the 1920s.

In making the move into more adult genres, producers traversed the line between exploitation and education. Lisa M. Rabin has argued that the use of *Black Legion* in the Human Relations Film Series provided an early example of the role of educational film in addressing race relations and in engineering debate amongst multi-class and multi-ethnic groups.

4.6. Suggested advertising from the pressbook for *Black Legion*
(1936). *Reprinted courtesy of BFI National Archive.*

The film program catered to diverse immigrant student bodies and their
families. In this way, these industry films reworked non-theatrical methods previously used by the Klan when it had attempted to present film in
schools as a way to educate America's youth.[131]

   Yet while producers emphasized the pedagogical function of these
films, they still retained much of their tabloid sensationalism even as
they purported to present film as a political and moral tool. The films
borrowed heavily from sensational newspaper headlines. *Legion of Terror* was "ripped red-hot from the revelations that shocked all America!"

while *Nation Aflame* was "virtually lifted bodily from the sensational headlines of recent months." Posters for *Black Legion* also stated that "the story the nation whispered now thunders from the screen!" (fig. 4.6).[132] The representation of the Klan had seemingly shifted, but producers continued to exploit the Klan as a source of excitement. In the case of *Legion of Terror,* advertisements exclaimed "Extra! Hooded Killers exposed!" while reviews noted that the film reached "an exciting climax with a murderous night ride of the Legion." Posters for *Nation Aflame* contained pictures of Klansmen (in white) beneath the words "Sensational! Startling!" Even in the seemingly serious drama of *Black Legion,* the Klan was still sold as a sensation. In publicity materials for the film, Warners suggested ways to exploit the Klan image, telling exhibitors that "cut-outs of hooded figures on your marquee can be made doubly effective if lit up at night with flaming torches."[133]

Exploitation for the "Klan cycle" also mirrored many of the methods used in the 1920s. For example, Columbia suggested hiring men dressed in the black hooded costumes of the film to travel through shopping districts shortly before the release of *Legion of Terror.* "Without benefit of signs on their backs," Columbia advised, "have them wander mysteriously around, whispering to passers by: 'MEETING TONIGHT RIALTO THEATER!'" The films offered direct attacks on modern Klan groups, but the exploitation still highlighted a commercial fascination with these costumed figures. Warners also recognized the public excitement generated by the appearance of Klansmen. As one of its seven selling points for *Black Legion,* Warners suggested the following: "Running Gag on your opening day – have a comedian carried out of the theater on a stretcher by two hooded figures, and into ambulance. Pull stunt every hour or so."[134]

While producers and exhibitors sought to exploit fears about new vigilante groups, the Klan also recognized an opportunity for publicity, as attested by its lawsuit with Warners over the Black Legion insignia. Popular and industry responses were largely cemented against modern vigilante groups, but the Klan still attempted to engage with film, to promote and redefine itself, as it had done so successfully before. The Klan cycle itself would prove to be short-lived, however; in an October 1937 review of *Nation Aflame, Motion Picture Daily* commented on the "secret society debunking propaganda, the cycle of which by this time has undoubtedly spun its course." Nevertheless, Klan groups continued to exploit other films, most notably *The Birth of a Nation*.[135]

By the late 1930s, with the Klan redefining itself as a predominantly anticommunist and anti-union group, the Klan used debates over *The Birth of a Nation* to highlight and condemn the communist threat. Janet Staiger has argued that toward the end of the 1930s, *Birth* was reconfigured by critical leftist and communist publications as a propagator of capitalism. The Klan appeared to embrace this reinterpretation of the film, though from a radically opposed ideological position. Glenn Feldman has observed that the film played regularly in Alabama "at the height of Birmingham's communist hysteria." Local Klan groups often supported and aligned themselves with these screenings. For example, in 1936 the Robert E. Lee Klavern placed advertisements for itself alongside posters for *The Birth of a Nation,* employing the same publicity method that William Simmons had used to launch the Klan in Atlanta twenty-one years earlier. By the end of the 1930s the film once again served as a battleground on which the Klan and its opponents confronted one another. As Staiger notes, early in 1940 the official communist newspaper, the *Daily Worker,* and its supporters "participated with blacks in picketing theaters reviving The Birth of a Nation."[136]

The repositioning of *Birth* in a modern social context may have renewed interest in the film, but it also altered its reception once more. When the *Portsmouth New Haven Herald* advertised a screening of *Birth* in January 1939, it contained a picture of a Klansman on a horse. Above the picture was the tagline, "The dreaded Ku Klux Klan rides again!" A few months earlier a piece in the *New Yorker,* entitled "Other Times, Other Morals," discussed a recent screening of *The Birth of a Nation* near Times Square. The writer explained that in 1915, "when the Klan rode out to save Lillian Gish the audience stood and cheered. Last week a new generation hissed the Klan and applauded ironically when Miss Gish repressed the foul mulatto."[137]

The Klan "remade" *Birth* ideologically throughout this period, as propaganda for the modern Klan and as an anticommunist text. Yet at the same time, the film industry was rewriting the history offered in *Birth*. First, in 1938, Paramount released the Randolph Scott western

The Texans, set in the Reconstruction era. At the end of the film, Alan, a Southerner who is unable to accept that the war is over, announces his latest plan to his female interest, Ivy. "We've got a new secret organization," he excitedly reveals. "It's springing up everywhere in the South. It's called the K K K – Ku Klux Klan." He states that the purpose of the group is "to drive the Yankees out of the South," explaining that "we meet at night and we wear masks." Ivy dismisses the heroic presentation of the group offered in *Birth*: "How childish! . . . This is America. We govern by law not night-riding . . . You're just a boy playing at soldiers." *The Texans* offered the same romantic view of Reconstruction shown repeatedly in films (most famously in *Birth*), yet the role of the Klan in this myth, shaped by the memory of the group's most recent incarnation, had irrevocably changed.

A year later, in 1939, David O. Selznick released the film adaptation of the hugely successful Margaret Mitchell novel *Gone with the Wind.* Selznick's epic effectively supported and retold Dixon and Griffith's history of the post–Civil War era. Yet, while Griffith had placed the Klan as central to his story of Reconstruction, Selznick removed the Klan from this history entirely. Significantly, Mitchell's novel largely endorsed the history of Reconstruction presented in *Birth*. She herself acknowledged the influence of Dixon on her work in a letter to him in 1936. "I was practically raised on your books," she wrote, "and loved them very much." She also recalled putting on plays from Dixon's books, which featured local neighbors dressed as clansmen.[138] The influence of Dixon was also apparent in Mitchell's attitude toward the original Klan: her novel presents the group as honorable and necessary. In the novel, India Wilkes tells Scarlett that "of course, Mr. Kennedy is in the Klan, and Ashley too, and all the men we know. They are men aren't they? And white men and southerners." India adds that "you should have been proud of him [Mr. Kennedy] instead of making him sneak out as though it were something shameful." Mitchell subsequently defended her sympathetic presentation of the Klan: "I have not written anything on the Klan which is not common knowledge to every Southerner."[139] This "common knowledge" was popularized by *The Birth of a Nation,* but by 1939 the legacy of the modern group that the film had helped to develop prevented a sympathetic presentation of the Klan on-screen.

Selznick determined at a very early stage to remove the Klan from the film version of *Gone with the Wind*. At a time in January 1937 when *Black Legion, Legion of Terror,* and *Nation Aflame* were all playing across the country, Selznick wrote a memo to screenwriter Sidney Howard, outlining his reservations about the Klan scenes. "I personally feel quite strongly that we should cut out the Klan entirely," he wrote. "It would be difficult if not impossible, to clarify for our audiences the difference between the old Klan and the Klan of our times."[140]

Selznick did not challenge the romanticized history offered in the novel (and in *Birth*), but he recognized that the modern Klan had reshaped the memory of the original group: "A year or so ago I refused to consider remaking *The Birth of a Nation,* largely for this reason." "Of course we might have shown a couple of Catholic Klansmen," he added regarding *Gone with the Wind,* "but it would be rather comic to have a Jewish Kleagle." Selznick did not feel audiences would distinguish the Klan on-screen from the vilified modern group and, unlike the producers of the 1920s, he suggested that the Klan could not be separated from issues of race and religion.[141]

The Klan press once more saw this on-screen revision as evidence of an ongoing attack by the film industry. "It is no secret," the *Fiery Cross* editorialized in 1941, "that the movie moguls have always fought the Ku Klux Klan because of its outstanding advocacy of Americanism and its opposition to affiliating with alien groups." Recalling the "vicious and greatly exaggerated propaganda" of *Black Legion,* the paper noted the complete elimination of the Klan from *Gone with the Wind,* which it suggested illustrated that "Jews will even stoop to [a] distortion of history to carry out their propaganda." However, a year earlier the same paper had celebrated *Gone with the Wind's* "uncanny accuracy and fidelity" and labeled the film "a celluloid epoch comparable with that other great screen story, 'The Birth of a Nation.'" This is indicative, once more, of the Klan's opportunism, reworking film discourses to define and position itself against its modern opponents. While its criticisms in 1941 served its antisemitic agenda, the Klan's praise in February 1940 furthered its anticommunist program and was primarily motivated by the very public condemnation of the film by the Communist Party newspaper, the *Daily Worker.* The *Daily Worker's* film reviewer, Howard Rushmore, famously left his role with the paper after ignoring his editor's instructions to "blister" *Gone with the Wind* and to urge his readers to boycott it. The Klan celebrated Rushmore's conversion "back to old fashioned American Americanism," while the subsequent review in the *Daily Worker* reimagined the historical film in relation to contemporary politics. The paper provocatively labeled Selznick's film "a glorification of the Ku Klux Klan," despite the removal of all direct references to the Klan, and suggested that the film's premiere in Atlanta was fitting, as the city "is the national headquarters of the Ku Klux Klan which this picture so insidiously glorifies."[142]

However, while Atlanta remained the spiritual and operational center of the Klan, the Klan's erasure from Atlanta history in *Gone with the Wind* reflects the group's faltering position in the city. On the eve of the film's celebrated world premiere there – at Loew's Grand Opera House, the same theater that first presented Dixon's play *The Clansman* in 1905 – a parade was arranged down Peachtree Street, but this time without a Klansman in sight. Indeed, while the events – the parade, a *Gone with the Wind* ball, and the premiere itself with invited Civil War veterans in attendance – brazenly celebrated Atlanta's Confederate past, the Klan's position both as part of this romanticized past and in contemporary Atlanta was increasingly unstable. Perhaps the single most damning example could be found on Peachtree Street itself, where the Imperial Palace, once the center of Klan operations, now served as the Cathedral of Christ the King after having been sold to an insurance company in 1936 and then to the Catholic archdiocese.[143]

Whilst Selznick cut the Klan from the film entirely, the group responded by attempting to put itself back in, to reinsert itself into film culture. It did so by returning to a strategy first utilized in 1915, when William Simmons unveiled the modern Klan by burning a fiery cross on Stone Mountain just outside Atlanta. Then, the launch of the Klan had effectively coincided with the Atlanta premiere of *The Birth of a Nation*. In 1939, shortly before *Gone with the Wind* premiered in Atlanta, representatives of the Klan contacted MGM with a similar idea. The Klan, keen to align itself with the film and looking to generate publicity, offered to burn a fiery cross on top of Stone Mountain to mark the film's opening. The difference in the Klan's reputation between 1915 and 1939 was palpable, however, and the Klan's offer was dismissed out of hand, with the story appearing only as a brief anecdote in local papers.[144]

The incident highlights both the Klan's marginalized position and its continued attempts to use film and the media to regain influence in American society. When James Colescott succeeded Hiram Evans as Imperial Wizard in June 1939, he launched a new "program of action" that he hoped would reinvigorate the Klan. One of his very first moves was to reintroduce the *Fiery Cross,* which would run for twenty-nine issues over the next three years, from July 1939 to October 1942. Labeled "The voice of Americanism," the *Fiery Cross* outlined Klan policies (for example, the "Klan opposes every ism of alien origin") and circulated directives (such as the removal of visors from the Klan costume after 1940). It reprinted reports on the Klan from the popular press, circulated tales of Klan activity, and sought to mobilize local groups behind Americanization campaigns.[145]

From the outset, Colescott outlined the need to regain control of the representation of the Klan. In a speech given in Florida in 1939, under the theme "Rebirth of the Nation," Colescott complained that the "Old Klan was severely hindered by adverse propaganda, principally in the form of atrocities committed in the name of the Klan. One of the principle missions of the new Klan will be the elimination of the sources of false propaganda." While making both a familiar defense for and a distinction from the discredited Klan of the 1920s, Colescott still recognized this control of "propaganda" as a racial and religious issue. The *Fiery Cross* described Hollywood as a "veritable honeycomb of foreign, alien, radical – even subversive elements" and, in October 1939, published the names of fifty actors and actresses who, it suggested, did not reveal their "true colors." Those stars, listed along with their birth names, included Joan Crawford (Lucille LeSueur), Mary Astor (Lucille Langhanke), Fred Astaire (Frederick Austerlitz), and Edward G. Robinson (Emanuel Goldenberg).[146]

A few months later, when discussing the "stream of propaganda" emanating from "alien" interests, the *Fiery Cross* outlined what it saw as "one of the jobs of the Klan." "Fill the minds of the American people with thoughts of their own country," the paper decreed, "and warn them to be on guard against the insidious influence of the movie where certain groups never lose an opportunity to advance their teachings at the expense of America." By promoting what it saw as positive American values and simultaneously monitoring "alien" messages, the Klan was again attempting to position itself on the front line of a battle over on-screen representation. A year later in July 1941, the Klan sought to materialize these anxieties into a larger national campaign, with Colescott announcing "the Million Dollar Americanization Program." An advertisement in the *Fiery Cross* explained that, through this fundraising campaign, the Klan aimed to promote Americanism "by means of sound trucks, newspapers, magazines, radio, motion pictures, booklets, speakers and every legitimate means available."[147]

While the Klan was no longer in a position to make any feature films, it did look to broadcast its message over the radio. On occasion, it manufactured ways to maneuver itself onto established shows. For example, a delegation turned up at WSB in Atlanta as part of the station's Christmas charity drive and gave a donation "fat enough to ensure happiness for a lot of needy folk." The *Fiery Cross* noted that the Klan was thanked before it made a short statement to the "million radio listeners throughout the south." The Klan's charity donation might best be interpreted as a form of sponsorship, effectively paying for airtime and for an affiliation with an established charitable campaign and radio station. Other Klan groups would pay for airtime more explicitly, as was the case with a weekly broadcast in Michigan; similarly, at the start of 1941, Ben E. Adams, the editor of the *Fiery Cross* (and Grand Dragon of South Carolina), launched *The Klan Speaks,* a fifteen-minute broadcast every Sunday on WFBC in Greenville, South Carolina, sponsored by three local Klan groups. Each week's program would begin with a verse of "America" before the music faded and the Grand Dragon began to speak in a studio full of applauding Klansmen. The broadcast was, unsurprisingly, widely celebrated in the *Fiery Cross,* where Colescott described it as "one of the most worthwhile efforts in all Klan history." This hyperbolic statement might be understood either as an indication of the continued importance of media to the modern Klan or as a damning indictment of the previous seventy-five years of Klan history.[148]

The Klan continued to rally against the "Jewish controlled press, radio and motion picture," complaining, for example, that Klan broadcasts were often kept off the air under pressure from Jewish advertisers. However, the terms in which the Klan articulated these antisemitic fears had subtly shifted in light of the encroaching global crisis that would climax in World War II. First, the Klan, in a return to discourses circulating around the Red Scare in 1920, presented the Jewish influences in relation to a greater communist threat, arguing that most of the propaganda "thrown on the screen by the Jew-controlled motion picture industry comes as a result of Communists in the industry." Second, its fears of "complete" Jewish control of the film industry were tied up in escalating fears of war. The Klan still referred to the "Jewish owned" industry's attempts "to break down the Christian Sunday and ridicule Protestant Clergymen," but, as a group vehemently opposed to war (before December 1941), it saw a Jewish industry "attempting to embroil the nation in another European conflict," forcing "America to bankrupt itself and spill its blood in a foreign war in which America has no part."[149]

The Klan remained acutely sensitive to how it was represented in the media. Colescott urged readers to send him any news reports of the Klan, which he would then publish in the *Fiery Cross* along with his response. Not all coverage was negative: Colescott celebrated *Life*'s four-page spread regarding the Klan's initiation ceremony at Stone Mountain in July 1939 as an "outstanding journalistic achievement." In general, newspapers helped Colescott to publicize his modern Klan to a wider audience, whether through accounts of Klan activities or through the Klan's response – but he would seize an even better opportunity in 1942 when the House Committee on Un-American Activities (widely known as the Dies Committee) launched an investigation into the group and called him to face the committee. Perhaps recognizing a parallel with the platform William Simmons had used when he was called before the House Rules Committee in 1921, Colescott welcomed the investigation as an opportunity to publicize the Klan's American credentials.

The Dies Committee was set up in 1938 to investigate subversive and disloyal activities in America, and from the outset the Klan championed its work. In 1939, Colescott wrote a telegram to its chairman, Martin Dies, congratulating him on the "splendid results you have achieved" and thanking him for the "graphic picture you have given America of enemies within our gates and government." "Every true American, and

that includes every Klansman," he added, "is behind the Dies Committee in its efforts to turn the country back to the honest, freedom-loving,
God-fearing Americans to whom it belongs." A few months later in January 1940, the *Fiery Cross* published Dies's keynote address delivered at
Madison Square Garden in its entirety ("Marxists shall not take away
God-given America," thundered Dies) and appropriated his speech as
"the keynote of the 1940 program of action laid down by the Ku Klux
Klan." Throughout its three-year run, the *Fiery Cross* would praise the
work of the Dies Committee, championing the "patriots" that served on
it and excoriating those senators who voted against its continuation.[150]

   In 1941, when a Senate subcommittee turned its attentions more
directly to the motion picture industry, the hearings articulated many
of the Klan's well-established anxieties. In investigating evidence of anti-
Nazi, war-mongering "propaganda" in the movies, the committee was
widely accused of antisemitism. "Those primarily responsible for the
propaganda pictures are born abroad," stated Senator Gerald Nye, further suggesting that in their desire to aid "certain causes abroad," these
figures "lose sight of what some Americans might call the first interests
of America."[151] Colescott recognized a Senate committee largely sympathetic to Klan ideals, and he provocatively suggested that the names
of committee members "would be found to be similar to if not the same
as former Klansmen."[152]

   While these investigations offer a reminder that the traditional values of the Klan still resonated at all levels of American political life,
the Klan's appearance before the Dies Committee also reveals its increasingly precarious position as an arbiter and embodiment of traditional American values. Indeed, when Dies announced the decision to
investigate the Klan, after meeting with Colescott at the end of January
1942, Henry Ford was threatening the Klan with legal action, a further
indication of the ideologically volatile context in which the Klan was
operating.[153]

   At the height of its growth and expansion in the early 1920s, the Klan
had embraced and reworked Ford's antisemitic writings. Twenty years
later, in 1941, it would again look to latch onto Ford's writing (and celeb-
rity), republishing a batch of old antisemitic essays from his *Dearborn
Independent* in a collection entitled *The International Jew*. Ford objected

to the "intentional misrepresentation" of his views, while the Klan countered by stating that the book merely collected articles that had been featured in the *Dearborn Independent*. The issue was clearly exacerbated by recent American participation in the war. The Klan wrote to Ford at the start of January explaining that it had withdrawn the booklet on the day war was declared, but reports suggested that the booklet had reached Germany, where it was reprinted by the Nazis.

The incident drew attention to an ideological alliance between the Klan and the Nazis, which threatened the Klan's American credentials in the midst of war. This was particularly damaging in the light of earlier widespread coverage of an outdoor meeting involving members of the German-American Bund and the Klan on the Bund's grounds in New Jersey in August 1940. On that occasion, Colescott had quickly launched an investigation and removed the participating officers but, as with the *Black Legion* case, the Klan faced criticisms that it was "un-American" at a moment when the country was enveloped in patriotic fervor and when the oft-repeated Klan anxieties around foreign threats were most acutely realized. Indeed, rather than initiating a new beginning for the Klan as might be imagined, American participation in the war would accelerate its decline. The production of the *Fiery Cross* was scaled down from eight pages to four, ostensibly to conserve paper as part of the war effort. In addition, a number of Klan leaders announced their intention to step down in order to enlist, while the Imperial Klonvokation in 1942 was postponed so that those who had intended to travel could spend their money instead on war bonds. The end, or at least an end, would soon follow, and in an entirely befitting way. After years of seeking legitimacy from the government and recognition as an American institution, the Klan received a tax bill in 1944 for $685,325. Backdated from the 1920s, when the Klan's commercial dealings had brought forward untold wealth, Colescott's moneymaking enterprise had become a financial noose. Thus constrained, he called a Klonvocation and formally disbanded the Klan.[154]

Epilogue

On the evening of May 9 1946 at 8 PM a mob of fully grown men solemnly
paraded up to a wide plateau on Stone Mountain, outside Atlanta, Ga., and
got down on their knees on the ground before 100 white-sheeted and hooded
Atlantans. In the eerie light of a half-moon and a fiery 200-by-300 foot cross
they stumbled in lock step up to a great stone altar and knelt there in the dirt
while the "Grand Dragon" went through the mumbo jumbo of initiating them
into the Ku Klux Klan.

Life, 27 May 1946

The launch of a new Klan in postwar America – one not crippled by tax
debts – was covered across the national media, including in a three-page
spread in *Life*. While the report was scathing of the "mumbo jumbo"
spoken and the "childish rituals and secretiveness," the magazine also
published eleven photographs, showing both private rituals and scenes
of the initiates on Stone Mountain. The widespread media coverage of
the event highlighted and inadvertently celebrated the performance and
profitable visual iconography of the group.

The photographs in *Life* included staged pictures of an individual
Klansman, and offered an insight into the inner workings of the Klan by
showing, for example, a Klan greeting and the pledge of secrecy. They
also included a photograph of the Grand Dragon, Samuel Green, posing
directly for the camera. The Klan was, once more, using the mainstream
media to relaunch before the American public. Indeed, in the build up to
the event, Green even placed advertisements in the local papers inviting
the public to Stone Mountain.[1]

In many respects, this may appear to be the start of a familiar story, one that this book has already told. The performance on Stone Mountain, and the interest it generated among the public and the media, intentionally recalled William Simmons's launch thirty-one years earlier. Of course, this was a Klan for a new era, one increasingly dislocated from the romanticism in the novels of Thomas Dixon (who died barely a month before this latest launch on Stone Mountain). Yet while the new Klan would become increasingly removed from the earlier incarnation, from the outset it again looked to film and the media to promote, define, and publicize itself both locally within Atlanta and also on the national stage.

In this instance, the Klan had invited *Life* to the meeting and seemed to grant them exclusive rights and free rein to photograph the ceremony. Newspaper reports explained that other photographers were compelled to shoot pictures from the upper slopes of Stone Mountain, away from the action, while two newsmen from the United Press were "seized and manhandled by a 'goon squad'" of Klansmen. Another figure was also blocked – cameraman Oscar Goodman – and his film camera taken. However, as *Film Daily* reported, the Klansmen who returned the camera forgot to remove the film. The resulting footage appeared in a Paramount Newsreel.[2]

The example shows the Klan literally attempting to take control of film and, more broadly, its own representation. While it failed to do so, the coverage that followed, regardless of its editorial stance, provided nationwide publicity from this modest, local Klan-orchestrated event. The media response attests to the continued interest and exportability of the Klan and, in particular, of images of the group. Beyond this, the discourses that circulated around the event – reporters blocked, cameras seized, "exclusive" inside pictures secured – illustrate the particular ways in which the Klan maintained a public profile and interest, as a source of mystery and excitement. From the very beginning, in 1915, when the Klan image was manufactured and advertised through the work of Thomas Dixon and D. W. Griffith, film had served to foster and maintain the Klan's public profile.

A month after this latest launch, on 10 June 1946, a barely concealed version of the Klan – the so-called "Clan of the Fiery Cross" – featured in a popular children's radio serial, broadcast across the nation. The fifteen-part story pitted a contemporary Klan against the celebrated all-American figure of Superman. In so doing, it consolidated the representation offered in the social problem films of the 1930s, with the Klan now repositioned as a threat to, rather than a protector of, Americanism. In this instance, the Klan targeted a Chinese American boy selected to play for a junior baseball team. The baseball team served once more as a microcosm of the American nation and, more specifically, as a junior team, of a new postwar America. The Klan was operating outside of this nation, both exorcized and ostracized, but attempting once more to regain a foothold within it.

The show, which famously exposed authentic Klan secrets courtesy of an infiltrator, Stetson Kennedy, marked an attempt on the part of the Klan's opponents to use the media to bring down the group at the exact moment of its attempted rebirth. In the radio series it was the *Daily Planet*, the newspaper where Clark Kent works, that sought to expose the group, offering a $1,000 reward for information. Furthermore, the Klan directly targeted and kidnapped newspaper reporters, burning a fiery cross on the lawn of editor Perry White. The central role of the media in creating, promoting, and undermining the Klan – so integral to the history told within this book – was now evidenced both on and off the air as a new Klan appeared.[3]

Furthermore, the ways in which the radio show sought to mold public opinion of the Klan recalled approaches deployed by the Klan in the 1920s, for example in revealing the inner workings of the group and directly targeting and looking to inculcate children. In ridiculing the rituals of the group and exposing its commercial motivations, the radio show sought to use the media to unmask and demystify the group, as Klan opponents had also done decades earlier.

At its height in the 1920s, the Klan helped shape and define modern America, utilizing cinema in all its forms to recruit and create Klan citizens, to promote and define itself, and, moreover, to position itself usefully within the nation's rapidly changing social and political landscape. The emergence of a new Klan in the spring of 1946 – a local group brought to national attention by the media – returns us to a beginning. The Klan would not disappear. It would regenerate within new social contexts, transformed once more yet retaining a connection to its previous lives through its images. The role of film and new forms of media in these later incarnations of the Klan is a story for another book.

Similarly, the Klan's practices in the 1920s and, indeed, its self-identity at the time – not as extremists but as 100 percent Americans and Protestants – were significant precursors to the ways in which conservative groups subsequently sought to use media to normalize new forms of conservatism and to position themselves within mainstream America. Heather Hendershot has eloquently explored how other conservative groups, such as the John Birch Society, used 16mm film in the 1960s to recruit members and how the popularization of broadcast media served to realign right-wing extremist and fundamentalist discourse into the mainstream.[4]

If we take a final leap forward to today, at the centenary of *The Birth of a Nation* and the modern Klan, we can see the legacies of these initial interactions between the Klan and cinema stretching across the American media landscape. The Klan image, constructed and contested through cinema, remains one of the most loaded and recognizable in American popular culture. The public furor over the reported (though ultimately unsubstantiated) sighting of a person in a Klan costume at Oberlin College in 2013, which prompted the school to cancel classes and precipitated nationwide media coverage, attests to the continued, politically charged potency of the image, even though the group attached to it is now little more than a discredited and insignificant curiosity.

This popular fascination with the Klan image has certainly been noted by film producers, although most films of the twenty-first century, in their attempts to ridicule the group, have sought to desensitize and demystify the costume. The distinctive Klan image more often serves as a visual shorthand for American extremism, depicting uneducated, localized social lepers, blown up and scattered across the screen in slow motion or destroyed by their own cinematic constructs. In *O Brother Where Art Thou?* (2000), it is the fiery cross that crushes and incinerates Big Dan, the one-eyed Klansman, while in *Django Unchained* (2012), the Klansmen are barely able to see as they come under attack, squinting through misplaced eyeholes due to their poorly designed hoods. The images that sustained the Klan, established through film almost a century ago, are now exposed, as is (in the example of *Django Unchained*) the century-long process of manufacturing and mythologizing this costume.

From the historically elastic appearance in *Django Unchained* to *O Brother Where Art Thou?*, *The Butler* (2013), and *Bad Boys II* (2003), the Klan has been depicted in films at very different historical moments (the nineteenth century, the 1930s, the 1960s, the present day). The Klan and its costume now encapsulate 150 years of history, covering at least three distinct historical movements. The image-making, or perhaps image-destroying, process has become somewhat reductive, serving to perpetuate the image and, at the same time, to disconnect it from specific historical movements. Certainly the public memory of the Klan, shaped by the civil rights movement, by more recent Klan activities, and, to an extent, cinema representation, has now erroneously reimagined the modern Klan of the 1920s as a renegade and marginal racist group. This is an understandable but dangerous revision, which impedes constructive discussion of how and why the Klan flourished. It is a revision that began in the period of this study, when the dominant visual representations of the Klan took shape. Indeed, the interwar period marks the last moment in which the image, function, and moral rectitude of the Klan was fully contested on a national stage. In many respects this book reveals an early ideological battle fought through the media, over the control and meaning of an image. It was a battle that the Klan would appear to lose, although even in apparent defeat it would retain sufficient notoriety to regenerate.

Beyond mere image making, the questions and issues raised in this study find uncomfortable echoes in contemporary America. In a country gripped by the corrosive forces of modernity, burdened by a fear of outsiders, and beset by a media-made panic toward – to borrow a phrase widely used in Klan literature – "the enemy within"; at a moment when the right-wing media have become the dominant voice in citizenship debates and in discussions over American national identity; and in a technological climate that sees extremist groups turning to new forms and sites of visual media (in particular online videos) to connect, propagate, and publicize their activities across the world, the experiences of the Klan almost a hundred years ago reveal a battle that has, in many respects, already been fought. It was a battle that helped both to shape modern America and determine the state and function of film, as part of the media, in this process.

Notes

Preface

Parts of chapter 2 previously appeared in "Protecting Protestantism: The Ku Klux Klan vs. The Motion Picture Industry," *Film History* 20:3 (2008), 367–380.

Parts of chapter 3 previously appeared in "'The True Story of the Ku Klux Klan': Defining the Klan through Film," *Journal of American Studies* 42:3 (December 2008), 471–488. Copyright © 2008 Cambridge University Press.

1. Seymour Stern, "Griffith: 1 – The Birth of a Nation," *Film Culture* 36 (Spring/Summer 1965), 80, 67. I have not found any references to the parade in contemporary newspaper reports.

2. *Atlanta Constitution*, 9 December 1915, 2; *Atlanta Journal*, 9 December 1915.

3. The original Klan enjoyed a short life. David Chalmers suggests that it was founded on Christmas Eve 1865, while Allen Trelease argued it was May or early June 1866. It spread across the South in 1867, before the Grand Wizard of the Klan, General Nathan Bedford Forrest, ordered its disbandment in January 1869. Although unofficial Klan forces continued for a few more years, by 1872 the Klan was an outdated and now historical monument of the Reconstruction era. See David Chalmers, Hooded Americanism: The History of the Ku Klux Klan, 3rd ed. (Durham, NC: Duke University Press, 1987), 8; Allen W. Trelease, *White Terror: The Ku Klux Klan Conspiracy and Southern Reconstruction* (Baton Rouge: Louisiana State University Press, 1995), 3.

4. "Klan Members to March," *Columbus Dispatch*, 5 January 1924.

5. "Mutual Film Corporation v. Industrial Commission of Ohio," 236 U.S. 230, 1915, 244.

6. Richard Barry, "Five Dollar Movies Prophesied," *New York Times,* 28 March 1915, SM16.

7. Lee Grieveson, *The Cinema and the Wealth of Nations* (Berkeley: University of California Press, forthcoming).

8. Recent studies that acknowledge the prominence of media to the modern Klan include Craig Fox's local study, *Everyday Klansfolk: White Protestant Life and the KKK in 1920s Michigan* (East Lansing: Michigan State University Press, 2011), and Thomas R. Pegram, *One Hundred Percent American: The Rebirth and Decline of the Ku Klux Klan in the 1920s* (Chicago: Ivan R. Dee, 2011). Significant recent collections on non-theatrical cinema include Charles R. Acland and Haidee Wasson's edited collection, *Useful Cinema* (Durham, NC: Duke University Press, 2011);

and Devin Orgeron, Marsha Orgeron, and Dan Streible eds., *Learning with the Lights Off: Educational Film in the United States* (New York: Oxford University Press, 2012).

9. Klantauquas were the Klan's version of the popular Chautauqua, traveling shows that might include a combination of lectures, music, and, on occasion, film. These are discussed in chapter 3.

1. Re-*Birth*

1. *Spotlight*, 15 January 1923, 3. The article contains a photographic reproduction of the telegram. The telegram, in the form of an interoffice message, is also held in the David W. Griffith Papers, 1897–1954 (DWGP) (Frederick, MD: University Publications of America, 1982). Microfilm accessed at the British Film Institute.

2. "Klan is Denounced by the Clansman," *New York Times*, 23 January 1923, 23. The speech was widely reported in regional newspapers throughout the country. See, for example, in Statesville, NC, "Dixon spits on Ku Klux.," *The Landmark*, 25 January 1923, 1.

3. "Peddling stock for Anti-Klan picture," *Imperial Night-Hawk*, 25 April 1923, 4; Anthony Slide, *American Racist: The Life and Films of Thomas Dixon* (Lexington: University Press of Kentucky, 2004), 172–173; "Motion Picture to Show Work of Klan," *Imperial Night-Hawk*, 22 August 1923, 4.

4. *Bridgeport Telegram*, 7 October 1924, 2; *Baltimore Afro-American*, 21 April 1922, 7.

5. *Spotlight*, 15 January 1923, 3; "Kansas Governor Asked by NAACP to Bar 'Birth of a Nation' Film" (press release), 8 June 1923, File C302, NAACP Archives, Library of Congress, Washington, DC.

6. Henry Jenkins, *Textual Poachers: Television Fans and Participatory Culture* (New York: Routledge, 1992). Jenkins develops a term that was previously explored by Michel de Certeau.

7. *Atlanta Constitution* (AC), 31 October 1905, 2. Dixon regularly appeared at this point, inserting himself into the narrative. The audience at the Atlanta premiere included Governor Terrell and the "leading representatives of Atlanta's political and social circles." *AC*, 30 October 1905, 9.

8. "Grand Gallery God Descends to Earth during 'Clansman,'" *Atlanta Independent*, 4 November 1905, 3. Frank Harper, "a Negro boy," was arrested and was "hit [with] several blows to compel submission" after the scene in the Klan cave. John Dittmer, *Black Georgia in the Progressive Era, 1900–1920* (Urbana: University of Illinois Press, 1977), 66–67; *Atlanta News*, 31 October 1905. In discussing a staging in Lexington, Kentucky, the *Lexington Herald* outlined the racial tensions and confrontation evident within the auditorium as "unconsciously the crowd became a part of the cast." *Lexington Herald*, 25 January 1906, 1.

9. "Tom Dixon Talks of The Clansman," *AC*, 29 October 1905, 2.

10. "A Challenge for Booker T.," *Kansas Vindicator*, 26 January 1906, 1.

11. *AC*, 29 October 1905, 2.

12. This was not the first production at the Grand to feature the Klan. William Haworth's *On The Mississippi* in February 1896 had depicted a villainous Reconstruction Klan embarking on the "chase and attempted execution of an innocent man." *AC*, 24 February 1896, 5.

13. *The State* (SC), 8 October 1905, 22; *Augusta Chronicle*, 8 October 1905, 8.

14. *AC*, 29 October 1905, D3. The review refers to the "impressive ritual" in the cave.

15. Quoted in Slide, *American Racist*, 63.

16. Slide, *American Racist,* 60; *AC,* 29 October 1905, 2.

17. "Let Us Postpone Clansman," *Atlanta Georgian,* 26 September 1906, 6.

18. *AC,* 27 September 1906, 14; Rebecca Burns, *Rage in the Gate City: The Story of the 1906 Race Riots* (Athens: University of Georgia Press, 2009), 147.

19. See Mark Bauerlein, *Negrophobia: A Race Riot in Atlanta, 1906* (San Francisco: Encounter Books, 2001); Joel Williamson, *A Rage for Order: Black-White Relations in the American South Since Emancipation* (Oxford: Oxford University Press, 1986), 141–151; Walter White, *A Man Called White: The Autobiography of Walter White* (1948; reprint, Athens: University of Georgia Press, 1995), 8. In closely referencing the themes of Dixon's work, the papers connected the perceived rise of the "African American rapist" to fears surrounding urban modernity, social mobility, and the proliferation of black saloons.

20. Thomas Cripps, *Slow Fade to Black* (New York: Oxford University Press, 1977), 58. The racial anxieties presented within the film helped to configure the response of the NAACP as evidence of a "black group" attempting to demonstrate power.

21. *Atlanta Georgian,* 26 September 1906, 6.

22. *AC,* 27 September 1906, 14; Slide, *American Racist,* 60; *Atlanta Georgian,* 6 April 1907, 4.

23. It is perhaps pertinent, given that a number of the reported African American attacks on white women proved to be unfounded, that the "negro villain" Gus did not actually rape Flora in *The Clansman.* Anthony Slide credits her death to "misadventure," as she throws herself to her death, fueled "by a deep distrust and fear of all African Americans." Slide, *American Racist,* 59.

24. Bauerlein, *Negrophobia,* 108–110; *Atlanta Journal,* 28 August 1906.

25. "Blacks Form 'White Caps'; Terror Reigns," *Atlanta Georgian,* 30 October 1906, 1. The White Cap movement operated in a number of states between the first and second Klan movements (1888–1906), its members donning white hoods. A vigilante group, it was ostensibly concerned with regulating moral transgressions, but evidently in some states it selected its targets on racial grounds. See Michael Newton, *White Robes and Burning Crosses: A History of the Ku Klux Klan from 1866* (Jefferson, NC: McFarland and Company, 2014), 28.

26. "The Clansman Causes Riot," *Oakland Tribune,* 11 November 1906, 6; David Mayer, *Stagestruck Filmmaker: D. W. Griffith and the American Theatre* (Iowa City: University of Iowa Press, 2009), 156.

27. *Atlanta Georgian,* 14 November 1908.

28. *Atlanta Georgian,* 6 February 1909, 9; *AC,* 31 January 1909.

29. *AC,* 31 January 1909.

30. *AC,* 9 December 1915, 2; *Atlanta Journal,* 9 December 1915;

31. "Where Will It End?," *New York Age,* 16 December 1915.

32. *New York Age,* 16 December 1915; *Variety* (12 March 1915) described the film as a "great epoch in picturemaking," while advertisements proclaimed "the dawn of a new epoch in the theatres of the world." *AC,* 29 October 1905.

33. Nancy MacLean, "The Leo Frank Case Reconsidered: Gender and Sexual Politics in the Making of Reactionary Populism," *Journal of American History* 78 (December 1991), 920, 938; David Chalmers, *Hooded Americanism: The History of the Ku Klux Klan,* 3rd ed. (Durham, NC: Duke University Press, 1987), 70.

34. *AC,* 21 August 1915, 1,3; *Fort Wayne Sentinel,* 20 August 1915.

35. MacLean, "Leo Frank Case"; Matthew Bernstein, *Screening a Lynching: The Leo Frank Case on Film and TV* (Athens: University of Georgia Press, 2009); Williamson, *A Rage for Order,* 239–247; Jeffrey Melnick, *Black-Jewish Relations on Trial: Leo Frank and Jim Conley in the New South* (Jackson: University Press of Mississippi, 2000), 34–35.

36. Nancy MacLean, "Leo Frank Case," 919.

37. In positioning their film as a high-class attraction within middle-class theaters – for example, by charging up to two dollars, playing "only" at leading established theaters, and including a thirty-piece symphony orchestra – Griffith and Dixon would seek to present cinema as a social response to, rather than cause of, the fears surrounding social modernity that are expressed both within *Birth* and the Leo Frank case.

38. Bernstein, *Screening a Lynching,* 16–17; Richard Maltby, "The Social Evil, the Moral Order and the Melodramatic Imagination, 1890–1915," in *Melodrama: Stage, Picture, Screen,* ed. Jacky Bratton, Jim Cook, and Christine Gledhill (London: BFI, 1994), 216; George Kibbe Turner, "The Daughters of the Poor," *McClure's* 34 (1909), 57–58. Turner distinguished from the native-born Western European Jews, but government reports made no such qualification, with the United States Immigration Committee Report in 1911 stating, "There are a large number of Jews scattered throughout the United States who seduce and keep girls."

39. Bernstein, *Screening a Lynching,* 17–20. The chief of police stopped the street advertisement and the censorship board ordered that the Frank sequence be removed on grounds of public policy.

Film was also used to direct and influence attitudes both toward the case and, more broadly, to the issues of lynching and capital punishment. Hal Reid, the father of Wallace Reid, who played a Klansmen in *Birth,* produced a fifteen-minute film featuring authorized footage of Frank in prison. As advertisements noted, the film was intended "to aid in a humanitarian campaign for the national abolition of capital punishment."

40. MacLean, "Leo Frank Case," 920, 938.

41. Gregory A. Waller, *Main Street Amusements: Movies and Commercial Entertainment in a Southern City, 1896–1930* (Washington, DC: Smithsonian Institution Press, 1995), 151.

42. William G. Shepherd, "How I Put Over the Klan," *Collier's* (14 July 1928), 35.

43. Ibid.; *Bridgeport Telegram,* 7 October 1924, 2. The *Bridgeport Telegram* suggests that "the Fiery Cross appears for the first time in connection with the Klan some forty years after its dissolution."

44. Agreement signed and accepted between Goldstein Company of Los Angeles and DW Griffith, 3 August 1914, DWGP. Goldstein was arrested in 1917 for violating the recently introduced Espionage Act after screening a version of his 1917 film of the American Revolution, *The Spirit of 76,* in California. The film included brief sequences that had been previously rejected by the Chicago censors and, at a moment of intense paranoia, was deemed "unpatriotic" to the war effort for its critical presentation of the British. Amidst speculation that he was a German spy and that this was a deliberate attempt to undermine the American military effort, Goldstein was sentenced to ten years in prison (subsequently reduced to three) and would leave America for Europe upon his release.

45. For more on Klan costumes see Kelly Baker, *Gospel according to the Klan: The KKK's Appeal to Protestant America, 1915–1930* (Lawrence: University Press of Kansas, 2011), 55–63. Newspaper reports stated that 25,000 yards of white muslin was used for the Klan regalia in the film.

46. Melvyn Stokes, *D. W. Griffith's The Birth of a Nation: A History of the Most Controversial Picture of All Time* (Oxford: Oxford University Press, 2008), 233; Wyn Craig Wade, *The Fiery Cross: The Ku Klux Klan in America* (New York: Simon and Schuster, 1987), 138–139.

47. Nancy MacLean, *Behind the Mask of Chivalry: The Making of the Second Ku Klux Klan* (New York: Oxford University Press, 1994), 7–8; Wade, *Fiery Cross*, 141–142.

48. Simmons was based in Brunswick at this stage. See *Thomasville Daily Times Enterprise*, 9 April 1913, 1.

49. Stokes, *The Birth of a Nation*, 233.

50. Wade, *Fiery Cross*, 145; Shepherd, "How I Put Over the Klan"; *Atlanta Journal*, 28 November 1915, 8.

51. Shepherd, "How I Put Over the Klan."

52. An article in the *Atlanta Constitution* (30 December 1915, 6) noted that, following the recent production of *Birth*, the meeting would touch on the history of "the real Ku Klux Klan, the accurate portrayal of which was the crowning feature of this famous film." *AC*, 13 December 1915, 5; *AC*, 14 December 1915, 14; *AC*, 19 December 1915, 16A; *AC*, 20 December 1915, 5.

53. *AC*, 12 December 1915, 10A; *AC*, 7 December 1915, 7. The film, Macintosh added, "is built to arouse your emotions and it does it. It is designed to educate you and it does it so much more than many hours of studying books." After claiming that the film "makes you love and hate," Macintosh concluded that "it is not de-signed to arouse your prejudices, and if you are fair minded and not predisposed, it will not do so."

54. *Atlanta Journal*, 7 December 1915.

55. Brock (sometimes listed as Brocj) was sentenced to life imprisonment in January 1917. The court heard that Brock was drunk at the time and had previously said he would "get myself a nigger before night." *Elkert Daily Review*, 20 January 1917, 6; *Chicago American*, 24 April 1916.

56. Linda Williams, *Playing the Race Card: Melodramas of Black and White from Uncle Tom to O. J. Simpson* (Princeton, NJ: Princeton University Press, 2001), 120; Vachel Lindsay, *The Art of the Moving Picture* (New York: Macmillan, 1915), 152–153.

57. Wade, *Fiery Cross*, 147.

58. *AC*, 5 December 1915, 12M.

59. *AC*, 13 December 1915, 5.

60. Kenneth T. Jackson, *The Ku Klux Klan in the City 1915–1930* (New York: Oxford University Press, 1967).

61. For example, *AC*, 12 December 1915, 10A.

62. In considering the impact of the film's exhibition on African Americans, *The Freeman*, an African American newspaper from Indianapolis, asked, "What does this prohibitive price mean? Is it a war on the races begun in high places?" *The Freeman* suggested that this prohibitive pricing, both in production and exhibition, further limited the African American's access to this "war," as the white producers, exhibitors, and audiences were "battling over our heads, in the skies – Zeppelins or aeroplanes – where there is small hope for those who must creep on the ground." *Freeman*, 17 April 1915, 4.

63. For more on African American cinema attendance, see for example Charlene Regester, "From the Buzzard's Roost: Black Movie-Going in Durham and Other

North Carolina Cities during the Early
Period of American Cinema," *Film History*
17:1 (2005), 113–124; Mary Carbine, "'The
Finest Outside the Loop': Motion Picture
Exhibition in Chicago's Black Metropolis, 1905–1928," *Camera Obscura* 23 (May
1990), 9–42; Waller, *Main Street Amusements;* Jan Olsson, "Modernity Stops at
Nothing: The American Chase Film and
the Specter of Lynching," in *A Companion
to Early Cinema,* ed. Andre Gaudreault,
Nicolas Dulac, and Santiago Hidalgo
(Malden, MA: Wiley-Blackwell Publishing, 2012), 261; Cara Caddoo, *Envisioning
Freedom: Cinema and the Building of Modern Black Life* (Cambridge, MA: Harvard
University Press, 2014).

64. Stephen Weinberger, "The Birth
of a Nation and the Making of the
N.A.A.C.P.," *Journal of American Studies*
45:1 (2011), 77–93.

65. These figures are reprinted in
Carole Marks, "Black Workers and the
Great Migration North," *Phylon* 46:2 (2nd
Quarter, 1985), 148. See also Ann Douglas,
*Terrible Honesty: Mongrel Manhattan in
the 1920s* (London: Picador, 1996), 73. The
migration of African Americans to the
urban North provoked anxiety particularly amongst many poorer whites who
saw this movement as a direct threat to
their social and economic positions. For a
brief contemporary consideration of this
process, see Guy B. Johnson, "The Negro
Migration and Its Consequences," *Journal
of Social Forces* 2:3 (March 1924), 404–408.
It is difficult to offer a date at which this
"great migration" began, but a number
of historians have used 1915 as a starting
point for their studies. For example, see
Spencer R. Crew, "The Great Migration
of Afro-Americans, 1915–1940," *Monthly
Labor Review* 111 (1987).

66. Lee Grieveson, *Policing Cinema:
Movies and Censorship in Early Twentieth*

Century America (Berkeley: University of
California Press, 2004), 139.

67. Thomas Cripps, *Slow Fade to Black:
The Negro in American Film, 1900–1942*
(New York: Oxford University Press,
1977), 61; "Letter from Thomas Dixon to
Joseph Tumulty," 1 May 1915; "Letter from
Thomas Dixon to Woodrow Wilson,"
5 September 1915, the latter two quoted
in John Hope Franklin, "Birth of a Nation – Propaganda as History," *Massachusetts Review* (Autumn 1979), 431.

68. *Marietta Journal,* 24 November
1916, 2; *AC,* 26 November 1916, C7; *AC,* 28
November 1916, 7.

69. *AC,* 20 January 1918, C2; *AC,* 27
January 1918, B10. It was again held over
for a second week.

70. *AC,* 7 March 1919, 12; *AC,* 9 March
1919, 2; *AC,* 11 March 1919, 10.

71. *AC,* 5 February 1922, D4; *Searchlight,* 18 February 1922, 8; *AC,* 22 April 1923,
C7. In 1925, it would play at the Alamo No.
2, the Palace Theatre, and the Alpha Theatre, reportedly setting house records at
each venue.

72. The *Coshocton Tribune* (21 November 1917, 3) reported that "New Philadelphia 'Y' fund workers have organized a Ku
Klux Klan for intimidation of tightwad
citizens." The *Bismarck Tribune* (2 November 1917, 1) in North Dakota noted the
emergence of a new group – the Liberty
Bands – that "recalls acts of [the] old Ku
Klux Klan," two weeks before *Birth* was
screened locally. A local review for the
film (*Bismarck Tribune,* 13 November 1917,
8) now stated that "the rides and rescues
of the Ku Klux Klan so graphically, dramatically set forth in *The Birth of a Nation*
are those of the original, right-enforcing
organization of the true sons of the old
South." The *Evening State Journal* (30
July 1919, 2) explained that in Virginia 113
citizens, "fashioned after the historic Ku

Klux Klan," banded together in a secret organization. These groups were, for the most part, not directly affiliated with Simmons's Knights of the Ku Klux Klan.

73. These articles and notices are all found in the *Montgomery Advertiser:* 8 May 1918, 1; 2 June 1918, 13; 10 June 1918, 5; 2 July 1918, 3; 22 September 1918, 1; 12 October 1918, 2, 8, 13 February 1918, 10; 12 April 1918, 2; 22 April 1918, 4. The Klan's reappearance was further marked through a series of advertisements in the local press before parades, for example, in the *Montgomery Advertiser* on 12 October. "Back to Life and very active after 40 years," the paper noted, listing the routes for the parade and presenting the Klan's work as an extension of the war effort ("This Is War, You Hear!").

74. Robert Alan Goldberg, *Hooded Empire: The Ku Klux Klan in Colorado* (Urbana: University of Illinois Press, 1981), 4.

75. Jackson, *The Ku Klux Klan in the City,* 10, 194.

76. For more on Powell, see Trevor Griffey, "The Washington State Klan in the 1920s," accessed 1 August 2013, Seattle Civil Rights and Labor History Project, http://depts.washington.edu/civilr/kkk _powell.htm.

77. *Exhibitors Trade Review,* 1 October 1921, 1264; *AC,* 31 July 1921, 35; *Columbus Ledger,* 21 August 1921, 8; *Columbus Daily Enquirer,* 22 August 1921, 2, 8;

78. *Augusta Chronicle,* 24 August 1921, 3. The letter from William Simmons to William Fox was dated 22 April 1921 and sent from Atlanta. The advertisement, along with the correspondence between Fox and the NAACP, is in the Records of the NAACP, box 1, C 312, Library of Congress, Washington, DC.

79. The letter, written by J. M. McArthur, King Kleagle of Tennessee, was sent on 24 May 1921. It was reprinted in the

New York World, 21 September 1921, 2, and was mentioned in film papers including *Wid's Daily,* 22 September 1921. The syndicated exposé further served to publicize and circulate these Klan policies.

80. *Jewish Criterion,* 10 November 1922, 36 A-B.

81. Goldberg, *Hooded Empire,* 14. An advertisement for the film appeared in the *Denver Post* (2 July 1921, 6), crediting the film's return to the Klan.

82. *Denver Post,* 3 July 1921, sec. 2, 6. Klan parades often used theaters as a central starting point. For example, in Dallas in May 1921, the Klan rented out the newly reopened Majestic Theatre, and at 9 PM on a Saturday night almost a thousand members walked from the venue in single file around the town. See *Dallas Daily News Herald,* 22 May 1921, 1–2; Laura Lee Mohsene, "The Women – God Bless Them: Dallas Women and the Ku Klux Klan in the 1920s" (Ph.D. dissertation, University of Texas, 2011), 84.

83. *Anniston Star,* 10 July 1921, 2.

84. Jackson, "The Ku Klux Klan in the City," 198. An advertisement for this event appeared in the *Sunday Oregonian* (18 December 1921), 9. The lecture by Reverend R. H. Sawyer, a part-time pastor and popular Klan speaker, was published as a pamphlet entitled "The Truth about the Invisible Empire, Knights of the Ku Klux Klan" in 1922 (Portland, Oregon: Northwest Domain). The attendance figure comes from the front page of this pamphlet. *Searchlight* (7 January 1922, 4) reported that *The Ku Klux Klan Rides Again* was also shown after the lecture, while the *Sunday Oregonian* referred to this film as *The Knights of the Ku Klux Klan Ride Again.* It described the film program as "eight reels of thrilling pictures, with a message of warning to American Manhood and Womanhood." Luther I. Powell was again prominent

here in bringing the film to Oregon, and such was his influence that a local chapter was named the Luther I. Powell Klan. *The Face at Your Window* played at the Eugene Theatre, with local Klansmen presented onstage and again serving as ushers. Eckard V. Toy, "Robe and Gown: The Ku Klux Klan in Eugene, Oregon, during the 1920s," in *The Invisible Empire in the West*, ed. Shawn Lay (Urbana: University of Illinois Press, 1992), 153–154; *Eugene Daily Guard*, 12 January 1922, 5.

85. *Sunday Oregonian*, 2 April 1922, 18. At this time, *The Birth of a Nation* returned to Portland and was held over for a second week at the Blue Mouse Theatre.

86. Letter from the NAACP to William Fox, 30 August 1921; letter from Fox to the NAACP, 23 September 1921, both in Records of the NAACP, box 1, C 312, Library of Congress, Washington, DC.

87. *Augusta Chronicle*, 26 August 1921, 5. Without directly referring to the Klan, the management adopted a phrase that would be widely used by Klan film promoters over the next few years, claiming that the film was instead "all American and one that every man, woman and child should see."

88. *State* (Columbia, SC), 8 May 1921, 2.26.

89. For example, a Klan recruiting newsletter reported that the film "shows the hooded figures of the Knights of the Ku Klux Klan riding to the rescue," while electric lights and large displays at the Regent in Kansas City promoted the film as "All about the Ku Klux Klan." All films dealing with the Klan were banned in Kansas and so, while the film could still play, the City Censor ordered the removal of the signs. *Variety*, 14 July 1922, 44.

90. See *Augusta Chronicle*, 26 August 1921, 5.

91. Ben Singer, "Movies and Ascendant Americanism," in *American Cinema of the 1910s: Themes and Variations*, ed. Charlie Keil and Ben Singer (New Brunswick, NJ: Rutgers University Press, 2009), 225–248; Kevin Brownlow, *Behind the Mask of Innocence* (Berkeley: University of California Press, 1990), 444, 445. Steven Ross looks in more depth at these films, particularly *Bolshevism on Trial*, in his book *Working Class Hollywood: Silent Film and the Shaping of Class in America* (Princeton, NJ: Princeton University Press, 1998), 138–144.

92. Stephen W. Bush, "Uncle Sam Takes a Hand," *Billboard*, 3 May 1919, 72; *Exhibitors Herald and Motography*, 3 May 1919, 26.

93. *News-Sentinel*, 23 September 1921, 5.

94. *Moving Picture World*, 25 December 1920, 948; *Entertainment Trade Review*, 27 November 1920. *Variety* stated in 1920 that President Wilson was eager to attend a day of film screenings organized by the Legion. *Variety*, 12 November 1920, 34.

95. "Woods Accepts Chairmanship of Americanism Committee and Will Work Out Plan of Co-operation," *Moving Picture World*, 11 December 1920, 704.

96. Lee Grieveson, "The Work of Film in the Age of Ford Mechanization," *Cinema Journal* 51:3 (Spring 2012), 25–51.

97. See for example James Burns, "American Philanthropy and Colonial Film-making: The Rockefeller Foundation, the Carnegie Corporation and the Birth of Colonial Cinema," in *Empire and Film*, ed. Lee Grieveson and Colin MacCabe (London: BFI, 2011), 55–72.

98. Letter from Knights of the Ku Klux Klan to David W. Griffith, 16 May 1921, DWGP.

99. "Ku Klux Klan Exposé Hits Birth of a Nation's Tour," *Variety*, 23 September 1921, 45.

100. "Hooded Klansmen Attend Picture Birth of a Nation," *Mexia Evening News,* 10 January 1922, 8; *Searchlight,* 28 January 1922, 8; "Living Klansmen Add Big Thrill at Exhibit of 'Birth of a Nation,'" *Searchlight,* 25 February 1922, 7; *Greensboro Record,* 21 February 1922, 7; see also "Local Klansmen Attend Theatre," *The Bee,* Danville, Virginia, 13 September 1923. Klansmen also used productions of *The Clansman* to launch the group in the early 1920s. When the play appeared under the title *Ku Klux Klan* for two days in Decatur in March 1922, the local paper published an article on opening night, asking, "Has the Ku Klux Klan invaded Decatur?" The play also was performed at the Klan-supported Classic Theatre in December 1922 and was advertised in the *Elwood Call Leader* on the same day that the paper reported a big Klan parade on its front cover. See *Decatur Review,* 19 March 1922, 21 and 22 March 1922, 8; *Elwood Call Leader,* 11 December 1922, 6.

101. Records of the NAACP, box 1, C 301, Library of Congress, Washington, DC; Nickieann Fleener-Marzec, *D. W. Griffith's The Birth of a Nation: Controversy, Suppression and the First Amendment as it Applies to Filmic Expression, 1915–1973* (New York: Arno, 1980), 188–189, 209n74. See also *New York Times,* 7 and 9 May 1921.

102. "Despite 16 Weeks Played Once, 'Birth' Barred in Riot Charge," *Variety,* 20 May 1921, 47.

103. Stokes, *The Birth of a Nation,* 235–241.

104. Alan Gevinson, ed., *Within Our Gates: Ethnicity in American Feature Films, 1911–1960* (Berkeley: University of California Press, 1997), 95; "Foes of Klan fight Birth of a Nation," *New York Times,* 3 December 1922, 5.

105. "Griffith's 'Birth of a Nation' Remains 'The Daddy of 'Em All,'" *Variety,*

8 December 1922; Roy E. Aitken, *The Birth of a Nation Story* (Middleburg, VA: Delinger, 1965), 61. I have not found any evidence of the Klan editing *Birth* directly, although Anthony Slide (*American Racist,* 77–78) notes the long held, though unsubstantiated, claim that the Klan owned a print featuring a final, additional sequence showing the mass deportation of African Americans.

106. *New York World,* 5 December 1922; *Variety,* 8 December 1922.

107. *Moving Picture World,* 17 May 1924, 297.

108. Stokes, *The Birth of a Nation,* 241; "United Artists to Release 'The Birth of a Nation,'" *Billboard,* 23 December 1922, 54.

109. *Noblesville Daily Ledger,* 5 September 1923, 3; *Noblesville Daily Ledger,* 13 August 1923, 6; *Elwood Call Leader,* 5 November 1923, 6; *Fiery Cross,* 10 August 1923.

110. Craig Fox, *Everyday Klansfolk: White Protestant Life and the KKK in 1920s Michigan* (East Lansing: Michigan State University Press, 2011), 42–43, 145–146.

111. Maxim Simcovitch, "The Impact of Griffith's 'Birth of a Nation' on the Modern Ku Klux Klan," *Journal of Popular Film* 1:1 (Winter 1972), 49. Simcovitch reports the Richmond Klan No.1 and Robert E. Lee Klan No.4 "attending en masse a showing of *The Birth of a Nation.*" Luther I. Powell Klan in Portland, Oregon, also attended screenings of *Birth.*

112. Goldberg, *Hooded Empire,* 153; Simcovitch, "Impact of 'Birth of a Nation,'" 49.

113. "'Birth of a Nation' to Be Shown for Church Benefit," *Searchlight,* 18 October 1924, 1, 5; *Searchlight,* 25 October 1924, 4; *Exhibitors Herald,* 19 January 1924, 62.

114. Josh Glick analyzes these cartoons in "Mixed Messages: D. W. Griffith and the Black Press, 1916–1931," *Film History: An International Journal* 23:2 (2011),

174–195. See *Chicago Defender*, 24 July 1915, 8, and 9 February 1924, 2:8.

115. *Spotlight*, 15 January 1923, 3.

116. *Imperial Night-Hawk*, 6 August 1924, 6.

117. Ibid., 25 April 1923, 4.

118. Ibid.

119. Letter from National Society of the Daughters of American Revolution to Jason Joy, Public Relations Committee of the MPPDA, DWGP, 1982.

120. See publicity book for *America* in DWGP, 1982.

121. Letter from Chief of Staff for the Grand Dragon of the Realm of Ohio to Harry Aitken, Epoch Producing Company, 4 December 1925, DWGP, 1982.

122. Paul McEwan, "Lawyers, Bibliographies and the Klan: Griffith's Resources in the Censorship Battle over The Birth of a Nation in Ohio," *Film History* 20:3 (2008), 357–366.

123. *Dawn*, 13 October 1923, 10; *Searchlight*, 7 October 1922

124. Letter dated 4 December 1925, DWGP, 1982.

125. "Klan Refused Right to Exhibit Picture," *Ohio State Journal*, 4 March 1926, 3. In 1925 the Ohio Supreme Court had upheld a ban on the film, explaining that the film "is not true to history, appeals to race prejudice and portrays scenes of crimes." See *Ohio State Journal*, 3 June 1925, 1. See also Gevinson, *Within Our Gates*, 95. Conway wrote to Lawrence and explained that Harry Aitken would handle the matter to ensure that there was no "conflict of authority." While Aitken's response is not known, the Klan did proceed with its request to show the film "privately."

126. *Dawn*, 9 February 1924, 10–11. The city also objected to "shots of the Klansmen." The Klan scenes were now problematic for censors, but they were also exciting and lucrative. After the case against the film was indefinitely adjourned, *Variety*

reported that the film played at the theater for four weeks and "set a box office attendance record for the theatre." Fleener-Marzec, *D. W. Griffith's The Birth of a Nation*, 139–141; *Variety*, 21 February 1924, 2. See also *Chicago Daily News*, 12 February 1924, 12, which reports that "hundreds of Klansmen were in attendance"; Simcovitch, "Impact of 'Birth of a Nation,'" 51.

2. The Battle

1. "Klan Sues Warner's on 'Legion' Emblem," *Hollywood Reporter*, 11 August 1937, 2.

2. "Kluxers Sue WB on 'Black Legion' Insignia," *Variety*, 18 August 1937.

3. Ibid.

4. In responding to the case, Ebenstein stated, "I need hardly say that it is both funny and sad to think that an organisation like the Ku Klux Klan has legal rights and a standing in court." All references to the *Black Legion* case come from the Warner Bros. archives at the University of Southern California. The first of these quotes comes from a letter from Morris Ebenstein to Roy Obringer (30 August 1937), while the other quotes come from an earlier letter from Ebenstein to Obringer (27 August 1937).

5. Letter from Captain Ramsay to Warner Bros. Motion Picture Co., 22 August 1937, Warner Bros. Archives, University of Southern California. Captain Ramsay had carried out many investigations of the Klan and was at this time traveling the country as publicity officer for the Clyde Beatty Circus. Ultimately Warners decided that his evidence was insubstantial.

6. Ebenstein to Obringer, 27 August 1937.

7. "Movie Weekly Writer Receives Official Communication from Ku Klux Klan," *Movie Weekly*, 14 July 1923, 4. See also *Imperial Night-Hawk*, 9 May 1923; "Kansas Klan Bars Chaplin," *Searchlight*,

23 June 1923, 2; "Klans Determined to Clean Up the Movies," *Imperial Night-Hawk,* 6 June 1923; "Charlie Too Funny: Censors Slash Film," *Port Arthur News,* 14 April 1923, 8.

8. "Memphis Klansmen Protest," *Searchlight,* 5 May 1923, 2; *Moving Picture World,* 2 June 1923, 384; *Moving Picture World* (19 May 1923, 221) reported the Klan's protests against *The Pilgrim* in similar terms, under a heading "Klan Now Censoring."

9. "300 Initiates Accept Vows of Klan Auxiliary," *Kokomo Daily Dispatch,* 26 July 1923, 1.

10. "Ridiculing Protestant," *Searchlight,* 6 January 1923, 2. The letter was sent from Comanche, Oklahoma, on 27 December 1922. "Ridiculing Protestants," *Searchlight,* 13 January 1923, 2.

11. *Imperial Night-Hawk,* 4 April 1923, 3; *Imperial Night-Hawk,* 9 May 1923.

12. *Movie Weekly,* 14 July 1923, 4.

13. *Dawn,* 26 May 1923, 14.

14. "Klansman Halt Chaplin Film at Walla Walla," *Searchlight,* 14 April 1923; *Fiery Cross,* 13 April 1923, 1; *Searchlight,* 6 January 1923, 2; *Searchlight,* 2 June 1923.

15. "Movie Propaganda is Beyond Real Ideas: Foreign Scenes Favored," *Searchlight,* 23 March 1924, 7; *Searchlight,* 26 April 1924, 1. This article also appeared in *Ohio Fiery Cross,* 2 May 1924, 8.

16. *Imperial Night-Hawk,* 19 March 1923, 3; *Imperial Night-Hawk,* 9 April 1923, 2; *Dawn,* 24 March 1923, 5.

17. "What Would Jesus Say?," *Dawn,* 16 December 1922, 5.

18. *Port Arthur News,* 14 April 1923, 8; "Pastors' Protest Fails to Stop Chaplin Film," *Atlanta Constitution,* 13 April 1923, 3.

19. *Christian Century,* 13 October 1921, 23. The Board also adopted a resolution commending managers for refusing to show Fatty Arbuckle pictures.

20. "Presbyterians Ask for Clean Movies," *New York Times,* 24 May 1922, 18.

21. *Minutes of the General Assembly of the Presbyterian Church in the United States of America,* 1922.

22. "Movie Clean-Up Sought by Best U.S. Citizenship," *Dawn,* 29 December 1923, 9.

23. William Romanowski, *Reforming Hollywood: How American Protestants Fought for Freedom at the Movies* (New York: Oxford University Press, 2012), 34.

24. "Jewish Supremacy in Motion Picture World," *Dearborn Independent,* 19 February 1921. A series of articles, entitled "Baring the Heart of Hollywood," appeared later that year, further critiquing the Jewish involvement within the film industry.

25. Ibid.; Anthony Slide, *American Racist: The Life and Films of Thomas Dixon* (Lexington: University Press of Kentucky, 2004), 125. As another point of curiosity, D. W. Griffith briefly played the role of Reverend Gordon in an early stage incarnation of *One Woman.*

26. "The Producer, the Distributor, the Exhibitor," *Dearborn Independent,* 5 November 1921, 6; Lee Grieveson, "The Work of Film in the Age of Ford Mechanization," *Cinema Journal* 51:3 (Spring 2012), 47.

27. "Mr Ford and the Eighteenth Amendment," *Kourier,* October 1925, 10; In December 1924, *Kourier* (p. 7) quoted the *Atlanta Georgian,* which described Ford as "the most remarkable man in the most remarkable country in the world."

28. *Fiery Cross,* 2 February 1923, 7; "Henry and Edsel Ford Sincerest Patriotic Americans," *Fiery Cross,* February 1940, 2, where Ford is described as the "first great employer to recognize his workers as human beings."

29. *Dearborn Independent,* 5 November 1921, 2. The Jewish press, including *Jewish Criterion* (29 August 1924), quoted Ford as saying, "The Klan is a victim of a mass of lying propaganda and that is the reason why the Klan is in some circles looked upon with dissatisfaction. The truth is that the Klan is an organization that has in its aim only the welfare and future of America."

30. See, for example, in *Tolerance,* "Ford Backs Ku Klux, Jews Charge," 17 June 1923, 8; 24 June 1923, 7; 8 July 1923, 2. The cover cartoon is found in *Tolerance,* 5 August 1923; the 1924 book was written in Yiddish by David Louis Meckler.

31. Upton Sinclair, *The Flivver King* (New York: Phaedra, 1937), 73–76.

32. *Dawn,* 12 May 1923, 16.

33. *Searchlight,* 6 January 1923, 2.

34. *Fiery Cross,* 11 May 1923, 8; *Searchlight,* 13 January 1923, 2.

35. *Dawn,* 12 May 1923.

36. "Al and the Movies," *Searchlight,* 31 May 1924, 3. The "Al" in the title refers to New York governor Al Smith, a prominent Catholic and a longstanding Klan target.

37. *Fiery Cross,* 11 May 1923, 8. The report also appeared in *Searchlight,* 19 May 1923, 4.

38. *Searchlight,* 23 March 1924, 7; "Official Censoring," *Dawn,* 13 October 1923.

39. *Imperial Night-Hawk,* 6 June 1923, 4; *Searchlight,* 5 May 1923, 2.

40. *Movie Weekly,* 14 July 1923, 4.

41. "Chaplin Movies Bring Reported Klan Threats, Withdrawn in New York," *Fresno Bee,* 28 March 1927, 4. "Chaplin Film Banned by Klan," 28 March 1927, held in the Press Release File on the divorce between Chaplin and Lita Grey, accessed through the Charlie Chaplin Archive at the Cineteca di Bologna library.

42. *Dawn,* 12 May 1923.

43. "Catholic Propaganda in Movie Organization," *Dawn,* 27 October 1923, 21. This was originally featured in *Imperial Night-Hawk* (10 October 1923, 4) under the title "Catholic Propaganda Clutches Movies."

44. "Romanizing the Theatrical World Goes on Merrily," *Searchlight,* 23 August 1924, 3; "Rome at Hollywood," *Fiery Cross,* 2 May 1924, 4.

45. *Fiery Cross,* 26 October 1923, 4.

46. "Hierarchy's Use of Movies for Propaganda Protested," *Ohio Fiery Cross,* 2 May 1924, 8; *Variety,* 11 June 1924, 22. *Fiery Cross* also complained about a radio lecture in New York addressing the film. It urged action by hitting the producers at the box office, suggesting once more that producers and exhibitors would respond on financial rather than moral grounds. See also *Searchlight,* 2 June 1923; *Searchlight,* 31 May 1924, 3.

47. Among the other films criticized for "mocking" the Protestant religion were *The Inside of the Cup* and *Hell's Hinges,* which *Imperial Night-Hawk* accused of ridiculing Prohibition, the very manifestation of the Klan and Protestant cause in the 1920s. "How the Commercialized Movies are Undermining Morals in America," *Imperial Night-Hawk,* 1 October 1924, 2.

48. *Exhibitors Herald,* 23 February 1924, 94; 22 March 1924, 83; 15 March 1924, 70.

49. "Unable to Interest Picture Industry," *Imperial Night-Hawk,* 28 May 1924, 6.

50. *Searchlight,* 31 May 1924, 6; *Searchlight,* 7 June 1924, 7. Schenck was a highly influential producer who produced many of Fatty Arbuckle's films and would later co-found Twentieth Century–Fox.

51. "Propaganda in Theatres," *Dawn,* 1 December 1923, 14. *Dawn* complained of two plays. One depicted "a Protestant minister, a missionary who is portrayed

in the odious role of a rapist," while the other addressed a Catholic priest who falls passionately in love with a gypsy girl. Despite being based on a popular novel, the Catholic character was cut from the stage version "in order not to wound the religious feelings of a considerable part of the audience," yet the other play continued unaffected.

52. "Jew-Jesuit Propaganda in 'The Miracle,'" *American Standard,* 1 August 1924, 17–19. The Klan again stressed the involvement of the Jewish manager, Max Reinhardt. These protests also extended to other media. In May 1929 *Kourier* urged Klansmen and Klanswomen to take action against "Romanist and Anti-American Propaganda" on an Iowa radio station, WNAX, by initially writing letters of protest. The article stated that "if this station is going to praise the Roman Catholics and fling nasty remarks at Protestantism and Protestant men, it is time we should make ourselves known."

53. *Fiery Cross,* 28 March 1924, 6; "Theatregoers are Awakened," *Fiery Cross,* 28 November 1924, 7. The article also noted that attendance for *Simon Called Peter,* another piece of "Roman Catholic propaganda," had fallen after the *Fiery Cross* had alerted Protestant theatergoers of the content of the play.

54. "Jew Movies a Moral Menace," *American Standard,* 15 April 1925, 173.

55. *Dawn,* 6 January 1923, 2.

56. "Best Show in Town," *Dawn,* 6 January 1923.

57. *Dawn,* 27 January 1923, 10; *Dawn,* 9 February 1924, 10–11. When a Klan-supported radio broadcast by the Fellowship Forum was halted in 1928 after someone cut the antenna cable, *Kourier* (February 1928) presented this vandalism as a deliberate religiously motivated attack on the

"national voice for Protestant fraternal America."

58. *Dawn,* 6 January 1923.

59. *Chicago Daily Journal,* 2 January 1923, 23; *Chicago Evening Post,* 4 January 1923.

60. *Fiery Cross,* 27 April 1923, 4; *Dawn,* 12 May 1923.

61. *Searchlight,* 22 March 1924, 1; *Fiery Cross,* 28 February 1924, 4; Glenda Frank, "Tempest in Black and White: The 1924 Premiere of Eugene O'Neill's *All God's Chillun Got Wings,*" *Resources for American Literary Study* 26:1 (2000), 79, 86. According to Stephen Black, O'Neill responded by scribbling "Go fuck yourself" at the bottom of the death threat and sending it back to the Klan leader who had sent it. See Stephen Black, *Eugene O'Neill: Beyond Mourning and Tragedy* (New Haven, CT: Yale University Press, 1999), 301.

62. *Movie Weekly,* 14 July 1923, 4.

63. Richard DeCordova, *Picture Personalities: The Emergence of the Star System in America* (Urbana: University of Illinois Press, 1990), 120; *Movie Weekly,* 16 February 1924, 9; *Movie Weekly,* 19 April 1924, 8–9.

64. *Kourier,* March 1927, 8; David M. Chalmers, *Hooded Americanism: The History of the Ku Klux Klan,* 3rd ed. (Durham, NC: Duke University Press, 1987), 122.

65. "A Lesson for the Negro and the Jew," *Dawn,* 12 May 1923.

66. *Fiery Cross,* 27 April 1923, 4.

67. "Paramount's Titles and Matter Viscously Attacked in Pamphlet," *Variety,* 9 July 1924, 17.

68. Ibid.

69. *Searchlight,* 31 May 1924, 3; *American Standard,* 15 November 1925, 519–520; *Dearborn Independent,* 5 November 1921, 6 and 14.

70. *Searchlight* (6 May 1924, 5) also published an extensive advertisement for

Paramount in May 1924, which stated, "If it's a Paramount picture, it's the best show in town."

71. *American Standard,* 1 July 1924, 5–6.

72. *Searchlight,* 26 April 1924, 2.

73. *American Standard,* 1 July 1924, 5–6.

74. Ibid.

75. "Patriots Make War on Jew Movies," *American Standard,* 1 February 1925, 54.

76. *Searchlight,* 11 November 1922, 4; *American Standard,* 1 July 1924, 5–6.

77. *New York Times,* 23 January 1921; *New York Times,* 2 May 1921; *Imperial Night-Hawk,* 1 October 1924, 2.

78. *Kourier,* May 1925, 22–24.

79. *Searchlight,* 12 July 1924, 7.

80. *Variety,* 9 July 1924, 17; *Kourier,* September 1933, 9–11.

81. *Photoplay,* March 1927, 28–31; Ruth Waterbury, "Don't Go to Hollywood!," *Photoplay,* March 1927, 50–51; *Movie Weekly,* 16 February 1924, 6–7; *Movie Weekly,* 22 March 1924; "Mary Pickford Gives Tip to Movie Struck," *Fiery Cross,* 7 December 1923, 4.

82. Christopher N. Cocoltchos, "The Invisible Empire and the Search for the Orderly Community: The Ku Klux Klan in Anaheim, California," in *The Invisible Empire in the West,* ed. Shawn Lay (Urbana: University of Illinois Press, 1992).

83. *American Standard,* 1 July 1924, 5–6; *Variety,* 9 July 1924, 17.

84. Wade, *The Fiery Cross,* 80.

85. These cartoons can be found in Bishop Alma White, *Heroes of the Fiery Cross* (Zarephath, NJ: The Good Citizen, 1928), 37, 74.

86. Mark Lynn Anderson, *Twilight of the Idols: Hollywood and the Human Sciences in 1920s America* (Berkeley: University of California Press, 2011), 18.

87. "Is There a Ku Klux Klan in the Movies?," *Movie Weekly,* 24 March 1923, 1, 4–5, 27.

88. Chalmers, *Hooded Americanism,* 3. *Imperial Night-Hawk,* 24 October 1924, 5, discusses Klan growth in California, while the assassination plot is reported on 23 July 1924.

89. *Los Angeles Times,* 8 June 1922, 1; *Los Angeles Times,* 26 August 1922.

90. *Variety,* 29 July 1925, 1, 9; *Variety,* 3 September 1924, 1.

91. "Hollywood Klan to Welcome All Races," *Afro American* (Baltimore), 13 February 1926, 3.

92. Lewis Milestone, transcript of an interview by Kevin Brownlow (1970), 49–50, kindly provided by Kevin Brownlow; "Calif. State Police Captain after K.K.K. Sign Painters," *Variety,* 10 September 1924, 29; *Variety,* 6 August 1924, estimated that there were 125,000 Klan members in the state.

93. *Movie Weekly,* 24 March 1923, 4.

94. Rob King, "Roscoe 'Fatty' Arbuckle: Hollywood's Starring Scapegoat," in *Flickers of Desire: Movie Stars of the 1910s,* ed. Jennifer M. Bean (New Brunswick, NJ: Rutgers University Press, 2011). A syndicated front-page report straight after Arbuckle's arrest, written by Ellis H. Martin, described him as "the life of the party . . . not only in real life, but in a recently enacted comedy." See *Pittsburgh Post-Gazette,* 12 September 1921, 1.

95. *Kourier,* November 1927, 30.

96. "At Hollywood, California, is a colony of these people," complained Senator Myers of Montana, "where debauchery, riotous living, drunkenness, ribaldry, dissipation, free love, seem to be conspicuous." *Congressional Record* 9657, 29 June 1922. See also Sam Stoloff, "Normalizing Stars: Roscoe 'Fatty' Arbuckle and Hollywood Consolidation," in *American Silent Film: Discovering Marginalized Voices,* ed. Gregg Bachman and Thomas J. Slater

(Carbondale: Southern Illinois University Press, 2002), 164.

97. *Variety,* 9 July 1924, 5.

98. *Fort Worth Star Telegram,* 24 January 1922, 2; *Tulsa World,* 2 June 1922, 5; Mark Lynn Anderson, "Tempting Fate: Clara Smith Hamon, or, The Secretary as Producer," in *Looking Past the Screen: Case Studies in American Film History and Method,* ed. John Lewis and Eric Smoodin (Durham, NC: Duke University Press, 2007).

99. William G. Shepherd, "Ku Klux Koin," *Collier's,* 28 July 1928, 38. Simmons acknowledged that the membership ("only" 125,000 members) and finances of the Klan were considerably lower than reported in the press. The report also notes how Simmons actively pushed for a full investigation. "I had spent over $2,000 for telegrams to congressmen, demanding an investigation of the Klan, as soon as gossip of an investigation began." Chalmers, *Hooded Americanism,* 38; Kathleen Blee, *Women of the Klan: Racism and Gender in the 1920s* (Berkeley: University of California Press, 1991), 5.

100. Hilary Hallett, *Go West, Young Women: The Rise of Early Hollywood* (Berkeley: University of California Press, 2013), 199.

101. Stoloff, "Normalizing Stars."

102. *Imperial Night-Hawk,* 4 April 1923, 3; 31 May 1923, 3, 5; 11 July 1923, 4.

103. *Dawn,* 21 April 1923. Wrigley attempted to sue *Tolerance,* the Catholic newspaper, for claiming he was a Klan member. The Klan, not entirely helpfully, supported this action, noting that "we are for Mr. Wrigley and we hope that he will push his suit to the limit." *Searchlight,* 10 February 1923, 2.

104. *Photoplay,* August 1918, 14; *Photoplay,* December 1918, 30–31.

105. Years later the Vernon Tigers would be rebranded the Hollywood Stars. Greg Merritt, *Room 1209: The Life of Fatty Arbuckle, the Mysterious Death of Virginia Rappe, and the Scandal That Changed Hollywood* (Chicago: Chicago Review Press, 2013).

106. Eliot Asinof, *Eight Men Out: The Black Sox and the 1919 World Series* (New York: Henry Holt, 1963), 135–136.

107. "Jewish Gamblers Corrupt American Baseball," *Dearborn Independent,* 3 September 1921; *Kourier,* March 1927, 14, quoting *Washington Evening Star,* 29 December 1926.

108. Harold Brackman, "The Attack on 'Jewish Hollywood': A Chapter in the History of Modern American Anti-Semitism," *Modern Judaism* 20:1 (2000).

109. *Kourier,* September 1933, 9–11.

110. "Movie Weekly Writer Threatened by Ku Klux Klan," *Movie Weekly,* 2 May 1923, 4–5, 27. The reference to Kelly as a "fighting Irishman" appeared in a preview to the article on the contents page of *Movie Weekly,* 28 April 1923.

111. "Movie Weekly Writer Received Official Communication from Ku Klux Klan," *Movie Weekly,* 14 July 1923, 4–5, 30. *Movie Weekly* suggested that this referred to the Rudolph Valentino film *The Sheik,* but given the language used and the timing of the letter, the Klan was evidently referring once more to *Bella Donna.*

112. *Movie Weekly,* 14 July 1923, 4–5, 30.

113. Ibid.

114. "The Folly of 1921," *Motion Picture Magazine,* August 1921, 21; "Shall the Ku Klux Klan Censor the Movies?," *Movie Weekly,* 7 July 1923.

115. Frederick James Smith, "Foolish Censors," *Photoplay,* October 1922, 39–41.

116. *Searchlight,* 25 February 1922, 4; *Dawn,* 6 January 1923.

117. *Dawn,* 13 October 1923, 10.

118. *Kourier,* December 1926, 5. The quotation comes from Dr. Hiram Evans, who succeeded William Simmons as Imperial Wizard in 1922.

119. *Kourier,* August 1925, 3; *Film Daily,* 15 July 1924, 1.

120. *American Standard,* 1 February 1925, 53–55.

121. Carr, *Hollywood and Anti-Semitism,* 70.

122. *Motion Picture News,* 13 March 1926, 1168; Thomas R. Pegram, *One Hundred Percent American: The Rebirth and Decline of the Ku Klux Klan in the 1920s* (Chicago: Ivan R. Dee, 2011), 149.

123. William D. Upshaw, Hearings of the U.S. House of Representatives, 1926, quoted in Lamar Beman, *Selected Articles on Censorship of the Theater and Moving Pictures* (New York: H. W. Wilson Company, 1931), 107.

124. Letter from Turner Jones to Wilton A. Barrett, 30 May 1923, from *The National Board of Review of Motion Pictures Records,* New York Public Library.

125. Letter from H. J. Mandeville to National Committee for Better Films, 23 April 1923, ibid.

126. Letter from Mrs. Livengood to National Board of Censorship, 6 March 1925, and reply dated 11 March 1925, both ibid.

127. "Organization of Women Want Clean Films," *Fiery Cross,* 30 March 1923, 5.

128. Raymond Moley, *The Hays Office* (Indianapolis: Bobbs-Merrill Company, 1945), 33–34. Gregory Black added that as a "teetotaler, elder in the Presbyterian church, Elk, Moose, Rotarian, and Mason, Hays brought the respectability of mainstream middle America to a Jewish-dominated film industry." Gregory Black, *Hollywood Censored: Morality Codes, Catholics and the Movies* (New York: Cambridge University Press, 1994), 31.

129. *Dawn,* 21 July 1923, 13.

130. "Sex Film Title 'Clean-Up,'" *Variety,* 2 July 1924, 1, 21; *Fiery Cross,* 27 April 1923, 4.

131. *American Standard,* 1 February 1925, 54; *American Standard,* 15 February 1925, 81.

132. Romanowski, *Reforming Hollywood,* 47.

133. Anne Morey, *Hollywood Outsiders: The Adaptation of the Film Industry, 1913–1934* (Minneapolis: University of Minnesota Press, 2003), 124.

134. *Variety,* 13 May 1921, 47; *Variety,* 20 May 1921, 1. The film was replaced by an American production, *The Money Changers* (1920).

135. Louis Pizzitola, *Hearst over Hollywood: Power, Passion and Propaganda in the Movies* (New York: Columbia University Press, 2013), 399; *Indianapolis News,* 25 January 1924.

136. "Film Service Gets Generous Approval," *Pinedale Roundup,* 6 March 1924. The article also appeared in *Ruthvern Free Press,* 27 February 1924, 3.

137. Letter from Will Hays to Commander Alvin Owsley, 1 May 1923; Resolution, 10 December 1924; Will Hays to General James Drain, 22 January 1925, all accessed at the American Legion Library, Indianapolis. I am indebted to Joseph J. Hovish for his help in accessing these materials.

138. Frank Walsh, *Sin and Censorship: The Catholic Church and the Motion Picture Industry* (New Haven, CT: Yale University Press, 1996), 30–35, 18. When the Vatican abolished the National Catholic Welfare Council in 1922, a group that had actively supported calls for better films and on-screen "decency," supporters convinced the pope to reverse the decision, "citing the resurgence of the Ku Klux Klan" as evidence of forthcoming anti-Catholic persecution.

139. *Imperial Night-Hawk,* 1 October 1924, 2; *Exhibitors Herald,* 29 April 1922, 37.

140. *Kourier,* May 1925, 22–24; *Imperial Night-Hawk,* 1 October 1924, 2.

141. Blee, *Women of the Klan,* 85–86.

142. "Jew Movies a Moral Menace to America," *American Standard,* 15 April 1925, 173.

143. *Kokomo Daily Dispatch,* 26 July 1923, 1; "Speaker Defines Klan in Address," *Kokomo Daily Dispatch,* 11 August 1923, 1.

144. *Dawn,* 9 June 1923, 13. *Dawn* reported that the theater owner could lose his license if he let the Klan use his theater. *Official Monthly Bulletin of the Knights of the Ku Klux Klan* issued by the Realm of Mississippi, April 1927.

145. James S. Hirsch, *Riot and Remembrance: America's Worst Race Riot and its Legacy* (Boston: Mariner Books, 2003), 167.

146. *Kourier,* October 1927, 29. "Are these facts an indication of our progress?" asked *Kourier,* adding, "Does America care more for entertainment than for culture, which is represented by a public library or a scientist's laboratory?"

147. Steven J. Ross, *Working Class Hollywood: Silent Film and the Shaping of Class in America* (Princeton, NJ: Princeton University Press, 1998), 21–23. Ross talks more specifically of earlier films, with the quotation referring to the Alhambra Theatre in Massachusetts in 1912. Reformers in the 1920s expressed these concerns about mixed audiences, yet Klan literature based its criticisms on the perceived Jewish control of the theaters.

148. Ben Singer, *Melodrama and Modernity: Early Sensational Cinema and Its Contexts* (New York: Columbia University Press, 2001), 295.

149. In his case study of Lexington, Kentucky, *Main Street Amusements: Movies and Commercial Entertainment in a Southern City, 1896–1930* (Washington, DC: Smithsonian Institution Press, 1995), Gregory Waller discusses sabbatarian campaigns each year from 1912 to 1915 and then again in 1918 and 1921, noting both the durability of this issue and the very localized responses to it.

150. Alma White, *The Ku Klux Klan in Prophecy* (Zarephath, NJ: The Good Citizen, 1925), 53. "The Great Jewish syndicates, the rulers and promoters of the motion picture industry, are striking death-blows to the morals of society and to American traditions and principles," she wrote, adding that the greatest menace to the nation's youth was the "movies."

151. *Moving Picture World,* 29 March 1919, 1776; "The Lord's Day and Commercialized Recreation," *Christian Century,* 24 February 1921, 5; "Would Undo Pennsylvania Blue Laws," *Moving Picture World,* 8 March 1919, 1332.

152. *Kokomo Daily Dispatch,* 28 February 1924, 1.

153. "K.K.K. Sunday Bill by Payne in Indiana," *Variety,* 3 December 1924, 2; *Film Daily,* 4 December 1924, 1.

154. *Moving Picture World,* 22 March 1924, 294; *Variety,* 15 March 1924, 1.

155. "To Paint Town Blue," *Moving Picture World,* 15 December 1923, 602; *Moving Picture World,* 19 January 1924, 204; "Ministers Ask Help of Klan to Abolish Sunday Movies," *Kourier,* 20 June 1924, 1.

156. *Variety,* 9 March 1924, 1. Further attempts to restrict the presentation of movies on Sundays were reported in the Klan press throughout 1924. For example, the *Fiery Cross* (12 December 1924, 8) alerted readers to an attempt in New Jersey to reopen theaters on Sundays.

157. Alexander McGregor, *The Catholic Church and Hollywood: Censorship and Morality in 1930s Cinema* (London: I. B. Taurus, 2013), 15.

158. "Jew Calls His Brethren to Fight Catholic Control," *Dawn*, 21 July 1923, 12. This was originally featured in *Fellowship Forum*.

159. *Jewish Criterion*, 25 November 1927, 33. For more on the production history of the film, see Richard Maltby, "*The King of Kings* and the Czar of All the Rushes: The Propriety of the Christ Story," in *Controlling Hollywood: Censorship and Regulation in the Studio Era*, ed. Matthew Bernstein (New Brunswick, NJ: Rutgers University Press, 1999), 60–86; Romanowski, *Reforming Hollywood*, 59–61.

160. McGregor, *The Catholic Church and Hollywood*, 17–20.

161. See Robert H. Wiebe, *The Search for Order* (New York: Hill and Wang, 1967).

162. Richard Maltby, "The Production Code and the Hays Office," in Tino Balio, *Grand Design: Hollywood as a Modern Business Enterprise, 1930–1939* (New York: Charles Scribner's Sons, 1993); also see Romanowski, *Reforming Hollywood*, 100.

163. *Syracuse Herald*, 25 June 1934, 9. Joseph Breen, the head of the Production Code Administration, was strongly anti-semitic and blamed the Jewish moguls for the "decadence on screen." See Black, *Hollywood Censored*, 39, 70.

164. *Fiery Cross*, April–May, 1940, 5. The article claimed that pictures always showed Catholic clergymen "in the most favorable light" and listed films in which Catholic priests were inserted "for the sole purpose of making the unsuspecting public a prey for Catholic propaganda."

165. Black, *Hollywood Censored*, 189; Walsh, *Sin and Censorship*, 113.

166. *Kourier*, September 1933, 9–11.

167. "White Legion Mob Beats Ex-Film Star, Companion," *Modesto Bee*, 3 June 1936, 1.

168. *Daily Courier* (Pennsylvania), 1 June 1934, 13; "New Klan Terrorizes Mid West," *Indiana Democrat* (Pennsylvania), 24 June 1934, 3. The *Charleston Gazette* (7 February 1924, 6) labeled the White Legion a "rechristened Ku Klux Klan." Glenn Feldman, *Politics, Society and the Klan in Alabama, 1915–1949* (Tuscaloosa: University of Alabama Press, 1999), 279.

169. *Gettysburg Times*, 2 September 1936, 1; *Port Arthur News*, 24 May 1936, 1–2. The Black Legion group had originally formed under the title of "Klan guard" in Ohio in the mid-1920s. Judge Hartrick emphasized the links between the two groups, claiming that "the first 200 members [of the Black Legion] were Klansmen who dyed their white robes black." See *Fitchburg Sentinel*, 1 September 1936, 1, 6.

170. *Variety*, 18 August 1937.

171. The legal action was resolved in favor of Warners as the court determined that the insignia was not used for the purpose of sale, even if publicity for the film, which contained phrases like "Their insignia . . . a cowardly hood!," did use the image and costume as a commercial selling point to attract audiences. Ultimately the Klan had to pay costs. The court brief is contained within the *Black Legion* file at the Warner Bros. archives at the University of Southern California.

172. Letter from Bernard Cruse to Warner Bros., 7 February 1937, Warner Bros. archives, University of Southern California.

3. Klan Cinema

1. *New York World* (*NYW*), 25 September 1921, 2.

2. *Variety*, 25 March 1921, 47.

3. *NYW*, 19 September 1921; *NYW*, 21 September 1921; *Wichita Daily Times*, 2 December 1921, 6.

4. *Hartford Courant*, 11 September 1921, 4:1. The holder of this box had opened Wheeler's letters and dropped them in the

mail chute with the label "Ku Klux Klan mail not for this box."

5. *New Haven Register,* 23 September 1921, 1. According to biographies, Wheeler was a "Yale man" who was in military and diplomatic sevice for the French, Czechoslovak, and Imperial Russian armies during the war. He moved to Hollywood and directed a number of independent productions, such as *The Love Wager* for Platinum Pictures in 1927 and the James Ormont war picture *Comrades,* set in France. He subsequently wrote and directed various films in Europe, providing Italian, English, and Spanish versions. See *Oakland Tribune,* 29 December 1927, 1; 19 January 1929, 23; *Film Daily,* 5 August 1940, 3; *Film Daily Production Guide and Directors' Annual Number 1941.*

6. *Englewood Times,* 9 September 1921, 5, 7. *The White Riders,* a western featuring Edmund Cobb, was released more widely in 1923 as *Riders of the Range.*

7. *Searchlight,* 8 April 1922, 2; *Miami District Daily News* (Oklahoma), 30 June 1922, 4; *Connersville News-Examiner,* 1 December 1922, 6.

8. A censor report in Kansas listed the producers as B & S Producing Company (*Tulsa World,* 7 May 1922, 14). McComb died in Texas in 1930 in a fishing accident.

9. *News-Sentinel,* 25 October 1922, 17.

10. *Connersville News-Examiner,* 29 November 1922, 8.

11. See, for example, *Alton Evening Telegraph,* 16 December 1922, 10; *Fort Wayne News Sentinel,* 21 October 1922, 9.

12. *Logansport Pharos-Tribune,* 11 October 1922, 9.

13. *Indianapolis Star,* 24 September 1922; *Noblesville Daily Ledger* (*NDL*), 4 November 1922, 3.

14. A version of *The Mysterious Eyes of the Ku Klux Klan* was playing on the night after the parade at the Idle Hour Theatre

in Drumright (see *Drumright Evening Derrick,* 31 March 1922, 1) and had likely played at the Broadway the previous week. Even if the film did not show this specific parade, its release in Oklahoma directly responded to the Klan's public performances in town.

15. *Tulsa World,* 2 April 1922, 2:1; James S. Hirsch, *Riot and Remembrance: America's Worst Race Riot and Its Legacy* (Boston: Mariner Books, 2003), 166.

16. *Tulsa World,* 28 September 1921, 2; *Miami District Daily News,* 16 February 1922, 8.

17. Hirsch, *Riot and Remembrance,* 166–167.

18. *Tulsa World,* 8 April 1922, 10; *Tulsa World,* 13 April 1922, 10.

19. *Miami District Daily News,* 30 June 1922, 2. It was advertised in Ohio with the tagline "Are you for or against them [the Klan]?"; *Hamilton Evening Journal,* 25 April 1923, 2.

20. *Logansport Pharos-Tribune,* 9 October 1922.

21. *Daily Ardmoreite,* 22 May 1922, 16; *Modesto Evening News,* 15 August 1922, 12; *Modesto Evening News,* 14 August 1922, 3.

22. *Wichita Daily Times,* 30 May 1922; *Bonham Daily Favorite,* 30 June 1922, 1; *Houston Chronicle,* 14 August 1922; *Port Arthur Daily News,* 28 August 1922, 2.

23. *San Antonio Evening News,* 16 October 1922, 1.

24. *Modesto Evening News,* 15 August 1922, 12. At Fort Wayne, it was listed as "The Inside Story of the Famous Ku Klux Klan," while in Indianapolis a slogan declaring it "the only picture ever made positively showing the inner workings of the KU KLUX KLAN" appeared in place of a title. See *Fort Wayne Journal Gazette,* 28 October 1922; *Indianapolis Star,* 24 September 1922, 60.

25. *Lincoln Sunday Star,* 6 December 1925, 6; *Lincoln Sunday Star,* 7 December 1925; *Lincoln Sunday Star,* 8 December 1925. The film was described as "the Klan moving picture" and as "a new photoplay," but it is evident from publicity materials that this was a reworking of *The Mysterious Eyes of the Ku Klux Klan.*

26. Ohio Division of Film Censorship Records, Ohio Historical Society. *The Mysterious Eyes of the KKK* (certificate no. 2666) was submitted by A. B. Seymour of Houston, Texas, in Cincinnati on 26 December 1922, as a three-reel film, with the maker listed as D. S. Prod. The film was "reconstructed[,] reviewed and approved" on 27 February 1923.

27. *Variety,* 2 June 1922, 37.

28. *Searchlight,* 12 August 1922, 1.

29. *Modesto Evening News,* 14 August 1922, 3.

30. *Fiery Cross,* 7 September 1923, 5; *NDL,* 15 October 1923, 3.

31. *Exhibitors Herald,* 1 March 1924, 76.

32. *Kansas City Star,* 2 May 1922, 1; *Connersville News-Examiner,* 28 November 1922, 6. The *Indianapolis Star* (26 September 1922, 4) dismissed the film as "a rambling account of what the Ku Klux Klan is supposed to do."

33. *Movie Weekly,* 6 October 1923, 4–5, 29. Kelly claimed, in what can hardly be termed an exclusive, that a "reliable source" had informed him that the film was "built upon a patriotic theme."

34. *Moving Picture World,* 22 September 1923, 324; *Columbus Dispatch,* 22 November 1923, 25.

35. *Columbus Dispatch,* 22 November 1923, 25. *Moving Picture World,* 22 September 1923, 324, 25. The Florida Feature Film Company produced a picture with Walter Miller and Irva Ross entitled *The Toll of Justice* in 1916 which, contrary to a few er-roneous reports, did not feature the Klan and bore no relation to the later film.

36. *Fiery Cross,* 20 July 1923, 1, 10.

37. *Canton Repository,* 7 August 1924, 6.

38. *NYW,* 14 April 1923, 9. Ricord Gradwell, "owner of Producers Security Corporation," had a contract to market the films if he approved of them. See also *Film Daily,* 16 April 1923, 1.

39. Thomas G. Dyer, "The Klan on Campus: C. Lewis Fowler and Lanier University," *South Atlantic Quarterly* 77 (Fall 1978), 453–469.

40. *Mooresville Times,* 20 July 1923, 1. The *Plainfield Messenger* (19 August 1923, 1, 5) discussed this second ceremony at length, but focused on the excellent work of those directing traffic, save for one incident. "During the ceremonial a woman fainted," the paper explained, "and when being rushed to the emergency hospital in an automobile, the car plunged down a ravine and collided with a tree, resulting in one woman suffering a broken arm and the other occupants being somewhat cut and bruised."

41. *Kokomo Daily Dispatch,* 11 August 1923, 1.

42. *Fiery Cross,* 10 August 1923, 12; *Middleton Daily Herald,* 30 January 1924, 1; *Fiery Cross,* 14 December 1923.

43. Walter Lippmann, *Public Opinion* (New York: Macmillan, 1922). See also Lee Grieveson, "Cinema Studies and the Conduct of Conduct," in *Inventing Film Studies,* ed. Lee Grieveson and Haidee Wasson (Durham, NC: Duke University Press, 2008), 50.

44. *Moving Picture World,* 1 December 1923, 458.

45. *Moving Picture World,* 22 September 1923, 324; *Newark Advocate,* 17 December 1923, 5, 13. *The Toll of Justice* was submitted to the Ohio Film Censorship board as a seven-reel film by C. and S. Pictures and

was viewed on four occasions between 20 November 1923 (card 3744) and 24 February 1925.

46. Wilbert Pictures Co., *The Toll of Justice Press Matter Exploitation Advertising Campaign Book* (1924). The booklet was uncovered in a barn in Columbus, Ohio, and was wrapped inside a copy of the *Franklin County News* (17 October 1924), which included a report and advertisement for the film on its front page. There was also a reel of film found with the material, which had been destroyed by the weather. I am enormously grateful to Thomas R. Pegram for alerting me to this and for sending me a copy of the campaign book.

47. *Film Daily*, 16 April 1923, 1; *NYW*, 14 April 1923, 9. The report stated that Haywood was a school friend of Dixon's from Wake Forest College.

48. *Ohio State Journal*, December 1923, 5:1; *Moving Picture World*, 1 December 1923, 458.

49. *Moving Picture World*, 1 December 1923, 458; *Fiery Cross*, 14 December 1923, 1; *Kokomo Daily Dispatch*, 11 August 1923, 1; *Winchester Journal Herald*, 7 February 1924, 4.

50. *Fiery Cross*, 14 December 1923, 1.

51. A version of *The Toll of Justice* is available at the University of North Carolina, Chapel Hill.

52. *NDL*, 17 January 1924, 2; *Fiery Cross*, 14 March 1924, 7; *Movie Weekly*, 6 October 1923, 4.

53. *Chicago Daily Journal*, 2 January 1923, 23; *Chicago Evening Post*, 4 January 1923, accessed at the Billy Rose Theatre Collection in New York. The play was heavily advertised and discussed in *Dawn*, 6 January 1923, 2.

54. *Chicago Evening Post*, 4 January 1923, explained that the enemy thus "stands not only for the menace of Japa-

nese Imperialism but also for the threat of Russian Bolshevism."

55. *NDL*, 24 April 1924, 6.

56. A tagline for the film stated, "A foolish school girl tries to be a sleuth and is caught." See Wilbert Pictures Co., *Toll of Justice Campaign Book*.

57. Kathleen M. Blee, "Women in the 1920s' Ku Klux Klan Movement," *Feminist Studies* 17:1 (Spring 1991), 60.

58. *Muncie Sunday Star*, 17 February 1924, 7.

59. *Film Daily*, 17 August 1922, 3; *Columbus Dispatch*, 22 November 1923, 25. *The Traitor Within* (certificate 116) was submitted by Hoosier Distributors of Indianapolis and was rejected on 14 April 1924 "on account of being harmful." The censor was V. M. Riegel. Ohio Division of Film Censorship Records, Ohio Historical Society.

60. *Ohio State Journal*, 23 November 1923, 2; *Fiery Cross*, 8 March 1924, 1. Klan newspapers regularly contained articles discussing the "proper use of bunting" or "the salute to the flag." See for example *Kourier*, July 1925.

61. Wilbert Pictures Co., *Toll of Justice Campaign Book*.

62. *Daily Northwestern*, 17 July 1924, 3; *NYW*, 25 September 1921, 2; *Lincoln Sunday Star*, 6 December 1925, 6.

63. *Newark Advocate*, 17 December 1923, 5; *Fiery Cross*, 14 March 1924; *Fiery Cross*, 25 January 1924, 1.

64. *Searchlight*, 24 March 1923, 6; *Imperial Night-Hawk*, 4 July 1923, 8; *Searchlight*, 19 May 1923, 4.

65. *Behind the Mask* was written by C. Anderson Wright, a man described on posters as "exposer of and former Grand Goblin" of the Klan. Wright produced another even shorter-lived play exposing the Klan, entitled *Masked Men*, later in 1922. See *Variety*, 23 December 1921, 24; *Syracuse*

Herald, 25 December 1921; *Syracuse Herald,* 17 December 1921, 6; *Variety,* 6 January 1922, 19; *Variety,* 8 December 1922, 23.

66. Wilbert Pictures Co., *Toll of Justice Campaign Book.* The booklet also offers some insights into the operating practices of independent exhibitors and the press. One suggestion is to "mail a neatly typewritten copy of reviews to each critic so that it will be available in case he lacks time to write his own."

67. Ibid.

68. *Perry Journal,* 20 May 1925, 4; *Corsicana Daily Sun,* 27 June 1925, 6.

69. Wilbert Pictures Co., *The Toll of Justice Campaign Book.*

70. *Columbus Dispatch,* 10 December 1923, 10.

71. *Canton Evening Repository,* 1 August 1924, 19; 2 August 1924, 3; 5 August 1924; 6 August 1924, 14; 8 August 1924, 22; 9 August 1924, 3.

72. *Canton Evening Repository,* 1 August 1924, 19; Wilbert Pictures Co., *The Toll of Justice Campaign Book.*

73. *Charleston Gazette,* 21 September 1924, 4; *Franklin County News,* 17 October 1924, 1.

74. *Newark Advocate,* 17 December 1923, 5; *Kluxer,* 5 January 1924, 29.

75. *Fiery Cross,* 14 March 1924; *Protestant Home Journal,* 4 March 1925, 1.

76. *Columbus Dispatch,* 2 January 1924, 23; *Mansfield News,* 20 February 1924, 11; *Ashland Times-Gazette,* 20 February 1924, 12.

77. *Muncie Evening Press,* 16 February 1924, 7; *NDL,* 15 January 1924, 3; *Greencastle Herald,* 13 February 1924, 5; *Anderson Daily Bulletin,* 9 January 1924, 8.

78. *Tipton Tribune,* 13 May 1925, 2; *Lincoln Sunday Star,* 6 December 1925, 6.

79. *Muncie Post-Democrat,* 11 January 1924, 1.

80. *Columbus Dispatch,* 5 January 1924.

81. *Portsmouth Daily Times,* 18 March 1924, 14; *Fiery Cross,* 29 February 1924, 1; *Greencastle Herald,* 13 February 1924, 5.

82. The advertisement for "America's Greatest Klan Photoplay" appeared regularly within the *Fiery Cross* (for example, 2 May 1924, 7) and also, with a different contact address, in *Searchlight* (16 August 1924).

83. *Decatur Review,* 17 July 1924, 12.

84. *Newark Advocate,* 17 December 1923, 5; *Ashland Times-Gazette,* 19 February 1924; *Portsmouth Daily Times,* 18 March 1924, 14; *Lima News,* 19 May 1924, 2; *Chronicle-Telegram,* 26 February 1924, 2; Frank D. Myers, "Lucas County and the Ku Klux Klan," http://lucascountyan .blogspot.co.uk/2012/07/lucas-county -ku-klux-klan-part-2.html, accessed 29 July 2012.

85. *Dawn,* 2 February 1924; *Decatur Daily Democrat,* 18 January 1924, 1; *Fiery Cross,* 25 January 1924, 1. The *Fiery Cross* suggested that the theft had led to a "great influx" in new members as it convinced many "that an organization such as the Klan is needed in America at this time."

86. *Searchlight,* 1 November 1924, 5; *Mansfield News,* 17 February 1924, 4.

87. *Chronicle Telegram,* 3 March 1925, 1–2; *Youngstown Citizen,* 19 March 1925.

88. *Decatur Review,* 17 July 1924, 12; *Kokomo Daily Tribune,* 31 January 1924, 12.

89. *Movie Weekly,* 6 October 1923, 5.

90. *Muncie Morning Star,* 22 February 1924; *Ashland Times Gazette,* 19 February 1924, 12.

91. *Muncie Morning Star,* 16 February 1924; *Fiery Cross,* 18 April 1924, 6; *Logansport Press,* 2 May 1924, 3.

92. *Fiery Cross,* 21 March 1924, 2.

93. *Indiana Catholic and Record,* 21 March 1924, 4.

94. *Indianapolis Star,* 8 June 1924, 10.

95. *Fiery Cross,* 21 March 1924, 5; *Tolerance,* 8 April 1923, 3. A month before screening *The Traitor Within,* the Imperial Wizard, Dr. Hiram Evans, delivered a speech at the Tabernacle in which he widely condemned Catholic influence in education. See *Indianapolis Star,* 14 February 1924, 12. *Tolerance* wrote an extensive piece in 1923 reporting that E. Howard Cadle was on the "Klan roll," but subsequently suggested that there were divisions within the Tabernacle's management over its Klan affiliation. *Fiery Cross,* 18 April 1924, 6; *Muncie Sunday Star,* 17 February 1924; *Muncie Morning Star,* 19 February 1924, 4; *Muncie Morning Star,* 21 February 1924; *Muncie Morning Star,* 26 February 1924, 7.

96. *Lincoln Daily Star,* 8 December 1925, 6.

97. *Variety* suggested that the film's poor box office in Topeka, Kansas, indicated that "all the Topka Klansmen failed to view their own picture." "Klux film real Cluck," *Variety,* 14 January 1925, 13.

98. *Fiery Cross,* 23 January 1925, 7; *Fiery Cross,* 30 January 1925, 2.

99. *Decatur Review,* 10 December 1924; *Evening Gazette,* 13 April 1925, 3. Advertisements also contained the caption "Like a Cloud by Day and Pillar of Fire by Night," a widely used phrase within Klan literature. See *Mexia Daily News,* 16 November 1924, 7.

100. *Protestant Home Journal,* 4 March 1925, 1, 8; *Fiery Cross,* 23 January 1925, 7; *Fiery Cross,* 30 January 1925, 1, 2.

101. *Evening Gazette,* 13 April 1925, 3; *Hutchinson News,* 7 March 1925, 9.

102. Poster for screening at Hiawatha Auditorium, accessed on 1 June 2014 at http://www.worthpoint.com/wortho pedia/1924-the-fifth-horseman-silent -movie-flyer.

103. *Iowa City Press-Citizen,* 2 September 1925, 5.

104. The Fifth Horseman script accessed at the Moving Image Section, Library of Congress, Washington, DC.

105. Ibid.

106. *Melbourne Argus,* 26 April 1924, 25.

107. For more on Ford, see Lee Grieveson, "The Work of Film in the Age of Ford Mechanization," *Cinema Journal,* 51:3 (Spring 2012), 25–51. The Church Film Company provided titles such as *The Life of Christ* and *The Servant in the House* to a wide range of churches. A report on the company in the *Bismark Tribune* (20 September 1921, 4) suggested that "many ministers will not approve of the idea, but it seems a sure-fire way for bringing lost sheep back into the fold." Church groups also wrote to the Board of Review, which supplied a pamphlet with films suitable for church exhibition.

108. *Indianapolis Star,* 11 August 1921, 16; *Variety,* 19 August 1921, 88.

109. The figure is quoted in the *Pinedale Roundup,* 6 March 1924, 6.

110. *American Legion Weekly,* 20 October 1922, 17; *Visual Education,* April 1923, 125.

111. *American Legion Weekly,* 20 October 1922, 17. For example, a 1925 screening in Ohio for *The Whipping Boss* was "for the benefit of the Mansfield High School band." See *Mansfield News,* 15 June 1924, 4; *Moving Picture World,* 23 February 1924, 636.

112. *American Legion Weekly,* 24 November 1922, 15; *American Legion Weekly,* May 18 1923, 27.

113. *American Legion Weekly,* 7 September 1923, 17. Rental prices were dependent on the size of the community's population. *American Legion Monthly,* April 1929, 33.

114. The Film Service Director wrote, "There is no stronger argument in favor of

adjusted compensation than the camera's story of the war." *American Legion Weekly,* 24 November 1922, 15.

115. *Visual Education,* March 1923, 92; *Fiery Cross,* October 1940, 7.

116. *Visual Education,* January 1923, 16; *American Legion Monthly,* September 1929; *The American Legion Presents Old Glory: An Educational Classic That Every American Should See* (American Legion Film Service, 1929).

117. *Ohio Knights of the Ku Klux Klan Records 1923–24,* Ohio Historical Society. The advice offered by the entertainment bureau was very detailed, including such insights as "Do not have artificial lights too close to the speaker's head, they draw insects and may spoil the speech."

118. Letter from Mrs. Livengood to the National Board of Censorship, 6 March 1925, the National Board of Review of Motion Pictures Records, New York Public Library.

119. Telegram dated 7 May 1924. Films requested include *Thomas J. Morgan.* Fort Wayne Ku Klux Klan Records, Indiana Historical Society.

120. *Searchlight,* 6 May 1922, 6; "Pilgrim Photoplay Exchange," box 1, folder 6, Fort Wayne Ku Klux Klan Records, Indiana Historical Society. Although it distributed religious, factual, and feature films, including *Birth,* Pilgrim was not catering entirely to Klan or Protestant groups. The pamphlet included a film like *The Parish Priest,* which was said to be "especially suitable for Catholic presentation."

121. The catalogue contained a diverse set of titles ranging from *Should I Buy a Tractor?* which promised to present "the tractor question, pro and con," to *Making a Ukelele.* "Bureau of Visual Instruction – Indiana University Extension Division 1925–26," box 2, folder 8, Fort Wayne

Ku Klux Klan Records, Indiana Historical Society.

122. *Searchlight,* 21 June 1924, 2; *Daily Northwestern,* 17 July 1924, 3. *The Traitor Within* played at the Shelbyville Chautauqua in August 1924, which was not officially a Klan gathering. See *Decatur Review,* 8 August 1924, 4.

123. *Davenport Democrat and Leader,* 14 September 1925, 3.

124. *Variety,* 6 August 1924, 1, 50.

125. Charlotte M. Canning, *The Most American Thing in America: Circuit Chautauqua as Performance* (Iowa City: University of Iowa Press, 2005), 10.

126. *Variety,* 16 July 1924, 1, 26. The Chautauquas advanced various resolutions in response, including adopting the patriotic slogan "Better Citizen." See *Variety,* 18 February 1925, 38.

127. *Youngstown Citizen,* 6 March 1925; *Youngstown Citizen,* 7 May 1925, 3; *Imperial Night-Hawk,* 23 July 1924, 5.

128. *Ohio Knights of the Ku Klux Klan Records 1923–24; Imperial Night-Hawk,* 9 July 1924, 4.

129. *Fiery Cross,* 10 August 1923, 12; *Fiery Cross,* 5 October 1923; *Fiery Cross,* 2 November 1923; *Protestant Home Journal,* 7 October 1924, 2; *Imperial Night-Hawk,* 12 November 1924. For more on the fire, see also J'Nell L. Pate, *North of the River: A Brief History of North Fort Worth* (Fort Worth: Texas Christian University Press, 1994), 93–96.

130. *Port Arthur News,* 12 May 1924, 3; *Port Arthur News,* 16 June 1924 12.

131. *Port Arthur News,* 27 May 1924, 1; *Dallas Morning News,* 1 September 1924, 2:16.

132. "The Awakening. Presention [*sic*] by Dick Dowling Klan No. 25, Port Arthur, Tex., June 23rd to July 3rd inclusive, a James H. Hull production," Photographic Print, Prints and Photographs Division,

Library of Congress, Washington, DC, http://www.loc.gov/pictures/item /2006679231; *Dallas Morning News*, 1 September 1924, 2:16.

133. *Charleston Gazette*, 18 June 1927, 3; *Protestant Home Journal*, 25 February 1925, 1.

134. Craig Fox, *Everyday Klansfolk: White Protestant Life and the KKK in 1920s Michigan* (East Lansing: Michigan State University Press, 2011), 181.

135. "The Awakening: Program: a Musical Patriotic, Dramatic Spectacular Extravaganza in 23 Scenes with Cast of 500 People" (Lynchburg, VA: Lynchburg Klan No. 11, Realm of Virginia, 1924).

136. *Richmond Times Dispatch*, 8 August 1926, 39. The advertisement described the play as "Better than Birth of a Nation."

137. *Imperial Night-Hawk*, 4 July 1923, 8; *Searchlight*, 19 May 1923, 4; *Fiery Cross*, 9 November 1923, 1; *Lawrence Journal World*, 14 February 1925; *Beatrice Daily Sun*, 20 September 1925, 2; *Lincoln Star*, 10 September 1925, 10; *Variety*, 25 February 1925, 46. The play was "written by a Klansman [Floyd P. Lee], is being produced by a Klansman, and all of the male characters in the production are members of the Invisible Empire."

138. *Canton Repository*, 24 March 1925, 21. See also *Gettysburg Times*, 22 July 1926, 9.

139. The play had been presented by Marion County Klansmen in August 1924 with a cast of 250. It was also put on by the Ashland Klan at the Opera House. *Canton Repository*, 26 July 1924, 10; *Cleveland Plain Dealer*, 26 July 1924, 8.

140. *Protestant Home Journal*, 18 February 1925, 1, 5; *Protestant Home Journal*, 25 February 1925, 8; *Youngstown Citizen*, 26 February 1925, 1.

141. Fox, *Everyday Klansfolk*, 180.

142. *Bonham Daily Favorite*, 3 March 1924, 3; *Fiery Cross*, 6 February 1925; *Fiery Cross*, 13 February 1925, 1; *Variety*,

25 February 1925, 1, 46. While the *Fiery Cross* claimed that the play was "being enthusiastically received by Klansmen," *Variety* countered that it had performed poorly in Indianapolis. The play's narrative would certainly have been familiar to all viewers of *The Toll of Justice* – the rescue of a young girl from an opium den by "real Americans" with a final act set in a Klan Klavern – while its author, J. Lamb Perry of Fort Worth, also wrote the official American Legion play, *Comrades*.

143. *Fiery Cross*, 23 January 1925, 7; *Fiery Cross*, 30 January 1925, 2; *Fiery Cross*, 6 February 1925.

144. *Urbana Daily Courier*, 20 October 1923, 2; *Imperial Night-Hawk*, 14 November 1923, 6; 5 December 1923, 5; *Urbana Daily Courier*, 7 November 1923, 3; *Urbana Daily Courier*, 13 December 1923, 4. For more on the fire that destroyed the venue, see *Daily Illini*, 3 April 1927, 1.

145. *Indiana Citizens' Post*, 3 May 1924, 1, 2. Michael E. Brooks notes that Clark M. Young, who owned a number of theaters in Bowling Green, Ohio, joined the Klan at the beginning of 1924, and the local Klan would use his Del-Mar Theatre for events before it was destroyed by fire in 1926. See Michael E. Brooks, *The Ku Klux Klan in Wood County, Ohio* (Charleston, SC: History Press, 2014), 97.

146. The advertisements for the Classic Theatre appeared regularly in the *Fiery Cross*, most notably through April 1923. The Classic showed *The Ku Klux Klan Play*, a version of *The Clansman*, for two nights in December 1922, offered "Klark's Kute Kids" in *My Broken Hearted Girl* in January 1924, and used musical performers, such as "Pete Sulliven Entertainers" and "Keith Entertainers," who had appeared on the bill with *The Traitor Within* and *The Toll of Justice* elsewhere in the state. It also presented a run of *The Birth*

of a Nation in February 1924. *Elwood Call Leader,* 13 December 1922; *Elwood Call Leader,* 8 and 28 January 1924.

147. *Searchlight,* 4 November 1922, 8. There was no mention of the Klan in any of the posters in the *Atlanta Constitution.*

148. Letter from Mrs. Livengood to the National Board of Censorship, 6 March 1925, *The National Board of Review of Motion Pictures Records,* New York Public Library.

149. Allen Safianow, "You Can't Burn History: Getting Right with the Klan in Noblesville, Indiana," *Indiana Magazine of History* 100:2 (June 2004), 109–154.

150. *NDL,* 4 November 1922, 1, 3; *NDL,* 7 November 1922, 6.

151. *NDL,* 9 February 1923, 8.

152. *NDL,* 24 June 1923, 1; *NDL,* 26 June 1923, 1. The other directors of the American Amusement Company were R. S. Truitt and Gray Truitt.

153. *NDL,* 30 June 1923, 3; *NDL,* 5 September 1923, 3, 7.

154. *NDL,* 13 August 1923, 6; *NDL,* 14 August 1923. Advertisements for the film at the Opera House and The American Theatre appeared regularly over the next two weeks.

155. *NDL,* 16 November 1923, 6; *NDL,* 12 November 1923, 3.

156. *NDL,* 16 November 1923, 6; *NDL,* 18 January 1923, 1.

157. *NDL,* 12 November 1923, 3; *NDL,* 28 November 1923, 3.

158. *NDL,* 28 November 1923, 3. McConaughy explained that "we promised you clean pictures and have proven it."

159. *NDL,* 14 October 1923, 3; *NDL,* 6 August 1924, 3; *NDL,* 24 October 1923, 3; *NDL,* 25 October 1923; *NDL,* 12 November 1923, 3; *NDL,* 31 July 1924, 4.

160. *NDL,* 15 October 1923, 3.

161. *NDL,* 14 January 1924; *NDL,* 15 January 1924, 1, 3; *NDL,* 16 January 1924, 6; *NDL,* 17 January 1924, 2.

162. *NDL,* 24 April 1924, 6; *NDL,* 26 April 1924, 3.

163. *NDL,* 2 July 1924, 2. For more on Heiny, see *NDL,* 30 January 1924, 1.

164. *NDL,* 2 August 1924, 3.

165. *NDL,* 6 August 1924, 3.

166. *NDL,* 26 June 1923, 1; *NDL,* 18 August 1924, 3.

167. NDL, 26 August 1924, 1. The theater attempted to reopen a week after its last performance on 30 August, with advertisements explaining that it would be "Absolutely 100% and Absolutely Free." The program was apparently attended by almost fifteen hundred people, but within three days The American was again described as a "thing of the past." On 5 September, Thompson announced plans to clear the theater's debts of around $1,000 and to reopen soon, having met with the other local stockholders. *The Ledger* reported in September that the Thompson family had taken over the theater and assumed all "obligations of [the] American Amusement Company." *NDL,* 29 August 1924, 8; *NDL,* 2 September 1924, 1; *NDL,* 5 September 1924, 1; *NDL,* 6 September 1924, 1.

168. *NDL,* 23 September 1924.

169. *Ohio State Journal,* 17 August 1924, 2; *Ohio State Journal,* 21 October 1924, 8. The film was the only one produced by Miafa, but a report in the *Fiery Cross* on 11 April 1924 had hailed the film as a success, claiming that Ray Wareham, the Miafa manager, had decided to take the film on tour because of the "many demands from other points."

170. M. William Lutholtz, *Grand Dragon: D.C. Stephenson and the Ku Klux Klan in Indiana* (West Lafayette, IN: Purdue University Press), 1991, 287–289. Ralph Roudebusch, a poultry farmer and a local

stockholder in the company, revealed in court that he had chatted with Stephenson in January 1925 "about the Moving Picture Company in which Mr. Stephenson was the heaviest stockholder." *Stephenson v. Indiana,* Appellant's Brief, Vol. 2, Case 25310, Indiana Supreme Court, 2218–2219, 2235–2239.

171. *Variety,* 21 January 1925, 42; *Variety,*15 April 1925, 1. Palmer had announced that he was employing fifty-two advance agents who would all attend a "special K.K.K. school for two weeks."

172. Carpenter was listed in 1924 with "Hoosier Distributors," the related company now responsible for distributing *The Traitor Within.* By 1925 Curtis C. Hendren was listed as Hoosier president and Frank G. Hous as general manager. Hoosier was housed at 217 Wimmer Building, surrounded by other film companies like Selznick Distribution Company and the National Film Exchange. *Indianapolis Directory 1924,* 485; *Indianapolis Directory 1925,* 813, 892, and 1589.

173. *Indianapolis Star,* 2 July 1925, 2. The Marion County grand jury, when compiling information about Stephenson, mentioned the company in a note, dated 26 August 1926, which explained that Martha Yoh Marson "was around Stephson's [sic] offices all the time. She is now in Florida. She went down there with Edward Young Clarke in connection with the Twentieth Century Motion Picture Corporation." See Marion County Grand Jury notes, box 3, folder 6, D. C. Stephenson Collection (M264), Indiana Historical Society.

174. *Indianapolis Star,* 2 July 1925, 1–2; *Variety,* 27 May 1925, 1, 10. The Twentieth Century Motion Picture Company was a subsidiary of Twentieth Century Enterprises. While Clarke was in charge of the movie company, Stoughton Fletcher was

president of the Twentieth Century Land Company.

175. *Hammond Times,* 19 July 1934, 5.

176. Adam Laats, *Fundamentalism and Education in the Scopes Era* (New York: Palgrave Macmillan, 2010), 109–110; *Hamilton Evening Journal,* 27 March 1926, 24.

177. *Davenport Democrat and Leader,* 4 April 1926, 3.

178. Randy Moore, Mark Decker, and Sehoya Cotner, *Chronology of the Evolution-Creationism Controversy* (Santa Barbara, CA: Greenwood Press, 2009), 198.

179. *Oakland Tribune,* 14 February 1926.

180. *Imperial Night-Hawk,* 16 May 1923, 8; *Protestant Home Journal,* 15 April 1924; *Broad Ax* (Chicago), 11 July 1925, 2. *Kourier,* February 1928; See also Fox, *Everyday Klansfolk,* 145.

181. *Kourier,* February 1928, 10–12. The contrast was made with the work of the "Romanized press and some Jewish publications."

182. *Oakland Tribune,* 14 February 1926; *Evansville Courier and Press,* 21 March 1926, 47.

183. Moore, Decker, and Cotner, *Evolution-Creationism Controversy,* 198.

184. *Variety,* 14 October 1921, 47. At the same time, Dintenfass was also trying to exploit Jack Johnson "in a comedy showing certain adventures of the colored ex-champion in Europe." See *Lincoln State Journal,* 14 August 1921, B5.

185. *Variety,* 1 February 1923, 1.

186. *After Dark,* 21 May 1923, New York State Archives, Motion Picture Division.

187. Letter from Frank B. Coigne to N.Y. State Censor Board, 5 October 1923. Report and Correspondence of the Motion Picture Commission of New York for *The Knight of the Eucharist* (Serial 5715 – 8/22, file 7915, box 2689) and *Mask of the Ku Klux Klan* (Serial 49838 – 11/23, file 9115,

box 2709). From New York State Archives, Motion Picture Division.

188. Pearl Bowser and Louise Spence, *Writing Himself into History: Oscar Micheaux, His Silent Films, and His Audiences* (New Brunswick, NJ: Rutgers University Press, 2000), 158–159. The tagline beneath the image in the *New York Age* said, "See the murderous ride of the insidious Ku Klux Klan." The poster also promised "Gripping Action, Love, Thrills, Suspense." While critiquing and exposing the Klan, Micheaux's work also exploited a popular interest in its cinematic image, using taglines that could equally have applied to *The Toll of Justice* ("See the Night Riders, Big Fights, Thrills, Pathos and Comedy"). *Kansas City Sun*, 11 December 1920, 5.

189. Charlene Regester, "Black Films, White Censors," in *Movie Censorship and American Culture*, ed. Francis G. Couvares (Amherst: University of Massachussetts Press, 1996), 176, 179.

190. Willis N. Huggins, "The Editor's Mail Box," *Chicago Defender*, 17 January 1920, 16.

191. *Indiana Catholic* (3 August 1923, 8) described *The Man without a Country* as "the American Legion film . . . shown under the auspices of the Knights of Columbus." Further examples include the Schubert-Murat Theatre, which put on *The Heart of Paddy Whack* for the "Knights of Columbus Theatre Party" in January 1924. See *Indiana Catholic*, 4 January 1924.

192. Steven J. Ross, *Working Class Hollywood: Silent Film and the Shaping of Class in America* (Princeton, NJ: Princeton University Press, 1998), 35.

193. *Davenport Democrat and Leader*, 9 March 1923, 12.

194. Bowser and Spence, *Writing Himself into History*, 28. Micheaux had emphasized in advertising materials that his first

film, *The Homesteader*, "cannot be booked through regular exchanges on the usual basis."

4. On Mainstream Screens

1. Memorandum from Lamar Trotti to Will Hays, 28 August 1928, MPPDA Digital Archive, http://mppda.flinders.edu.au/records/396/scan/1050.

2. Peter S. Harrison, *Harrison's Reports and Film Reviews, 1919–62* (Los Angeles: Hollywood Film Archives, 1997); *The Motion Picture Almanac* (Chicago: Quigley Publishing Company, 1929), 198.

3. Milliken to Hays, 24 August 1928, MPPDA Digital Archive, accessed on 1 October 2013, http://mppda.flinders.edu.au/records/396/scan/1053; Melvyn Stokes, *D. W. Griffith's The Birth of a Nation: A History of the Most Controversial Picture of All Time* (Oxford: Oxford University Press, 2008), 243.

4. Memorandum, 17 August 1928, Serial Number L38089, State of New York Education Department, Motion Picture Division. The censor's concerns centered on the social reactions to the Klan image, whether through the formation and recruitment of Klan groups or through the potential violence and unrest generated by these Klan appearances.

5. Trotti to Hays, 28 August 1928; *Variety*, 10 October 1928.

6. *Atlanta Constitution*, 26 December 1915; *Variety*, 17 March 1916, 25. An advertisement in *Frederick Daily News* (20 October 1913, 2) for a screening in Maryland in October 1913 explained that the film focused on the "last exciting days of the famous Ku Klux Klan" in North Carolina, suggesting that the action took place after the scenes depicted in *Birth*. Richard Alan Nelson stated that Gene Gauntier had earlier penned *The Northern Schoolmaster* in 1909, which was advertised in *Moving Pic-*

ture World (10 April 1909, 429, and 17 April 1909, 477) as "a powerful story of reconstruction days in the South, and depicts a raid of the Ku Klux Klan." The film offered a sympathetic presentation of a persecuted Northerner heading south. See Richard Alan Nelson, *Florida and the American Motion Picture Industry 1898–1980* (New York: Garland, 1983), 394.

7. Sumiko Higashi, *Cecil B. DeMille and American Culture: The Silent Era* (Berkeley: University of California Press, 1994), 137.

8. *Motography*, 28 October 1916, 861; *Moving Picture World* (*MPW*), 7 October 1916, 22; *Kansas City Star*, 16 January 1921, 14C; *Oakland Tribune*, 13 March 1918, 11.

9. *Wid's Daily*, 22 February 1917. The review is also referenced in Richard Alan Nelson, "Commercial Propaganda in the Silent Film," *Film History* 1 (1987), 161.

10. *Sandusky Register*, 15 April 1919, 2. The film is also listed as *The Eyes of Truth*.

11. Reviews described *Bolshevism on Trial* as "the picture of the hour" and "the most timely picture of the year." *Fort Wayne Journal-Gazette*, 10 July 1919, 10; *Deming Headlight*, 20 June 1919.

12. *Wid's Daily*, 30 March 1919, 19.

13. *MPW*, 5 April 1919, 126; *Kansas City Star*, 13 June 1919, 25.

14. Leslie Debauche, "Mary Pickford's Public on the Home Front," in *Film and the First World War*, ed. Karel Dibbets and Bert Hogenkamp (Amsterdam: Amsterdam University Press, 1995), 149.

15. Eileen Whitfield, *Pickford: The Woman Who Made Hollywood* (Lexington: University Press of Kentucky, 1997), 338.

16. *Heart o' the Hills* publicity book (1919), Moving Image Section, Library of Congress, Washington, DC.

17. *Photoplay*, July 1922, 103. The official synopsis for the film, registered on 22 June 1922, refers to the "quaint Alabama town."

18. *Kingston Daily Freeman*, 28 May 1920, 6; *MPW*, 1 July 1922, 58.

19. Jacqueline Najuma Stewart, *Migrating to the Movies: Cinema and Black Urban Modernity* (Berkeley: University of California Press, 2005), 222–225.

20. Thomas Cripps, *Slow Fade to Black* (New York: Oxford University Press, 1977), 61.

21. DeBauche, "Mary Pickford's Public," 150–155. Christine Gledhill argues that Pickford provided "the world's first experience of full-blown *film* stardom." Christine Gledhill, "Mary Pickford: Icon of Stardom," in *Flickers of Desire: Movie Stars of the 1910s*, ed. Jennifer M. Bean (New Brunswick, NJ: Rutgers University Press, 2011), 43.

22. *Pictures and Picturegoer*, 10 July 1920, 35. Magazines endorsed (and preserved) Pickford's reputation as the sexless big sister and as a positive force for moral good. A typical report in *Bioscope* (13 March 1920) recounts a tale of Pickford politely telling off a little boy who called her "Mary Pigfeet." The boy apologized and Pickford not only wrote back to him, but also phoned his school to ensure that he was settling in well. She was told that he "was one of the best boys in school."

23. *Motion Picture Magazine*, July 1918, 18.

24. *Heart o' the Hills* publicity book. A further "catch line" stated that the jury's response will "warm your heart in the trial of Mary Pickford for murder."

25. *Heart o' the Hills* publicity book.

26. John Fox Jr., *The Heart of the Hills* (New York: Scribner's, 1913), 106, 108, 118.

27. An early draft referred to "a secret band of night riders . . . [who] depend upon the disguise of their masks to protect them from discovery and arrest."

28. Fox, *The Heart of the Hills*, 51, 119.

29. *Washington Post*, 8 December 1919.

30. The best and most exhaustive account on the WKKK remains Kathleen Blee, *Women of the Klan: Racism and Gender in the 1920s* (Berkeley: University of California Press, 1991).

31. Michael Rogin, "'The Sword Became a Flashing Vision': D.W. Griffith's The Birth of a Nation," in *The Birth of a Nation,* ed. Robert Lang (New Brunswick, NJ: Rutgers University Press, 1994), 193.

32. Kevin Brownlow, *Mary Pickford Rediscovered* (New York: Harry N. Abrams, 1999), 168.

33. Memorandum of Agreement between John Fox Jr. and Gladys Mary Moore (Mary Pickford), 16 June 1919, Margaret Herrick Library, Academy of Motion Picture Arts and Sciences, Beverly Hills, CA.

34. The Los Angeles papers were quoted in the 1 April edition of *Kinematograph Weekly* as saying that "Mary Pickford says she will devote her life to the screen and will never marry again," yet Pickford had actually remarried three days earlier. Pickford admitted in her autobiography *Sunshine and Shadow* (New York: Doubleday, 1955) that "we were warned that our pictures might become total failures at the box office, that our hard-earned prestige would be buried under an avalanche of malignant gossip and denunciation" (204).

35. *Variety,* 5 December 1919, 61; *Wid's Daily,* 7 December 1919, 7.

36. *New York Age,* 25 December 1920; Stewart, *Migrating to the Movies,* 224; Henry Sampson, *Blacks in Black and White: A Source Book on Black Films* (Metuchen, NJ: Scarecrow Press, 1995), 272.

37. "Film Censors and Other Morons," *The Nation,* 12 December 1920. This can be found in *Cinema Nation: The Best Writing on Film from "The Nation,"* ed. Carl Bromley (New York: Thunder's Mouth Press/ Nation Books, 2000), 63.

38. *New York Times,* 18 September 1921, 21:3.

39. *Wid's Daily; Exhibitors Herald,* 19 November 1921, 64. *Law and Order* copyright material 17084, 12 October 1921, Moving Image Section, Library of Congress, Washington, DC.

40. *Exhibitors Herald,* 20 January 1923, 62; *New York Times,* 5 December 1922, 24:3; *Variety,* 8 December 1922, 33.

41. John Moffatt Mecklin, *The Ku Klux Klan: A Study of the American Mind* (New York: Harcourt, Brace and Company, 1924), 25–29. See also David Chalmers, *Hooded Americanism: The History of the Ku Klux Klan,* 3rd ed. (Durham, NC: Duke University Press, 1987), 36–38.

42. Mecklin, *The Ku Klux Klan,* 25–29.

43. *Galveston Daily News,* 15 November 1921, 2; *Tulsa World,* 26 August 1921, 7. *Exhibitors Herald* (10 September 1921, 67) commented during the Klan's exposé in the *New York World* that while the film does not deal directly with the Klan, "the advertising value of the title is especially appealing at this time."

44. *Wisconsin Rapids Daily Tribune,* 17 January 1923, 4.

45. *Chicago Tribune,* 17 June 1922.

46. File of The Motion Picture Commission of the State of New York, August 1922, Serial Number 5715, New York State Archives.

47. *MPW,* 27 November 1920, 513.

48. The censor board in Ohio rejected the film on 29 December 1920. It was resubmitted on 4 April 1922 but was again rejected. See Record 878, Ohio Division of Film Censorship Records, Ohio Historical Society.

49. *MPW,* 10 June 1922, 579; *Motion Picture News,* 3 June 1922, 3020–3021.

50. *The Fifth Horseman* was approved with this cut on 17 November 1924. Ohio

Division of Film Censorship Records, Ohio Historical Society.

51. The presentation of Reconstruction, put forward initially by the Dunning School of historians, and subsequently presented most powerfully in *Birth*, was not significantly challenged during this period. Claude Bowers's hugely popular *The Tragic Era* and U. B. Phillips's influential *Life and Labor in the Old South* were both released in 1929. David Levering Lewis, in *W.E.B. Du Bois: The Fight for Equality and the American Century, 1919–1963* (New York: Henry Holt, 2000), suggests that "educated people of color" saw Bowers's work as "tantamount to a lynching in prose" (360).

52. "The Order" appeared not in the "ghostly looking" white robes of the novel, but in black.

53. Rex Beach, *The Mating Call* (London: Hutchinson and Co., 1928), 49, 77.

54. Ibid., 195.

55. Lester Friedman, *Hollywood's Image of the Jew* (New York: Frederick Ungar, 1982), 3.

56. Steven J. Ross, *Working Class Hollywood: Silent Film and the Shaping of Class in America* (Princeton, NJ: Princeton University Press, 1998), 141.

57. *New York Times*, 2 August 1923, 14.

58. *Variety*, 23 June 1922.

59. The Fifth Horseman script, Moving Image Section, Library of Congress, Washington, DC.

60. Alan Gevinson, ed., *American Film Institute Catalogue. Within Our Gates: Ethnicity in American Feature Films, 1911–1960* (Berkeley: University of California Press, 1997), 236.

61. *Photoplay*, October 1922, 39–41.

62. Report of the Motion Picture Commission of the State of New York, June 1922, Serial Number 2936, New York State Archives. The commission also viewed the Klan as "mob violence" and criticized its secret methods, which were often exploited on-screen by corrupt individuals imitating the Klan for their own violent purposes.

63. *Kourier*, October 1925, 10.

64. *MPW*, 22 March 1924.

65. *New York Clipper*, 14 October 1905, 876.

66. *Portsmouth Daily Herald*, 20 February 1906, 2.

67. *Altoona Mirror*, 17 September 1906, 1.

68. Michelle Wallace and Charles Musser briefly discuss *The White Caps* on the DVD release of *Edison: The Invention of The Movies* (Kino Video, 2005).

69. A stage play entitled *The White Caps* by Owen Davis appeared around the same time as Porter's film.

70. *New York Herald*, 19 June 1922.

71. Rex Beach's 1927 novel presents the original Klan as a "necessity" and again attributes crimes not to the genuine group but to corrupt individuals ("they're not real Ku-Kluxers ... They're just plain rowdies"). The genuine Klan, according to Swallow, "was made up of the very best people; ministers, judges – people like that whose motives were patriotic and whose actions were above suspicion" (77, 90).

72. In the novel there is a hint of Rose's foreign background: her maiden name is Burkhardt but in the film this is never mentioned or referred to.

73. *Kansas City Star*, 19 August 1928, 10.

74. *The Mating Call* was aligned in publicity with Thomas Meighan's last picture for Howard Hughes, the tough gangster film *The Racket*, moving away from the more youth-oriented genres of the previous decade.

75. *Mexia Evening News*, 10 August 1922, 2.

76. *Variety*, 23 June 1922. A favorite review of *One Clear Call* comes from an

exhibitor, quoted in *MPW*. He described it in five words as "slow, draggy, depressive. Otherwise Good."

77. *Lincoln State Journal*, 1 October 1922, B1; *Mexia Evening News*, 10 August 1922, 2.

78. This advertisement appears in a number of local papers, including *Noblesville Daily Ledger*, 9 February 1923, 8.

79. *MPW*, 4 June 1922; *New York Times*, 18 June 1922; *Chicago Tribune*, 16 May 1922.

80. "One Clear Call" by Frances Nimmo Greene, fictionalized by Jerome Shorey, *Photoplay*, July 1922, 77–78, 103–104.

81. Letters from Earl Wayland Bowman to Agnes Just Reid, 26 February 1922 and 16 April 1922. The lengthy quote comes from a letter from Bowman to Reid, 30 May 1921. All letters are collected at Boise State University Library, Special Collections and Archives, MSS4 box 1, folder 26. Bowman described the film industry as "the crookest rottenest game I ever saw in my life" and wrote that if they wanted any further stories they should "say it with MONEY." "I won't be expecting anything from them," he concluded, "and won't be disappointed."

82. *MPW*, 30 September 1922.

83. *Oakland Tribune*, 3 July 1919, 12; *Oakland Tribune*, 7 July 1919, 5; *Kingston Daily Freeman*, 28 May 1920, 7.

84. *Black Mask*, 1 August 1923, 118.

85. *Black Mask*, 1 June 1923, 32.

86. *Chronicle Telegram*, 25 February 1920, 5.

87. As in the later westerns, John Hogue exploited the anonymity offered by the Klan costume, although in this case his motive (to save his daughter) is one that the audience is encouraged to identify with.

88. *Black Mask*, 1 August 1923 and 1 September 1923.

89. *Black Mask*, 15 June 1923, 66. Even the critical Klan literature recognized the appeal of the Klan. In this instance, Whetland had been drawn to the Klan by the failings of secular and religious leadership and by the image of the Klan: "To Whetland there was a romance and mystery about these silent, secret figures that gave him the first thrill he had had in years."

90. Beach, *The Mating Call*, 82, 83.

91. The burglars "organize a Klan for their own protection" as they steal cars, paint them in their garage, and then sell them back to their original owners. The Klan also controls the legal system as "the jury usually consists of twelve good and faithful 'Ku Klux.'" Copyright material 17084, 12 October 1921, Moving Image Section, Library of Congress, Washington, DC.

92. Richard Koszarski, *An Evening's Entertainment: The Age of the Silent Feature Picture* (Berkeley: University of California Press, 1990), 28.

93. Peter Stanfield, *Horse Opera: The Strange History of the 1930s Singing Cowboy* (Urbana: University of Illinois Press, 2002), 143.

94. See, for example, Michael Denning, *Mechanic Accents: Dime Novels and Working-Class Culture in America* (New York: Verso, 1987).

95. Sean McCann, *Gumshoe America: Hard-Boiled Crime Fiction and the Rise and Fall of New Deal Liberalism* (Durham, NC: Duke University Press, 2000), 40, 52.

96. See Joanna Hearne, "'The Cross-Heart People': Race and Inheritance in the Silent Western," *Journal of Popular Film and Television* (Winter 2003), 181–196.

97. *Exhibitors' Trade Review*, 26 March 1921, 1559; *Sheboygan Press-Telegram*, 22 April 1922, 10.

98. *Bridgeton Evening News,* 11 November 1922, 2. The film was based on a 1910 short story by E. H. Corr.

99. *Middletown Daily Herald,* 26 June 1923, 8.

100. *MPW,* 24 March 1923, 466. Initially released in 1916, *The Night Riders* was reissued as a two-reeler in 1923.

101. *Bisbee Daily Review,* 31 July 1921, 4.

102. Both *Heart o' the Hills* and *The Cambric Mask* presented the Klan in relation to land development. In *The Cambric Mask,* the night riders try to force the central protagonist to sell valuable land.

103. *Exhibitors Trade Review,* 9 September 1922, 984.

104. *Kinematograph Weekly,* 21 September 1922, 66; *MPW,* 31 March 1923, 543.

105. *Motion Picture News,* 2 September 1922, 1141

106. *Motion Picture News,* 23 September 1922, 1493.

107. *Motion Picture News,* 2 September 1922, 1148; *Exhibitors Herald,* 29 July 1922, 49; *Exhibitors Herald,* 24 June 1922, 85.

108. *Motion Picture News,* 2 September 1922, 1150; *Motion Picture News,* 26 August 1922, 1114; *Motion Picture News,* 9 September 1922, 1264.

109. *Film Daily,* 5 August 1922, 4.

110. *Daily Clarion Ledger,* 20 September 1922; *Exhibitors Herald,* 25 November 1922, 75; Jerry Dallas, "Movie Theatres in Twentieth-Century Jackson, Mississippi," *Journal of Mississippi History* (Spring 2007).

111. *Film Daily,* 16 September 1922, 4; *New Market Herald,* 24 July 1924, 3.

112. *Motion Picture News,* 9 September 1922, 1265.

113. *Exhibitors Herald,* 17 December 1921, 47.

114. *MPW,* 1 December 1923, 486; *MPW,* 14 April 1923, 743.

115. *MPW,* 3 November 1923, 146.

116. *MPW,* 8 September 1923, 150.

117. *Film Daily,* 3 October 1923.

118. Amy Louise Wood, *Lynching and Spectacle: Witnessing Racial Violence in America, 1890–1940* (Chapel Hill: University of North Carolina Press, 2009), 248.

119. Wood, *Lynching and Spectacle,* 223, 252.

120. *Liberty,* 20 November 1937; *Look,* 21 December 1937.

121. *Hammond Times,* 13 March 1937, 37.

122. *Independent Exhibitors Film Bulletin,* 4 November 1936, 2.

123. *Legion of Terror* publicity book, BFI, London; *Black Legion: Warner Bros. Campaign Plan,* BFI, London.

124. *Black Legion* campaign plan.

125. Ibid.; Legion of Terror Publicity Book; *Florence Morning News,* 6 December 1936, 2.

126. Matthew H. Bernstein, *Screening a Lynching: The Leo Frank Case on Film and Television* (Athens: University of Georgia Press, 2009), 78–82, 107–109.

127. Anthony Slide, *American Racist: The Life and Films of Thomas Dixon* (Lexington: University Press of Kentucky, 2004), 197. The PCA added that "the fact that the victims of the Klan's vengeance are members of another race, accentuates the problem."

128. Bernstein, *Screening a Lynching,* 94; Slide, *American Racist,* 175; letter from Ebenstein to Obringer, 13 August 1936, Warner Bros. Archives, University of Southern California, Los Angeles.

129. Bernstein, *Screening a Lynching,* 61.

130. Slide, *American Racist,* 176; Gregory D. Black, *Hollywood Censored: Morality Codes, Catholics and the Movies* (New York: Cambridge University Press, 1994), 269.

131. Lisa M. Rabin, "The Social Uses of Classroom Cinema: A History of the Human Relations Film Series at Benjamin Franklin High School in East Harlem,

New York City, 1936–1955," *Velvet Light Trap* 72 (Fall 2013), 58–71; Craig Kridel, "Educational Film Projects of the 1930s: Secrets of Success and the Human Relations Film Series," in *Learning with the Lights Off: Educational Film in the United States,* ed. Devin Orgeron, Marsha Orgeron, and Dan Streible (New York: Oxford University Press, 2012), 215–229.

132. *Burlington* (NC) *Daily Times News,* 19 December 1936, 3; *Wisconsin Rapids Daily Tribune,* 14 July 1937, 6; *Black Legion* campaign plan. British documentary pioneer Basil Wright offered a succinct summary of *Black Legion* in *World Film News,* August 1937, 9:

> He [Bogart] proceeds by easy stages to the murder of his best friend, squeals on his fellow legionaries, and departs with them all on a life-sentence. Close-up of wife, and fade-out.
>
> Let us not omit to record a sententious speech by the judge summing up the principles of American democracy and quoting extensively from Abraham Lincoln, while the audience, realizing the horrors are over, gropes for its hat and coat.

133. *Hammond Times,* 13 March 1937, 37; *Florence Morning News,* 6 December 1936, 2; *Black Legion* campaign plan.

134. *Legion of Terror* publicity book; *Black Legion* campaign plan.

135. *Motion Picture Daily,* 22 October 1937, 8.

136. Janet Staiger, *Interpreting Films* (Princeton, NJ: Princeton University Press, 1992), 139–153; Glenn Feldman, *Politics, Society and the Klan in Alabama, 1915–1949* (Tuscaloosa: University of Alabama Press, 1999), 280.

137. *Portsmouth New Haven Herald,* 11 January 1939, 6; reported in *Modesto Bee,* 2 June 1938, editorial page.

138. Letter from Margaret Mitchell to Thomas Dixon, 15 August 1936. This is discussed in Roy E. Aitken, *The Birth of a Nation Story* (Middleburg, VA: Derlinger, 1965), 9.

139. Margaret Mitchell, *Gone with the Wind* (New York: Macmillan, 1936), 798; Jim Cullen, *The Civil War in Popular Culture: A Reusable Past* (Washington, DC: Smithsonian Institution Press, 1995), 82.

140. Rudy Behlmer, ed., *Memo from David O. Selznick* (New York: Viking Press, 1972), 147.

141. Ibid. In the film, the characters instead go off to a "political meeting."

142. *Fiery Cross,* October 1941, 6; *Fiery Cross,* February 1940, 6; *Miami News,* 24 December 1939, 6.

143. Chalmers, *Hooded Americanism,* 317. The Klan would instead take up residence at its old robe factory on 3155 Roswell Road in Buckhead, Atlanta, with the robes still manufactured on the second floor. *Fiery Cross,* December 1939, 1.

144. *Syracuse Herald Journal,* 3 January 1940, 15. The article explained that a member of the Klan slipped a note under "one Metro official's hotel room door" late at night.

145. Colescott sought to relate the contemporary situation in 1939 to the two previous moments when the Klan emerged in 1865 and 1915. "Betrayed at home and beset abroad," he wrote, "America is tottering like a grand old mansion whose once-solid foundations have changed to quicksand." *Fiery Cross* claimed at the end of 1939 that in the six months since Colescott came to power, membership had increased 22 percent. By the summer of 1941, *Fiery Cross* claimed that paid-up membership was up 15–20 percent from June 1939 when

Colescott took over. *Fiery Cross*, September 1939, 4; *Fiery Cross*, December 1939, 2; *Fiery Cross*, July 1941, 8.

146. *Fiery Cross*, October 1939, 1, 7.

147. *Fiery Cross*, April-May 1940, 4; *Fiery Cross*, July 1941, 1, 3.

148. *Fiery Cross*, January 1940, 1; Chalmers, *Hooded Americanism*, 319; *Fiery Cross*, first quarter 1941, 1.

149. *Fiery Cross*, October 1941, 6. *Fiery Cross* (June 1940, 1) also republished and commented on a report of "Motion Pictures of Germany's war machine" (specifically *Der Westwall/The West Wall*, 1939), which were applauded when shown at a fundraiser in Rhode Island. The report noted that on one side of the screen was a Nazi flag with an American flag on the other.

150. *Fiery Cross*, November 1939, 4; *Fiery Cross*, January 1940, 1; *Fiery Cross*, November 1940, 4. The *Fiery Cross* further explained that the committee members "have had the support of the Ku Klux Klan" from the day the committee was created.

151. "U.S. Senate Subcommittee Hearings on Motion Picture and Radio Propaganda, 1941," in *Hollywood's America: Twentieth Century America through Film*, 4th ed., ed. Steven Mintz and Randy W. Roberts (Chichester: Wiley Blackwell, 2010).

152. Stetson Kennedy, *Southern Exposure: Making the South Safe for Democracy* (1946; reprint, Tuscaloosa: University of Alabama Press, 2011), 177. The *Fiery Cross* (November 1940, 1) reported on the findings of the committee, listing more than a dozen prominent actors named in grand jury testimony, including James Cagney and Humphrey Bogart.

153. *Wisconsin State Journal*, 27 January 1942, 4; 1 January 1942, 1.

154. *Fiery Cross*, January 1942, 3; Wyn Craig Wade, *The Fiery Cross: The Ku Klux Klan in America* (New York: Simon and Schuster, 1987), 272–275.

Epilogue

1. "The Ku Klux Klan Tries a Comeback," *Life*, 27 May 1946, 42–44; *Augusta Chronicle*, 10 May 1946, 1; *Kansas City Star*, 10 May 1946, 10; *Register* (IL) *Republic*, 10 May 1946, 1; Wyn Craig Wade, *The Fiery Cross: The Ku Klux Klan in America* (New York: Simon and Schuster, 1987), 276–289.

2. *Film Daily*, 15 May 1946, 9.

3. *Augusta Chronicle*, 12 June 1946, 1. The full series is available online at https://archive.org/details/Superman_page09, accessed 5 February 2014. There are numerous accounts of Superman's exposé of the Klan, including Richard Bowers, *Superman versus the Ku Klux Klan: The True Story of How the Iconic Superhero Battled the Men of Hate* (Washington, DC: National Geographic Society, 2011).

4. Heather Hendershot, *What's Fair on the Air: Cold War Right Wing Broadcasts and the Public Interest* (Chicago: University of Chicago Press, 2011).

Selected Bibliography

MANUSCRIPT COLLECTIONS

American Legion Library (Indianapolis, Indiana)
    American Legion Weekly and selected papers
Boise State University Library (Idaho)
    Earl Wayland Bowman Collection
British Film Institute (London, UK)
    Black Legion and *Nation Aflame* publicity books
    David W. Griffith Papers, 1897–1954 (Frederick, MD: University Publications of America, 1982)
Cineteca di Bologna library (Bologna, Italy)
    Charlie Chaplin Archive
Indiana Historical Society (Indianapolis)
    D. C. Stephenson Collection
    Fort Wayne Ku Klux Klan records
Indiana State Library (Indianapolis)
    D. C. Stephenson Collection
    Homer Showalter Oral Transcription
Library of Congress (Washington, DC)
    Records of the National Association for the Advancement of Colored People
    Prints and Photographs Division
Library of Congress, Motion Picture, Broadcasting and Recorded Sound Division (Washington, DC)

Heart o' the Hills and *The Mating Call* publicity books
    Copyright, publicity material, and scripts for films including *The Fifth Horseman*
Margaret Herrick Library at the Academy of Motion Picture Arts and Sciences (Beverly Hills, California)
    Mary Pickford Collection
New York Public Library (New York)
    The National Board of Review of Motion Pictures Records
    Billy Rose Theatre Collection
New York State Archives (New York)
    Film Censorship Records, Motion Picture Scripts Collection
Ohio Historical Society (Columbus)
    Ohio Division of Film Censorship Records
    Ohio Knights of the Ku Klux Klan Records, 1923–24
Warner Bros. Archives (University of Southern California, Los Angeles)
    Black Legion File

NEWSPAPERS AND PERIODICALS

Altoona Mirror (Pennsylvania)
American Legion Monthly
American Legion Weekly
American Standard (New York)

Anderson Daily Bulletin (Indiana)
Anniston Star (Alabama)
Appleton Post-Crescent (Wisconsin)
Ashland Times-Gazette (Ohio)
Atlanta Constitution
Atlanta Georgian
Atlanta Independent
Atlanta Journal
Atlanta News
Augusta Chronicle (Georgia)
Baltimore Afro-American
Beatrice Daily Sun (Nebraska)
Billboard
Bioscope (United Kingdom)
Bisbee Daily Review (Arizona)
Bismarck Tribune (North Dakota)
Black Mask
Bonham Daily Favorite (Texas)
Boston Advertiser
Boston American
Bridgeport Telegram (Connecticut)
Broad Ax (Chicago)
Burlington Daily Times (North Carolina)
Camera
Canton Repository (Ohio)
Catholic Columbian (Ohio)
Charleston Gazette (West Virginia)
Chicago American
Chicago Daily Journal
Chicago Daily News
Chicago Defender
Chicago Evening Post
Chicago Tribune
Christian Century (Illinois)
Chronicle-Telegram (Ohio)
Clearfield Progress (Pennsylvania)
Cleveland Plain Dealer (Ohio)
Columbus Daily Enquirer
Columbus Dispatch
Columbus Ledger
Connersville News-Examiner (Indiana)
Corsicana Daily Sun (Texas)
Coshocton Tribune (Ohio)
Cumberland Evening Times (Maryland)
Daily Ardmoreite (Oklahoma)

Daily Courier (Pennsylvania)
Daily Illini (Illinois)
Daily Kennebec Journal (Maine)
Daily Northwestern (Illinois)
Dallas Morning News
Danville Bee (Virginia)
Davenport Democrat and Leader (Iowa)
Dawn (Chicago)
Dearborn Independent (Michigan)
Decatur Daily Democrat (Indiana)
Decatur Review (Indiana)
Deming Headlight (New Mexico)
Drumright Evening Derrick (Oklahoma)
Edwardsville Intelligencer (Illinois)
Elkhart Daily Review (Indiana)
Elwood Call Leader (Indiana)
Englewood Times (Colorado)
Entertainment Trade Review
Eugene Daily Guard (Oregon)
Exhibitors Herald
Exhibitors Trade Review
Fiery Cross (Indiana/Ohio editions)
Film Daily (previously *Wid's Daily*)
Fitchburg Sentinel (Massachusetts)
Florence Morning News (South Carolina)
Fort Wayne Journal-Gazette (Indiana)
Fort Wayne News Sentinel (Indiana)
Franklin County News (Ohio)
Franklin Evening Star (Indiana)
Frederick Daily News (Maryland)
Frederick Post (Maryland)
Galveston Daily News (Texas)
Gettysburg Times (Pennsylvania)
Gleaner (Jamaica)
Greencastle Herald (Indiana)
Greenville Morning Herald (Texas)
Hamilton Evening Journal (Ohio)
Hammond Times (Indiana)
Helena Daily Independent (Montana)
Hertford Courant (Connecticut)
Hollywood Reporter
Houston Chronicle (Texas)
Hutchinson News (Kansas)
Imperial Night-Hawk (Atlanta)
Independent Exhibitors Film Bulletin

Indiana Catholic and Record
Indiana Citizens' Post
Indiana Democrat (Pennsylvania)
Indiana Evening Gazette (Pennsylvania)
Indianapolis News
Indianapolis Star
Indianapolis Weekly Messenger
Iowa City Press-Citizen
Ironwood Daily Globe (Michigan)
Jewish Criterion (Pittsburgh)
Kansas City Star
Kansas Vindicator
Kinematograph Weekly
Kingsport Times (Tennessee)
Kingston Daily Freeman (New York)
Kluxer (Ohio)
Kokomo Daily Dispatch (Indiana)
Kourier
Landmark (North Carolina)
Lawrence Journal World (Kansas)
Lexington Herald (Kentucky)
Liberty Magazine
Life
Lima News (Ohio)
Lincoln (Daily) Star (Nebraska)
Lincoln (Evening) State Journal (Nebraska)
Lincoln Sunday Star (Nebraska)
Logansport Pharos-Tribune (Indiana)
Logansport Press (Indiana)
Look Magazine
Los Angeles Herald
Los Angeles Times
Mansfield News (Ohio)
Marietta Journal (Georgia)
Marion Daily Star (Ohio)
Melbourne Argus (Australia)
Mexia Daily (Evening) News (Texas)
Miami District Daily News
Middletown Daily Herald (New York)
Modesto Bee (California)
Modesto Evening News (California)
Monthly Film Bulletin (UK)
Mooresville Times (Indiana)
Morning Oregonian
Motion Picture Daily

Motion Picture Magazine
Motion Picture News
Movie Weekly
Moving Picture World
Muncie Evening Press (Indiana)
Muncie Morning Star (Indiana)
Muncie Post Democrat (Indiana)
Muncie Sunday Star (Indiana)
Nevada State Journal
New Haven Register (Connecticut)
New Market Herald (Iowa)
New Republic
New York Age
New York Clipper
New York Herald
New York Times
New York Tribune
New York World
Newark Advocate (Ohio)
Noblesville Daily Ledger (Indiana)
Oakland Tribune (California)
Official Monthly Bulletin of the Knights of
    the Ku Klux Klan (Mississippi)
Ohio State Journal
Oklahoman
Perry Journal (Oklahoma)
Photoplay
Pictures and Picturegoer (United
    Kingdom)
Pinedale Roundup (Wyoming)
Plainfield Messenger (Indiana)
Port Arthur Daily News (Texas)
Portsmouth Daily Herald (New
    Hampshire)
Portsmouth Daily Times (Ohio)
Portsmouth New Haven Herald (Illinois)
Protestant Home Journal (Ohio)
Register Republic (Illinois)
Richmond Times-Dispatch (Virginia)
Riverdale Pointer (Illinois)
Ruthvern Free Press (Iowa)
San Antonio Evening News (Texas)
Sandusky Register (Ohio)
Sandusky Star Journal (Ohio)
Searchlight (Atlanta)

Sheboygan Press-Telegram (Wisconsin)
Southtown Economist (Chicago)
Spotlight (Minneapolis)
State (South Carolina)
Stevens Point Daily Journal (Wisconsin)
Sun Herald (Iowa)
Sunday Oregonian
Syracuse Herald Journal (New York)
Thomasville Daily Times Enterprise (Georgia)
Time
Tipton Tribune (Indiana)
Tolerance (Chicago)
Tulsa World (Oklahoma)
Urbana Daily Courier (Illinois)
Variety
Visual Education (Chicago)
Warren Tribune (Ohio)
Washington Evening Star
Washington Post
Wichita Daily Times (Texas)
Williamsport Gazette and Bulletin (Pennsylvania)
Winchester Journal Herald (Indiana)
Wisconsin Rapids Daily Tribune
Woodland Daily Democrat (California)
World Film News (United Kingdom)
Youngstown Citizen (Ohio)

BOOKS AND ARTICLES

Acland, Charles R., and Haidee Wasson, eds. *Useful Cinema.* Durham, NC: Duke University Press, 2011.

Aitken, Roy E. *The Birth of a Nation Story.* Middleburg, VA: Delinger, 1965.

Allen, Michael. *Family Secrets: The Feature Films of D. W. Griffith.* London: British Film Institute, 2000.

Anderson, Mark Lynn. "Tempting Fate: Clara Smith Hamon, or, The Secretary as Producer." In *Looking Past the Screen: Case Studies in American Film History and Method,* edited by Jon Lewis and

Eric Smoodin. Durham, NC: Duke University Press, 2007.

——. *Twilight of the Idols: Hollywood and the Human Sciences in 1920s America.* Berkeley: University of California Press, 2011.

Archer, Leonard C. *Black Images in the American Theatre: N.A.A.C.P. Protest Campaigns – Stage, Screen, Radio and Television.* New York: Pageant-Poseidon, 1973.

Asinof, Eliot. *Eight Men Out: The Black Sox and the 1919 World Series.* New York: Henry Holt, 1963.

Bachman, Gregg, and Thomas J. Slater, eds. *Discovering Marginalized Voices.* Carbondale: Southern Illinois University Press, 2002.

Baker, Kelly. *Gospel according to the Klan: The KKK's Appeal to Protestant America, 1915–1930.* Lawrence: University Press of Kansas, 2011.

Bauerlein, Mark. *Negrophobia: A Race Riot in Atlanta, 1906.* San Francisco: Encounter Books, 2001.

Beach, Rex. *The Mating Call.* London: Hutchinson and Co., 1928.

Behlmer, Rudy, ed. *Memo from David O. Selznick: The Creation of Gone with the Wind and Other Motion Picture Classics, as Revealed in the Producer's Private Letters, Telegrams, Memorandums and Autobiographical Remarks.* New York: Viking Press, 1972.

Bernardi, Daniel, ed. *The Birth of Whiteness: Race and the Emergence of U.S. Cinema.* New Brunswick, NJ: Rutgers University Press, 1996.

Bernstein, Matthew. *Screening a Lynching: The Leo Frank Case on Film and TV.* Athens: University of Georgia Press, 2009.

Black, Gregory D. *Hollywood Censored: Morality Codes, Catholics and the Movies.* New York: Cambridge University Press, 1994.

Black, Stephen. *Eugene O' Neill: Beyond Mourning and Tragedy*. New Haven, CT: Yale University Press, 1999.

Blake, Aldrich. *The Ku Klux Kraze: A Lecture*. Huntington, IN: A. Blake, c. 1924.

Blee, Kathleen. *Women of the Klan: Racism and Gender in the 1920s*. Berkeley: University of California, 1991.

———. "Women in the 1920s' Ku Klux Klan Movement." *Feminist Studies* 17:1 (Spring 1991).

Bogle, Donald. *Toms, Coons, Mulattoes, Mammies, and Bucks: An Interpretive History of Blacks in American Film*. New York: Continuum, 2001.

Bowers, Claude G. *The Tragic Era: The Revolution after Lincoln*. Cambridge, MA: Literary Guild of America, 1929.

Bowers, Richard. *Superman versus the Ku Klux Klan: The True Story of How the Iconic Superhero Battled the Men of Hate*. Washington, DC: National Geographic Society, 2011.

Bowman, Earl Wayland. "High Stakes." *American Magazine* (September 1920), 56–59, 194–202.

Bowser, Pearl, and Louise Spence. "Identity and Betrayal: The Symbol of the Unconquered and Oscar Micheaux's Biographical Legend." In *The Birth of Whiteness: Race and the Emergence of U.S. Cinema*, ed. Daniel Bernardi. New Brunswick, NJ: Rutgers University Press, 1996.

———. *Writing Himself into History: Oscar Micheaux, His Silent Films and His Audiences*. New Brunswick, NJ: Rutgers University Press, 2000.

Brackman, Harold. "The Attack on 'Jewish Hollywood': A Chapter in the History of Modern American Anti-Semitism." *Modern Judaism* 20:1 (2000).

Brooks, Michael E. *The Ku Klux Klan in Wood County, Ohio*. Charleston, SC: The History Press, 2014.

Brownlow, Kevin. *Behind the Mask of Innocence*. Berkeley: University of California Press, 1990.

———. *Mary Pickford Rediscovered: Rare Pictures of a Hollywood Legend*. New York: Harry N. Abrams, 1999.

———. *The Parade's Gone By*. Berkeley: University of California Press, 1968.

Burns, Rebecca. *Rage in the Gate City: The Story of the 1906 Race Riots*. Athens: University of Georgia Press, 2009.

Butters, Gerald R. Jr. "*The Birth of a Nation* and the Kansas Board of Review of Motion Pictures: A Censorship Struggle." *Kansas History* 14:1 (Spring 1991), 2–14.

Caddoo, Cara. *Envisioning Freedom: Cinema and the Building of Modern Black Life*. Cambridge, MA: Harvard University Press, 2014.

Calney, Mark. "D. W. Griffith and 'The Birth of a Monster': How the Confederacy Revived the KKK and Created Hollywood." *American Almanac*, 11 January 1993.

Campbell, Craig W. *Reel America and World War I: A Comprehensive Filmography and History of Motion Pictures in the United States, 1914–1920*. Jefferson, NC: McFarland, 1985.

Campbell, Edward D.C. Jr. *The Celluloid South: Hollywood and the Southern Myth*. Knoxville: University of Tennessee Press, 1981.

Canning, Charlotte M. *The Most American Thing in America: Circuit Chautauqua as Performance*. Iowa City: University of Iowa Press, 2005.

Carbine, Mary. "'The Finest Outside the Loop': Motion Picture Exhibition in Chicago's Black Metropolis, 1905–1928." *Camera Obscura* 23 (May 1990), 9–42.

Carr, Steven. *Hollywood and Anti-Semitism: A Cultural History up to World War II*. Cambridge: Cambridge University Press, 2001.

Chadwick, Bruce. *The Reel Civil War: Mythmaking in American Film.* New York: Vintage, 2002.

Chalmers, David. *Hooded Americanism: The History of the Ku Klux Klan.* 3rd ed. Durham, NC: Duke University Press, 1987.

Chandler, James. "The Historical Novel Goes to Hollywood: Scott, Griffith, and Film Epic Today." In *The Birth of a Nation,* ed. Robert Lang. New Brunswick, NJ: Rutgers University Press, 1994.

Cocoltchos, Christopher N. "The Invisible Empire and the Search for the Orderly Community: The Ku Klux Klan in Anaheim, California." In *The Invisible Empire in the West,* ed. Shawn Lay. Urbana: University of Illinois Press, 1992.

Cohen, Paula Marantz. *Silent Film and the Triumph of the American Myth.* Oxford: Oxford University Press, 2001.

Cook, Raymond A. *Thomas Dixon.* New York: Twayne Publishers, 1974.

Courtney, Susan. *Hollywood Fantasies of Miscegenation: Spectacular Narratives of Gender and Race, 1903–1967.* Princeton, NJ: Princeton University Press, 2005.

Couvares, Francis G., ed. *Movie Censorship and American Culture.* Washington, DC: Smithsonian Institution Press, 1996.

Crew, Spencer R. "The Great Migration of Afro-Americans, 1915–1940." *Monthly Labor Review* 111 (1987).

Cripps, Thomas. *Slow Fade to Black: The Negro in American Film, 1900–1942.* New York: Oxford University Press, 1977.

Cullen, Jim. *The Civil War in Popular Culture.* Washington, DC: Smithsonian Institutional Press, 1995.

Debauch, Leslie Midkiff. "Mary Pickford's Public on the Home Front." In *Film and the First World War,* ed. Karel Dibbets and Bert Hogenkamp. Amsterdam: Amsterdam University Press, 1995.

———. *Reel Patriotism: The Movies and World War One.* Madison: University of Wisconsin Press, 1997.

DeCordova, Richard. *Picture Personalities: The Emergence of the Star System in America.* 1990. Reprint, Urbana: University of Illinois Press, 2001.

Denning, Michael. *Mechanic Accents: Dime Novels and Working-Class Culture in America.* New York: Verso, 1987.

Dessommes, Nancy Bishop. "Hollywood in Hoods: The Portrayal of the Ku Klux Klan in Popular Film." In *Journal of Popular Culture* 32:4 (Spring 1999), 13–22.

Dinnerstein, Leonard. *The Leo Frank Case.* New York: Columbia University Press, 1968.

Dittmer, John. *Black Georgia in the Progressive Era, 1900–1920.* Urbana: University of Illinois Press, 1977.

Dixon, Thomas Jr. *The Black Hood.* New York: Appleton and Co., 1924.

———. *The Clansman: An Historical Romance of the Ku Klux Klan.* New York: Doubleday, 1905.

Douglas, Ann. *Terrible Honesty: Mongrel Manhattan in the 1920s.* London: Picador, 1996.

Dyer, Richard. "Into the Light: The Whiteness of the South in *The Birth of a Nation.*" In *Dixie Debates: Perspectives on Southern Cultures,* ed. R. H. King and H. Taylor. New York: New York University Press, 1996.

Dyer, Thomas G. "The Klan on Campus: C. Lewis Fowler and Lanier University." *South Atlantic Quarterly* 77 (Fall 1978), 453–469.

Eyman, Scott. *Mary Pickford: America's Sweetheart.* New York: Donald I. Fine, 1990.

Feldman, Glenn. *Politics, Society and the Klan in Alabama, 1915–1949.* Tuscaloosa: University of Alabama Press, 1999.

Fleener-Marzec, Nickeanne. *D. W. Griffith's The Birth of a Nation: Controversy, Suppression and the First Amendment as It Applies to Filmic Expression, 1915–1973*. New York: Arno, 1980.

Forman, Henry James. *Our Movie-Made Children*. New York: Macmillan, 1933.

Fox, Craig. *Everyday Klansfolk: White Protestant Life and the KKK in 1920s Michigan*. East Lansing: Michigan State University Press, 2011.

Fox, John Jr. *The Heart of the Hills*. New York: Scribner's, 1913.

Frank, Glenda. "Tempest in Black and White: The 1924 Premiere of Eugene O'Neill's *All God's Chillun Got Wings*." *Resources for American Literary Study* 26:1 (2000), 75–89.

Franklin, John Hope. "Birth of a Nation – Propaganda as History." *Massachusetts Review* 20 (Autumn 1979), 417–433.

Friedman, Lester. *Hollywood's Image of the Jew*. New York: Ungar, 1982.

Frost, Stanley. *The Challenge of the Klan*. Indianapolis: Bobbs-Merrill, 1924.

Gabler, Neal. *An Empire of Their Own: How the Jews Invented Hollywood*. New York: Crown Publishers, 1988.

Gaines, Jane M. *Fire and Desire: Mixed Race Movies in the Silent Era*. Chicago: University of Chicago Press, 2001.

Gevinson, Alan, ed. *American Film Institute Catalogue. Within Our Gates: Ethnicity in American Feature Film, 1911–1960*. Berkeley: University of California Press, 1997.

Gilman, Sander. *The Jew's Body*. New York: Routledge, 1991.

Gish, Lillian. *The Movies, Mr Griffith and Me*. London: W. H. Allen, 1969.

Gledhill, Christine. "Mary Pickford: Icon of Stardom." In *Flickers of Desire: Movie Stars of the 1910s*, ed. Jennifer M. Bean.

New Brunswick, NJ: Rutgers University Press, 2011.

Glick, Josh. "Mixed Messages: D. W. Griffith and the Black Press, 1916–1931." *Film History* 23:2 (2011), 174–195.

Goldberg, Robert Alan. *Hooded Empire: The Ku Klux Klan in Colorado*. Urbana: University of Illinois Press, 1981.

Goldschmidt, Henry, and Elizabeth McAlister, eds. *Race, Nation and Religion in the Americas*. New York: Oxford University Press, 2004.

Grant, Madison. *The Passing of the Great Race*. New York: Scribner's, 1916.

Green, J. Ronald. *Straight Lick: The Cinema of Oscar Micheaux*. Bloomington: Indiana University Press, 2000.

Grieveson, Lee. *The Cinema and the Wealth of Nations*. Berkeley: University of California Press, forthcoming.

——. "Cinema Studies and the Conduct of Conduct." In *Inventing Film Studies*, ed. Lee Grieveson and Haidee Wasson. Durham, NC: Duke University Press, 2008.

——. *Policing Cinema: Movies and Censorship in Early Twentieth Century America*. Berkeley: University of California Press, 2004.

——. "The Work of Film in the Age of Ford Mechanization." *Cinema Journal* 51:3 (Spring 2012), 25–51.

Griffith, D. W. *The Man Who Invented Hollywood: The Autobiography of D. W. Griffith*. Louisville: Touchstone, 1972.

Hall, Prescott F. "The Recent History of Immigration and Immigration Restriction." *Journal of Popular Economy* 21:8 (October 1913).

Hallett, Hilary. *Go West, Young Women: The Rise of Early Hollywood*. Berkeley: University of California Press, 2013.

Harrison, Peter S. *Harrison's Reports and Film Reviews, 1919–62*. Los Angeles: Hollywood Film Archives, 1997.

Hays, Will. *Memoirs*. New York: Doubleday, 1955.

Hearne, Joanna. "'The Cross- Heart People': Race and Inheritance in the Silent Western." *Journal of Popular Film and Television* (Winter 2003), 181–196.

Hendershot, Heather. *What's Fair on the Air: Cold War Right Wing Broadcasts and the Public Interest*. Chicago: University of Chicago Press, 2011.

Higashi, Sumiko. *Cecil B. DeMille and American Culture: The Silent Era*. Berkeley: University of California Press, 1994.

Higham, John. *Strangers in the Land: Patterns of American Nativism, 1860–1925*. New Brunswick, NJ: Rutgers University Press, 1955.

Hirsch, James S. *Riot and Remembrance: America's Worst Race Riot and Its Legacy*. Boston: Mariner Books, 2003.

Horowitz, David A., ed. *Inside the Klavern: The Secret History of a Ku Klux Klan of the 1920s*. Carbondale: Southern Illinois University Press, 1999.

Indianapolis City Directory. Indianapolis: R. L. Polk, 1924, 1925, 1927.

Inscoe, John. "*The Clansman* on Stage and Screen: North Carolina Reacts." *North Carolina Historical Review* 64:2 (April 1987).

Jackson, Kenneth T. *The Ku Klux Klan in the City, 1915–1930*. New York: Oxford University Press, 1967.

Jenkins, Henry. *Textual Poachers: Television Fans and Participatory Culture*. New York: Routledge, 1992.

Jenkins, William D. *Steel Valley Klan: The Ku Klux Klan in Ohio's Mahoning Valley*. Kent, OH: Kent State University Press, 1990.

Johnson, Guy B. "The Negro Migration and Its Consequences." *Journal of Social Forces* 2:3 (March 1924).

———. "A Sociological Interpretation of the New Ku Klux Movement." *Social Forces* 1 (May 1923), 440–445. Reprinted in *The Sociology of Race Relations*, ed. Thomas F. Pettigrew. New York: Free Press, 1980.

Kennedy, Stetson. *Southern Exposure: Making the South Safe for Democracy*. 1946. Reprint, Tuscaloosa: University of Alabama Press, 2011.

King, Rob. "Roscoe 'Fatty' Arbuckle: Hollywood's Starring Scapegoat." In *Flickers of Desire: Movie Stars of the 1910s*, ed. Jennifer M. Bean. New Brunswick, NJ: Rutgers University Press, 2011.

Koszarski, Richard. *An Evening's Entertainment: The Age of the Silent Feature Picture, 1915–1928*. New York: Scribner's, 1990.

Kridel, Craig. "Educational Film Projects of the 1930s: Secrets of Success and the Human Relations Film Series." In *Learning with the Lights Off: Educational Film in the United States*, ed. Devin Orgeron, Marsha Orgeron, and Dan Streible. New York: Oxford University Press, 2012.

Laats, Adam. *Fundamentalism and Education in the Scopes Era*. New York: Palgrave Macmillan, 2010.

Lacey, Robert. *Ford: The Men and the Machine*. London: Heinemann, 1986.

Lang, Robert, ed. *The Birth of a Nation*. New Brunswick, NJ: Rutgers University Press, 1994.

Lantzer, Jason S. "Dark Beverage of Hell: The Transformation of Hamilton County's Dry Crusade, 1876–1936." PhD dissertation, Indiana University, 2006.

———. "*Prohibition Is Here to Stay*": The Reverend Edward S. Shumaker and the Dry Cause in America. South Bend, IN: University of Notre Dame Press, 2009.

Lay, Shawn, ed. *The Invisible Empire in the West: Towards a New Historical Appraisal of the Ku Klux Klan of the 1920s*.

Urbana: University of Illinois Press, 1992.

Lears, T. J. Jackson. *No Place of Grace: Antimodernism and the Transformation of American Culture, 1880–1920.* New York: Pantheon, 1981.

Levy, Eugene. "'Is the Jew a White Man?': Press Reaction to the Leo Frank Case, 1913–1915." *Phylon* 35:2 (2nd quarter, 1974).

Lewis, David Levering. *W.E.B. Du Bois: The Fight for Equality and the American Century, 1919–1963.* New York: Henry Holt, 2000.

Lewis, Michael, and Jacqueline Serbu. "Kommemorating the Ku Klux Klan." *Sociological Quarterly* 40:1 (1999), 139–157.

Lindsay, Vachel, *The Art of the Moving Picture.* New York: Macmillan, 1915.

Lippmann, Walter. *Public Opinion.* New York: Macmillan, 1922.

Loucks, Emerson H. *The Ku Klux Klan in Pennsylvania: A Study in Nativism.* Harrisburg, PA: Telegraph Press, 1936.

Lutholtz, M. William. *Grand Dragon: D. C. Stephenson and the Ku Klux Klan in Indiana.* West Lafayette, IN: Purdue University Press, 1991.

Lutz, Tom, and Susanna Ashton, eds. *These "Colored" United States: African American Essays from the 1920s.* New Brunswick, NJ: Rutgers University Press, 1996.

MacLean, Nancy. *Behind the Mask of Chivalry: The Making of the Second Ku Klux Klan.* New York: Oxford University Press, 1994.

——. "The Leo Frank Case Reconsidered: Gender and Sexual Politics in the Making of Reactionary Populism." *Journal of American History* 78 (December 1991).

Maltby, Richard. "*The King of Kings* and the Czar of All the Rushes: The Propriety of the Christ Story." In *Controlling Hollywood: Censorship and Regulation in the Studio Era,* ed. Matthew Bernstein, 60–86. New Brunswick, NJ: Rutgers University Press, 1999.

——. "The Social Evil, The Moral Order and The Melodramatic Imagination, 1890–1915." In *Melodrama: Stage, Picture, Screen,* ed. Jacky Bratton, Jim Cook, and Christine Gledhill. London: BFI, 1994.

Mayer, David. *Stagestruck Filmmaker: D. W. Griffith and the American Theatre.* Iowa City: University of Iowa Press, 2009.

McEwan, Paul. "Lawyers, Bibliographies and the Klan: Griffith's Resources in the Censorship Battle over *The Birth of a Nation* in Ohio." *Film History* 20:3 (2008), 357–366.

McGregor, Alexander. *The Catholic Church and Hollywood: Censorship and Morality in 1930s Cinema.* London: I. B. Taurus, 2013.

McLean, Adrienne L., and David A. Cook, eds. *Headline Hollywood: A Century of Film Scandal.* New Brunswick, NJ: Rutgers University Press, 2001.

Mecklin, John Moffatt. *The Ku Klux Klan: A Study of the American Mind.* New York: Harcourt, Brace, and Company, 1924.

Melnick, Jeffrey. *Black-Jewish Relations on Trial: Leo Frank and Jim Conley in the New South.* Jackson: University Press of Mississippi, 2000.

Merritt, Greg. *Room 1209: The Life of Fatty Arbuckle, the Mysterious Death of Virginia Rappe, and the Scandal That Changed Hollywood.* Chicago: Chicago Review Press, 2013.

Merritt, Russell L. "Dixon, Griffith and the Southern Legend." *Cinema Journal* 12 (Fall 1972), 26–45.

Milestone, Lewis. Interview by Kevin Brownlow, 1970. Transcript provided by Kevin Brownlow.

Mitchell, Margaret. *Gone with the Wind.* New York: Macmillan, 1936.

Mohsene, Laura Lee. "The Women – God Bless Them: Dallas Women and the Ku Klux Klan in the 1920s." PhD dissertation, University of Texas, 2011.

Moley, Raymond. *The Hays Office.* Indianapolis: Bobbs-Merrill Company, 1945.

Moore, Leonard Joseph. *Citizen Klansmen: The Ku Klux Klan in Indiana, 1921–1928.* Chapel Hill: University of North Carolina Press, 1991.

Moore, Randy, Mark Decker, and Sehoya Cotner. *Chronology of the Evolution-Creationism Controversy.* Santa Barbara, CA: Greenwood Press, 2009.

Morey, Anne. *Hollywood Outsiders: The Adaptation of the Film Industry, 1913–1934.* Minneapolis: University of Minnesota Press, 2003.

Negra, Diane. "Immigrant Stardom in Imperial America: Pola Negri and the Problem of Typology." *Camera Obscura* 16:3 (2001), 159–195.

Nelson, Richard Alan. "Commercial Propaganda in the Silent Film: A Case Study of *A Mormon Maid* (1917)." *Film History* 1 (1987).

———. *Florida and the American Motion Picture Industry, 1898–1980.* New York: Garland, 1982.

Nesteby, James R. *Black Images in American Films, 1896–1954: The Interplay between Civil Rights and Film Culture.* Washington, DC: University Press of America, 1982.

Newton, Michael. *White Robes and Burning Crosses: A History of the Ku Klux Klan from 1866.* Jefferson, NC: McFarland and Company Inc., 2014.

Newton, Michael, and Judy Ann Newton. *The Ku Klux Klan: An Encyclopaedia.* New York: Garland, 1991.

Olsson, Jan. "Modernity Stops at Nothing: The American Chase Film and the Specter of Lynching." In *A Companion to Early Cinema,* ed. Andre Gaudreault, Nicolas Dulac, and Santiago Hidalgo. Malden, MA: Wiley-Blackwell, 2012.

Orgeron, Devin, Marsha Orgeron, and Dan Streible, eds. *Learning with the Lights Off: Educational Film in the United States.* New York: Oxford University Press, 2012.

Pascoe, Peggy. "Miscegenation Law, Court Cases, and Ideologies of 'Race' in Twentieth Century America." *Journal of American History* 83:1 (June 1996), 44–69.

Pegram, Thomas R. *One Hundred Percent American: The Rebirth and Decline of the Ku Klux Klan in the 1920s.* Chicago: Ivan R. Dee, 2011.

Pickford, Mary. *Sunshine and Shadow.* New York: Doubleday, 1955.

Pizzitola, Louis. *Hearst over Hollywood: Power, Passion and Propaganda in the Movies.* New York: Columbia University Press, 2013.

Presbyterian Church of the United States of America. *Minutes of the General Assembly of the Presbyterian Church in the United States of America, 1922.* Philadelphia: Office of the General Assembly, 1922.

Rabin, Lisa M. "The Social Uses of Classroom Cinema: A History of the Human Relations Film Series at Benjamin Franklin High School in East Harlem, New York City, 1936–1955." *Velvet Light Trap* 72 (Fall 2013), 58–71.

Randel, William Pierce. *Ku Klux Klan: A Century of Infamy.* Philadelphia: Chilton Books, 1965.

Regester, Charlene. "Black Films, White Censors." In *Movie Censorship and American Culture,* ed. Francis G. Couvares. Washington, DC: Smithsonian Institution Press, 1996.

———. "From the Buzzard's Roost: Black Movie-going in Durham and Other North Carolina Cities during the Early Period of American Cinema." *Film History* 17:1 (2005), 113–124.

Roberts, Randy. *Papa Jack: Jack Johnson and the Era of White Hopes.* New York: Free Press, 1983.

Robinson, David. *Chaplin: His Life and Art.* 2nd ed. London: Penguin, 2001.

Rogin, Michael. *Blackface, White Noise: Jewish Immigrants in the Hollywood Melting Pot.* Berkeley: University of California Press, 1996.

———. "'The Sword Became a Flashing Vision': D. W. Griffith's The Birth of a Nation." In *The Birth of a Nation,* ed. Robert Lang. New Brunswick, NJ: Rutgers University Press, 1994.

Romanowski, William. *Reforming Hollywood: How American Protestants Fought for Freedom at the Movies.* New York: Oxford University Press, 2012.

Ross, Steven J., ed. *Movies and American Society.* Oxford: Blackwell, 2002.

———. "The Unknown Hollywood." *History Today* 40 (April 1990).

———. *Working Class Hollywood: Silent Film and the Shaping of Class in America.* Princeton, NJ: Princeton University Press, 1998.

Safianow, Allen. "You Can't Burn History: Getting Right with the Klan in Noblesville, Indiana." *Indiana Magazine of History* 100:2 (2004), 109–154.

Schickel, Richard. *D. W. Griffith: An American Life.* New York: Simon and Schuster, 1984.

Schlereth, Thomas J. *Victorian America: Transformations in Everyday Life, 1876–1915.* New York: HarperCollins, 1991.

Shepherd, William G. "How I Put Over the Klan." *Collier's* (14 July 1928).

Shull, Michael Slade. *Radicalism in American Silent Films, 1909–1929: A Filmography and History.* Jefferson, NC: McFarland, 2000.

Silva, Fred, ed. *Focus on "The Birth of a Nation."* Englewood Cliffs, NJ: Prentice Hall, 1971.

Silverman, Joan. "The Birth of a Nation: Prohibition Propaganda" In *The South and Film,* ed. Warren French. Jackson: University Press of Mississippi, 1981.

Simcovitch, Maxim. "The Impact of Griffith's 'Birth of a Nation' on the Modern Ku Klux Klan." *Journal of Popular Film* 1:1 (Winter 1972).

Sims, Patsy. *The Klan.* New York: Stein and Day, 1978.

Sinclair, Upton. *The Flivver King.* New York: Phaedra, 1937.

Singer, Ben. *Melodrama and Modernity: Early Pulp Cinema and the Social Contexts of Sensationalism.* New York: Columbia University Press, 2001.

———. "Movies and Ascendant Americanism." In *American Cinema of the 1910s: Themes and Variations,* ed. Charlie Keil and Ben Singer, 225–248. New Brunswick, NJ: Rutgers University Press, 2009.

Slide, Anthony. *American Racist: The Life and Films of Thomas Dixon.* Lexington: University Press of Kentucky, 2004.

———, ed. *D. W. Griffith: Interviews.* Jackson: University Press of Mississippi, 2012.

Staiger, Janet. *Interpreting Films: Studies in the Historical Reception of American Cinema.* Princeton, NJ: Princeton University Press, 1992.

Stamp, Shelley. *Movie-Struck Girls: Women and Motion Picture Culture after the Nickelodeon*. Princeton, NJ: Princeton University Press, 2000.

Stanfield, Peter. *Horse Opera: The Strange History of the 1930s Singing Cowboy*. Urbana: University of Illinois Press, 2002.

Stern, Seymour. "The Birth of a Nation Centenary Issue." *Film Culture* no. 36 (Spring/Summer 1965).

———. "The Birth of a Nation in Retrospect." *International Photographer* 7 (April 1935).

Stewart, Jacqueline Najuma. *Migrating to the Movies: Cinema and Black Urban Modernity*. Berkeley: University of California Press, 2005.

Stokes, Melvyn. *D. W. Griffith's The Birth of a Nation: A History of the Most Controversial Picture of All Time*. Oxford: Oxford University Press, 2008.

———. "The Ku Klux Klan as Good and Evil in American Film." In *Les Bons et Les Méchants*, ed. Francis Bordat and Serge Chauvin, 215–228. Paris: University of Paris X-Nanterre, 2005.

Stoloff, Sam. "Normalizing Stars: Roscoe 'Fatty' Arbuckle and Hollywood Consolidation." In *Discovering Marginalized Voices*, ed. Gregg Bachman and Thomas J. Slater. Carbondale: Southern Illinois University Press, 2002.

Taylor, Helen. *Scarlett's Women: Gone with the Wind and Its Female Fans*. New Brunswick, NJ: Rutgers University Press, 1989.

Trelease, Allen W. *White Terror: The Ku Klux Klan Conspiracy and Southern Reconstruction*. Baton Rouge: Louisiana State University Press, 1995.

Tucker, Richard K. *The Dragon and the Cross: The Rise and Fall of the Ku Klux Klan in Middle America*. Hamden, CT: Archon Books, 1991.

Turner, George Kibbe. "The Daughters of the Poor." *McClure's* 34 (1909), 57–58.

Upshaw, William D. "House Hearings, 1926." In *Selected Articles on Censorship of the Theater and Moving Pictures*, ed. Lamar Beman. New York: H. W. Wilson Company, 1931.

"U.S. Senate Subcommittee Hearings on Motion Picture and Radio Propaganda, 1941." In *Hollywood's America: Twentieth Century America through Film*, 4th ed., ed. Steven Mintz and Randy W. Roberts, 170–174. Chichester: Wiley Blackwell, 2010.

Vasey, Ruth. *The World according to Hollywood, 1918–1939*. Madison: University of Wisconsin, 1997.

Wade, Wyn Craig. *The Fiery Cross: The Ku Klux Klan in America*. New York: Simon and Schuster, 1987.

Waller, Gregory A., *Main Street Amusements: Movies and Commercial Entertainment in a Southern City, 1896–1930*. Washington, DC: Smithsonian Institution Press, 1995.

Walsh, Frank. *Sin and Censorship: The Catholic Church and the Motion Picture Industry*. New Haven, CT: Yale University Press, 1996.

Weinberger, Stephen. "The Birth of a Nation and the Making of the N.A.A.C.P." *Journal of American Studies* 45:1 (2011), 77–93.

Wexman, Virginia Wright. "The Family on the Land: Race and Nationhood in Silent Westerns." In *The Birth of Whiteness: Race and the Emergence of U.S. Cinema*, ed. Daniel Bernardi. New Brunswick, NJ: Rutgers University Press, 1996.

White, Bishop Alma. *Heroes of the Fiery Cross*. Zarephath, NJ: The Good Citizen, 1928.

———. *The Ku Klux Klan in Prophecy*. Zarephath, NJ: The Good Citizen, 1925.

White, Walter. *A Man Called White: The Autobiography of Walter White*. 1948. Reprint, Athens: University of Georgia Press, 1995.

Whitfield, Eileen. *Pickford: The Woman Who Made Hollywood*. Lexington: University Press of Kentucky, 1997.

Wilbert Pictures Co. *The Toll of Justice Press Matter Exploitation Advertising Campaign Book*. N.p., 1924.

Williams, Linda. *Playing the Race Card: Melodramas of Black and White from Uncle Tom to O. J. Simpson*. Princeton, NJ: Princeton University Press, 2001.

Williamson, Joel. *A Rage for Order: Black-White Relations in the American South since Emancipation*. New York: Oxford University Press, 1986.

Wood, Amy Louise. *Lynching and Spectacle: Witnessing Racial Violence in America, 1890–1940*. Chapel Hill: University of North Carolina Press, 2009.

SELECTED FILMOGRAPHY

After Dark aka The Hooded Mob (Jack Noble, 1923)

Alice and the Dog Catcher (M. J. Winkler Prod., 1924)

Alice's Mysterious Mystery (M. J. Winkler Prod., 1926)

Ashes of Vengeance (Norma Talmadge Film Corporation, 1923)

Bella Donna (Famous Players-Lasky, 1923)

Big Stakes (East Coast Films, 1922)

The Birth of a Nation (David W. Griffith Corporation, 1915)

Black Legion (Warner Bros., 1937)

Bolshevism on Trial (Mayflower Photoplay Corp., 1919)

The Cambric Mask (Vitagraph Co., 1919)

Cotton and Cattle (Westart Pictures, 1921)

An Eastern Westerner (Rolin Films, 1920)

The Face at Your Window (Fox Film Corp., 1920)

The Female (Famous Players- Lasky, 1924)

The Fifth Horseman (E. M. McMahon Prod., 1924)

For the Freedom of the East (Betzwood Film Company, 1918)

Gone with the Wind (Selznick International Pictures, 1939)

Heart o' the Hills (Mary Pickford Co., 1919)

Hell's Hinges (New York Motion Picture Corporation, 1916)

The High Sign (Metro, 1921)

The Hill Billy (Jack Pickford Prod., 1924)

In the Clutches of the Ku Klux Klan (Gene Gauntier Feature Players, 1913)

Inside of the Cup (Cosmopolitan Productions, 1921)

Janice Meredith (Cosmopolitan Pictures, 1924)

Joan the Woman (Cardinal Film Corp., 1916)

Kid Speed (Chadwick Pictures Corp., 1924)

Knight of the Eucharist (Creston Feature Pictures, 1922)

Law and Order (Hal Roach Studios, Inc., 1921)

Legion of Terror (Columbia, 1936)

Lodge Night (Hal Roach Studios Inc., 1923)

The Man without a Country (Thanhouser Film Corp., 1917)

Manhandled (Famous Players-Lasky, 1924)

The Mask of the Ku Klux Klan (Hopp Hadley, 1923)

The Mating Call (Paramount, 1928)

The Midnight Riders (Universal, 1920)

A Morman Maid (Jesse L. Lasky Feature Play Co., 1917)

Mountain Justice (Warner Bros., 1937)

The Mysterious Eyes of the Ku Klux Klan aka The Inside Story of the Ku Klux Klan (Bernard McComb, 1922)

Nation Aflame (Treasure, 1937)

Northern Schoolmaster (Kalem Co., 1909)

One Clear Call (First National, 1922)

The Pilgrim (Charles Chaplin Film Co., 1923)

The Prodigal Judge (Vitagraph Co., 1922)

Riders of the Dawn (Zane Grey Pictures, Inc., 1920)

The Rose of Kentucky (Biograph, 1911)

Shadows of the West (Cinema Craft, 1921)

The Symbol of the Unconquered (Micheaux Film Corp., 1920)

The Texans (Paramount, 1938)

Three Ages (Metro Pictures Corp., 1923)

The Toll of Justice (Miafa Picture Company, 1923)

The Traitor Within (Cavalier Pictures, 1924)

When Knighthood Was in Flower (Cosmopolitan Pictures, 1923)

The White Caps (Edison, 1905)

The White Masks (William M. Smith Prod., 1921)

The White Rose (D. W. Griffith Inc., 1923

The White Sister (Inspiration Pictures, 1923)

Within Our Gates (Micheaux Film Corp., 1920)

Young Sherlocks (Hal Roach Studios, Inc., 1922)

Index

TOM RICE is a lecturer in Film Studies at the University of St. Andrews, Scotland. He previously worked as the senior researcher on a major archival project on Colonial Film, (www.colonialfilm.org.uk). His articles have been featured in a number of edited collections and journals, including *Film History, Journal of British Cinema and Television, Historical Journal of Film, Radio and Television,* and *Journal of American Studies.*